# Ten Political Ideas that Have Shaped the Modern World

# Ten Political Ideas
# that Have Shaped
# the Modern World

Sanford Lakoff

*for Mary Walshok
with admiration*

*[signature]*

*October 2014*

ROWMAN & LITTLEFIELD PUBLISHERS, INC.
*Lanham • Boulder • New York • Toronto • Plymouth, UK*

Published by Rowman & Littlefield Publishers, Inc.
A wholly owned subsidiary of The Rowman & Littlefield Publishing Group, Inc.
4501 Forbes Boulevard, Suite 200, Lanham, Maryland 20706
http://www.rowmanlittlefield.com

Estover Road, Plymouth PL6 7PY, United Kingdom

British Library Cataloguing in Publication Information Available

**Library of Congress Cataloging-in-Publication Data**
Lakoff, Sanford A.
    Ten political ideas that have shaped the modern world / Sanford Lakoff.
        p. cm.
    Includes bibliographical references and index.
    ISBN 978-1-4422-1201-5 (cloth : alk. paper) — ISBN 978-1-4422-1203-9
(electronic)
    1. Political science—History. 2. Political science—Philosophy—History.
I. Title.
    JA83.L28 2010
    320.01—dc22                                                2011014228

♾™ The paper used in this publication meets the minimum requirements of
American National Standard for Information Sciences—Permanence of Paper for
Printed Library Materials, ANSI/NISO Z39.48-1992.

Printed in the United States of America

*For the Clan:*
Deb, George, Kathleen, Andrew, Daniela, and especially Natalia

# Contents

# Preface and
# Acknowledgments

In an essay entitled "Essentially Contested Concepts," the British philosopher W. B. Gallie contended that differing interpretations of certain widely used concepts could not be resolved by analysis but are "nevertheless sustained by perfectly respectable arguments and evidence." As examples, he cited Christianity, art, democracy, and social justice. That some concepts or systems of ideas can be variously interpreted with plausible arguments is undoubtedly true, and to this extent the account to be presented here will often vindicate Gallie's contention—one that was very much in keeping with the relativistic tenor of the time. But differences of interpretation are not always beyond analytic resolution. A number of the political ideas to be examined in these chapters need not be considered *essentially* contested. In many instances, core meanings can be objectively discerned. No one would disagree, for example, that fascism exalts the state above the individual and calls for dictatorship and the crushing of all dissent. Or that according to the socialist ideal, gross inequality of wealth is fundamentally unjust. Even in such instances as the definitions of liberalism and conservatism, where the core meanings have changed over time and hybrids have developed—in one case "social liberalism," in the other "liberal conservatism"—it is possible to discern essential elements that are distinctive and beyond dispute. Liberals see equal liberty and equal opportunity as the moral foundations of a good society. Conservatives fear that radical forms of equality and liberty are likely to promote relativistic nihilism, a tyranny of the majority, and cultural debasement. As to democracy, while there are sharp differences (as well as continuities) between the ancient and modern understandings of the term, and while cynical appropriations (such as "guided democracy") have made it seem a meaningless shell for propagandistic abuse, it now has a core of concrete and widely accepted meaning. Everyone would agree that democracy requires free, fair, and frequent elections based upon universal suffrage. Some analysts continue to believe, however, that democracy per se does not guarantee individual liberty—indeed that the two may be so incompatible as to produce "illiberal democracy." I will try to show here that because the core value of democracy is universal autonomy, "illiberal democracy" is an oxymoron: even the procedural requirement of free and fair elections implies freedom of speech and assembly. On this concept, then, while there is still disagreement, at least the issues in contention can be readily identified.

Above all, however, the aim of these chapters is to clarify the meaning these terms have received and the impact they have had by examining their history and interpretation. The late Isaiah Berlin once mentioned that a teacher of his at Oxford had introduced a course on philosophy by expressing the hope that when it was over, the students enrolled in it "would no longer talk rot." This book is offered in the same spirit, in homage to my own teachers, who, like Berlin, explored the history of ideas not only out of scholarly curiosity but to clarify our thinking, display the folly of intolerant absolutisms, and honor speculation that contributes to the progress of civilization. Its premise is that when we think about political ideologies, both those we may endorse and those we may deplore, our understandings are shaped by ideas developed over time, in a process of which we are apt to be only dimly aware without historical study. These ideas will have originated in response to prior conditions but often remain relevant because they express values or ways of thinking that have continuing appeal, for good or ill. We will be better able to adopt, reject, or modify them if we appreciate how they originated and how they have contributed to shaping the modern world.

Some social theorists, notably Emile Durkheim, have suggested that certain major ideas enter into "collective consciousness." He showed, for example, in his classic study of suicide, that religious predispositions help explain differential patterns of behavior on that score. But while political ideas are often adopted by groups and may be inculcated by socialization in families and other groups, the notion that there is a collective consciousness risks confusing the empirically demonstrable fact that certain beliefs are widely held and are influential on believers with the unwarranted inference that they constitute an immaterial or phantom reality of their own—one that possesses the minds of adherents like some sort of demon. When I refer here to "the modern mind," I am thinking of the consciousness of all those in modern times influenced or at least aware of much-discussed social ideas and ideologies. Everyone who fits this general classification is apt to be conversant with general social ideas that have gained currency since the end of the medieval era—conventionally taken as the beginning of modernity. Political ideas stand out because they are often used as labels and are embedded in institutions such as nation-states, political parties, and movements, and in policy prescriptions and preferences. Some are widely accepted, others are rejected and denounced, but all form part of a general awareness. In that very limited sense, there is a "modern mind."

In some instances, modern political ideas have evolved from premodern beginnings, like Christian social teachings and democracy. Others, like fascism and "Islamism"—the highly politicized and radical version of traditional Islam—are new in origin. Some, like socialism, have received elaborate formulations; others, like nationalism, are only perceptions of identity, that is, feelings of belonging to some "imagined community," in Benedict Anderson's insightful phrase; they receive elaborate intellectual formulation only in theories developed to account for them.

The ten political ideas to be examined here do not exhaust the category. Others could be included, among them progressivism, pluralism, populism, anarchism, and technocracy. Each of these is problematic, however. "Progressivism" is an American term that expresses a form of liberalism emphasizing competitive enterprise (against monopoly) and "grass-roots democracy" (against bossism and machine politics) and allowing for state regulation of the market economy and provisions for social welfare. It is therefore best understood as a modified blend of democracy and liberalism. Anarchism, either in its libertarian or communitarian form, is by definition an antipolitical idea. "Populism" is a term applied to expressions of protest (in Europe against autocracy or taxation, and in the United States against the "eastern bankers" or against racial and ethnic minorities) rather than a coherent ideal. Pluralism, while originally a call (by theorists like Léon Duguit and G. D. H. Cole) for a form of government that would create a "parliament of groups," has been absorbed in modified form into the modern concept of democracy, where it stands for plural forms of autonomy. It is implied by the existence of a sphere of "civil society" distinct from the state in which such subgroups as churches, corporations, professional associations, and trade unions are allowed to govern their own affairs (through what is sometimes called "private government"). It is also reflected in such constitutional techniques as power sharing (also known as "consociational" or "consensual" democracy), federalism, and devolution, all of which aim to respect diversity on regional, ethnic, or linguistic grounds and to provide forms of self-government that counteract the effects of overcentralization. Technocracy is an idea that has been bruited mainly in literary fantasies, from Francis Bacon's *New Atlantis* and Thomas Campanella's *City of the Sun* to Aldous Huxley's *Brave New*

*World.* However much the modern dependence on science and technology makes such fantasies more relevant than in the past, the idea of technocracy has entered political discourse only peripherally.

The presentation of the ten major ideas reviewed here has been structured chronologically to take account of their origins but not to suggest that there is a scheme of progression in which the later ideas succeed the earlier ones. The patterns of interconnection among political ideas are much more complex than can be captured in that sort of formula. A better way to think about their interaction is as a kind of ongoing dialogue. The Christian concept of equality, at first both ambiguous and ambivalent, has become the bedrock of modern democratic belief, sometimes with its transcendental moorings intact, otherwise secularized with a philosophical rationale. While the schism between fundamentalist and reformed ("demythologized") Christianity sharply divides the faithful today, the belief in human equality bequeathed by the Judeo-Christian tradition (and shared by the mainstream Islamic tradition) has come to be widely accepted, except in societies still divided by tribalism and drawn to such antiegalitarian ideologies as fascism and Islamism. The civic humanism that appeared as the political ideology of the Renaissance played an important role in setting this belief in a social context, divorcing it from the church's acceptance of hierarchy and monarchy, and restoring the classical belief in citizenship. Today civic humanism finds expression not only in the advocacy of "participatory democracy" but also in the call for "world citizenship," as a recognition of common humanity and the need for cooperation to preserve the global environment—sometimes thought of, thanks to modern extraterrestrial exploration, as "spaceship earth."

In the seventeenth and eighteenth centuries, civic humanism found expression in liberalism—even though the name itself only appeared early in the nineteenth century. It emerged as the hatreds spawned by religious schism made toleration seem more advisable than insistence on orthodoxy, and as feudalism yielded to a new economy of independent landowners, farmers, merchants, and factory owners and workers. Preoccupied at first with the need to protect religious liberty and the property rights of an emerging middle class, liberals called for a new "social contract" in which certain basic natural rights—life, liberty, and property—would be respected as the foundation of the social order. Government was to be held accountable to the governed—or at least to those entitled to vote because their possession of property showed that they were rational enough to govern themselves and had a "stake" in legislative outcomes. Today, liberalism stands for the protection of civil liberties and civil rights for all, not just the propertied. As "social liberalism," it also calls for a limited but active state that regulates the economy, promotes opportunity, and assures a "safety net" providing basic welfare without discouraging individual initiative.

Conservatism emerged in reaction to what was perceived as the upheaval of traditional ways of life ("the Old Order"). That upheaval, dramatically evident in the excesses of the French Revolution, entailed a radical attack on the privileges and power of the landowning aristocracy, on the assertion of authority by absolute monarchy, and on the truth claims of religion and the social role and privileges of the clergy. Conservatives rallied to the defense of the Old Order and denounced those who supposed that it could be replaced root and branch by untried novel systems based on nothing but abstract "reason." They warned that the use of violence in the name of civic virtue would leave a poisonous residue that would only encourage further violence and result in new forms of Caesaristic dictatorship. In the late nineteenth and early twentieth centuries, some conservatives embraced racist and ethnocentric attitudes, and eventually fascism, to defeat what they considered the menace of liberalism, democracy, socialism, and anarchism. Even early on, however, this reaction against movements aimed at mass emancipation was attenuated by the development of a hybrid "liberal conservatism" (evident in the thinking of Edmund Burke and Alexis de Tocqueville) that sought to make common cause with liberalism against forces much further to the left and considered far more threatening to the established order. Today, European and American conservatives are more apt to be adherents of this hybrid than of the earlier antiliberal version of the doctrine.

Like an earthquake, the upheaval wrought by the French Revolution brought to the surface two other ideas that were to gain strength throughout the nineteenth century and into the twentieth. One was socialism, the other nationalism.

"Socialism" is a term deliberately invented (in the 1830s) to represent a contrast to the liberal focus on the individual. Its origins can be discerned much earlier, in reveries about the "Golden Age," before the emergence of social hierarchy and private property, and in religious movements inspired by the rejection of materialism in favor of the pursuit of a life of poverty and prayer. From the middle of the nineteenth century onward, socialism took two forms. One was devoted to the construction of ideal communities (after the example of Thomas More's "Utopia" and other similar accounts). The other, advanced chiefly by Karl Marx, saw socialism (and its highest form, communism) as the inevitable outcome of a grand historical evolution, marked by epochal conflicts among social classes, in which advances in the "mode of production" would entail changes in "relations of production." Socialism would be achieved, either peacefully or by revolution, when the forces of production were removed from control by the owners of property and given to the "proletariat" or working class. The result would be the end of "class struggle" and the beginnings of a new phase of history in which the ultimate rule would be "to each according to his needs." In the "command economies" of the Soviet Union and other socialist states that have followed its example, however, socialism has become an opportunity for rule by a "new class" (as Milovan Djilas called the members of the Communist Party) led by authoritarian rulers, vindicating the warnings of those who saw the abolition of private property as an invitation to totalitarian dictatorship. In democratic societies, experiments with the nationalization of industry have revealed that it is hardly an economic panacea. Even socialists now concede that the regulated competitive market is a better engine for innovation and economic growth. As an ideal, however, socialism nevertheless continues to inspire the belief that fairness requires a social system in which inducements to work and enterprise are balanced by provision of public goods and private welfare for all.

Nationalism sprang up in Western Europe and spread eastward, and then to the areas of the world colonized by the European powers, for reasons that are probably best explained in compound form. Cultural and political nationalism had begun to emerge even earlier, as a result of the breakup of the Roman Empire and the emergence of separate nation-states. The resulting emphasis on ethnic, cultural, and linguistic differences reinforced the sense of separateness, provoking chauvinist claims of national superiority. But the French Revolution gave nationalism a democratic coloration. The belief in democracy unleashed by the Revolution, and by others like it, including the American Revolution, called for "the people" to become sovereign. The French Declaration of the Rights of Man and the Citizen stated that "the principle of sovereignty resides essentially in the nation: no body of men, no individual, can express authority that does not expressly emanate from it." Because of this assertion of popular sovereignty, France came to be called "*la grande nation*," the paradigm of nationalism and at the same time the standard-bearer for the cause of liberty. National self-determination thus became an expression of democracy, as well as an extension of the liberal principle of individual self-determination. The democratic revolutions of the late eighteenth and early nineteenth centuries dovetailed with movements for national unification and the breakup of empires in a period that came to be called the "springtime of nations." When national groups inspired by this sense of belonging were subordinated by foreign dynasties or imperial powers, they often rebelled and demanded independence. The example of France, newly empowered by its revolution, was not lost on its German neighbors, who recognized that their division into separate states weakened them against the force of Napoleon's army. Nationalistic fervor spread eastward throughout Europe and into the colonial domains marked out by the European powers during the ages of exploration. The result was that nationalism became a powerful rallying cry and a rival to other ideologies for popular loyalty—sometimes exploited for the sake of these other ideologies. Nationalism today remains a potent force despite epochal transnational innovations, such as the United Nations and the European Union, which are aimed at fostering an overarching sense of loyalty. The efficacy of the United Nations rests on the will of the member states. And, paradoxically, the very achievement of European unity has made it more practical for subnational groups—which now have less to lose by detaching themselves—to demand greater autonomy and even separate nationhood.

In the twentieth century, critiques of democracy in the form of racism, elitism, hero worship, and chauvinistic nationalism coalesced in fascism. The term was invented in Italy to describe the antiparliamentary and economically syndicalist movement led by Mussolini, and it came to describe similar movements in Germany and elsewhere. The German "National Socialist" movement gave the doctrine a defining if eclectic meaning. Nazism was a pastiche of ideologies, a loose amalgam of nationalism, racial exclusivism, hero worship, and a belief in economic and social coordination for the purposes of enhancing the power of the state. It was properly described at the outset as a "revolution of nihilism" because it expressed an abhorrence of intellectual sophistication and traditional Judeo-Christian and secular values (whether those of Kantian ethics or political liberalism, socialism, and conservatism). In their place it put a vaguely defined creed emphasizing will and a total subordination to the fatherland and its all-powerful *"führer,"* as well as a supposed historic mission to dominate the world and purify it of racial inferiority. Fascism is today widely seen as the rationale of a ruthless effort to create a totalitarian empire that caused incalculable suffering, but it retains a lurking appeal for those prey to ethnic and racial prejudices and those so frustrated and insecure in their private and public lives as to suppose that an order imposed and maintained by violence and repression will somehow bring salvation.

Realism in international relations and foreign policy is an idea that arose in academic study and came to be widely accepted among scholars, policy makers, and commentators. An outgrowth of German "realpolitik," it posited that "moralism" is out of place in relations among states, for reasons rooted in the egoistic tendencies inherent in human nature and in the anarchy of interstate relations. Hans J. Morgenthau, the leading theorist of realism, strongly criticized foreign policy goals and methods like those of President Woodrow Wilson that were guided by the belief that traditional "power politics" and "balance of power" diplomacy had failed and must be replaced. Wilson wanted to "make the world safe for democracy" by strengthening the rule of international law, to be enforced by a new international organization, the League of Nations, which would be charged with the authority and power to curb aggression and assure national self-determination, dismantling the imperialism that had led to a scramble for colonies and the oppression of the colonized. Morgenthau and others contended that such attitudes and expectations had proven naive and had in fact only led to World War II, and that they would prove still more destructive in an age of nuclear weapons. Instead, he proposed that security and peace are best obtained by policies guided by sober and pragmatic consideration of national interest coupled with a willingness to promote mutual accommodation. Today, the realist perspective continues to find adherents—lately in response to the much criticized effort by the United States to establish democracy in Iraq by military intervention—even as concern for such evils as genocide and "ethnic cleansing" lead critics of realism to contend that concern for human rights should also enter into the equation in formulations of foreign policy.

"Islamism" is a term now in wide use to describe a radical and highly politicized version of Islam that has grown up since the 1920s and calls for the re-creation of the ancient Islamic caliphate, uniting mosque and state. The most radical Islamists call upon believers to engage in jihad—meaning, for them, war to the death against the "infidels" who stand in their way, as well as against "corrupt" and supposedly apostate Muslims who do not accept their version of the faith. Although the doctrine was originally advanced by Sunni Muslims, it has gained resonance among Shiites as well thanks to the success of Iranian religious leaders in overthrowing that country's secular monarchy and replacing it with an "Islamic republic." This regime resembles the ancient caliphates that arose in the immediate wake of the prophet Muhammad in giving ultimate authority to religious leaders and in requiring that secular law conform to religious teachings. The repressive record of Islamist regimes such as those of the Taliban in Afghanistan and the Iranian theocracy underscores the conflict between, on the one hand, the belief that all law comes from God alone and must therefore be interpreted by those most qualified, and on the other, the democratic belief that secular lawmaking must be the work of self-governing communities guided by their own moral and practical judgments.

This belief in self-government is of course at the heart of democracy, the political idea that is now the most widely held of all. Although democracy was a dormant ideal in the period after the fall of the Greek *polis* and the Roman *civitas*, it was revived in principle in small-scale republican experiments beginning in medieval times and finally emerged full blown as authoritarian regimes were overthrown and the suffrage was gradually extended in Europe and North America, and then in many other regions. The essence of the democratic idea is that all people, suitably educated, are capable of and deserve the opportunity to be autonomous—that is, to govern their own lives, separately and in common, under the rule of law established by majorities, with respect for the rights and liberties of the individual and minorities. Autonomy takes several forms—individual, plural, and collective—and this combination, differently expressed, can be found in all examples of institutional and procedural democracy. Experience has shown that democracy is unlikely to emerge or survive unless a number of preconditions and conditions are in place, such as widespread literacy; religious toleration; a muting of tribal, sectarian, and regional hostilities; and above all a will to respect its principles, but also that once established it commends itself as the best way to achieve stability and prosperity. As has often been noted, democracies are far less likely to make war against other democracies than nondemocratic states have been in their disputes with other states. American democracy, as the epilogue suggests, exhibits the three forms of autonomy as a direct result of the impress of three historic influences—British individualism, Roman pluralism, and Athenian communalism. Clashes over policy and political structure and the compromises reached on divisive issues reflect the dynamic interplay of these influences.

Clarification of the meaning of political ideas cannot necessarily promote toleration or peaceful accommodation among those holding different points of view. Adherents of one or more of these ideas may well find others abhorrent and threatening. At the very least, however, a better understanding of what each of these ideas entails will mitigate the tendency to confuse them and use them inappropriately as labels in ideological battles. In the case of one idea, that of democracy, now approaching universal acceptance, better appreciation of its meaning may help protect efforts to promote self-government and cooperation based on common respect for the equal dignity of human life. That alone would amply reward the efforts of both the author and the reader of this study.

---

The chapters that follow draw on previous writings and lectures. The writings include two books, *Equality in Political Philosophy* (1964) and *Democracy: History, Theory, Practice* (1997); a volume edited with Maurice Cranston entitled *A Glossary of Political Ideas* (1979); and several articles, book chapters, and encyclopedia essays: "Democracy," *Encyclopedia of Nationalism*; "Autonomy and Liberal Democracy," *Review of Politics*; "Christianity and Equality," *Nomos 9* (© 1967, Transaction Publishers); "The Origins of Liberal Conservatism," *Review of Politics* (1989); "Liberalism in America: Hartz and His Critics," http://www.informaworld .com, *Critical Review of Social and Political Philosophy*; and "The Reality of Muslim Exceptionalism," *Journal of Democracy*. Most of the material in chapter 6 is drawn from my entry, "Socialism from Antiquity to Marx," in *Dictionary of the History of Ideas*, ed. Philip P. Wiener (© 1973, Gale, part of

Cengage Learning). It is reproduced here by permission (www.cengage. vom/permissions). Barbara Selby, research and information manager at the Alderman Library of the University of Virginia, graciously identified a copyright holder. Chapter 8 draws on a lecture on "Morality in Foreign Policy: Hans Morgenthau and the Modern Predicament," presented at a symposium at the University of San Diego and reproduced in a privately printed collection of essays edited by George Mazur. Material in the epilogue is drawn from a review for *Historically Speaking: The Bulletin of the Historical Society* and a lecture to the Society for the Preservation of the Greek Heritage in Washington, D.C., arranged by my friend Professor Athanasios Moulakis. Earlier versions of the chapters were presented in 2008 as lectures in a course on "The Battle of Ideas" for the Osher Institute for Lifelong Learning at the University of California, San Diego. I am indebted to Jack Schaps and Stan Faer for inviting me to present the course and to all those who listened so attentively and honored me with a lifetime membership. I am also grateful to colleagues at the University of California, San Diego, and friends who offered comments and encouragement, including William Atherton, Aida Gold, the late Paul Roazen, Anita Safran, Jean Edward Smith, Theodore J. Stahl, and Sheila Tobias.

Sanford Lakoff

# 1

~~~

# Christianity and Equality

When Alexis de Tocqueville sought to explain the rise of democracy in the West, he reflected that its core value, the belief in equality of condition, seemed to have unfolded as if by divine plan: "The gradual progress of equality is something fated. . . . God does not Himself need to speak for us to find sure signs of His will."[1] Tocqueville did not claim that this will was revealed in the Christian Gospels, but Christianity did introduce into Western consciousness a belief, however ambiguous, in the ideal of human equality. The apostles did not propound a program for the reform of earthly government, but the assumption of human equality before God was certainly latent in their universalistic claim that conventional distinctions of identity and status were now to be overcome. Paul made this announcement with startling force: "There is no such thing as Jew and Greek, slave and freeman, male and female; for you are all one person in Christ Jesus" (Galatians 3:28).[2]

Even in the somewhat muted, donnish tones of the New English Bible, Paul's declaration keeps its dramatic ring. But drama apart, what did he mean? Was he suggesting that the new freedom purchased by the sacrifice of the redeemer was already in itself emancipation from the customary distinctions of the world and the flesh? Was he announcing a new doctrine of human equality, and did he intend it to stand as a challenge both to Judaic "chosenness" and to Greco-Roman notions of the necessity of hierarchy in nature and society?

We have some help from Paul himself, but unfortunately not quite enough. The passage appears in the midst of an effort to explain to the backsliding Galatians how it is that they can consider themselves part

1

of the issue of Abraham and therefore beneficiaries of the promises covenanted by God with the Jewish patriarch. It is not necessary, Paul contends, that they adopt the provisions of the Mosaic law. This law was promulgated, he points out, 430 years after the promise was made. To become the children of God and therefore his heirs, they must only have faith in Christ. Through faith they may achieve union with the messiah and thereby become themselves sons of God. Paul explains,

> This is what I mean: so long as the heir is a minor, he is no better off than a slave, even though the whole estate is his; he is under guardians and trustees until the date fixed by his father. And so it was with us. During our minority we were slaves to the elemental spirits of the universe [or the elements of the natural world, or elementary ideas belonging to the world], but when the term was completed, God sent his own Son, born of a woman, born under the law, to purchase freedom for the subjects of the law, in order that we might attain the status of sons. (Galatians 4:1–5)[3]

In offering this analogy, Paul is less concerned with describing the inheritance that now awaits the liberated believer than he is with persuading the insecure to pay no attention to rival evangelists. He urged them to ignore the "agitators" who insist that no one can enjoy the patrimony of Israel without assuming the yoke of the law, who warn that they cannot be considered people of God unless they observe the holy days and circumcise all male issue. (As for such circumcisers, Paul tartly observes, "they had better go the whole way and make eunuchs of themselves!") It is only necessary, he insists, that they accept the guidance of the spirit of God. Given a sincere faith and righteous comportment, all may join in the hope that "if we do not slacken our efforts we shall in due time reap our harvest" (Galatians 6:10).[4]

For all its ambiguity, Paul's letter to the Galatians helps explain not only how the "good news" of Christianity contributed to the development of egalitarian ideas but also how it came to inspire an endless succession of movements for emancipation, from the medieval mystics and sectaries to the modern secular rebels in politics and art—all of whom have felt the yearning for a new identity, a new wholeness, a new communion, in which the frustrating and petty limitations of the human species would somehow be overcome. Whatever the nature of the supernatural "inheritance" Paul has in mind but does not specify, the burden of his message is surely that the inheritance is available to any and all, circumcised or not, and without regard to sex or station, provided only that they dedicate themselves to a new life in the image of God—a life exemplified in the savior who was God in the form of man.

It was to prove a message of extraordinary force, particularly among the Gentiles to whom, as Paul declared, he had been called by God to proclaim a new dispensation. In some sense it must surely have been received as a doctrine of equality. If, as R. W. and A. J. Carlyle could assert, the Stoic doctrine of natural equality stood in epochal contrast to the Aristotelian idea of natural inequality,[5] how much more of an affront to received dogma must the Christian conception have been? Not to the Jews, to be sure, for Jesus was hardly the first Jewish teacher to announce that human beings created in the image of their maker ought to love their neighbors as themselves or that, as the children of Israel, they were all alike the covenantal people of the God of Abraham. This much of the Christian message was nothing new to them, and the rest struck fundamentally at the very roots of their existence—their ties as a people, the law embodying their relation to God, and their expectation of a world transformation to be ushered in by the coming of the messiah. In the more fractious and unstable Greco-Roman world, where narrow civic and kinship loyalties, evanescent cults, and exclusive mystery religions stood in embarrassing contrast to the unitary power of the empire, the universalism of the Christian doctrine was understandably attractive. Nor could its chiliastic egalitarianism fail to elicit interest in cultures where the myth of a golden age was a persistent theme.

## TWO INTERPRETATIONS OF CHRISTIAN EQUALITY: ANTIPATHETIC AND ANTICIPATORY

The Greco-Roman world had of course already developed in Stoicism a doctrine that served the same universalistic purpose as Christianity and that also included a belief in equality. But the weakness of Stoicism as a rival to Christianity is nowhere more apparent than in their different ideas of equality. Although Stoicism too challenged elitist pretensions, it did so by using the same terms of argument that had traditionally served to support the belief in aristocracy. Thus, whereas Aristotle had argued that differences in rational capacity made some fit to rule and others fit only to obey, the Stoics asserted that the very possession of the capacity to reason made men more alike than different. Christianity in effect undercut the entire argument by contending that degrees of rationality made no difference. What mattered was that every man had a soul and that in the eyes of God all souls were equally worthy. In this respect, as in others, it is easy to understand why Christianity was more attractive to larger masses of people than Stoicism, which could only have had great appeal for an educated minority. Once the powerful edifice of Greek philosophy, which had already developed a concept of the immortality of the soul,[6] was fused with the revealed ethic of Christianity by the Neoplatonists, the intellectual and moral appeal of the Christian conception of equality over that of Stoicism was assured. The message of Paul could then become the firm belief not only of the Galatians but also of all the peoples of the great civilization that arose upon the foundations laid by Greece and Rome.

And yet, even as it triumphed in history, the Pauline Christian conception of equality was never a very clear guide to thought or action. It was one thing to proclaim that all human beings were equals in the eyes of God; it was another to assert that all should be equal in the eyes of the world. Was the Christian revelation to be considered a call for social and political equality? Or was it, like the Stoic conception of natural equality,[7] merely a wistful invocation of paradise lost, implying no sanction of egalitarianism in the present? There have been plausible answers on both sides of the question. Indeed, these answers can be divided into two broad theories of the Christian conception of social equality: the *antipathetic* and the *anticipatory*.

The antipathetic view has been put forward both by politically conservative theological fundamentalists and hostile critics of Christianity. In its mildest form, this interpretation maintains that Christianity is no sponsor of secular ideals. Insofar as the Christian revelation announces a doctrine of equality, the term is said to refer only to the inner soul and not to the external envelopes which, in the eyes of the world, distinguish one soul from another. The promise of emancipation is therefore not to be taken as a prophecy of democracy, communism, or a liberal equality of rights, but simply and solely as a pledge that God loves all his creatures equally and holds out to all of them the hope of eternal life. As Rudolf Bultmann observes, succinctly if perhaps too dogmatically, "The negation of worldly differentiations does not mean a sociological program within this world; rather it is an eschatological occurrence which takes place only within the eschatological Congregation."[8]

Others have argued, on the same side of the question but with a still stronger belief in the opposition of Christianity to secular social reform, that a religious and a social conception of equality are incompatible. Søren Kierkegaard contended that the effort to achieve an egalitarian social order was bound to be in vain. The world, he argued, is necessarily the realm of the separate and the diverse. In spirit, however, men are identical. In a Christian sense, therefore, there can be no distinctions among men, whereas in worldly respects, differences are inherent and unavoidable. As a result, when Christian pietists hold property in common and a group of secular communists does the same, the contrast is fundamental, despite appearances, because in the one case the property is a thing indifferent (as a characteristic of worldly vanity and imperfection) whereas in the other it is all important (as the desired good that is to relieve all suffering). Where material things are considered important, Kierkegaard suggests, there is bound to be contention and separateness of interest. Only insofar as the world is negated does equality become an appropriate standard for human relations. Christianity is therefore egalitarian but only in a spiritual sense. Otherwise it is opposed to all secular efforts at leveling—a phenomenon Kierkegaard condemned as a debasement of all higher values.[9]

Ironically, this rather fundamentalist and otherworldly interpretation of Christian egalitarianism is shared by the leading modern sponsors of atheistic alternatives to religion, Karl Marx and Sigmund Freud. In Marx's view, Christianity—indeed all religion—serves to deflect and dampen the outrage of the lower classes at the misery of their lot. Deluded by promises of far-off bliss (and revenge against their oppressors), they can be taught to accept present exploitation with patient endurance. The Christian conception of an ultimate equality of souls is therefore precisely the enemy of social progress, an ideology that must be overcome rather than the inspiration of an ethical ideal that awaits implementation.[10] Freud held what amounts to a similar view. In a study of the cohesiveness of the social system,[11] he described the Christian doctrine of equality as a myth of order that serves to support the most hierarchical of social institutions by persuading adherents that God loves them all equally. Unlike Marx, of course, Freud could not conceive of a viable society that would in fact be built upon egalitarian principles, but he had no doubt that the Christian ideal of equality was, if anything, a barrier to egalitarianism of a structural kind. Thus, despite other differences, Bultmann, Kierkegaard, Marx, and Freud all share a conception of Christian equality as at least indifferent to social equality and at most quite hostile to it.

According to the anticipatory theory, by contrast, the Christian doctrine of equality is far from indifferent to society. Even though in itself it is a declaration of spiritual equality, Christianity is said to have clear implications for the social order—implications that have in fact been drawn in the course of Western history. By stressing the dignity of man, the immortality of the soul, and the promise of redemption held out to the low as well as the high, Christianity is said to have implanted the ethical seeds that ultimately blossomed in the various social conceptions of equality. The Christian idea of equality, according to this interpretation, should be understood as having anticipated a more explicitly stated ideal of social reform. As historian Gordon S. Wood has observed, in the course of the eighteenth century an enlightened and republicanized gentry came to recognize that inferiors had realities equal to their own and "in effect secularized the Christian belief in the equality of all souls before God."[12]

Ernst Troeltsch is perhaps the best exponent of the anticipatory theory. Troeltsch readily admitted that there is nothing directly socially revolutionary about the teachings of the New Testament. "The message of Jesus," he points out, "is not a programme of social reform. It is rather the summons to prepare for the coming of the Kingdom of God."[13] But Troeltsch also recognizes that in terms of historic impact, Christianity cannot be said to have simply issued a call for quietistic adjustment. "At first," he observes, "the revolutionary power of the idea of equality is hidden" in the Christian emphasis on inner, spiritual equality, but in time the "realistic question" is bound to be asked: "whether there are not grades and kinds of poverty which make it impossible to rise to this kind of equality, and whether external uplifting is not necessary."[14]

Unlike Bultmann, then, who argues that Christianity is in intention a call to otherworldly values, Troeltsch holds that this very summons was bound to raise the question of the need for social reform in this world. There is, of course, no necessary contradiction between these two interpretations. The one, which is shared as far as it goes by both Bultmann and Troeltsch, refers entirely to the inner logic of the Christian message; the other refers to its reception and to the train of thoughts it inspired. And yet the difference is important. If Christian doctrine is in itself indifferent or even hostile to the reform of society, any effort to achieve social equality of whatever kind may be labeled unchristian or anti-Christian and, by some definitions, idolatrous. But if Christian ethics requires or permits action to reform the world, then it may be the religious duty of the Christian to promote the cause of social equality as a means of infusing grace into worldly existence.

A variation on the same theme is what might be called the protoproletarian theory of the Christian conception of equality. According to this point of view, Christianity was virtually from the start a doctrine of mass emancipation. Inasmuch as the message of the Gospels was particularly addressed to the lowly, who were promised bliss in the afterlife, whereas the rich and powerful were warned that they would come to grief (see especially Luke 6:20–26), was it not in inception a doctrine of social equality—or, at any rate, was it not bound to be understood as such? Friedrich Nietzsche believed that it was. Judaism and Christianity were the very embodiment of the "slave morality" because both doctrines promised to turn the natural state of affairs upside down so that the meek and victimized could lord it over the high and mighty. The victory of Christianity, he maintained, was a victory for the slave morality because where Christianity was adopted, the belief in strength and glory was replaced by the exaltation of weakness and pity: "The wretched are alone the good; the poor, the weak, the lowly, are alone the good; the suffering, the needy. The sick, the loathsome . . . are to be saved, and not the powerful and rich."[15] Later on, the masses would turn upon the priests who had first persuaded them of this new morality and had inspired in them a wish for revenge. Not content with far-off satisfaction, they would demand immediate redress; they would become revolutionaries. Christianity, Nietzsche theorized, far from being indifferent to the social order, had actually been the source of all the egalitarian movements that, in modern times, were threatening to transform Western civilization into a mass society—from democracy and utilitarianism to anarchism and communism. He condemned them all, religions and secular philosophies alike, as agents of degeneration.

There is hardly much point in trying to decide between these two lines of interpretation. As is so often the case with major historical movements, even contradictory or incompatible theories turn out to have some plausibility. The Christian attitude toward the ideal of equality is a good example of how ideas can be said to be essentially contested. That attitude is certainly not wholly one of indifference or hostility; neither is it steadfastly and thoroughly sympathetic. But that very inner tension points to a deeper understanding. Perhaps the best one can say is that the Christian attitude toward equality is profoundly dualistic. On the one hand, the identity of all souls and the equal promise of divine grace stand as the quintessence of the Christian revelation; and on the other, the Christian is counseled to accept the inequalities of the world as inevitable consequences of sin.

From the start, Christian doctrine combines both elements, either of which could be stressed to the virtual exclusion of the other. The monastic orders and the sectarian movements put the promise of ultimate equality at the very center of Christian teaching. To ignore this goal or to postpone its achievement, they believed, was to lead an unchristian life. To put aside all distinctions of rank, vocation, and dress, and to keep all goods in common was to demonstrate the possession of *pneuma* and to set an example for the sinful world without. But the fathers of the church and the canonists who came after them put the stress on the other element of Christian belief. Preoccupied as they were with the absorption of peoples ill prepared for perfection, and apprehensive for the unity and the moral authority of the church in an unredeemed world, they venerated hierarchy as a synonym for order. All advocates of equality, whether obedient to the discipline of the church or disdainful of it were bound to appear to them as either real or potential heretics.

In exhibiting this dualistic attitude toward human equality, Christianity was scarcely unique. The major Greek and Roman philosophers, from Socrates on, all looked on equality either as the hallmark of some distant and irrecoverable past or as an ideal to which only the few best—Plato's guardians, for instance—might aspire. Neither the democracy of Athens nor the ascetic communism of Sparta, in practice so important in the Greek experience, won favor with the philosophers. Equality might be recognized as a valid standard in the sphere of ideals—whether as an expression of the lost wholeness of humanity or of justice—but as a practical goal it was condemned for degrading the superior to the level of the inferior. Classical political philosophy, like Christianity, is a source of support both for those who believe in the ultimate merit of egalitarianism and for those who hold that as an immediate proposal it is impractical and pernicious.

With this ambivalence between ultimate and operative values, the Christian attitude was surely no radical departure from convention in the sphere of social philosophy. At the same time, it is easy to see how it might have been regarded as a radical departure by those who choose to consider only the ultimate side of its message. The Christian message *is* a doctrine of equality to the extent that it includes, as an extremely important element, the promise that in the victory over mortal limitations, the distinctions of the world are annulled and count for nothing. The love feats celebrated by Christ and the apostles symbolized this ideal of equality, as does the ethical injunction, adopted from Judaism, to love one's neighbor and to demonstrate this love by the performance of works of charity. The incarnation can also be understood as a token of the belief in equality inasmuch as the annihilation of the distance between God and man is evidence of the essential and common divinity of the human spirit. It raises, and it answers, the question of whether, if there is no barrier between God and man, there should be barriers between man and man.

This message, moreover, *was* directed especially to those who were both poor in worldly goods and deficient in the training that the priests of Israel claimed necessary for piety and that the philosophers of the "pagan" world claimed necessary for virtue. Christianity was an appeal, as the King James translators awkwardly but perceptively put it, to the "poor in spirit" (Luke 6:20), to the vulgar "people of the land" (*am haaretz*).[16] It could not have been received as anything but a revolutionary doctrine by those who were looked upon, and had come to look upon themselves, as the wretched and despised of the earth but whom Christ singled out for particular affection. The "poor in spirit" must surely have understood the radical social implications in the description of the original Christian communion in Acts 4:

> The whole body of believers was united in heart and soul. Not a man of them claimed any of his possessions as his own, but everything was held in common, while the apostles bore witness with great power to the resurrection of the Lord Jesus. They were all held in high esteem; for they had never a needy person among them, because all who had property in land or houses sold it, brought the proceeds of the sale, and laid the money at the feet of the apostles; it was then distributed to any who stood in need.

From this it might surely be concluded that the practice of Christian love required not only a belief in ultimate spiritual equality but also a willingness to put into practice the principle of the abolition of social distinctions associated with the realization of perfect community in the kingdom of God.

Other Christians might nevertheless demur, understandably, from drawing such conclusions. Until the evils of the world were actually annulled by God, what right did any of its people have to pretend that they were already living in a state of redemption? While human relations remained under the curse of the fall, and were therefore inevitably imperfect, was not the obedient Christian obliged to accept inequalities as God's judgment upon sinful humanity? The incarnation was experienced by one man for all. But to the believer it remained an achievement with which he could only identify indirectly and at a great distance. The new being exemplified by Christ would remain for other men only an aspiration and a hope. The ethical commandment to love one's neighbor was designed for, and would only be necessary in, a social structure riven with distinctions between the rich and the poor, the lettered and the illiterate, the wellborn and the lowly. Because of the doctrine of predestination, moreover, even the promise of salvation was not ambiguously egalitarian. As Troeltsch observes, "The idea of predestination cuts the nerve of the absolute and abstract idea of equality. . . . In spite of the equality of all in their sinful unworthiness and in their possession of grace . . . the equal claim of all to an equal share in the highest life-value through equal working out of vocation and destiny, is invalidated."[17]

Combined, however tenuously, both lines of thought were characteristic of early Christianity. There is no better statement of this dualistic attitude toward equality than that of St. Augustine, the most authoritative and most influential of the fathers of the church. God, he declares, had originally intended that men should rule over "irrational creation," but not over other men. "The righteous men in primitive times were made shepherds of cattle rather than kings of men, God intending thus to teach us what the relative passion of the creatures is, and what the desert of sin."[18] Slavery and other forms of inequality were therefore not intended by the creator. Nevertheless, the inequalities in the world are ordained by God as "the result of sin." Slaves are therefore not to revolt but to remain in subjection, not in "crafty fear but in faithful love, until all unrighteousness pass away, and all principality and every human power be brought to nothing, and God be all in all."[19] The Christian is expected to strive for justice in the earthly city, but he should entertain no illusions about the possibility of achieving it; the weight of his energies ought to be withdrawn from the world and concentrated on the love of God.

Even St. Ambrose, who is often celebrated for his denunciation of wealth, did not call for the abolition of private property. He merely offered a Christian gloss on the Stoic idea of a golden age in which there were no distinctions of rank and fortune, adding that present inequalities had come about through the fall from grace. Ambrose did not contend that these inequalities were unjust or that they should be done away with. Like Augustine, he was content to identify them as the consequence of sin. Ambrose's counsel was no different from that of the Stoics. A good man was obliged to behave charitably toward all, whatever their condition, but he was not compelled to pursue an unrealistic egalitarian goal. Equality, with paradise, would be restored by God in his good time.[20]

Conditioned by feudalism and wracked by fear of disunity, Christianity underwent in medieval times an intensification of its antipathetic strain. Hierarchy was said by the spokesmen of the church to be as essential in human affairs as in the structure of the cosmos and the ordering of the personality. As the heavens rose above the earth and the soul was higher than the body, so the pope was superior to the emperor, the clergy to the laity, the secular nobility to its subjects. Thus refined and elaborated, Christianity could serve as a pillar of feudal aristocracy. Only with the revolt against hierarchy within the church, culminating in the Protestant Reformation, did the anticipatory egalitarian strain emerge again into the open as a respectable and widely held position. Until then it had been relegated to the eschatological underground—to the heretical sects in which the impatient and the thoroughly alienated sought release from earthly imperfections.

The Protestant Reformers were not all as radical in their interpretations as these earlier heretics, but they too were moved to withdraw from the existing church, and in some instances from existing society, by what they felt was a scandalous disparity between the ideals of Christianity and the practices of Christendom. Given this perspective, it is not surprising that in elaborating a Christian conception of equality, the Reformers should have sought to make this ideal, no less than the others, operative as well as ultimate. This is not to say that all of them sought to reform the whole of society in an egalitarian direction. In most cases the Reformers' advocacy of equality was restricted to the church. But even in these cases, the reasoning advanced contributed to and prefigured the later development of the secular theory of equality in its three major variants: liberal, conservative, and socialist.[21]

Martin Luther, perhaps the foremost in influence, offered a view of Christian equality that in a number of crucial ways resembled and presaged a modern liberal view. Much of what Luther had to say, in his conservative moods, about politics and society was quite conventional. But what is novel in his social theory tends in a distinctly liberal direction. In his celebrated advocacy of a "priesthood of believers," Luther squarely opposed the effort of the Roman church to distinguish among Christians according to their clerical or lay status and according to whether their vocations were "spiritual" or "carnal." In opposition to the Roman practice of hierarchical co-optation and designation, Luther argued that the congregation should ordain its own minister and that it should have the right to hold him responsible for the conduct of his office. Referring to the different treatment accorded clerics and laymen in law, Luther exclaimed: "Whence comes this great distinction between those who are equally Christians? Only from human laws and inventions!"[22]

In economic and conjugal matters, Luther was similarly emancipated from the medieval association of the worldly with the demonic.[23] Max Weber has properly described his position as one of "inner-worldly asceticism" according to which the individual Christian is called upon to demonstrate the strength of his faith by a diligent pursuit of his calling and by pursuing a mode of life in which ordinary activities are regarded as opportunities and challenges for virtuous conduct.[24] Although he generally stopped short of extending to politics and economics the egalitarian reforms he advocated for the church, Luther's reasoning is in principle quite close to what became the basis for the secular liberal doctrine of equality. Like Luther, liberals such as John Locke and John Stuart Mill would argue that all men were capable of governing themselves and that social life should be regarded as a kind of competition in virtue in which each individual was called upon to use his talents to the fullest extent possible.

John Calvin used a quite different argument in his assault on Catholic hierarchy. At the center of Calvin's opposition to hierarchy was his belief in universal depravity. This pessimistic assumption contrasts sharply with Luther's relatively far more optimistic belief that all Christians were capable of spiritual discernment. Historically, Calvin's doctrine of equal depravity led to two rather different positions. Congregationalist disciples read his argument to mean that no one was to be trusted with prolonged or unlimited authority and that all matters of importance should be left to the disposition of the congregation at large. Presbyterians saw in Calvin's stress on predestination a profound modification of this concept of equal depravity and drew the conclusion that, in view of the sinfulness of most men, it was essential for the few saints who were God's elect to rule over the others in strict and unquestioned authority. Calvin himself had drawn a republican conclusion in theory (in his *Institutes of the Christian Religion*) but had provided a practical example, in his Genevan theocracy, of dictatorial elitism.

Neither of these groups of epigonic exegetes captured the essential logic of Calvin's argument, however, as well as did that most impious of political philosophers, Thomas Hobbes (even though he did so unintentionally). As Calvin and Hobbes both recognized, if men are equal only or primarily in the sense that they are all driven by their base passions and are all similarly incapable of achieving their egoistic goals, they are bound to be tormented by constant anxiety. Self-government will prove impossible; security or tranquility will seem the most desirable of goals. The only way they could hope to put an end to their fears and perpetual insecurity would be to abandon all pretensions to self-reliance and to surrender themselves in utter and complete obedience to an omnipotent ruler, who alone can give them the greatest of gifts, the gift of life itself. It is only necessary to substitute for Calvin's God the conception of an all-powerful earthly sovereign—a "Mortall God"—and for his belief in salvation the ideal of security to see how this theological conception of equality can lead to a secular conservatism.

The Reformation also produced an incipiently socialist conception of equality in the doctrines of the so-called left-wing Reformers. Many of those on this left wing were pietists and mystics who wished only to escape society, not reform it. The social activists, however, like Thomas Müntzer and Gerrard Winstanley, were left-wingers in the modern sense of the term. What sets them apart from previous sectarian advocates of Christian communism is that they did not simply wish to withdraw from society into communities of the perfect, there to await the transformation of the rest of the world, but instead saw themselves as agents of social revolution.

Thomas Müntzer and his peasant army were convinced that they had been chosen by God to serve as the vanguard of the millennium. As both Marx and Lenin of that movement, Müntzer offered to his followers a theory of the historical development toward the millennium and a justification for a revolutionary suspension of ordinary ethical standards. The spirit of God, he declared, had entered human history in the incarnation. It would grow stronger despite oppression until it would finally topple the devilish powers of persecution. He and his followers, Müntzer declared, were instruments of the spirit whose mission was to bring about that kingdom of God, if necessary by exterminating the godless.[25] Gerrard Winstanley, who was a much more pacifistic and democratic communist, also believed that the millennium would come in time and space through the work of the spirit of God in history, aided and put into effect by human effort. The time was approaching, Winstanley prophesied, when the spirit would begin to appear in the flesh and "every one shall look upon each other as equall in the Creation."[26] The New Jerusalem, he said, was not to be sought in the hereafter but in this world and this life. While man and the divine spirit are still alien to each other, man mistakenly imagines that redemption is to be achieved after death. But when the spirit finally succeeds in taking hold of him, "man is drawne up into himself again, or new Jerusalem . . . comes down to Earth."[27]

At the base of this socialistic conception of Christian equality is plainly a stress on the spiritual identity of mankind. It is this identity which, in the eyes of the radicals, calls for a total transformation—not only of the church but of secular society as well. This transformation must be guided by the effort to make the egalitarian example of the original Christian community the goal of all mankind. The similarity between the theological statement of this doctrine in historicist and dialectical terms and the later expressions of socialist egalitarianism is arresting evidence of the significance of the Reformation as a turning point in the history of social thought and of the links connecting seemingly diverse theories that are at bottom expressions of the same ethical impulse.

As an ultimate ideal, then, equality was very much an element of Christian teaching from the outset. Just because it was regarded as an ultimate ideal, however, without direct and general bearing on life in the world, it was allowed to remain an abstract and undifferentiated goal. While Christian thought hovered uncertainly between heavenly hopes and earthly resignation, no significant effort was made to define the possible meaning of Christian equality in terms that would be relevant to society. Only when the demand for a socially relevant creed became a full-scale revolt with the Protestant Reformation was such an effort undertaken by recognized spokesmen for large sectors of the Christian community. The outcome was not one Christian ideal of equality but several. The Reformers thus provided a strong foretaste of the rival theories of equality that were to emerge in open contest only in the nineteenth century. Although these egalitarian principles were for the most part applied only within the church, the spectrum of possibility they represented was the same as that which was to define the pattern of political speculation in later times. The Reformers may therefore be said to have contributed to and prefigured the development of the liberal, conservative, and socialist theories of equality.

To some present-day Christians these applications of Christian doctrine will appear as a laudable effort to spiritualize social relations. To others they will appear as improper secularization. To the student of intellectual history, however, perhaps the most intriguing aspect of the matter is what it reveals of the parallel between religious thought and political philosophy. When political philosophy is dualistic with respect to equality, so is Christianity; when Christianity exhibits several ideas of social equality, so, not long afterward, does political philosophy. In matters of social ethics at least, the same tides seem to have carried both traditions in Western thought.

Indeed, it is tempting to speculate that what leads the socially sensitive religious thinker and the ethically sensitive political thinker to the same conclusion must be a fundamentally similar set of assumptions. What both wish to know, in the final analysis, is how to arrange human affairs in the way that best suits the aspirations and limitations of the human species. There are optimists, pessimists, and meliorists among religious thinkers, as there are among political thinkers. How understandable, therefore, that when they consider the possible shape of an egalitarian society, they should arrive at conclusions that reflect their various predilections. The very fact of the convergence should at least make us aware that the distance between religious and political ideals is not as great as is sometimes imagined. The apostles and their master may well have intended their message of equality to refer only to life in a world to come. But those who take this message of emancipation to heart are bound to wish to see it fulfilled in the world in which they live, especially among those in whom the expectation of a transformed world recedes into the distant future. Inevitably, they will also differ as to precisely how it ought to be realized. In this sense, the Christian dilemma with respect to equality is the universal and ever present human dilemma.

The inner character of the message contrasts strikingly with what has happened institutionally to the church founded to maintain and spread the faith. The church has been rent apart into hundreds if not thousands of fragmentary sects. Formal religiosity has lost its once unchallenged grip over civil and political life. Most of the recent expositors of Christian doctrine have reversed older teachings that made secular government subordinate to the authority of the church. These changes, however, have not necessarily affected underlying standards of morality. Some historians have argued that the secular philosophies that emerged with the Enlightenment only amounted to "old wine in new bottles," that is, secularized versions of Judeo-Christian teachings. In view of this long and profound influence, the historian Arnold Toynbee had reason to characterize Western civilization as Christian, even though that designation gives short shrift to the pre-Christian influences that reemerged during and after the Renaissance.

In more recent times, however, the influence of Christianity has become attenuated and ambiguous. Paradoxically, although it has become a world religion, it has lost the coherence and centrality to ordinary life in the West that it once enjoyed. It is not simply that rival churches and sects offer competing versions of its dogmas, but that these churches and sects are caught in a double dilemma that gravely weakens their influence. First, Christianity is a house divided, torn between fundamentalism and modernism, or between an evangelical, literalist tendency and a more ecumenically minded reformist tendency. Second, its validity and bearing are now challenged by a host of hard-to-reconcile changes in attitudes and lifestyles— many of them secularistic, naturalistic, and materialistic—and by competing methods and forms of knowledge, both philosophical and scientific.

In view of these changes, extracting a single timeless Christian message on the social order would seem hard enough, but it is made even harder by internal changes over time. After the apostolic era, in which faith in the resurrection made the end of the world seem imminent and the reform of the social order a secondary matter, patristic writers and canonists sought to adapt the teachings to an enduring world. As the papacy became the recognized seat of ecclesiastical authority, the hierarchical and monarchical order of society gained religious endorsement. From the fifteenth century onward, the Protestant Reformation not only undermined the hold of church dogmas but substituted a new attitude of engagement with secular activities. The Puritan Revolution brought Protestantism into the political order by challenging the alliance of throne and altar and pressing the case for a transfer of authority to the laity. In the nineteenth century, Christian teachings changed again when religion was confronted by the challenges of liberalism, socialism, and evolutionary science. The Catholic Church restated its traditional doctrines, issuing a "syllabus of errors" in the 1860s, denouncing secularism, liberalism, and socialism and ignoring Darwinism, but Protestants divided into religious liberals and conservative literalists. The liberals tried to modernize Christianity by demythologizing it, while the fundamentalists resisted, insisting on the full literal truth of the Bible.

In its first phase, Christianity stood squarely against the legacies of Greece and Rome. Athenian democracy and Roman republicanism were civic ideologies that served as a foundation of loyalty, heroic self-sacrifice in battle, and pride. Pericles, in his famous funeral oration, boasted that Athens was a school to all Hellas and predicted quite accurately that future generations would marvel at its accomplishments. Romans gloried in their advanced way of life and their conquests, which they attributed to their manly ethos. These civic ideologies were complemented and enhanced by naturalistic attitudes toward the body and sexuality and the release of animal spirits in games and festivals. They were also accompanied by mythical pantheistic beliefs and cultural rites that survived from earlier times. Christianity was very different. It came from the east, where there were no strong civic ideologies but only tribal cults. It adopted Judaic monotheism and the prophetic belief that a savior would be sent to establish the kingdom of God on earth. But whereas Judaism was grounded in a covenant tied to a particular people and their particular way of life, the original version of the new Christian belief repudiated everything earthly, "carnal," and particularistic. Instead, it stressed universality, faith, and spirituality, and sought to do away with or minimize the emphasis on ritual and codes of law. Christianity transformed Roman *virtù* into Christian virtue.

Christianity began as an apolitical faith. "The well known antagonism between early Christianity and the *res publica*," Hannah Arendt pointed out, was well summed up in the formula of Tertullian, the church father, *"nec ulla magis res aliena quam publica"* (no matter is more alien to us than what matters publicly).[28] "Political activity," she observes, "which up to then had derived its greatest inspiration from the aspiration toward worldly immortality, now sank to the low level of an activity subject to necessity, destined to remedy the consequences of human sinfulness on one hand and to cater to the legitimate wants and interests of earthly life on the other." The life of the individual "now came to occupy the position once held by the 'life' of the body politic."[29]

Saint Augustine made the opposition between Christianity and Roman beliefs starkly clear by contrasting the city of man with the city of God—the one resting on self-love, the other on love of God; the one celebrating earthly virtue and aiming for fame and power, the other piety and hope of eternal life after death. The city of man had been founded by Cain, the fratricide: "It is recorded of Cain that he built a city, but Abel, being a sojourner, built none. For the city of the saints is above, although here below it begets citizens, in whom it sojourns till the time of its reign arrives, when it shall gather all in the day of the resurrection."[30] Between the two symbolic cities, there could be no Ciceronian compromise. The Christian lived "like a captive and a stranger" in the earthly city and would remain so until the Second Coming.[31] Augustine was not simply attacking the Roman Empire as a departure from republican civic virtue as that ideal had been stated by Cicero or deploring the corruption of Roman morals and manners. He was rejecting the very rationale for Roman citizenship as it had been presented by Cicero, who followed Plato by making justice the basis of communal life and defining justice as giving everyone his due. Augustine insisted that true justice meant not only giving all men their due but above all giving God his due, and therefore that pagan Rome was not a republic, as Cicero had claimed, because it was not founded on justice.[32] The Augustinian message held that humanity was faced with a radical choice between two loyalties, and that for Christians there could be no compromise between them. Submission to temporal authority was a religious obligation, but only because political authority was instituted as a remedy for sin, not because government was a natural necessity or an opportunity to fulfill some divine gift for autonomy. Early Christianity counseled indifference to the civic function. In sharp contrast to the Greek and Roman perspective, the human relationship to the earthly city was redefined so that it did not include commitment to the *polis* or *civitas*, except as a necessary and transitory evil. As a result, there was little in early Christian teachings that amounted to a political theory and no concern at all that political authority be based in any way upon the consent of the governed.

As Rome was weakened by attacks from the German tribes, Christianity came to replace the old civic ideology, which had been hollowed out and weakened by the corruption for which Rome became infamous. Christianity not only filled the vacuum but did so in a way that, as Nietzsche said, entailed a transvaluation of values. Now it was the meek who would inherit the earth, not the proud Roman legions. Now the gladiatorial combats and killings of the coliseum were replaced by the view that murder was sinful and life sacred. After Constantine made Christianity the official religion of the Empire, it became the core belief system of Western civilization. While democratic Athens and republican Rome eventually had a great influence on modern forms of popular government, for the better part of two millennia Christianity had a much stronger influence on Western moral and political thinking. As a result, the belief in popular self-government all but disappeared in Europe. It was replaced by acceptance of what was called the *Respublica Christiana*, a vision of the social order in which obedience to hierarchal authority was thought the key to harmony and godliness. The clergy, led by the pope, were made superior to the laity in temporal as well as spiritual matters. Laymen were considered subjects of authority with no right to govern themselves. Self-determination was thought to violate the very structure of the divinely ordained universe. Law was said to be laid down by God and interpreted by the church; its sanctions were to be applied by clergy and temporal authorities. Subjects had political duties, not rights: "Man, in this system was always and necessarily a subject; he could not be a citizen."[33]

## A HOUSE OF WORSHIP DIVIDED:
## CHRISTIAN SOCIAL TEACHINGS TODAY

In modern times, Christians are apt to hold differing views of the social teachings of the faith. Most would surely agree that the essence of the teachings is the message of perfect love, or *agape*—much as in the Judaic moral teaching of Rabbi Akiba, "Love thy neighbor as thyself," and Rabbi Hillel, "What is hateful to you never do to your fellow man. That is the entire Torah; all else is commentary." Christianity, it is often said, created a universal faith founded on the message of brotherly love by removing the "stumbling blocks" of rituals like male circumcision and by reinterpreting the covenant with Israel as a metaphor for a promise to all who would accept it. But to begin to understand the message of the Gospels in its specifically Christian meaning, it is necessary to appreciate its emphasis on the dialectic of original sin and the hope of salvation based on the sacrifice of Christ on behalf of sinful humanity. In essence, the Christian message calls upon people to recognize that without God's grace they are lost souls, given over to the proverbial seven deadly sins, but that by accepting the sacrifice of the savior on their behalf, they may be saved from the evils of the human condition. Humanity is offered the all-precious gift of a gratuitous redemption from sinfulness and its terrible consequences by a merciful God who sacrifices his only son to redeem its sins. Believers are asked to credit the revealed understanding that human beings are created by God and given free will; that when they disobey his warning not to try to obtain knowledge of good and evil, they are banished from paradise and forced to live by the sweat of their brow and to suffer sickness and natural calamities; that they are finally rescued by the creator when he sends his son to be persecuted and killed, and by so doing offers believers an opportunity to renounce sin and achieve salvation.

To accept this narrative requires a leap of faith, since it can in no way be demonstrated scientifically, any more than can the miracles said to attest to the truth of the Gospels, but that leap has in fact been made in many generations. Later on, interpretive embellishments were added, including the doctrines of the Trinity, the virgin birth of Mary, the immaculate conception of Jesus, the resurrection of the body, the intercession of saints, the belief that in the Mass the believer can ingest in the wine and wafer the blood and body of the redeemer, and for Calvinists, the belief in predestination. Warranted or not, these are additions. The kernel of the message is that God created humanity in his image, but human beings, exercising their God-given gift of free will, have continued to disobey God's commandments—and that the savior promised in the Jewish scriptures has appeared and shown the only way out of their misery.

Apart from the credibility of this account, at least one profound question remains to be answered. Are the injunctions to piety and good behavior meant to promote a reform of life in the world or are they designed to win a reward in the afterworld? Many Christians would no doubt say they are for both ends, but the Gospels do not provide a clear answer. They suggest that if people accept the Christian message Christ will return in glory and reign over "the world to come." But is the world to come to be in this life or the afterlife? "My kingdom," Christ said in the Gospel according to John, "is not of this world." But did that mean that when he returned he would establish God's kingdom on earth, or rather that God's kingdom is not an earthly kingdom? That question was probably left open because the expectation then was that the world as it was would soon come to an end. The result is a deep ambivalence in the Christian attitude toward the social order.

Christianity today is a house divided not only because of sectarian and denominationalist rivalries but more importantly because Christians have fallen into sharp disagreement over the essential meaning and bearing of the Gospels, not just over theological nuances. In America, Garry Wills suggests, the conflict is between "Christianity of the head" and "Christianity of the heart."[34] That is a polite way of putting it, but of course there is more to the disagreement than this image suggests. Fundamentalists insist on the literal truth of the Bible, whatever science may say about such things as the history of the universe. They oppose efforts to revise its moral standards with respect, for example, to homosexuality to suit modern attitudes of toleration toward sexual choices. They believe that anyone who disagrees with any of its strictures is damned, whether they be Christian or non-Christian. The fundamentalists shut their eyes to what science and biblical criticism reveal. Onlookers can only shake our heads in wonder when a Baptist spokesman says with perfect confidence that God does not hear the prayers of a Jew; or when a leading minister tells the people of Orlando that they will suffer fiercer hurricanes for allowing a gay pride parade; or when the principal of Wycliffe College, Oxford, one of the leading schools of theology in the Anglican Church, announces that 95 percent of the people of Great Britain now face the prospect of hell because of their failure to follow the Christian faith (as he sees it); or when a best-selling author like Tim LaHaye tells his readers to prepare for the end of the world, which will not be all that bad if they are on the right side of God because they will be "raptured" up to heaven while others are "left behind."

Liberals or moderates want to preserve the mystery and moral teachings of the religion but ignore the mythological thinking and customs of a less enlightened age such as patriarchalism, slavery, capital punishment, and, for some, the condemnation of homosexuality. The status of women in the family and ecclesiastical callings is also very much a subject of contention. The head and the heart are hardly complementary. There appears to be no middle ground here, unless somehow the belief that stewardship requires Christians to save the environment provides a new platform for unity.

While these debates divide Christians, the influence of Christianity as a whole has become attenuated and gravely weakened. That process began when the legacy of classical antiquity was discovered and revived in the Renaissance. The church lost its moral compass in its vicious treatment of heretics, in its condemnation of Galileo, and when popes made a mockery of their vows of celibacy and cynically sold "indulgences" for sins. During the wars of religion, adherents of competing sects slaughtered each other with hardly a care for Christian love. Finally, in modern times, the churches failed abysmally even to try to stop the Holocaust—a tragedy above all for those who perished but also for what it revealed about the moral bankruptcy of the churches as institutions.

Christianity remains in parlous straits, despite superficial indices. Worldwide, the hold of religion, including that of Christianity, is strengthening. According to the *Economist*, the proportion of people attached to the world's four largest religions—Christianity, Islam, Buddhism, and Hinduism—rose from 67 percent in 1900 to 74 percent in 2005, and may reach 80 percent by 2050.[35] Fully a third of the world's peoples—or about 2 billion—subscribe to some form of Christianity, making it the largest confession in the world, followed by Islam with some 1.5 billion. These numbers are rising, however, because the growth rate of poorer, less educated areas of the world is considerably higher than that of more developed regions. Much of the growth in Christianity, moreover, is coming in the least sophisticated forms of belief, such as Pentecostalism, which is challenging institutionalized Catholicism and Protestantism alike. Europe and the United States are on opposite courses. In America, evangelical religion continues to play an influential role, whereas in Europe, fundamentalism, indeed even modernized Christianity, is in decline. As the *Economist* reports, only 20 percent of Europeans say that God plays an important role in their lives, compared with 60 percent of Americans. Only 44 percent of people in Britain believe in the existence of God, and only 15 percent go to church each week, against 40 percent of Americans. In England, Protestants are said to go to church when they are born, marry, and die and not otherwise. Even in the Catholic heartlands of Spain, Italy, and Ireland, church attendance rates have dropped below 20 percent. And in Dublin, home to 1 million Catholics, only one priest was ordained in 2004.[36]

One indication of the difficulty religion is in is that it is open season for attacks in the name of atheism. Christopher Hitchens goes so far as to say that "religion poisons everything."[37] This is the kind of polemical exaggeration that sells books but does not advance understanding and gives atheism a bad name. Religion is not always toxic. Sometimes it inspires kindness and compassion, the building of schools and hospitals, and acts of charity, compassion, and humility. In the United States, Quakers ran the "underground railway" for escaping slaves, and Unitarians like Harriet Beecher Stowe campaigned for abolition. Black churches inspired the civil rights movement and Martin Luther King's philosophy of nonviolence. Without the secularized Judeo-Christian values of benevolence and compassion, the Enlightenment would have left a moral vacuum in the wake of its assault on superstition and the belief in miracles. If Christianity is not simply reformed but argued out of existence, what is to replace it? The examples of Soviet communism and Nazi fascism suggest that the answer may be nihilistic political religions that would make the old religion seem invaluable. In this connection, it is well to recall the observation of Alexis de Tocqueville: "There are sections of the population in Europe where unbelief goes hand in hand with brutishness and ignorance, whereas in America the most free and enlightened people in the world zealously perform all the external duties of religion."[38]

For well over a millennium, following the appearance of the Gospels, Christian moral teachings eclipsed the civic precepts of Greece and Rome in Western consciousness, along with the pantheistic, naturalistic, and mythological cosmologies that informed classical religious perspectives. Despite the apparently egalitarian implications of these teachings, they were used to support monarchy, feudalism, and intolerance. Today, however, the social bearing they convey is radically different. Christianity now, in all its varieties, supports or is at least not hostile to democracy, social justice, and ecumenical brotherhood. As this contrast strongly suggests, there is no essential or inherent Christian teaching concerning the social order. But there is an evolved meaning on which there is now considerable agreement, despite continuing disagreement on the application of Christian teachings to specific issues and areas of social conduct, such as human reproduction, marriage and divorce, or economic systems and practices. Just as the early church was ambivalent toward the permanence of the social order, it was ambivalent about making the equality of souls the basis of social order. In time, that ambivalence has been overcome, and the message of Christianity for society has become decidedly egalitarian.

## NOTES

1. Alexis de Tocqueville, *Democracy in America*, trans. George Lawrence (Garden City, NY: Anchor Books, 1969), author's introduction, p. 12.

2. *New English Bible* (Oxford: Oxford University Press, 1961), p. 323, emphasis added.

3. Ibid.

4. Ibid., pp. 623–24.

5. *A History of Mediaeval Political Theory in the West* (New York: Barnes & Noble, 1953), vol. 1, p. 8.

6. See Werner Jaeger, "The Greek Ideas of Immortality," *Harvard Theological Review* 52, no. 3 (July 1959): pp. 135–48.

7. Cf. George H. Sabine and Stanley B. Smith, introduction, Marcus Tullius Cicero, *On the Commonwealth*, trans. Sabine and Smith (Columbus: Ohio State University Press, 1929), p. 25, and John Plamenatz, "Equality of Opportunity," in *Aspects of Human Equality, Fifteenth Symposium of the Conference on Science and Religion*, ed. Lyman Bryson et al. (New York: Harper, 1957), p. 87.

8. Rudolf K. Bultmann, *The Theology of the New Testament*, trans. K. Grobel (New York: Scribner, 1951), vol. 1, p. 309. Bultmann begs the question inasmuch as the "eschatological congregation" may conceivably mean the community of believers or, more narrowly, the church. If the term refers to either one, the belief in spiritual equality can be quite legitimately understood as an injunction to institutional equality, either within the social structure in general or within the *organization* of the church.

9. See Søren Kierkegaard, "On Authority and Revelation," *The Book on Adler, or a Cycle of Ethico-Religious Essays* (1848), trans. W. Lowrie (Princeton, NJ: Princeton University Press, 1955), pp. xxv–xxvi.

10. For a somewhat different Marxist view, however, see F. Engels, "On the History of Early Christianity" (1894–1895), in Karl Marx and Friedrich Engels, *Basic Writings on Politics and Philosophy*, ed. L. Feuer (New York: Doubleday, 1959), pp. 168–94. Here Engels discerns parallels between early Christianity and the early history of working-class movements but notes that, limited as it was by its time, Christianity introduced the idea of another world as a "religious way out" (p. 184).

11. *Group Psychology and the Analysis of the Ego*, trans. J. Strachey (New York: Norton, 1949), p. 43.

12. Gordon S. Wood, *The Radicalism of the American Revolution* (New York: Vintage, 1993), p. 235.

13. Ernst Troeltsch, *The Social Teaching of the Christian Churches*, trans. O. Wynn (New York: Harper, 1960), p. 61.

14. Ibid., p. 77.

15. *The Genealogy of Morals* (1887), trans. H. B. Samuel, in *The Philosophy of Nietzsche* (New York: Modern Library, 1927), p. 643.

16. See George Foot Moore, *Judaism in the First Centuries of the Christian Era, the Age of the Tannaim* (Cambridge, MA: Harvard University Press, 1962), vol. 2, pp. 72–73 passim.

17. Troeltsch, op. cit., pp. 74–75.

18. *The City of God*, trans. M. Dods (New York: Modern Library, 1950), p. 693.

19. Ibid., p. 694.

20. See C. Homes Dudden, *The Life and Times of St. Ambrose* (Oxford: Oxford University Press, 1935), vol. 2, pp. 502–54, and A. O. Lovejoy, "The Communism of St. Ambrose," *Essays in the History of Ideas* (Baltimore, MD: Johns Hopkins University Press, 1948), p. 298 passim.

21. This development is traced in Sanford A. Lakoff, *Equality in Political Philosophy* (Cambridge, MA: Harvard University Press, 1964).

22. *An Open Letter to the Christian Nobility of the German Nation, Concerning the Reform of the Christian Estate* (1520), in his *Three Treatises* (Philadelphia: Fortress Press, 1943), p. 14.

23. For Luther's novel views on "fleshly lust," see particularly his *A Commentary on St. Paul's Epistle to the Galatians* (1535), ed. P. S. Watson (London: James Clarke, 1953), p. 503. For his economic views, see in addition to *Three Treatises* his *On Trading and Usury, Works of Martin Luther* (Philadelphia: A. J. Holman, 1930), vol. 4, pp. 12–69.

24. See Max Weber, *The Protestant Ethic and the "Spirit" of Capitalism and Other Writings*, trans. Peter Baehr and Gordon C. Wells (New York: Penguin, 2002).

25. See particularly T. Müntzer, *Sermon Before the Princes* (1524), in *Spiritual and Anabaptist Writers*, ed. G. H. Williams and A. Mergal (Louisville, KY: Westminster John Knox Press, 2006). For a study of the entire left wing of the continental Reformation see George H. Williams's magisterial descriptive history, *The Radical Reformation* (Philadelphia: Westminster Press, 1964). See also the perceptive analysis of Müntzer and his movement in Norman Cohn, *The Pursuit of the Millennium* (New York: Oxford University Press, 1970).

26. *The New Law of Righteousness* (1648) in *The Works of Gerrard Winstanley*, ed. G. H. Sabine (Ithaca, NY: Cornell University Press, 1941), p. 159.

27. *Fire in the Bush* (1650), ibid., p. 458.

28. Hannah Arendt, *The Human Condition: A Study of the Central Dilemmas Facing Modern Man* (Garden City, NY: Doubleday Anchor, 1959), p. 65.

29. Ibid., p. 287.

30. Augustine, *The City of God*, trans. Marcus Dods (New York: Modern Library, 1950), p. 479.

31. Ibid., p. 696.

32. Ibid., p. 699.

33. William J. Bouwsma, *Venice and the Defense of Republican Liberty* (Berkeley: University of California Press, 1968), p. 6.

34. Garry Wills, *Head and Heart: American Christianities* (New York: Penguin Press, 2007).

35. *Economist*, 20 November 2007.

36. Ibid.

37. Christopher Hitchens, *God Is Not Great: How Religion Poisons Everything* (New York: Hachette, 2007), p. 12.

38. Tocqueville, op. cit., vol. 1, p. 295.

# 2

———— ❦ ————

# Civic Humanism

"Civic humanism" is a translation of the term *bürgerhumanismus* first advanced by the German historian Hans Baron during the time of the Weimar regime in the 1920s.[1] When introduced, it referred to a new consciousness featuring the advocacy of republican government in terms that harked back to the classical belief in active citizenship and resistance to tyranny. Baron also noted an emphasis on the study of Roman history and literature as a guide to institutional design and conduct. As a political ideology, it was an outgrowth of the belief in the dignity and creative potential of human life that animated Renaissance humanism, as well as a reaction to threats against the independence of Florence. It has continuing relevance insofar as it informs later conceptions of civic culture that emphasize a sense of community.

While civic humanism does not necessarily contest transcendental religious notions, it does focus attention on the here and now rather than on life after death, and on improving the human condition. It emerged alongside and as a result of the revival of the classical naturalism and secularism that had been eclipsed in medieval times by Christian strictures on carnal sinfulness. It gave rise to a broader revival of classical political values, especially pronounced in Britain and America, which has been called "the Atlantic Republican tradition"[2] and which aimed to limit monarchical absolutism or substitute it with republicanism. Like the Renaissance original, it championed liberty and self-government based on the capacity for reason and civic virtue on the part of the new self-reliant middle class. The civic humanists and republicans were not naive, however. With the classical experience very much in mind, they feared the dangers of factionalism, corruption, and Caesarism and engaged in constitutional engineering, such as checks and balances, to minimize the dangers.

Baron showed that civic humanism arose in Florence in the fifteenth century for reasons that are as much political as intellectual. The flowering of political speculation during this period was a response to threats to Florentine liberty from the Duke of Milan and others, extending from the late fourteenth century to the mid-fifteenth century. The threat ended when the independence of the Florentine republic was negotiated by Cosimo de Medici in 1453, but the repressive rule of the Medici brought republicanism into disfavor. The turmoil produced a "new type of humanism" emphasizing "political engagement" and a celebration of Florentine republicanism.[3]

Quentin Skinner has criticized Baron's thesis on the ground that it gives short shrift to the influence of the early "city republics" of Italy and "the wider movement of Petrarchean humanism which had already developed in the course of the fourteenth century."[4] Skinner shows persuasively that however much military threats may have focused the minds of Florentines on the preservation of civic liberty, they had been for some time preoccupied with the justification of republican liberty and the problems involved in maintaining it—not least the need to avoid reliance on mercenaries in favor of citizen armies. The general aim was to maintain "a free constitution under which every citizen is able to enjoy an equal opportunity of involving himself actively in the business of government."[5] This concern for citizen self-government led civic humanists to prefer the republic to monarchy. Whereas Baron believed that this preference represented a decisive break with early, late-medieval humanist thinking, Skinner contended that this sentiment can be found much earlier.

Whatever its lineage, however, civic humanism is undoubtedly an outgrowth of the general literary and artistic humanism that was an early feature of the Renaissance. It is rooted in the visionary celebration of human creativity of Gian Francesco Pico della Mirandola, whose "Oration on the Dignity of Man" has been called the manifesto of Renaissance humanism. Later, it takes explicitly political form in the thinking of the Florentine civic humanists, notably Francesco Guicciardini and Niccolò Machiavelli. Still later, it appears in the republican thinking that arose in England and America—notably in the political works of John Milton and James Harrington—in the seventeenth century. During the Age of Enlightenment, it was joined to the belief that reason, even if unaided by revelation, can establish universal moral values, and that thanks to the irreversible advance of knowledge, humanity is capable of "indefinite perfectibility." In this evolution, civic humanism became part of the ways of thinking that came to make up the modern sensibility in politics, morals, and aesthetics.

At its core is an idealization of human creative and empathetic potentialities, coupled with an injunction to civic engagement and philanthropy. Civic humanism achieved its clearest and strongest ethical formulation in Immanuel Kant's categorical imperative. Kant argued that reason suggests universal maxims, and that the will is fully autonomous only when it is guided by these maxims. "So act," the imperative holds, "that your conduct can be a maxim for all mankind." Civic humanism gives this moral philosophy political bearing. Montesquieu in particular made "civic virtue" the hallmark of republicanism, and the rise of parliamentary government, supported by British and American intellectuals—notably Milton, Harrington, and the American Founding Fathers—gave it political saliency in the eighteenth century and beyond. As popular government took hold, civic humanism provided its essential moral and practical foundation, creating confidence in the potentialities of ordinary people and challenging the claim that only those endowed with heroic or supernatural qualities could tame the sinful tendencies of the mass of fallen mankind.

## HUMANISM, AESTHETIC AND CIVIC

Renaissance humanism arose out of a fascination with the rediscovered legacy of classical civilization, especially "humane letters," or what today would be called the humanities. That classical legacy was summed up in the word *humanitas*. Hans Kohn has given an illuminating explanation of the Roman origins of Renaissance humanism:

> What the Greek Stoics brought to Rome has been defined by Cicero as *humanitas*. The Romans received Greek learning and Greek language and grew by it into something peculiarly Roman and at the same time universal. They molded it into the plasticity of the Latin language, developed through the creative genius of Catullus, Cicero, and Lucretius in the time of Caesar, and of Horace, Ovid, and Virgil in the time of Augustus. The word *humanitas* itself was in its new meaning an originally Roman word to which no close parallel existed in the Greek language. It came to mean in Rome the Greek *paidea*, culture in the sense of Isocrates, the refined manner, the benevolent attitude, the cultivated appreciation of the beautiful which distinguished the Greek from the barbarian. This meaning was combined with the meaning of the Greek word *philanthropeia*, love of man, so that humanitas came to mean a compound of the qualities of the human and the humane, that quality which makes man a man, "quidditas qua homo est quod est." Under Stoic influences it became both an individual norm that man might become a real man, might cultivate the human in himself; and, at the same time, a universal norm, the consciousness of the human quality common to all human beings, the oneness of humanity.[6]

First and foremost, humanism meant the rediscovery of the art and architecture and literature of ancient Greece and Rome. It started innocently enough and with a limited agenda—the rediscovery of the legacy of classical antiquity that had been ignored and condemned by the church as pagan. Petrarch is often said to have been the founder of humanism because he steeped himself in the classics, collecting everything he could find, including inscriptions and coins, and imitated classical forms in his writing. Others followed his example by trying to arrest the destruction of the remnants of classical art and architecture. The Italian humanists studied the Latin and Greek classics, formed book clubs to read them, and decorated busts of the great authors with garlands. Humanism inspired a new appreciation of the greatness of Rome and evoked nostalgia for a time when people could investigate all fields of knowledge and imagination without fear of reproof. It also produced a more joyous conception of life, free from religious strictures.

The early humanists were mainly imitative, until the recovery of the classical legacy inspired the most gifted to think that they could not only admire and ape the old achievements but add to them. Leon Battista Alberti, an architect and writer, spoke for this new boldness when he said, "Men can do all things if they will." Erasmus of Rotterdam criticized corruption in the church and kings who plundered society, but he did not challenge religion; instead he sought to explain what the Bible really meant. The historian Lorenzo Valla became famous for revealing that the so-called "donation of Constantine" was a forgery, by which he undermined one of the claims of the Roman see, created when the emperor Constantine in the fourth century converted to Christianity and made it the official religion of the Empire. The church did not react defensively; Valla was made an official of the papal curia.

As the treatment of Valla suggests, humanism was at first not perceived as hostile to religion or the church. On the contrary, major humanists like Erasmus saw the study of humane letters as one more revelation of God's works. In the same spirit Newton and Descartes studied nature and the mind. Newton spent much of his time trying to prove that the Bible was accurate. Descartes was a follower of the Jansenist version of Catholicism. The papacy encouraged not only religious art but secular art and embellishments as well. Great patrons emerged like Lorenzo di Medici and the Renaissance popes—who were well rewarded by the thousands of works of sacred art that today adorn the churches of Italy and the museums of the world.

At the same time, however, the Renaissance unleashed a spirit of criticism unknown in the Middle Ages, when the church had succeeded in stamping out deviations as heresies. Renaissance writers and scientists generally avoided censure—with the significant exception of Galileo—

because they did not make a frontal assault on church doctrine. Still, change was unmistakably in the air. Suddenly artists discovered the uniqueness of the human form rather than its Gothic uniformity, influenced by the belief in the equality of souls. Michelangelo's *David*, commissioned by the government of the city of Florence, celebrates a biblical figure but in a way that reveals his naturalness, heroic masculinity, and individuality. Leonardo da Vinci explored human anatomy, not the anatomy of the soul, and tried to understand how birds, not winged angels, managed to fly. He even designed a submarine but suppressed the plans "on account of the evil nature of men." Galileo investigated the heavens and challenged church orthodoxy, which foolishly relied on the Ptolemaic cosmology as support for the view that the earth had been created by God as the center of the universe. Boccaccio's *Decameron* described ambitious merchants, lecherous friars, and cuckolded husbands. The contempt of the worldly was replaced by a candid acknowledgment of the way people actually behaved. Readers may have been scandalized, but they were fascinated at the same time. Shakespeare was evidently a Christian, and possibly a hidden Roman Catholic, but his plays became a kind of literary scripture, a replacement for the stories told in the Bible that had preoccupied Western thinking until then. The new theater reproduced but went beyond the mystery plays and passion plays that had occupied the stage exclusively to that time. Small wonder that thespians were suspected of immorality and were required to be licensed. And no matter what the morals of Shakespeare's Macbeth, Hamlet, Richard III, or Othello, or of Mozart's Don Giovanni—dramas in which all villains had to be punished—the very portrayal of human villainy, and of ambition and jealousy, and even madness, enlarged the canvas on which people could see life displayed. The plays often celebrated the pagan fixation on fame and glory, which the church had denounced as pagan and carnal, however often the ambitious were brought down by tragic flaws. Shakespeare was no political revolutionary, as is obvious from his sympathetic treatment of Julius Caesar, but his exhibition of the human drama, in all its depths and shallows, was itself revolutionary, as were the romantic novels that followed. Literature became a mirror up to nature, not a window into the soul. Whereas medieval art had fastened on depicting scenes from the scriptures, like those depicted in the stained-glass windows of the churches, now painters examined the human form and painted people in respectable modes of life, aristocrats and businessmen who were their patrons, and the battles in which nations led by kings vied with each other. Eventually they would discover landscapes, seascapes, still-life domestic scenes, commoners, exotic natives, and nightmare visions. Nineteenth-century Impressionism seemed a rebellious attack on objective reality, and in some ways it was; but its emphasis was on the way of seeing that the artist saw, and eventually abstract art took the rebellion against so-called objectivity to its ultimate conclusion by making the vision of the artist the reality. Art historians David M. Robb and J. J. Garrison have incisively described the initial change wrought by the Renaissance:

> The character of Renaissance culture is an indication of the reorientation of European thought away from the abstract and spiritual values of medieval culture toward more material ones. In the Middle Ages, man was of no importance save as he was part of the church, and the physical earth was only a proving ground for the soul where it was prepared for the ultimate realities to be found in the next world. In the Renaissance, man's inherent dignity was once more perceived in a way comparable in some respects to that of classic antiquity, and in addition the world in which he lived was no longer thought to be only a symbol but was considered something of fundamental and intrinsic significance. The interest in nature that is apparent in Renaissance thinking may seem at first to be a logical outcome of the realistic view of material forms in the Middle Ages. But medieval realism is an outgrowth of the conception then prevalent of nature as a manifestation of divine purpose while that of the Renaissance is scientific in the modern sense in being born of a searching inquisitiveness about things which are believed to have meaning in and of themselves rather than merely as symbols in a previously determined order of an abstract nature. It was in the Renaissance that an objectively analytical point of view toward nature is found for the first time; and as the most important institution therein, man once more became the focal point of human interests rather than being reduced to the status of a cog in a theological machine. In its basic humanism, Renaissance thought is distinguished from that of the Middle Ages in a much more significant way than by its classicism.[7]

Over time, the Renaissance reoriented the Western mind from a preoccupation with piety and otherworldliness toward a focus on self-expression, the investigation of nature, and the improvement and enjoyment of life on earth. This was the first stage in a transformative process that was to be followed by the early flowering of the natural sciences in the sixteenth and seventeenth centuries, the glorification of reason as the fountain of progress in the eighteenth, and the artistic adventurism that began in the Age of the Baroque and included Romanticism, Impressionism, Modernism, and more recent movements. Popular sensibilities lagged these epochal developments, but eventually rationalism, science, and artistic license, often embedded in bohemian lifestyles, struck at the already decayed roots of medieval thinking and produced what is generally thought of as modernism—including capitalism, urbanization, and industrialization, along with the social protests they inspired; experimentation in the fine and popular arts; and a cultural fascination with novelty, hedonism, and the critical spirit. The nineteenth-century historian Jacob

Burckhardt was among the first to recognize the dramatic change that the Renaissance represented in creating these linked humanistic outlooks:

> In the Middle Ages both sides of human consciousness—that which was turned within as that which was turned without—lay dreaming or half awake beneath a common veil. The veil was woven of faith, illusion, and childish prepossession, through which the world and history were seen in strange hues. Man was conscious of himself only as a member of a race, people, party, family, or corporation—only through some general category. In Italy this veil first melted into air; an *objective* treatment and consideration of the State and of all the things of this world became possible. The *subjective* side at the same time asserted itself with corresponding emphasis; man became a spiritual *individual*, and recognized himself as such.[8]

Writing a century later, the popular historian Barbara Tuchman went further than Burckhardt in describing the Renaissance as "the period when the values of this world replaced those of the hereafter":

> Under its impulse the individual found in himself, rather than in God, the designer and captain of his fate. His needs, his ambitions and desires, his pleasures and possessions, his mind, his art, his power, his glory, were the house of life. His earthly passage was no longer, as in the medieval concept, a weary exile on the way to the spiritual destiny of his soul.[9]

At first, however, the "rebirth" of ancient letters and wisdom remained limited to the contemplative pleasure and edification of quietist poets and scholars. Gradually it merged with an assertive defense of the sovereign independence of the increasingly rich, powerful, and confident merchant cities of Italy. Ethical humanism served as a bridge from the study of humane letters to civic humanism. Pico Della Mirandola issued what amounted to a charter of ethical and civic humanism when he depicted man as a creator in the image of God. As Burckhardt put it, the state too became a work of art. Machiavelli's prince was a creator endowed with a kind of superhuman *virtù*—not Christian virtue but Roman *virtù*, connoting manliness, a quality that could become *virtu ordinata*, or common virtue in the successful republic. In the Italian city-states, republicanism grew out of the medieval commune, as institutions were created to organize civic participation and provide for executive leadership. As in antiquity, the belief took hold that political life, the life of the citizen, had high value, that the goal of life was to improve the here and now, not to wait to be rewarded for piety in the hereafter. Thus Pico said,

> Finally, the Great Artisan mandated that this creature who would receive nothing proper to himself shall have joint possession of whatever nature had been given to any other creature. He made man a creature of indeterminate

and indifferent nature, and, placing him in the middle of the world, said to him "Adam, we give you no fixed place to live, no form that is peculiar to you, nor any function that is yours alone. According to your desires and judgment, you will have and possess whatever place to live, whatever form, and whatever functions you yourself choose. All other things have a limited and fixed nature prescribed and bounded by our laws. You, with no limit or no bound, may choose for yourself the limits and bounds of your nature. We have placed you at the world's center so that you may survey everything else in the world. We have made you neither of heavenly nor of earthly stuff, neither mortal nor immortal, so that with free choice and dignity, you may fashion yourself into whatever form you choose. To you is granted the power of degrading yourself into the lower forms of life, the beasts, and to you is granted the power, contained in your intellect and judgment, to be reborn into the higher forms, the divine."

Imagine! The great generosity of God! The happiness of man! To man it is allowed to be whatever he chooses to be! As soon as an animal is born, it brings out of its mother's womb all that it will ever possess. Spiritual beings from the beginning become what they are to be for all eternity. Man, when he entered life, the Father gave the seeds of every kind and every way of life possible. Whatever seeds each man sows and cultivates will grow and bear him their proper fruit. If these seeds are vegetative, he will be like a plant. If these seeds are sensitive, he will be like an animal. If these seeds are intellectual, he will be an angel and the son of God. And if, satisfied with no created thing, he removes himself to the center of his own unity, his spiritual soul, united with God, alone in the darkness of God, who is above all things, he will surpass every created thing. Who could not help but admire this great shape-shifter? In fact, how could one admire anything else?[10]

This encomium to mankind did not directly or necessarily challenge the Christian conception of man as created in the image of God. On the contrary, it endorsed this belief but in a way that emphasized human creativity rather than sinfulness. Like Michelangelo's portrayal on the ceiling of the Sistine Chapel of God touching Adam with divine power, Pico saw humankind as having been given godlike powers that could be used to achieve good or evil—boundless creativity or destructiveness.

Pico's oration emphasized the creative potential of human beings in their social character. As Athanasios Moulakis points out, republican thinking emerged in a city that was very different from the medieval village. It had a lively commercial life and one in which learning and the exchange of ideas were encouraged. Political thinking, moreover, was not the monopoly of learned civil servants or of only a few thoughtful intellectuals:

Florence possessed an articulate and literate population who had ample opportunity to exercise their arguments on matters of state in a social frame of frequent consultation, discussion, and controversy in both formal and informal gatherings. There was also a tradition of composing memoranda for private and family use, or to circulate among small circles of friends who might share ideas and sympathies. Fathers made a habit of leaving books of observations, admonitions, and advice for the benefit of their children. Naturally there are great differences of tone and content, from homespun commonplace to gnomic shrewdness, to flights of eloquence and analytical insight. This is all part of the intellectual inheritance of men who cannot properly be called "humanists," though they were certainly schooled in Latin and the Roman classics, such as Machiavelli and Guicciardini.[11]

Machiavelli became famous and infamous for stripping the veil that masked the realities of princely cunning and ruthlessness, but it should not be forgotten that he was himself a republican, and that *The Prince* was one such memorandum intended to be part of a larger work that would devote more attention to the lessons of the Roman republic, as recorded in his *Discourses on the First Ten Books of Livy*. He and Guicciardini became the first modern expositors of republicanism, the predecessors of Montesquieu and the British "Commonwealthmen." In so doing, they anchored popular government in the ideal of civic humanism. Machiavelli saw Roman republicanism as the expression of a civic culture that valued liberty and the diversity it inevitably entailed. He understood that for this liberty to be protected, the mass of the citizenry must develop a sense of civic loyalty. Roman *virtù* provided that sense. It was in effect the basis of citizenship, an attitude overriding loyalty to family, clan, or region, and providing the community with a strength of purpose comparable to that which motivates princes. Although he recognized that princes can impose order by a combination of cunning and force, he warned that this order must come at the price of liberty. The key political question for him therefore was how to achieve both order and liberty, and the answer was to apply the lessons of Roman experience, above all the lesson that a patriarchal senate should be checked by a popular assembly. The "struggle of the orders," which seemed so calamitous to others, struck him as the very basis of Roman liberty because it prevented a concentration of power that could become oppressive. Recognizing that in times of crisis the republic might need to suspend its ordinary guarantees, he called attention to the Roman practice of allowing for constitutional dictatorship, that is, the suspension of ordinary civil liberties and political procedures to allow for rule by a single consul for a limited and prescribed period of time. In this way, reason of state could be made constitutional rather than a license for despotism. His fear, also drawn from Roman experience, was that civic humanism would lead the state to be so successful as to promote expansion, and expansion had been the downfall of Roman republicanism because popular government could not control an empire.

Like Machiavelli, Guicciardini recognized the need to separate political behavior from the sphere of individual behavior. The state, he observed, behaved in accordance with "reason of state," which sometimes entailed a violation of ethical norms. He counsels cities to avoid conquering others, if at all possible, because conquest will require suspension of ethical norms. That way, the city can serve as an opportunity for the expression of distributive justice among its citizens, and they can learn to exercise good judgment by taking part in its decisions. Guicciardini proposed that Florence provide for both a senate and a council of the people to allow for deliberation. Both would need to be kept relatively small so as to assure that deliberation was not overwhelmed by demagoguery. Guicciardini was no democrat; he wanted to restrict membership in both bodies to representatives of leading families. Moulakis contends that Guicciardini's "realist constitutionalism" is not properly civic humanism because it assumes that people who participate in politics do so because they are driven by ambition and calculation, rather than out of a sense of civic responsibility based on an ideal of civic virtue. Because rule is restricted to a limited group of fully entitled and politically active citizens, it departs from the model of classical republicanism. It emphasizes the leadership of exemplary statesmen, not the character or will of the public.[12] The point is well taken, but Guicciardini was ahead of his time, because republicanism became a creed that blended the emphasis on civic virtue with the interest-based political economy that would emerge after the age of the Italian city-states.

Before that blending became obvious, civic humanism put great stress on civic virtue, as Montesquieu, the most highly regarded writer on law and politics in the century, made clear at the outset of *The Spirit of the Laws*: "What I call virtue in a republic is love of homeland, that is love of equality. It is not a moral virtue or a Christian virtue, and this is the spring that makes republican government move, as honor is the spring that makes monarchy move."[13] In effect, Montesquieu made civic virtue the primary requisite for the success of the republican experiments that were to follow his midcentury writings.

In Britain and America, republicanism gained strength in the eighteenth century, reflecting a social and economic transition in which smallholders became more numerous and were endowed with the sterling qualities of the "yeoman farmer," in contrast to the corrupt, luxury-loving ways of absolutism and aristocracy. In the process, a new egalitarianism, couched in terms of republicanism and civic virtue, emerged to challenge the age-old distinction between the highborn few and the common many.

Baron saw the Weimar Republic as an expression of the spirit that had first appeared in the Italian city-states. Beyond seeking to identify the character of a particular time and place, he studied the political culture of Renaissance Florence as an instance of a transhistorically exemplary mode of communal existence relevant to his own times. As Moulakis has pointed out, Florentine civic humanism represented for him a decisive turning point in history . . . an epochal event that, by looking backward to antiquity, pointed forward to modernity, which he embraced wholeheartedly, without the misgivings of a Jacob Burckhardt or a Max Weber, as a liberating, civilizing, progressive process. The advent of civic humanism marked for Baron the victory of secular economic, social, and political ideals versus the asceticism, religious obscurantism, and hierarchy of the Middle Ages. Civic humanism provided the vital vehicle for the translation of the exalted ancient idea of citizenship to the modern age. The humanist defense of republican liberty against monarchical tyranny announced the beginnings of modern democratic thought, elevated by an educational ideal of classical inspiration, and accompanied by a renewed cultural creativity.[14]

The Renaissance challenge to the centrality of religion and theology also played a critical role in enabling the rise of modern physical science. Copernicus, Newton, and Descartes did not set out to challenge religious belief, but by making the study of nature independent of theology and placing man and his planet in a universe regulated by scientific laws that did not allow for intermittent miraculous intervention, they effectively dethroned theology as the queen of the sciences. Francis Bacon aphorized that knowledge and power coincide and urged reliance on inductive scientific method. Although he also reassured the religious authorities that while a little knowledge makes a man an atheist whereas more leads him to appreciate the wonders of the created universe, he offered a far more radical vision in his utopian account, *The New Atlantis*. There he imagined an island somewhere in the Pacific regulated by a different Christianity, a religion of "light," presided over by leading scientists, featuring laboratories for experiment and synthesizers of new knowledge, and dedicated to "the enlarging of the bounds of human empire, to the effecting of all things possible." John Locke may have been a believing Christian or at least a deist, but his philosophic system did not require belief in a transcendental deity. Benedict Spinoza was excommunicated by the Dutch Sanhedrin for heresy. Thomas Hobbes's books had been burned for the same reason. By the eighteenth century, the philosophers of the Enlightenment had no doubt that religion was an obstacle to reason and progress. They were apt to be deists who thought of the divinity as a clockmaker, a creator of the universe who set it in motion under a system of physical laws but did not intervene thereafter. They saw the history of humanity as a gradual progression from ignorance, superstition, and fear of the unknown to reliance on the advance of knowledge to achieve "indefinite perfectibility." Organized religion was a barrier to progress because it relied on supernatural dogmas that could not be questioned. "What is enlightenment?" Kant asked. His answer was "*Sapere Aude!*" (Dare to Know!), or what amounted to a defiant recasting of the story of the Garden of Eden; only this time, the result was not the expulsion from paradise but the promise of progress through the accumulation of scientific understanding and its applications. As Skinner remarks, the emphasis on man's creative powers so characteristic of Renaissance humanism not only helped foster a new interest in individual personality but also the belief that "man might be able to use his powers to bring about a transformation of the physical world."[15]

So important has civic humanism been to the modern spirit—in the concern for individual liberty, for creative freedom, for political self-government, and for a Promethean conquest of nature—that it has lost its narrowly political character. In modern times civic humanism is thought of politically as the sense of community, altruism, and tolerance—an ideal that should inform both civil society and the public sector. It may also be discerned in the belief in the importance of education and dialogue as a necessary condition for active citizenship and social progress.

## NOTES

1. See Hans Baron, *The Crisis of the Early Italian Renaissance: Civic Humanism and Republican Liberty in an Age of Classicism and Tyranny*, rev. ed., 2 vols. (Princeton, NJ: Princeton University Press, 1966).

2. See J. G. A. Pocock, *The Machiavellian Moment: Florentine Political Thought and the Atlantic Republican Tradition* (Princeton, NJ: Princeton University Press, 1975).

3. Baron, op. cit., vol. 1, p. 459.

4. Quentin Skinner, *The Foundations of Modern Thought* (Cambridge: Cambridge University Press, 1978), vol. 1, p. 71.

5. Ibid., p. 78.

6. Hans Kohn, *The Idea of Nationalism* (New York: Macmillan, 1944), p. 64.

7. David M. Robb and J. J. Garrison, *Art in the Western World* (New York: Harper & Brothers, 1942), pp. 180–81.

8. Jacob Burckhardt, *The Civilization of the Renaissance in Italy* (1860), trans. S. G. C. Middlemore (London: Phaidon, 1951), p. 81.

9. Barbara Tuchman, *The March of Folly: From Troy to Vietnam* (New York: Ballantine, 1984), p. 52. Not that she considers the Renaissance in Italy an unalloyed blessing: "To an unusual degree in the Renaissance good walked with evil in a wondrous development of the arts combined with political and moral degeneration and vicious behavior. Discovery of classical antiquity with its focus on human capacity instead of on a ghostly Trinity was an exuberant experience that led to a passionate embrace of humanism, chiefly in Italy, where it was felt to be a return to ancient national glories. Its stress on earthly good meant an abandonment of the Christian ideal of renunciation and its pride in the individual undermined submission to the word of God as conveyed by the Church. To the extent that they fell in love with pagan antiquity, Italians of the ruling class felt less reverence for Christianity, which, as Machiavelli wrote in *The Discourses*, makes 'the supreme felicity to consist in humility, abnegation and contempt of things

human,' whereas pagan religion found the chief good in 'grandeur of the soul, strength of body and all the qualities that make men redoubtable.'" "Strangely," she continues, "the efflorescence in culture reflected no comparable surge in human behavior but rather an astonishing debasement." Ibid., pp. 57–59. As part of an account of the "march of folly," she goes on to chronicle the vicious behavior of arbitrary rulers, secular and religious alike, with their inducements to self-indulgence and senseless violence.

10. Gian Francesco Pico della Mirandola, "Oration on the Dignity of Man," in Ernest Cassirer, Paul Oscar Kristeller, John Herman Randall, et al., eds., *The Renaissance Philosophy of Man* (Chicago: University of Chicago Press, 1948).

11. Athanasios Moulakis, introduction, *Republican Realism in Renaissance Florence: Francesco Guicciardini's "Discorso di Logrogno"* (Lanham, MD: Rowman & Littlefield, 1998), p. 14.

12. Ibid., p. 22.

13. Montesquieu, Charles Secondat, Baron de, *The Spirit of the Laws*, trans. Anne M. Cohler, Basia Carolyn Miller, and Harold Samuel Stone (Cambridge: Cambridge University Press, 1989), foreword.

14. Athanasios Moulakis, "Civic Humanism," *Stanford Encyclopedia of Philosophy* (Palo Alto, CA: Stanford University Press, 2007).

15. Skinner, op. cit., p. 98.

# 3

∞

# Liberalism

The nineteenth century has been called "the age of ideology" because so many competing social ideas clamored for acceptance as public opinion suddenly began to loom large in politics. Ideologies—simplified versions of philosophic doctrines better adapted to action than elaborate treatises—served to mobilize segments of the public by providing rationales for loyalty and militancy that joined principle to self-interest. One of the first to emerge came to be known as liberalism. Liberalism was one offshoot of Renaissance humanism, an outgrowth of its encouragement of freedom of inquiry and self-expression. In the spirit of Pico's oration on the dignity of man, liberalism broadened the connotation of liberation beyond creativity in artistic expression so as to extend emancipation to the lives and aspirations of the industrious middle class and eventually of all. The Enlightenment served as a link between Renaissance humanism and the emergence of liberalism by making liberty of thought critical to progress. Liberalism became the ideology of the champions of parliamentary government, free trade, and what were thought of as natural rights. As absolutism was challenged and rejected, as the democratic revolutions spread the ideals of natural or human rights and popular sovereignty, and especially as religious toleration became a necessity to avoid civil war, liberalism became a more and more attractive political ideal.

The etymological root of liberalism is the word "liberty," from the Latin *libertas*, among the terms revived in the Renaissance. The medieval church had made the freedom of the will the basis of moral responsibility, but the church authorities did not approve of "liberty of conscience" because it could lead believers into error and heresy. Indeed, it was indirectly as a result of the turmoil produced by the Reformation that freedom of the will became the basis of the belief in the right of conscience, that is, in the right of individuals to choose among the various Christian denominations. In effect, the zero-sum distinction between orthodoxy and heresy was dropped in favor of the view that for the sake of civil peace, divergent forms of faith had to be accepted as more or less equal competitors for the allegiance of the believer. The wars of religion eventually led to toleration, and toleration was the first expression of liberalism. The demand for toleration was couched in terms of the belief that whatever might be said for the truth claims of the various forms of Christian belief, it would be against the essential tenets of the faith to compel anyone to accept a particular version of Christian doctrine. This was a new, grudgingly accepted idea, forced upon Christians by the reality of the schisms, the hatreds, and the persecutions it engendered. The pragmatic spirit of toleration, with its encouragement of "denominationalism" and individual freedom of choice, laid the groundwork for the more general ideal of liberalism. Discontent with the imposition of orthodoxy by political authorities also produced a belief in the right of resistance, that is, the right to oppose political authorities that imposed beliefs that could not be accepted. From the right of resistance against religious imposition, it was only a short step to a claim of the right of revolution against tyrannical authority exercised in other respects as well. If forced belief was a basis for rebellion, then so was enforced taxation without representation.

The ideology that first came to sum up the resulting belief in the liberty of the individual was liberalism. The word "liberal" came into wide use politically in the 1820s after a political party in Spain called itself *los Liberales*. In England, the Whigs, or "Country Party," had already arisen in opposition to the Tory (or King's) Party. The Whigs had brought off the Glorious Revolution of 1688 that ended absolutism and produced limited monarchy, with power passing increasingly to a parliament dominated by an elected House of Commons. In the nineteenth century the Whigs were renamed Liberals. That party's most famous leader was William E. Gladstone. To stress their opposition to liberal ideas, the Tories called themselves Conservatives and found a major champion in Benjamin Disraeli. Oddly enough, when the term "liberal" was first introduced in England, it was used by Tories to smear the Whigs by associating them with Catholic Spain. The term stuck because the Whigs liked it. It enabled them to present themselves as champions of the liberty of the individual rather than of the propertied interests. Indeed "individualism" was another new word that arose in the early nineteenth century and was often used as a synonym for liberalism. Canada, which had become a British dominion, still has a Liberal Party and a Conservative one, except that the Conservatives changed their name to the oxymoronic Progressive Conservative Party.

As the ideology of the British Liberal Party, liberalism had several key elements: the legacy of natural rights/social contract theory as expounded by John Locke; a belief in free market economics expounded by Adam Smith and the Manchester School; and a belief in religious toleration that was greatly expanded to include freedom of speech and freedom of the press. Critics on the left said that what really concerned liberals most was the protection of property rights. According to Marx and Engels, liberalism was merely the "disguise of the bourgeoisie," that is, an attempt to make capitalism seem natural and justified by resting it on universal natural principles of justice. Following in their footsteps, Harold J. Laski in the twentieth century wrote an influential book on liberalism in which he contended that the liberty of liberalism is set in the context of property.[1] In the same vein, C. B. Macpherson defined liberalism not as the advocacy of individualism in all respects but of "possessive" individualism.[2] From the perspective of liberals themselves, economic freedom, or the right to hold private property and to acquire and dispose of it, is the expression of a more general belief in the liberty of the individual, which includes the civil rights to freedom of speech, assembly, and conscience, and the political right to consent to authority.

The Whigs believed in the principles formulated by John Locke, physician to Sir Anthony Ashley, the first Earl of Shaftesbury, who was the leader of the faction. Locke's *Two Treatises of Government*, which were begun earlier in the decade but published only later, came to be regarded as the rationale of the Glorious Revolution. Those principles were that government should protect natural rights—life, liberty, and property. Add to that a commitment to the antimercantilist, pro–free trade, antitariff, antiregulatory economics of Adam Smith's *Wealth of Nations*, published in 1776, to freedom of the press and freedom of religion, and the result is what it meant to be a liberal in England for most of the nineteenth century.

Although he did not use the term "liberal," Locke's analysis of the true origins of civil society became the bedrock for British and later American liberalism. In the first treatise, Locke attacked the ideas of Sir Robert Filmer, whose belief in patriarchalism claimed that civil authority was rooted in God's gift to Adam of dominion over nature. Filmer extended this belief so as to make fathers in the family and holders of royal authority the legitimate ruling figures in all societies. Without directly challenging the idea that fathers should regulate families, Locke ridiculed the idea that the authority of kings was somehow derived from God's gift of sovereignty to Adam. He argued that the belief that human beings must be subjected to a civic patriarch was incompatible with the natural liberty of the individual. It was, he said, a rationale for slavery that no freeborn Englishman should accept. Commentators have sometimes suggested that Locke deliberately chose to attack Filmer rather than Thomas

Hobbes, another defender of monarchy, because he was preparing to make use of Hobbes's theory for his own purposes, without acknowledging his debt to Hobbes lest he be accused of atheism and materialism; Filmer was an easier target. But Locke presented a view of human nature, the state of nature, and the social contract that was markedly different from Hobbes's. It is therefore quite misleading to see Hobbes, not Locke, as the founder of liberalism merely because he made an earlier effort to emphasize atomistic individualism as the condition of the state of nature. Hobbes used this technique of argument to support the conclusion that human beings should seek the protection of civil government in any form and could not complain of any infraction the sovereign committed so long as he protected their lives.

There was much more to patriarchalism, however, than a defense of the authority of the father in the family and of the king in society. In effect, patriarchalism was a theory of the social order which stressed the centrality of the nuclear family and groups in general rather than of the individual, and of custom and sentiment rather than contract and rationality. When Locke developed his alternative to patriarchalism, he did so in terms that made society an atomistic collection of individuals held together not by custom and tradition but by contract entered into by rational individuals operating out of a sense of self-interest, guided by moral law available to reason. In the second treatise, Locke argued that to discover the true original or rise of civil government, it was necessary to do a thought experiment in which we imagine what society would be like without it. In a "state of nature," people would be independent and equal in their capacities. They would be concerned to protect their lives and to draw from the bounty of nature what they needed to sustain themselves. As rational creatures, they were also born with the capacity to understand the moral law, that is, the injunction not to harm anyone else except in self-defense. The natural law would also acknowledge a right of property—the right the individual had to the sustenance he derived by his own labor by mixing his sweat with the soil. (As Macpherson points out, however, Locke assumed that even in a state of nature a man might acquire servants, and that these servants could be his agents in acquiring property.) The natural law imposed limits on the amount of property anyone could take from nature. He could take only enough to provide for his own needs, not so much as to deprive others of the opportunity to satisfy their own needs, or a surplus that would only spoil. But Locke acknowledged that the introduction of money had provided a way for people to get around these limitations, or at least to get around the spoilage limit. On this ground, he was accused by socialist critics of rationalizing "infinite appropriation."

Locke grounded the ideal of liberty on a contrived or imagined premise, or a thought experiment known as "state-of-nature thinking." He did not originate this way of thinking but drew on the prior work of theorists like Thomas Hobbes. Locke's portrait of the state of nature differed from that of Hobbes in that he did not think that a state of nature would necessarily be a state of war, and he presented a different view of the role of the law of nature and the rights it implied. With respect to the state of nature, Locke agreed with Hobbes that since by definition it would be one in which people lived without common government, they would rely on themselves for security and well-being. But he supposed that they might have few occasions for becoming aggressive toward others because there was enough land to satisfy their needs. Rather than having to encroach on his neighbor's property, an individual could simply relocate *in vacuo loco*, to an empty space. There was therefore no necessary reason why the state of nature should be an inevitable state of war, or why individuals should be so insecure in this state as to believe that they must do all they could to master everyone else.

Locke also argued that in a state of nature human beings would use their natural reason to discover the law of nature, which would teach them first of all that it would be in everyone's interest to agree to respect the right to life. Hobbes, too, thought that reason would enable human beings to recognize that it was in their interest to seek peace. But Locke buttressed the appeal to self-interest with the contention that the law of nature imposed a moral obligation because it was the law of God, and men were God's creatures, duty bound to follow his injunctions.

Locke also differed from Hobbes in drawing more than one corollary right from the law of nature. Hobbes had argued that only one natural right arose in the state of nature, which was the right to life, or more precisely the right to whatever was necessary to preserve one's life. Locke argued that the law of nature also gave human beings rights to liberty and property, or estate, on the ground that both liberty and property are necessary to the security of life. This is a critical difference, because it requires a private sector or civil society that checks any tendency of the state to be all encompassing, and allows for a right of revolution if a government does not protect the rights to liberty and property.

Philosophically, Locke became famous for arguing that there were no innate ideas, that the mind is a *tabula rasa*, a blank slate, on which impressions are formed which then become ideas. This put a great deal of emphasis on the environment and education. Liberals from then on become imbued with the idea that education was essential if people were to use their liberty wisely. It is no accident that liberals tend to be champions of public education, especially as society became more and more democratic. If people were to be given the suffrage, liberals believed, it was important that their rational faculties be developed. Education would do that. Conservatives were at first leery of educating the lower classes. They were afraid these classes would no longer be willing to be subservient to their masters and would become intoxicated with half-baked ideas of equality and even the superiority of numbers to quality.

Locke's discussion of the right of property is ambiguous. It has been interpreted as an effort to protect property from all state interference, that is, to make it an absolute right that would allow for infinite appropriation. But Locke also noted that in civil society, the laws regulate property. This could mean simply that the laws define and protect property rights, but it could also mean that the state could interfere, for example, to prevent any one individual from engrossing so much land as to deprive others of access to land. The introduction of money may indeed have enabled people to avoid the spoilage limitation, but the other limitation—the right of others to have access to land—runs up against the finitude of land, all the more so if one restricts land to states that own it. This prefigured the split that would develop later between those liberals who saw state interference with property rights, as determined by the play of the market, as "the road to serfdom," in Hayek's phrase, and those who believed that state intervention was necessary to preserve competitive equality in a world in which there was no longer empty space for people to go off and take their share of nature's bounty. Before that split developed, another movement of ideas developed that provided another platform for liberal thinking, which was utilitarianism.

In the thinking of Jeremy Bentham, liberalism acquired an alternative to natural rights/social contract theory, an alternative that was in some ways superior, in others not so. It was superior in the sense that it did not require acceptance of a fictitious state of nature that might be configured in a variety of ways to justify respect for individual liberty. Bentham argued in effect that it was only necessary to accept the idea that human beings are self-interested and that they aim to pursue happiness or pleasure and to avoid pain. He derided the resort to state-of-nature thinking as philosophical fiction and famously said that "natural rights are nonsense, natural and imprescriptible rights nonsense upon stilts."[3] Instead, Bentham proposed that by thinking in terms of the "felicific calculus," it was obvious that all human beings wished to maintain their lives, as the sine qua non for pursuing pleasure. Furthermore, in order to ascertain what individuals wanted, it was advisable to give them an opportunity to register their preferences by voting. Since representation would be needed to legislate in large societies, they would vote for representatives, But Bentham was leery of the possibility that the representatives would substitute their own interest for those of the voters; he therefore laid down that they must be "dislocable" in frequent elections. Bentham thus drew out the democratic implications of Locke's theory. Locke had argued for representation, but he had not clearly stipulated that the elections must be based on universal suffrage. He had allowed for a property qualification on the ground that otherwise the right of property would not be secured, as the majority of the poor and landless might expropriate property owners if they were enfranchised. Bentham believed that everyone should count for one and none for more than one. He also accepted the idea that although the recognition of property rights was valuable to the common welfare because it gave an incentive for people to work for the common benefit, it would be right for the legislature to limit property rights for the sake of the general welfare. That would certainly include inheritance taxes. Bentham saw no justification for passing wealth on from one generation that had earned it to another that had not. The point was to encourage everyone to use his industry for his own benefit and that of others.

Bentham's theory was disquieting to many liberals, because it made the issue of rights not a matter of nature or natural laws but of social convention. Suppose that happiness could be achieved without liberty or property? Would we not then return to the thinking of Hobbes? And indeed some of Bentham's disciples were close to Hobbes when they defined law as the command of the sovereign. Would a Benthamite be ready to sacrifice liberty for the sake of pleasure? Would he not suppose that the good of the greatest number might justify harm to individuals? John Stuart Mill sought to allay some of these misgivings by reinterpreting utilitarianism to make clear that it provided support to liberty. Liberty, Mill argued, is essential if people were to know the truth, and the truth would also help them understand their interests. On utilitarian grounds, then, happiness required liberty. It meant that in all matters that are self-regarding, individual judgment and action should be respected. Only in those matters where the exercise of liberty interfered with the like exercise by others, or caused harm to them, would it be right to restrict that liberty. The most important kind of liberty for Mill is intellectual liberty, because it is only through the free exchange of ideas and the competition of ideas in the marketplace, that human beings could discover truth and falsehood, and progress would be assured. Otherwise error and superstition would mislead people, and they would be at the mercy of demagogues and charlatans. Mill followed Bentham in arguing for representative government, though he preferred proportional representation as the fairest form of election. The one quarrel he had with Bentham was that Bentham made it seem that all pleasures were equal. Mill argued that there was a hierarchy of pleasure, that only those who had experienced the pleasure of a work of art, say, could realize that it was superior to some childish game. And he did not believe that the felicific calculus should be arranged so that all individual pleasures were assigned the same value. "Better Socrates dissatisfied than a pig satisfied," said Mill; "push pin" is not as good as poetry. This view undercut the democratizing impact of Bacon's utilitarian thinking, and then and since it has opened liberals to the charge that they are elitists. The answer is of course that utilitarian democrats or liberals in the John Stuart Mill mode aim to improve human understanding, to raise everyone as close as possible to the ideal of Socrates, rather than to reduce everyone to the lowest common denominator.

In the middle of the century, Mill became a pivotal and authoritative spokesman for British liberalism. He distinguished between two meanings of the term, the one English, the other continental. The other meaning Mill singled out as continental was derived from Rousseau rather than Locke. It put the emphasis on popular self-government through the state. Whereas Lockean liberalism leans toward laissez-faire, toleration, natural rights, and limited state sovereignty, continental liberalism leans more toward participatory democracy, toward an active role for the state, representing the community, and not for the idea that the state should leave the individual completely to his own devices.

Isaiah Berlin later did a gloss on Mill by distinguishing between two types of liberty, freedom from and freedom to.[4] He preferred freedom from over freedom to. The Rousseauean formula opens the door to coercion by an overpowerful state, which could require conformity rather than dissent and make the dissenter into what Ibsen called in his famous play of that name, an enemy of the people. Critics of Rousseauean liberalism say that at the very least it creates the nanny state that is always legislating new codes of individual behavior.

English liberalism, rooted in the thinking of John Locke and Adam Smith or the later ideas of Jeremy Bentham, gradually underwent a change. Some liberals remained unreconstructed champions of laissez-faire. The best example is Herbert Spencer, the champion of Social Darwinism. Spencer wrote books with titles like *The Man versus the State* to emphasize his fear that the state would encroach on the liberty of the individual in the name of advancing social welfare. By doing so it would interfere with the natural mechanism by which society made progress, the mechanism of the market. Spencer added the prestige of evolution to the traditional belief in the magic of the invisible hand. Others compromised with socialism and created social liberalism,[5] which was the foundation of the welfare state and also led to the transition from the Liberal Party to the Labor Party. The emergence of welfare state liberalism had everything to do with the advance of capitalism and the transformation of the industrial system from one that emphasized smallholdings to one that invoked the creation of giant corporations and industries. The fear of monopoly led many liberals, like the American progressives, to want to put a check on the growth of monopolies. At the same time, they came to feel that the terms of competition had become unequal. Most people were apt to be workers dependent on capitalist owners. If all that was done would be to protect the right of property, that inequality would result in a new kind of feudalism in which workers would become wage slaves and owners would be free to keep them at a minimal level of subsistence. The socialist critique of capitalism hit home, but liberals wanted to preserve the freedom that capitalism entailed by regulating it. Regulation would not only curb the excesses of property owning and the danger of monopoly, but it would also spread the benefits of industry by allowing for a safety net and for redistribution of wealth through taxation. Welfare state liberals like Leonard Hobhouse and T. H. Green argued that individuals had duties as well as rights and that the social contract had to be such as to allow for inequality of outcomes only on the premise that opportunity for different outcomes was equal and that everyone benefited from combined labor. The millionaire was allowed by society because his existence created jobs for many others. This was the social bargain.

This amalgam was highly important for the development of the "positive" state or "welfare state liberalism." It laid the groundwork for rationalized policies aimed at regulating the swings of the business cycle, curbing monopolistic practices, regulating food and drugs for public safety, and redistributing wealth through the progressive income tax and the inheritance tax. These measures were adopted in recognition that the liberty of the individual had to be balanced and integrated with the good of the society as a whole. It was not enough to leave the care of the indigent and injured to the benevolence of the wealthy; a safety net was needed that would be provided by the state through taxation. How extensive the safety net would become was a matter of intense debate. Many social liberals wanted greater equality, but others feared that to increase the tax rate would discourage initiative and entrepreneurial activity, and that it represented an overweening interference with the free play of individual actions. Liberals have never fully resolved the question of what constitutes the balance. As a result, societies influenced by social liberalism vary considerably in the tax burdens they impose and the benefits they provide. All modern societies now have social insurance systems, and most provide for universal health care either by mandating insurance coverage or by using taxation as a source of revenue. In the process, the definition of what constitutes liberal human rights has broadened considerably. Security of life is now understood to mean security against extreme poverty and against the ravages of illness and disease.

Liberalism also extends outward, via a concern for universalizing human rights. Liberal societies are therefore urged to champion human rights abroad, by providing aid to developing countries and assisting them to overcome poverty by other means, including access to markets and assistance with education. Liberals tend to want to promote peaceful conflict resolution out of respect for the right to self-determination of other people, in contrast to those who would tend to rely on force and make alliances with autocratic rulers out of national self-interest. In an increasingly dangerous world, liberals tend to champion efforts toward arms reduction and control.

Both in domestic and international terms, they tend to favor efforts to get at the root causes of discontent and to reform those who cause violence by substituting rehabilitation for imprisonment, by treating drug addiction as an illness rather than a crime, and by seeking to remove the causes of violence, including terrorism, by improving the conditions that are thought to breed antisocial behavior. Liberalism is of course more than an ideology and more than a philosophy; it is a temperament. The liberal tends to be passionate about invasions of civil liberties and civil rights but compassionate with regard to human suffering. Liberals have been in the forefront of efforts to desegregate society racially, to promote religious toleration, and to overcome xenophobic hostility to immigrants.

Liberals are also sensitive, however, to the criticism that they can sometimes be gulled by vicious people into supposing that by appeasing them, they can bring them to reform. A tough-minded liberal is one who is skeptical about such possibilities but nevertheless persists in believing that down deep human nature is good and needs environmental nurturing in order that the good will triumph over the inclination to do harm. A liberal society is one in which the spirit of live and let live is widespread, and in which there is both a strong encouragement of self-reliance, of the achievement of all that people are capable of, and at the same time a sense of fellow feeling or communal responsibility that leads to philanthropy—liberalism in the original sense of the word—and to altruistic behavior.

## LIBERALISM IN AMERICA:
## THE HARTZ THESIS AND ITS CRITICS

Many have noted that the United States is very much in the grip of liberalism, no one more provocatively than Louis Hartz in *The Liberal Tradition in America*.[6] His assertion that because of the virtual absence of feudalism in the New World, Lockean liberalism faced no ideological competitors and therefore became an unacknowledged but unchallengeable national creed, has been "enormously influential,"[7] even though it has not met with universal acceptance. Some of the resistance is warranted, but once the thesis is modified to take account of valid criticisms and subsequent developments, including scholarly studies, it remains indispensable to any understanding of American political thought, past or present.

Hartz was well aware of the differences between old or classical liberalism and its newer, more inclusive form, and of the conflict between right-wing liberals (whom he called Whigs) and left-wing liberals (whom he called, variously, "democrats," "reformers," or "the petit bourgeois giant"), but in his reductionist zeal to show that both factions were trapped within the magnetic field of "irrational Lockianism," he made too little of the differences. Nor did he give proper weight to other influences—including republicanism (both in its older and modern forms), racism, nativist xenophobia, and religious beliefs both compatible and incompatible with liberalism—which remain constant, often nagging companions. There is indeed an American consensus, centered on the ideal of equal liberty imbibed by the founding generation mainly from the natural rights/social contract theorists and enshrined in the Declaration of Independence, the Constitution, and the institutions of government and civil society arising on these foundations. This consensus is, as Hartz showed, demonstrably narrower than the spectrum of Western European thought—at least until recently, as Western Europeans and others elsewhere have come to think more like Americans. It has become a divided or pluralistic consensus, however, in which the common goal is equal liberty, but in which debate persists, often heatedly, over how equal liberty should be realized in practice and what means are appropriate to achieve and protect it. Paradoxically, the intensity with which Americans subscribe to the consensus makes them especially sensitive to the gap between ideal and real and apt to succumb at various periods to bouts of what Samuel P. Huntington called "creedal passion."[8]

Hartz saw the consensus as a threat to internal dissent and to realism in foreign policy. He hoped it would somehow be "transcended," possibly by a traumatic encounter with the outside world—a prescient observation, given that it was made well before both the American involvement in Vietnam and President Nixon's historic rapprochement with China. Whether the pluralistic character of the consensus will now lessen this threat remains to be seen, although there is already some evidence that in both respects that worried Hartz, American liberalism has become less dogmatic and more pragmatic, if not altogether tolerant—in his word, less "irrational." What Hartz did not foresee, and perhaps could not, in the early years of the Cold War and the rise of the third world, was that in large part as a result of the impact of America upon the world, liberalism has come to be "ascendant" throughout the Western world and in many developing countries as well, presenting an opportunity "in which many of the most critical political issues will be contested within the liberal framework."[9]

The flattest contradiction of the Hartz thesis has come from leading members of the latest generation of historians of the colonial and federal periods who contend that the revolt against British imperial rule was inspired by republican rather than liberal ideas. They have drawn upon and amplified Caroline Robbins's study of the English "Commonwealthmen," Bernard Bailyn's and Gordon S. Wood's examinations of their influence in seventeenth- and eighteenth-century America, and J. G. A. Pocock's assimilation of the Anglo-American school to the broader "Atlantic republican tradition."[10] Pocock went so far as to describe the American Revolution as "the last great act of the Renaissance."[11] He has put the criticism of the Hartz thesis especially bluntly. Against the "conventional wisdom" which sees the Puritan covenant reshaped into a Lockean social contract, to such an extent that Locke is made "a patron saint of American values," his interpretation

> stresses Machiavelli at the expense of Locke; it suggests that the republic—a concept derived from Renaissance humanism—was the true heir of the covenant and the dread of corruption the true heir of the jeremiad. It suggests that the foundation of independent America was seen, and stated, as taking place at a Machiavellian—even a Rousseauean—moment, at which the fragility of the experiment, and the ambiguity of the republic's position in secular time, was more vividly appreciated than it could have been from a Lockean perspective.[12]

Wood argues, in implicit criticism of Hartz, that Americans were not "born free" but became so as a result of a radical revolution—one that turned an agrarian, patriarchal society into a commercial republic.[13] Garry Wills downgrades the influence of Locke on the Declaration of Independence by contending that Jefferson's thinking was influenced much more by his study in college of the works of the Scottish moralists, Francis Hutcheson, Adam Smith, and David Hume.[14]

Other critics have found different shortcomings. On the political left, Hartz's view that Americans have been gripped by "this fixed, dogmatic liberalism of a liberal way of life"[15] has been rejected because it seems to shrug off the conflict between capital and labor and to rule out the possibility of radical reform. This criticism from the left is somewhat ironic. Although Hartz noted tartly that "the American Marxist learns nothing and forgets nothing," he drew heavily on Marxian theory—unlike professed Marxists like Granville Hicks, who "had a genius for evading the constructive uses to which Marxian analysis can be put in the American scene."[16] He also sharply criticized the national intolerance of "un-American" ideologies, especially the fear of socialism in any form. In the politically charged atmosphere of the 1960s and 1970s, however, his interpretation was sometimes dismissed as one of a number of "end-of-ideology" interpretations that had the effect of covering up the country's social conflicts. To critics on the left, all varieties of "consensus theory" smacked of status quo propaganda implying that fundamental reform could never succeed because American conditions "had eliminated the cultural bases for a collective approach to resolving social problems." This interpretation is said to have "resonated with the national mood of those Cold War years" and to have "tended to banish social conflict from United States history."[17] Leftist radicals preferred more conflict-oriented versions of the country's past, like Howard Zinn's,[18] and critiques of the country's selfish individualism like *Habits of the Heart*,[19] or more encouraging readings, notably Charles Reich's *The Greening of America*, according to which the country was shedding its traditional liberal obsession with the acquisition of wealth and adopting the eco-communitarian vision Reich called "Consciousness III."[20] William M. Sullivan has argued that contrary to Hartz, new historical research, coupled with post–World War II experience, including the civil rights movement and the anti–Vietnam War agitation, shows that the spirit of Puritan covenantalism and the republican civic virtue animating the American Revolution could be rekindled to support a new form of democratic socialism.[21]

The same opposition to liberal self-interest has led many American conservatives and neoconservatives either to ignore or reject Hartz's theory for neglecting entirely the founders' supposedly central preoccupation with civic virtue rather than with (liberal) individualism. The view of the founders is said by some conservatives to reflect a moral outlook running counter to the secularist and materialist implications of Locke's notion that life is, as Leo Strauss memorably put it, "the joyless quest for joy."[22] But some have sought to interpret the founders' liberalism so as to make it more acceptable to conservatives. To this end, Thomas G. West adopts the convoluted tactic of assimilating Lockean liberalism and democratic equality to the classical aristocratic ideal. "The evidence is overwhelming," he concedes, "that Locke was the leading authority on the principles of government for the Americans who made the Revolution," but in spirit, the founders were adhering to the classical view that political life must foster the end of virtue, by substituting "virtue as the chief public standard of right" for rule by the virtuous—a presumably prudential decision that classical philosophers would have sanctioned as a way of adjusting to egalitarian social conditions.[23]

Some historians and students of political theory intrigued by Hartz's thesis or willing to accept it in large part have expressed disagreements on particular counts. John Patrick Diggins, while recognizing the persuasiveness of Hartz's thesis, contends that American Lockeanism absorbed elements of New England Puritanism, rooting the American version of liberalism in a Christian tradition that made "moral ideas and culture more important than material interests and power as motives of human action."[24] Others have found Hartz's thesis overly reductionist. Thus, Richard Hofstadter—often identified as another exponent of "consensus" theory—disagrees with Hartz on two grounds. First, he argues that although American debates do indeed take place within a narrower compass than Europe's, they remain real and important in their own terms. "[T]he consensus point of view is limited in that it is only an assertion about the frame or configuration of history and not about what goes on in the picture. . . . Americans may not have quarreled over profound ideological matters, as these are formulated in the history of political thought, but they quarreled consistently enough over issues that had real pith and moment."[25] Second, he disagrees with Hartz's view that antebellum arguments between Northerners and Southerners did not reflect a breakdown of the liberal consensus but only proof of its hold. "One may differ," Hofstadter contends,

> as to whether to call the impassioned arguments of the North and South "ideological" differences—but if this was not an ideological conflict (and I think it was), we can only conclude that Americans do not *need* ideological conflict to shed blood on a large scale. In the face of this political collapse, what does it matter if Professor Hartz reassures us that, because the Southern states were simply adhering to their own view of the Constitution which they incorporated into the Confederate constitution, the Civil War does not represent a real failure of the American consensus? . . . I can best put my own dissent by suggesting a cartoon: A Reb and a Yank meet in 1865 to survey the physical and moral devastation of the war. "Well," says one to the other consolingly, "at least we escaped the ultimate folly of producing political theorists."[26]

Sharper dissent has been registered by those especially mindful of the nativist and racist strands of American history. In order to understand the broadening of the criteria for American citizenship, Judith N. Shklar observes, it is critically important not to overestimate the role of liberal ideals, as Hartz had done:

> America has not always marched single file down a single straight liberal highway as both the lamenters and celebrators of its political life have claimed, either in despair or in complacency. What has been continuous is a series of conflicts arising from enduring anti-liberal dispositions that have regularly asserted themselves, often very successfully, against the promise of equal rights contained in the Declaration of Independence and its successors, the three Civil War amendments.[27]

Orlando Patterson has put a similar complaint more dismissively: "In America, the pathways to freedom have been just as exceptional and paradoxical as those of Germany and, for African Americans, nearly as tragic. Louis Hartz's smooth linear curve from the Mayflower to the cold war champion of freedom cannot be taken seriously."[28] Those who see feminism or the campaign for homosexual rights as challenges to the notion that Americans have always been guided by liberal beliefs might pose comparable objections.

Some of this criticism is unwarranted or at least based on a superficial grasp of what Hartz was arguing and a failure to appreciate the strengths of his insight. When critics interpret him as contending that Americans are in the grip of a Lockean liberal consensus that limits the room to maneuver ideologically, they are certainly right, but it would be wrong to read him as supposing that as a result American history has been one long Arcadian idyll. He could hardly have denied that there had been serious conflicts and even bloody confrontations in American history, especially in the Civil War, but also in the later struggles between labor and capital. With respect to slavery, Hartz was under no illusion that it was in any way compatible with liberalism. His point was rather that Southern apologists, in their effort to preserve their "peculiar institution," erected a never-never land at odds with the national self-image. Because the neofeudal society they sought to justify was not authentic feudalism but plantation capitalism based on slavery, they were forced into all sorts of bogus romantic deceits. Their liberalism was "so traditional that even they could not get away from it." Drawn in one direction by Americanism and in another by their effort to preserve slavery, they found themselves in the utterly contradictory position of defending democracy for whites, while grounding it "on one of the most vicious and antiliberal doctrines of modern times"—an obvious reference to racism.[29]

It was the very hold of liberal doctrine over the American psyche, even in the face of antiliberal practices like slavery, that fascinated Hartz. He might also have cited the example of the nineteenth-century cry of "Manifest Destiny," when jingoists rationalized an aggressive war against Mexico as a liberal crusade to liberate its people from the yoke of feudalism and colonialism.[30] Over and over he drove home his central theme that, compared to the ideological conflicts that often convulsed Western Europe over roughly the same period, prevailing preconceptions compelled the major parties to American conflicts to occupy a relatively narrow space along the spectrum of political belief. This has been a space in the liberal middle between the poles of the conservative right and the socialist left, marked on the one side by aristocracy and absolutism and on the other by anarchism or collectivism. His aim was to show that from the early contests between Jeffersonians and Hamiltonians over the scope of central authority to those between Democrats and Republicans over the New Deal, American political battles have been waged ideologically within this constrained Lockean liberal framework, whereas European arguments had run the full gamut, from royalism to socialism and anarchism. Hartz also sought to show that Americans were unaware of their own fundamental agreement, polemically exaggerating opponents' views by casting them in European terms. As Irving H. Bartlett explains, contrasting Hartz's account with Parrington's, "Jacksonian Democrats likened the Whigs to the corrupt Old World aristocracy; the Whigs rejoined by comparing the Jacksonians to the bloodthirsty rabble of Europe. Yet both had immeasurably more in common with each other than with their alleged counterparts abroad."[31] Similarly, New Dealers were called "creeping socialists" by their critics, while they referred to their opponents as "Bourbon reactionaries" and stalking horses for fascism. Hartz's point is that both factions were essentially committed to the same liberal principles, despite their disagreements. In Europe the classical liberalism of Locke and Adam Smith had to compete with other ideologies to the left and right; in America it took sole possession of the popular mind. It had become so ingrained that it went altogether unrecognized. As if it had buried itself deep in some collective unconscious, it had become "a massive national cliché,"[32] thought of simply as "Americanism."

By recognizing the hold of the consensus, Hartz suggested, it was possible to appreciate certain peculiarities of American politics and social thought. The winner-take-all electoral format, with its bias toward a two-party system, has been sustained because it rests on an underlying ideological consensus. In Europe, the absence of such a consensus on political principles generated less adaptable ideological parties and the adoption of proportional representation. (Although PR is still being promoted in the United States as a fairer system and one apt to increase electoral participation, it is worth noting that after it was adopted for council elections in New York City, it was abandoned when a few Communists and Socialists won seats as a result.) Because of the agreement on principles, an appointed Supreme Court has been allowed to issue constitutional interpretations—a power vouchsafed elsewhere only to parliaments. Pragmatism became the one original American philosophical school because social ends could be presupposed. Against the consensus, socialism could make no headway, even though the oppressive conditions imposed by Gilded Age capitalism were at least as onerous to America's workers as to their counterparts in Europe. Trade union movements had produced major socialist parties in Europe, whereas here workers had followed Samuel Gompers in adopting a "pure and simple" unionism, demanding better wages and hours. They continually refused to engage in "political unionism," rejecting calls for "direct action" via a general strike to paralyze government or to turn their backs on the two established political parties in favor of a party of labor. Franklin Roosevelt, acutely sensitive to American expectations, penciled out of the drafts of his speeches prepared by his brain trusters references he thought smacked of collectivism. "Extremist" ideologies were denounced as necessarily alien, a notion symbolized perfectly by the deportation of radicals ordered by Attorney General A. Mitchell Palmer.

The very oddity of the term "un-American" demanded an explanation. (Can anyone imagine, Hartz asked, the French setting up an Un-French Activities Committee or the British an un-British Activities Committee to expose all those who voted for their leftist parties?)

Although Americans themselves scarcely realized that the spectrum of their views was cut off at the extremes, European-style conservatism failed to take root. What goes by the name here is much more an effort to hold on to classical liberalism, with its intense individualism and suspicion of big government—not the belief in a titled aristocracy, a paternalistic autocracy, or, in the twentieth century, a willingness to entertain fascism as a way of overcoming the presumed dangers of egalitarianism. Huey Long had had a great insight into the American ethos, Hartz thought, when he suggested that fascism would come to America denying it was fascism.[33]

Hartz thought he knew why this had happened. Oddly enough the answer could be summed up as "no feudalism, no socialism." Hartz was not simply endorsing the notion of "American uniqueness" as it had previously been advanced, without any linkage to European conditions. He was suggesting that Americans thought differently from Western Europeans because they had had only the faintest experience of feudalism. Here he drew upon an insight of Alexis de Tocqueville, who had remarked, in *Democracy in America*, that "the Americans were fortunate in having been born equal, without having to become so by revolution."[34] The observation is cited as an epigraph to the book because Hartz's analysis begins from just this premise, that unlike the inhabitants of the Old World, those of the New had no need to overcome a feudal past. Contrary to those like J. Franklin Jameson, who saw the American Revolution as a social revolution, Hartz contended that it was a rebellion of colonial liberation. It was in that sense that the United States was, as Seymour Lipset would later note, the "first new nation."[35] Its struggle against the mother country had not entailed a civil war over class structure but only a demand for independence, nor had it left a residue of bitterness and division or inspired conspiratorial factions intent either on restoring some preexisting order or on carrying the revolution to a more radical conclusion.

Because of the absence of competing visions, the nation the colonists founded when they separated from the mother country was conceived purely and entirely in the light of the natural rights/social contract principles expounded by Locke. As a result, Americans have been much closer to each other ideologically than to European contemporaries of either the left or the right. By comparing American political thinking with that of Western Europe at every period, Hartz showed that American political thinking has hardly matched the range of European debates, where every conceivable "ism"—from anarchism (libertarian and communitarian) to pluralism (religious and guild socialist) to socialism, communism, and fascism—struggled for supremacy, reflecting a wrenching struggle among economic and social classes unleashed by the revolt against feudalism and the *Ständestaat*. Americans were divided by income and social standing but, naively or not, refused to identify themselves as belonging to different social classes—at least after they ceased to be immigrants and became assimilated to the national insistence on denying the very existence of class distinctions. The United States was a society without aristocrats, peasants, or proletarians. Instead, Americans have thought of themselves as "individuals"—to such an extent that the ideology became a myth identified with nationality. An "irrational Lockianism" made other ideologies seem foreign—indeed "un-American."[36]

The contrast with Europe could not have been sharper. In France, as Patrice Higgonet would later observe, an ancient corporatist tradition accustomed people to resist individualism and think of themselves as belonging to estates or classes. As a result, "Babouvian socialism was a modern graft on an ancient trunk."[37] In America, the absence of a feudal past meant that each American would think of himself as an "independent entrepreneur"[38] and resist being consigned permanently to some caste or class.

Without explicitly acknowledging his debt, Hartz here drew upon work in the sociology of knowledge by Karl Mannheim, who had considerable influence on his entire approach to the study of the history of ideas. Like Mannheim, Hartz saw ideologies as rationalizations of group interests. Mannheim had shown that European conservatism arose in opposition to liberalism because in the aftermath of the French Revolution the aristocracy needed an ideology that would enable it to deny the universalistic claims of liberalism and to attack liberal economics, or capitalism. Instead of the atomism and rationalism of liberalism, conservatives embraced organicism and tradition. Like Mannheim,[39] Hartz argued that socialists borrowed the conservative critique of liberalism because they too wanted an ideology that would suit a working class whose interest lay in combating the liberal claim that individualism and self-interest were universal rational "laws." Relying on history rather than abstract principles would serve the interest of workers, as a similar reliance was serving the interest of aristocrats.

Hartz adapted this Mannheimian analysis in arguing that the old storybook version of American history was true, in the sense that from the founding onward, the American experience followed a very different course than that of the modern states of Western Europe. Why, for example, did the framers of the American Constitution seek deliberately to weaken the central government by hamstringing it with a division of powers and checks and balances? The answer was that unlike European revolutionaries, who had to overcome a feudal past, they had no need for a strong state with which to smash the remnants of an old order. "The action of England inspired the American colonists with a hatred of centralized authority; but had that action been a transplanted American feudalism, rich in the chaos of ages, then they would surely have to dream of centralizing authority themselves."[40] Eighteenth-century liberalism— the natural rights ideals of Locke coupled with the free-market ideals of Adam Smith—seized hold of the American mind to such an extent that it became a creed identified with nationality itself—"Americanism" or "the American way of life." Any other doctrines were considered alien. Social- ists were therefore fighting a losing battle trying to transplant a "Euro- pean" doctrine into American soil because Americans, whatever their actual conditions, refused to think of themselves in class terms. The same handicap doomed the later efforts of those like Lawrence Dennis who, in the 1930s, prophesied that Americans too would embrace the fascism that had come first to Europe.[41]

The exception that proved the rule, Hartz suggested, was the attempt of antebellum Southerners like John C. Calhoun and George Fitzhugh to repudiate Locke in favor of doctrines that would justify the "fraudu- lent" feudal society the South had created by substituting slaves for serfs and a "plantocracy" of "cotton snobs" for a titled nobility. The South's "reactionary Enlightenment" failed, however, because it was trapped in contradiction from the start, unable to make a clean break with the country's Lockean roots. Calhoun sought to modify the Lockean social contract by allowing for the rights of constituent groups, via his "doctrine of the concurrent majority," but he could hardly flatly deny individual rights and call for a return to the full-fledged estate theories of feudalism. Fitzhugh, the more trenchant critic of northern capitalism, seemed to echo Marx and Engels in denouncing it as economic cannibalism, but he too could do no more than celebrate the illusory romantic paternalism of the Southern way of life. He knew perfectly well that there was no going back to a thoroughgoing feudalism in which a presumably benevolent order of princes and dukes would lord it over a nation of peasants rather than independent American farmers. Besides, whatever credence white South- erners might give to rhetoric of this sort, such ideas were too far from the acceptable limits of "the American way of life" to gain acceptance in the North. In that sense, they were as foredoomed as the lost cause of the Confederacy they helped inspire.[42]

The triumph of the North reaffirmed the country's dogmatic com- mitment to "Americanism" and set the stage for the development of democratic capitalism. In reaction to the excesses of the Gilded Age, populists yearned to return to a simpler agrarian, egalitarian past, while progressives dithered between the old Jeffersonian ethos of economic de- centralization and grassroots democracy, and the more Hamiltonian and communal ethos of the new "social" liberalism expounded in England by T. H. Green and L. T. Hobhouse and by Herbert Croly in the United States.[43] On either side they were hemmed in by the liberal consensus. At first they contented themselves with the largely symbolic and unrealistic cause of attacking the trusts and bossism in the name of individualism in economics and politics. Because the middle-class progressives refused to make common cause with collectivists, American socialists found themselves utterly isolated from them on the one side and from the trade union movement on the other. With Edward Bellamy, they were forced to imagine utopias that would never be realized. The New Deal reoriented progressive thinking so as to make government into a positive tool for reform, but at the same time it made clear beyond doubt that "the failure of socialism in America stemmed from the ideologic power of the national irrational liberalism rather than from economic circumstance."[44] In practice, the New Deal made changes that deviated from the old liberal ethic but were disguised as "bold and persistent experiment" so that they would not appear to be deviations from "Americanism."

But Hartz was far from rhapsodic about the benevolent role of the consensus, as some critics of consensus theory may mistakenly suppose. As his pupil Paul Roazen has remarked, Hartz "was alarmed by the 'deep and unwritten tyrannical compulsion' contained in the unanimity of American liberalism."[45] Rather than celebrating the glories of the American consensus, out of a Panglossian denial of the realities of conflict, he saw its very "irrationality" as a mythic set of blinkers preventing Americans from recognizing the realities of their own social system and of other systems not constrained by the same historical origins. Under its hold, they were unable to recognize the empirical fact of social stratification, whatever sociologists like the Lynds and Warner might find. They became intolerant of dissent, punishing even pacifistic anarchists with imprisonment. That intolerance first produced the Alien and Sedition Acts and later the deportations resulting from the Palmer raids following World War I, and the assaults on civil liberties by the House Un-American Activities Committee and Senator Joseph R. McCarthy in the 1940s and 1950s. Enthralled by a dangerously naive Wilsonianism, they rationalized American imperialism as colonial liberation, imposing American liberal and democratic values on societies hardly prepared for them, and promoting self-determination in regions destined to become Balkanized hotbeds of competing ethnic nationalisms. Most important for the immediate future, the hold of the consensus was preventing modern Americans from acknowledging the validity of other, collectivistic approaches to economic and political development. Only if the experience with other countries, including the Soviet Union and the developing countries, engendered "a new level of consciousness"[46] might

Americans "transcend" the consensus and come to terms realistically with the rest of the world.

If a proper reading of Hartz's analysis clears his thesis of criticisms arising from misunderstanding, two problems of different sorts are presented by his style, or mode of presentation. One arises from the very fact that his analysis rests on a continual comparison of American and Western European thinkers and statesmen. Notwithstanding his brisk and crackling prose, some readers are bound to be disconcerted or even intimidated by the demands he makes upon their historical knowledge by constantly comparing Americans and Europeans of the same time periods. On one especially challenging early page (7), for example, the reader has a fleeting encounter with Samuel Adams, Mark Twain, Benjamin Disraeli, the Leveller John Lilburne, Sir Walter Scott, and the French *Doctrinaire*, Pierre Ballanche. Hartz cannot be faulted for any lack of preparation on the reader's part, but there is a related, more troubling problem, which is that he usually alludes to these figures symbolically, as though he were moving black or white figures on opposite sides of a chessboard, without explaining in detail exactly what they are supposed to represent.

Sometimes the technique works brilliantly, as in the provocative rhetorical question posed in the first chapter: "Is not the problem of Fitzhugh the problem of DeLeon?"[47] This is a wonderfully incisive way of jolting the reader into grappling with his central contention that because of the absence of feudalism and the uncontested acceptance of liberalism in the country's founding, Americans lacked the sense of class that in Europe drew many toward the alternatives to liberalism that emerged in the form of conservatism (symbolized by George Fitzhugh, the apologist for slavery), and socialism (symbolized by Daniel De Leon, the turn-of-the-century socialist theorist). Without a background of class division, Americans were bound to be uncomfortable with visions of society that presupposed a division into a landed aristocracy, a mercantile bourgeoisie, and a working-class proletariat. As a result, neither Fitzhugh's neofeudalism nor De Leon's socialism could find more than a marginal following. Both had the same problem of how to appeal to Americans trapped by Locke (symbolizing liberalism).

Readers are bound to be perplexed, however, if not altogether baffled, by other passages, like this one, illuminating as is its insight once deciphered:

> The victory of American Whiggery under the Horatio Alger dispensation was thus not due in the first instance to the spectacular growth of American capitalism after the Civil War, to "America's Economic Supremacy," as Brooks Adams put it, though a crash would end its reign and bring the American democrat to power with a distinctive New Deal. Actually capitalism was advancing in European countries as well during this era, most of

all in Germany where, needless to say, Alger was an even more alien figure than he was in England or France. The triumph of the new Whiggery came from the effect of an economic boom within the confines of the American liberal world, or more specifically, the effect of a boom on the peculiar mentality of that "petit bourgeois" giant who was its distinguishing product: the American democrat absorbing both peasantry and proletariat. If he was able to smash Whiggery in the age of Hamilton when it tried to use the European techniques, he was a pushover for its democratic capitalism, its pot of American gold, when it gave those techniques up. The line of Whig development from Edward Everett through Abraham Lincoln to Andrew Carnegie was the clue to his undoing.[48]

Translated into less colorful language, what Hartz was saying is that the rise of plutocracy in the Gilded Age was not due (as Marxists supposed) to the victory of capitalism (which was triumphing in Europe without producing social harmony) but to a willingness on the part of ordinary Americans (the "American democrat" or "petit bourgeois giant") to concede its legitimacy. These ordinary Americans had absorbed the liberal ("Horatio Alger") strive-and-succeed ideology and saw nothing wrong in successful entrepreneurs becoming millionaires. They had resisted the upper class (Whiggery) when it made the mistake of trying to impose a simulacrum of European aristocracy (à la Hamilton), but were quite ready to concede power to an economic upper class that could claim to have arisen legitimately as a result of its competitive success. Only the Great Depression seemed to bring this reign of plutocracy into question, as ordinary Americans succeeded in promoting a "democratic capitalism" in the New Deal. The line of development from Everett (symbolizing humanitarian compassion plus commerce) through Lincoln (symbolizing free labor) to Carnegie (symbolizing "Algerism") explains why ordinary Americans were willing to support the New Deal, understood as an effort to rescue capitalism rather than replace it.[49]

Once the prose is translated (and stripped, it must be admitted, of its peculiar stylistic zest), the problem with this analysis is that it makes it seem as though there were no obstacles to the triumph of plutocracy—no Homestead strike, no Haymarket Massacre—and that no significant changes were effected by progressivism and its offspring, the New Deal, because political thinking remained unwaveringly liberal in its basic preconceptions. By fixing his sights on the ideological continuity, Hartz did less than full justice to the social movements that arose in resistance to buccaneer capitalism, and to the great institutional changes begun in the New Deal with respect to social security (including, eventually, health care for the elderly), income transfers for the sake of social welfare, the rights of labor to bargain collectively, and the role of the "positive state" in regulating the economy to promote full employment and soften the swings of the business cycle. If all this was only a continuation of an underlying liberal tradition, it was a continuation with considerable differences of application—differences that would be felt in the improvement of the conditions of labor; the political role of trade unions; the encouragement of the civil rights movement; the strengthening of the regulatory, fiscal, and monetary leverage of the central government; and the adoption of a "safety net," if not in the whole panoply of welfare state guarantees envisioned by the more ardent champions of the New Deal, the Fair Deal, and the Great Society. To see all these changes merely as details, or applications of the same underlying principles, is to constrain the meaning of ideological consensus virtually to the breaking point.

Another troubling example of the perils of symbolic manipulation appears in Hartz's otherwise provocative and even brilliant account of the impossible task antebellum white Southerners faced in trying to assimilate slavery to the American creed:

> Locke, in other words, was too real, too empirical, too historical in America to attack: and the consequences of this are obvious. The God of the reactionaries was Himself on Locke's side, and the Southerners, when they assailed "metaphysicians," were committing a vigorous suicide. E. N. Elliott cherished the sociological relativism of Montesquieu, but the relative unfolding of America's culture had alas been liberal. Fitzhugh spoke of Burkean "prejudices," but the prejudices of America were alas the prejudices of liberty and equality. Indeed the "prejudice" argument was even more self-annihilating than the argument of cultural relativism. One might argue, insofar as slavery itself was concerned, that it was a historic institution, despite its sudden expansion after 1830, and that Montesquieu's lesson for the American Negroes was therefore different from his lesson for the American whites. But on the plane of "prejudice," the problem was not so simple: in its Jeffersonian youth the South had considered slavery bad. How then could Burke be used to assail Locke when even below the Mason-Dixon Line Burke actually equaled Locke?[50]

A literalist familiar with the texts being referred to here is bound to be uneasy with this passage. As to God, Southerners like Thornton Stringfellow had no difficulty finding biblical sources in which slavery is considered acceptable practice.[51] As for Locke, he considered slavery justified if the slaves were taken in war, a condition outside any social contract. Presumably, this critical qualification applied to the slaves imported into the American colonies. Literally speaking, Locke approved of the enslavement of Africans,[52] even though he attacked Sir Robert Filmer for supposedly wanting to enslave freedom-loving Englishmen; it was slavery for whites that aroused Locke's indignation. Montesquieu is hardly a sociological relativist pure and simple, whatever E. N. Elliott may have made of him; despite his relativism, he favored republican government founded on the principles of equality and civic virtue over the other forms, and he contended, with great effect on European opinion, that slavery violated the general principles that promoted human happiness. Jefferson, although he did indeed condemn slavery as immoral—notably in the draft passage subsequently deleted from the Declaration of Independence—was of course a Virginia slaveholder and no abolitionist. Southern apologists for slavery had as much right to claim him as a forebear as northern abolitionists. Finally, as Hartz almost admits, a Burkean belief in prejudice could readily include an acceptance of slavery inasmuch as slavery was an accepted fact of American life, tacitly sanctioned by the Constitution until the Thirteenth Amendment.

But Hartz worked on the level of ideology, which does not require philosophic exegesis or reference to empirical realities, and the point he is making here, by using these theorists as surrogates for public opinion, is astute. The white Southerners did indeed have a virtually impossible task in trying to persuade themselves and Northerners to allow a hybrid liberal/neofeudal ideology to flourish on American soil—in order to accommodate their "peculiar institution" in a country founded on the belief that all men are endowed with equal rights. Lincoln understood this fundamental paradox well and constantly cited that most famous passage of the Declaration, along with the Northern concern that "free labor" not have to compete against slave labor, to persuade Americans who were not abolitionists to recognize that to rationalize slavery for blacks was to undermine the way of life the country had been created to achieve.

Stylistically, then, Hartz's argument may cause readers some problems, but these are not insuperable and, with the important exception of the transformation of liberalism represented by the New Deal, do not seriously invalidate his point.

If stylistic criticisms can for the most part be deflected, are any of the substantive criticisms of Hartz's thesis fatal? Was he wrong to make Lockean liberalism rather than republicanism the key influence on the thinking that went into the Revolution and decisively shaped American thinking? Did he make it seem that the country has already been a shining example of liberalism, whereas in fact it has been exactly the opposite toward Native Americans and African Americans, toward immigrants who have suffered from nativism, toward women, and toward social nonconformists? Did he whitewash the country's divisive conflicts, or to vary the metaphor, smooth out its wrinkles? Does his thesis rule out all efforts to challenge the reigning orthodoxy of rugged individualism in the name of more compassionate ideals? Does not the modern revival of republicanism, in the form of governmental initiatives designed to promote social betterment, and the accompanying revival of communitarianism as an ideology, show that Hartz missed the essential point that American political thinking moves dialectically between republicanism and liberalism?

With respect to the influence of Locke, Carl L. Becker had already shown, prior to Hartz's work, that the Declaration of Independence was Lockean doctrine incarnate, strikingly similar in substance and language to the argument of the *Second Treatise* in treating the rights of nature and the social contract as "self-evident truths."[53] "I turned to neither book nor pamphlet while writing the Declaration," Jefferson wrote in his memoirs, but as the historian Samuel Eliot Morison points out, there was hardly any need for him to do so since "the principles and language of John Locke's Second Treatise of Government (1690) were so much a part of his mind that unconsciously he thought and wrote like Locke."[54] Jefferson recalled that in drafting the Declaration, he had not intended to be original but to sum up the American mind. "Locke's little book on government," he wrote, "is perfect as far as it goes. Descending from theory to practice, there is no better book than the Federalist."[55]

Other champions of the Revolution and framers of the Constitution showed the same Lockean impress. In *Common Sense*, Tom Paine exhorted the "inhabitants of America" to rise up against "a long and violent abuse of power" and to recognize that government—"like dress, the badge of lost innocence"—arises out of the prior creation of society "in a state of natural liberty," that it must be entrusted to an elected, representative legislature, and that it has as its end "freedom and security."[56] John Adams, in the preamble to the Massachusetts Constitution, observed, as if he were answering an examination question to show what he had learned from the social contract theorists:

> The body politic is formed by a voluntary association of individuals. It is a social compact, by which the whole people covenants with each citizen, and each citizen with the whole people, that all shall be governed by certain laws for the common good.[57]

Similarly, James Wilson of Pennsylvania, one of the most thoughtful of the framers, wrote of the ends of government in the purest Lockean strain:

> All men are, by nature, equal and free: no one has a right to any authority over another without his consent; all lawful government is founded on the consent of those who are subject to it: such consent was given to ensure and increase the happiness of the governed, above what they would enjoy in an independent and unconnected state of nature. The consequence is, that the happiness of society is the first law of every government.[58]

Wills' effort to father the Declaration on Hutcheson rather than Locke stretches credulity, as has been shown by Ronald Hamowy and Harry V. Jaffa.[59] Jaffa cites a particularly glaring example of the weakness of this claim with respect to this well-known passage in the Declaration:

But when a long train of abuses and usurpations, begun at a distinguished period and pursuing invariably the same object, evinces a design to reduce them under absolute despotism, it is their right, it is their duty, to throw off such government.

Wills claims that this passage shows the influence of a similar one from Hutcheson:

A good subject ought to bear patiently many injuries done not only to himself, rather than take up arms against a prince in the main good and useful to the state, provided the danger extends only to himself. But when the common rights of humanity are trampled upon, and what at first attempted against one is made precedent against all the rest, then as the governor is plainly perfidious to his trust, he has forfeited all the power committed to him.

But Jaffa cites the much closer parallel passage in the *Second Treatise*, which appears in chapter 19, significantly devoted to the "dissolution of government":

But if a long train of Abuses, Prevarications, and Artifices, all tending the same way, make the design visible to the People, and they cannot but feel, what they lie under, and see, whither they are going; 'tis not to be wonder'd, that they should then rouze themselves, and endeavour to put the rule into such hands, which may secure to them the ends for which Government was first erected.[60]

The fact that Jefferson's language shows similarities to Hutcheson's as well as Locke's should hardly be surprising. A recent study of the Declaration exploring its manifold sources points out that it drew on principles widely accepted among the colonists, principles

conveniently stated in John Locke's *Second Treatise of Government* and by many other seventeenth- and eighteenth-century English and Scottish writers. Colonists encountered those principles in the press and from the pulpit; even Blackstone's *Commentaries on the Laws of England* cited "the principles of Mr. Locke" in interpreting the English Revolution of 1689. By the late eighteenth century, "Lockean" ideas on government and revolution were accepted everywhere; they seemed, in fact, a statement of principles built into English constitutional tradition.[61]

Other studies of the impact of Lockean ideas have come to the same conclusion. A study of the framers of the Constitution notes that Locke's political philosophy exerted the "strongest pull" on their struggle to formulate their ultimate goals.[62] John Marshall, by far the most influential jurist in defining the Constitution, based his defense of the right of property on the "generally admitted" argument of the *Second Treatise*.[63]

Republicanism was certainly also influential before, during, and after the Revolution, as is evident not only from the pamphlet literature and sermons cited by Bailyn but from the pervasive reference to Roman experience in the thinking of the founding leaders—and even in the pen names they adopted—Publius, Cato, Brutus, and so forth. To a considerable extent, however, republicanism and liberalism entered the American mind in tandem. As Stephen M. Dworetz has observed, "Republicanism and liberalism coexisted at the founding."[64] Bailyn recognized that in reworking classical republicanism, the colonists drew heavily on the work of contract theorists, notably Locke, along with other Enlightenment theorists.[65] In so doing they gave republicanism a foundation in natural law and natural rights either lacking or muted in previous republican theory. When Jefferson observed that "the true foundation of republican government is the equal right of every citizen, in his person and property," he expressed this blending of the two traditions.[66] Recent biographical and textual studies of Algernon Sidney, along with Locke an important and often-cited influence on American thinking in the eighteenth century, suggest that republican and liberal influences were often combined. Sidney's *Discourse* combines liberal fascination with the social contract and natural rights with republican condemnation of monarchical corruption and exaltation of civic virtue. He cites Machiavelli's *Discourses* and evidence from Roman history, as one would expect from a republican, even as he devotes most of the work to an exposition of the origins of liberty and representative government in the state of nature and the social compact. "When attention is restricted to instances in which the influence of Sidney's ideas was strongest," Alan Craig Houston has remarked, "a striking conclusion emerges: virtually all of the 'republican' principles drawn from Sidney's writings—from the rule of law to the right of revolution—were perfectly compatible with Lockean liberalism."[67] The influence of republicanism, moreover, was limited because of its links to classical ideals of aristocracy, with its disdain for the banausic pursuits of ordinary citizens, and to the neoclassical belief in the desirability of government by hereditary oligarchies.[68] These ideals suited elitists like the Viscount Bolingbroke in the first half of the eighteenth century, Isaac Kramnick has pointed out, but they held much less appeal to a later generation of bourgeois radicals like Joseph Priestley in Britain and Tom Paine in America. The new "self-made" men whose views these later writers reflected and helped shape were active in commerce, unlike landed aristocrats, and were too concerned with the protection of their interests to entrust government to cliques of established families.[69]

Similarly, Wood's objection that Hartz minimized the radical character of the American Revolution is not as stark as it seems. Wood does not claim that America experienced full-fledged feudalism. Hartz anticipated such criticisms of his sweeping assertion that America bypassed feudalism by pointing out that America did not experience its two most fundamental features: the division of land into large estates and the division of labor and social status between a titled aristocracy and a peasantry. Although many colonists came as indentured servants, they were not serfs and did not become peasants upon emancipation. As industrialization spawned a class of "artisans and mechanics," they did not think of themselves as a proletariat distinct from the bourgeoisie and aristocracy. As a result, Americans never developed the same consciousness of class as Europeans took for granted. But Hartz took note of the way the liberalism of 1776 inspired attacks against the vestiges of feudal corporatism in the New World—"the disestablishment of the Anglican church, the abolition of quitrents and primogeniture, the breaking up of the Tory estates."[70] Wood, in his richly detailed study, shows that while the generation that made the Revolution was indeed inspired by republican ideals and rebelled not only against monarchy but more generally against the aristocratic and paternalistic order it had produced in the colonies, the next generation of Americans rejected "the revolutionaries' dream of building a classical republic of elitist virtue"[71] in favor of an enterprising, largely middle-class order held together by "new democratic adhesives in the actual behavior of plain ordinary people—in the everyday desire for the freedom to make money and pursue happiness in the here and now."[72] This characterization is not very different from Hartz's, though it shifts the onset of liberalism to the postrevolutionary period. Although Wood, like Kramnick, contends that the "new paradigm" was complex, he concedes that "there is no doubt that something changed in the late eighteenth century and that a mode of thinking we came to call liberalism emerged in the early nineteenth century."[73]

With respect to the Civil War, Hartz may fairly be criticized for putting so much emphasis on the power of ideas to make it seem that the North was bound to win the war simply because the Confederate cause was so much at odds with the national cause. In fact, as is widely recognized, the war was for some months a close-run affair and the North eventually won for other reasons, including its industrial superiority and Grant's dogged generalship. The outcome of the war ended the Southern challenge to the consensus, but the "lost cause" was not foredoomed, as Hartz makes it seem, by its ideological anachronism.

The charge that consensus theory covers up conflict rests to some extent on a misunderstanding of what "consensus theory" entails. To Hartz, it meant that liberalism in the eighteenth-century sense of the term had become a set of blinders. The same is true for Hofstadter, who is often yoked with Hartz as an advocate of consensus theory. Both Hartz and Hofstadter emphasized the hold of American liberalism (though Hofstadter preferred to call it the belief in the primacy of property rights) in order to criticize the country's myopia and its inability to cope with the modern world. This was a world, Hofstadter wrote, in which what is demanded is not America's traditional isolationism and insistence on laissez-faire but "international responsibility, cohesion, centralization, and planning." The "traditional ground," he thought, "is shifting under our feet."[74] Hartz had a similar view of the need to adjust American thinking to the realities of a world in which other nations were going to take collectivistic paths to development. As he observed in the final chapter,

> [T]he psychic heritage of a nation "born free" is as we have abundantly seen, a colossal liberal absolutism, the death by atrophy of the philosophic impulse. And in a war of ideas this frame of mind has two automatic effects: it hampers creative action abroad by identifying the alien with the unintelligible, and it inspires hysteria at home by generating the anxiety that unintelligible things produce. The red scare, in other words, is not only our domestic problem: it is our international problem as well. When the nation rises to an irrational anticommunist frenzy, it replies to the same instinct, which tends to alienate it from Western democratic governments that are "socialist." When it closes down on dissent, it answers the same impulse, which inspires it to define dubious regimes elsewhere as "democratic." This is the peculiar link that a liberal community forges between the world and domestic pictures: its absolute perspective, its "Americanism."[75]

Finally, the notion that the republicanism of the revolutionary period is the ancestor of a modern communitarianism different from and dialectically opposed to liberalism is open to serious question. For one thing, this claim takes two very different forms. Left-wing communitarians see republicanism as the basis of a movement for a more egalitarian social order.[76] Right-wing communitarians decry modern immorality, which they blame on liberalism, and call for a return to traditional moral standards emphasizing the inculcation of "virtue."[77] These two incompatible invocations of republicanism suggest that it is being rediscovered so as to serve as a "usable past" by critics of different aspects of liberalism anxious to find legitimacy in the country's founding experience. Neither movement moves very far from the core of the liberal consensus; both make common cause with elements of the consensus, the left with its emphasis on civil liberties and civil rights, the right with its emphasis on property rights. The idea that modern reform movements are somehow outgrowths of republicanism is hardly obvious. Progressivism did come to make more use of the state than traditional liberals called for, but only to restore liberal competitiveness and to attack monopolies and bossism. As was once said of them, they used Hamiltonian means for Jeffersonian ends. The modern regulatory state has been described as "a kind of post–New Deal republicanism" designed to allow a range of government activity to protect prosperity and the disadvantaged while respecting private property and freedom of contract,[78] but it might just as easily be understood as a pragmatic response to the vagaries of unrestrained capitalism and an ideological outgrowth of progressive left-of-center liberalism.

Hartz's emphasis on the repressiveness and intolerance of American liberalism as the "decisive domestic issue of our time"[79] makes clear that his work was designed with the period in which it was written very much in mind. But his thesis remains an indispensable guide to understanding American political thought. In the more than two centuries since the founding of the republic, the American fixation on liberal individualism and rejection of anything smacking either of conservative organicism or socialist collectivism has been nothing short of overwhelming. Ironically, some of the most telling evidence in favor of the thesis comes from socialists and conservatives themselves—socialists when they lament their inability to make headway against the stubbornly resistant American working class, presumably brainwashed into adopting "false consciousness"; conservatives when they champion liberal economic policies and oppose paternalistic government—positions once anathema to their European ideological forebears. If anything, Hartz's interpretation bears up well in the light of subsequent experience. Since the politically abortive countercultural ferment of the 1960s, the main political developments in succeeding decades have reaffirmed the ideological commitment of the great majority of the electorate to political and economic individualism, the core principle of Lockean liberalism. The rejection of the New Left— symbolized by the defeat of Eugene McCarthy and George McGovern in national politics—and the revulsion caused by the resort of some domestic left-wing movements to terrorism provoked a backlash that helped to put Ronald Reagan into the White Office. Subsequently, Democratic office seekers frightened of being labeled with the "L word" declared themselves "New Democrats"—that is, liberals who acknowledged that the era of big government was over and pledged to "reinvent" government by cutting its size and making it more accountable. The American electorate followed its usual pattern of seesawing between right of center and left of center, tacking the ship of state first one way and then the other. A campaign consultant astutely advised President Clinton that his best strategy was to "triangulate," or to find the center position and embrace it; Clinton followed the advice with considerable political success.

A survey of American opinion by McCloskey and Zaller in recent times found that Americans do indeed share a consensus with respect to the basic values of liberal democracy and capitalism, learning these values from the country's political elite

> in at least three different combinations, the nineteenth-century liberal pattern described by Louis Hartz and others as the prevailing tendency (strong support for the values of both traditions); the welfare state liberal pattern (strong support for democracy and qualified support for capitalism); or the pattern favored by many strong conservatives (strong support for capitalism and qualified support for certain democratic values).[80]

In other words, virtually all Americans accept the values associated with liberal democracy and the market economy, but differ on the emphasis they give to each of the two components. Another study, using interviews conducted in middle-class communities rather than survey research, found that on moral matters Americans were anxious above all not to be divided by "culture wars," but to be, despite their differences, "one nation, after all." They worry most that the country will be torn apart by its divisions and continue to think that the best society is one not divided by class but united by middle-class standards of personal responsibility and striving for a decent standard of living.[81] This study provides important evidence that American liberalism may well be losing what Hartz feared was its inherent intolerance of dissent and nonconformity.

Philosophically, both the consensus and the divisions are evident in the prodigious literature on liberalism that has been produced, mainly in the United States and Britain, over the past several decades.[82] It is especially pronounced in the writings of two of the most widely discussed American philosophers of the late twentieth century, John Rawls and Robert Nozick,[83] and even among some of their critics. Rawls's "original position" resembles Locke's state of nature, as does his assumption that in such a position people would reason that they had to establish liberty as the first priority as a principal of justice. Rawls differs from Locke in a number of particulars. He assumes that the "contractors" meet behind a "veil of ignorance" in the sense that they do not know their position in society or their talents or views on the ends of life. Locke made only the assumption that people in such a condition would be able to reason about the principles of justice, or what he referred to as the rights of nature. In keeping with the modification of the liberal theory of property rights introduced earlier by Hobhouse,[84] Rawls's contractors accept the "difference principle," whereby inequalities are justified if and only if they benefit "the least advantaged," whereas Locke assumed that private property had general benefits but ought not be limited unless others were precluded from taking what they needed from the common bounty of nature. Rawls has also noted that Locke's contract has undemocratic implications because "he assumes that not all members of society following the social compact have equal rights: citizens have the right to vote in virtue of owning property so that the propertyless have no vote and no right to exercise political authority." Rawls takes the side of Kant, arguing that "Locke's doctrine improperly subjects the relationships of moral persons to historical and social contingencies that are external to, and eventually undermine, their freedom and equality."[85] Nozick's contract is, as he himself admits, little different from Locke's. Individuals in a state of nature would join together to achieve security, much as they do in civil society when they buy insurance, but the social compact would lead only to the "minimal state"—a form of government devoted to the protection of the rights individuals enjoy in the state of nature. Its sole authority to redistribute their wealth would arise in cases where rectification of a specific injustice in the original acquisition of property could be shown. Otherwise, differences in wealth resulting from differential talent and industry and free exchange should be respected.

The liberal principles that frame the thinking of both Rawls and Nozick are reflected in myriad ways in American social values and institutions. In recent years alone, the liberal impulse has led to profound changes. For better and for worse, college students have overthrown the authority of the professoriate, winning the right to design their own curricula and inducing grade inflation. Patients expect doctors, once held to be beyond questioning, to respect their autonomy by explaining their diagnoses and treatment options, and lawyers are ready to hold them responsible for malpractice. An explosion of litigation has resulted from the "rights revolution."

Still, the Hartz thesis does need to be modified—to recognize that the meaning of liberalism has broadened over time, that the modern American consensus has come to be divided into liberal and conservative wings, and that other illiberal or nonliberal influences, such as republicanism (both in its older and modern, communitarian forms), racism and xenophobia, as well as religious beliefs with illiberal implications, remain strong if mostly peripheral forces. Hartz's analysis suffers from its very strength—a zeal for "single-factor analysis" aiming to show that every disagreement in the history of the republic has been argued within the rhetorical boundaries staked out by the *Second Treatise of Government*. To make this case, Hartz had to give short shrift to republican ideas and downplay the differences between the progressive and conservative wings of the liberal consensus. He failed to take proper notice of the great changes in the meaning and application of the liberal ideal—changes resulting from the struggles for inclusion waged by working people, minorities, women, and lately homosexuals. These changes may well have been latent in Lockean liberalism from the start,[86] but they did not become manifest until they were forced onto the public agenda by social forces left out of the previous versions of liberalism. In addition, he altogether ignored the lingering influence of prerevolutionary Puritan religious thinking, which at least some analysts contend predisposed American colonists to accept a political covenant and left a lingering moralistic strain, reinforced by several "Great Awakenings." Even if some of these tendencies are only contrapuntal to the larger theme or of only marginal significance, they need to be taken into account by any theory that claims to be comprehensive.[87]

Modification is needed first of all to take account of the changing meaning of liberalism as an ideal and a political label. The political liberalism that is traceable to Locke was originally biased toward the rights of the propertied, as critics from Harold Laski[88] to C. B. Macpherson[89] have shown. Nor did Locke rule out enslavement of captives taken in war, a convenient rationale for the European slave trade.[90] Over time, as a result of reformist struggles, liberalism has become more inclusive and democratic, excluding all forms of slavery and guaranteeing equal political and civil rights without regard to property, religious faith, race, or gender. As a liberal democracy, the United States has become, in Michael Lind's apt term, a "civic nation" founded not on ethnicity but on political values and symbols.[91] Although compounded for a time with the laissez-faire doctrines of economic liberalism, political liberalism has in modern times been bifurcated into two wings, now commonly called liberal and conservative, divided mainly by disagreement over the economic role of government and the balance between public and private sectors, but also over the extent to which personal autonomy should be restricted by prevalent but not necessarily universal moral standards.[92]

What remains altogether outside the Hartzian framework is American religiosity. Hartz paid too little attention to the importance of religious thinking in America, from the Puritans and Congregationalists of New England and the Anglicans of Virginia, through the Great Awakening to the Quaker abolitionists and the evangelical stirrings among modern fundamentalists and the turn toward social reformism in several Protestant denominations and among Jews and Roman Catholics. Although liberalism deliberately makes religion politically irrelevant, the relationship between religious and secular belief is significant and needs examination.[93] Tocqueville thought of American religiosity as an antidote to the concern for material betterment that he thought was at the core of American individualism.[94] The American dream as it developed in the post–Civil War era was increasingly not a reverie about establishing the New Jerusalem, despite occasional experiments with utopian communities, but with building a better life in the here and now, for oneself and one's progeny. Religious belief has exerted powerful influence over many aspects of American life, inspiring entrepreneurs and salesmen and great figures in the civil rights movement like Dr. Martin Luther King Jr. Overall, however, the history of American religion is a striking testimony to the validity of Hartz's thesis in that the social movements with which the various faiths have become engaged are often drawn to one side or the other of the liberal consensus. Thus, modern liberal believers adopt a "social gospel" approach (or one similarly inspired by the papal social encyclicals), while fundamentalists like the Christian Coalition make common cause with secular conservatives. American Catholicism, with its challenges to the traditionalism of the European church, is a particularly striking example of how American liberalism has influenced religious belief. A fuller examination of this relationship might well show that a Hartzian approach is even more far-reaching than he supposed.[95]

Hartz was certainly right to identify America's ideological uniqueness by using a comparative approach, vindicating G. K. Chesterton's remark that America is "the only nation that is founded on a creed."[96] Hartz's main error was in assuming that the American consensus would have to be modified to allow the country to come to terms with the outside world. Exactly the opposite seems to have happened: the outside world has come to terms with the American consensus. For a time it did seem that Hartz's analysis was correct. American policy was running into serious intellectual opposition in Latin America, for example, on the part of the *dependencia* theorists who argued that capitalist America was trying to impose its hegemonic capitalism on Latin America. The high-handed American role in the hemisphere reinforced this perception. But the pendulum began to swing the other way in the 1980s and 1990s. The election of Reagan, signaling the revival of liberal conservatism in the United States, was matched by the rise of Thatcherism in England and the resurgence of conservative parties elsewhere in Western Europe. With the fall of communism in Eastern Europe, the rise of market economies in Asia, including China, and the revival of democracy in Latin America (coupled with a less interventionist attitude on the part of the United States), liberalism has gained new respect. America's obsession with liberalism has not prevented the country from dealing realistically with the rest of the world, and the world has not moved, as many expected, toward collectivism. The American and Western European example of systems combining liberal democracy with a regulated market economy has been accepted as a fairer, freer, and more efficient system than collectivism on the Soviet model. It remains to be seen whether the transition to free markets and democracy will proceed successfully in the former communist countries, but for the time being, there is no reason to suppose that America's liberal consensus has handicapped the country in dealing with them. Hartz was right to warn against the intolerance of dissent at home and against parochialism in foreign policy, but he may well prove to have been wrong in underestimating the appeal of American liberalism, even in societies that did not spring into being in the absence of feudalism. As far as American thinking is concerned, however, his thesis continues to ring true, once it is modified to allow for divisions within the overall consensus.

## NOTES

1. Harold J. Laski, *The Rise of European Liberalism: An Essay in Interpretation* (London: Allen & Unwin, 1936).

2. C. B. Macpherson, *The Political Theory of Possessive Individualism: Hobbes to Locke* (Oxford: Oxford University Press, 1962).

3. See *Rights, Representation, and Reform: Nonsense upon Stilts and Other Writings on the French Revolution; The Collected Works of Jeremy Bentham*, ed. Philip Schofield, Catherine Pease, and Cyprian Blamires (Oxford: Oxford University Press, 2002).

4. Isaiah Berlin, *Liberty: Incorporating Four Essays on Liberty*, ed. Henry Hardy with an essay on Berlin and his critics by Ian Harris (Oxford: Oxford University Press, 2002).

5. See especially Leonard Hobhouse, *Liberalism* (New York: Oxford University Press, 1964).

6. Louis Hartz, *The Liberal Tradition in America: An Interpretation of American Political Thought since the Revolution* (New York: Harcourt Brace, 1955; reissued, Harcourt Brace Jovanovich, 1980).

7. Joyce O. Appleby, *Liberalism and Republicanism in the Historical Imagination* (Cambridge, MA: Harvard University Press, 1992), p. 163.

8. See Samuel P. Huntington, *American Politics: The Promise of Disharmony* (Cambridge, MA: Harvard University Press), p. 53, and especially chaps. 5 and 6, pp. 85–166.

9. William A. Galston, *Liberal Purposes* (Cambridge: Cambridge University Press, 1991), pp. 4–6.

10. Caroline Robbins, *The Eighteenth-Century Commonwealth-Man* (Cambridge, MA: Harvard University Press, 1959); Bernard Bailyn, *Ideological Origins of the American Revolution* (Cambridge, MA: Harvard University Press, 1967); Gordon S. Wood, *The Creation of the American Republic* (New York: Norton, 1972); and J. G. A. Pocock, *The Machiavellian Moment: Florentine Republican Thought and the Atlantic Republican Tradition* (Princeton, NJ: Princeton University Press, 1975).

11. J. G. A. Pocock, "Virtue and Commerce in the Eighteenth Century," *Journal of Interdisciplinary History* 3 (1972): p. 120. Cited in Appleby, op. cit., p. 323.

12. Pocock, *The Machiavellian Moment*, p. 45. See also Dorothy Ross, "The Liberal Tradition Revisited and the Republican Tradition Addressed," in *New Directions in American Intellectual History*, ed. John Higham and Paul K. Conkin (Baltimore, MD: Johns Hopkins University Press, 1979), pp. 116–31, and Appleby, op. cit.

13. Gordon S. Wood, *The Radical Revolution* (New York: Knopf, 1992).

14. Garry Wills, *Inventing America: Jefferson's Declaration of Independence* (New York: Vintage, 1979).

15. Hartz, op. cit., p. 9.

16. Ibid., pp. 277–79. Hartz's use of Marxian theory is well recognized by Diggins, op. cit.

17. William M. Sullivan, *Reconstructing Public Philosophy* (Berkeley: University of California Press, 1986), pp. 4, 185.

18. Howard Zinn, *A People's History of the United States* (New York: Harper, 1967).

19. Robert Bellah, Richard Madsen, William M. Sullivan, Ann Swidler, and Steven M. Tipton, *Habits of the Heart* (Berkeley: University of California Press, 1985).

20. Charles Reich, *The Greening of America: How the Youth Revolution Is Trying to Make America Livable* (New York: Random House, 1970).

21. Sullivan, op. cit., p. 224.

22. Leo Strauss, *Natural Right and History* (Chicago: University of Chicago Press, 1953), p. 251.

23. Thomas G. West, "The Classical Spirit of the Founding," in *The American Founding: Essays on the Formation of the Constitution*, ed. L. Jackson Barlow, Leonard W. Levy, and Ken Masugi (New York: Greenwood Press, 1988), pp. 4, 40–41.

24. John Diggins, *The Lost Soul of American Politics: Virtue, Self-Interest, and the Foundations of Liberalism* (New York: Basic Books, 1998), pp. 8–9.

25. Richard Hofstadter, *The American Political Tradition and the Men Who Made It* (New York: Vintage, 1989), preface, p. xxix.

26. Richard Hofstadter, *The Progressive Historians: Turner, Beard, and Parrington* (New York: Knopf, 1968), pp. 461–62. Quoted by Christopher Lasch, foreword to *The American Political Tradition*, p. xix.

27. Judith N. Shklar, *American Citizenship* (Cambridge, MA: Harvard University Press, 1991), p. 12.

28. Orlando Patterson, "The Liberal Millennium," *New Republic*, 8 November 1999, p. 60.

29. Hartz, op. cit., pp. 166–67. Hartz's implicit contention that the hold of the liberal consensus doomed slavery is partially supported by Wood's observation that the Revolution ended the climate that allowed black slavery, as well as other forms of servitude, to go unchallenged: "With the revolutionary movement, black slavery became excruciatingly conspicuous in a way that it had not been in the older monarchical society with its many calibrations and degrees of unfreedom; and Americans in 1775–76 began attacking it with a vehemence that was inconceivable earlier." Wood, op. cit., p. 186.

30. Frederick Merk, *Manifest Destiny and Mission in American History* (New York: Knopf, 1963), pp. 122–23, quotes an editorial supporting the war with Mexico from the *New York Sun* of 22 October 1847 that reflects this Lockean mind-set: "To *liberate* and *ennoble*—not to *enslave* and *debase*—is our mission. Well may the Mexican nation, whose great masses have never yet tasted liberty, prattle over their lost phantom of nationality. . . . If they have not—in the profound darkness of their vassal existence—the intelligence to accept the ranks and rights of freemen at our hands, we must bear with their ignorance. But there is no excuse for the man educated under our institutions, who talks of our 'wronging the Mexicans' when we offer them a position . . . in which, for the first time, they may aim at the greatness and dignity of a truly republican and self-governing people" (italics in original).

31. Irving H. Bartlett, *The American Mind in the Mid-Nineteenth Century* (New York: Thomas Y. Crowell, 1967), p. 3.

32. Hartz, op. cit., p. 140.

33. Ibid., p. 276.

34. In the original edition of the book, Hartz misquoted Tocqueville by substituting "free" for "equal"—a mistake corrected in subsequent editions.

35. Seymour M. Lipset, *The First New Nation* (Garden City, NY: Doubleday, 1963).

36. Hartz's Harvard colleague, Samuel H. Beer, a close student of British politics, agreed that "in contrast with European politics and certainly with British, American politics is, and always has been, overwhelmingly 'liberal.'" Beer noted that the absence of elements of Toryism and socialism "distinguishes American politics from British and puts all its significant forces and ideas within a broad liberal tradition." Samuel H. Beer, "Liberalism and the National Idea," in *Left, Right and Center: Essays on Liberalism and Conservatism in the United States*, ed. Robert A. Goldwin (Chicago: Rand McNally, 1965), p. 149.

37. Patrice Higgonet, *Sister Republics: The Origins of French and American Republicanism* (Cambridge, MA: Harvard University Press, 1988), p. 42.

38. Hartz, op. cit., p. 89.

39. "It is generally believed that the socialists were the first to criticize capitalism as a social system; in actual fact, however, there are many indications that this criticism was initiated by the right-wing opposition and was then gradually taken over by the left opposition. . . . Proletarian thought has in many ways a significant affinity with conservative and reactionary thought." Karl Mannheim, "Conservative Thought," *Essays on Sociology and Social Psychology*, ed. Paul Kecskemeti (New York: Oxford University Press, 1953), pp. 90–92.

40. Hartz, op. cit., p. 43.

41. Lawrence Dennis, *The Coming American Fascism* (New York: Harper, 1936).

42. Hartz, op. cit., pp. 145–77.

43. "The ideal of individual justice," Croly wrote, "is being supplemented by the ideal of social justice." Herbert Croly, *Progressive Democracy* (New York: Macmillan, 1914), pp. 148–49, cited in David W. Levy, *Herbert Croly of the New Republic* (Princeton, NJ: Princeton University Press, 1985), p. 168. See also L. T. Hobhouse, *Liberalism* (New York: Oxford University Press, 1964), and T. H. Green, *Lectures on Political Obligation* (London: Longmans, 1941).

44. Hartz, op. cit., p. 259.

45. Paul Roazen, "Louis Hartz's Teaching," *Virginia Quarterly Review* 64, no. 1 (Winter 1988): p. 115.

46. Hartz, op. cit., p. 308.

47. Ibid., p. 9.

48. Ibid., p. 204.

49. James A. Morone, *The Democratic Wish* (New York: Basic Books, 1998), p. 18, puts this point differently. He argues that the changing character of American policies and institutions results from a continuing tension between a dominant liberal tradition and the "recurring subordinate ideology" of republicanism.

50. Ibid., p. 153.

51. See Eric L. McKitrick, ed., *Slavery Defended: The Views of the Old South* (Englewood Cliffs, NJ: Prentice-Hall, 1963), pp. 86–98.

52. Locke and his patron, Lord Anthony Ashley Cooper, Earl of Shaftesbury, held shares in the corporation chartered to colonize Carolina. As secretary to the

"Lords Proprietor," Locke wrote temporary laws for the colony forbidding the enslavement of Indians but allowing the use of African slaves obtained in the slave trade. Barbara Amiel, *Locke and America* (Oxford: Oxford University Press, 1996), pp. 126–27.

53. Carl L. Becker, *The Declaration of Independence: A Study in the History of Political Ideas* (New York: Knopf, 1942).

54. Morison, *The Oxford History of the American People* (New York: Oxford University Press, 1965), p. 222.

55. Quoted in Wills, op. cit., p. 449.

56. Thomas Paine, *Collected Writings* (New York: Library of America, 1995), pp. 6–9.

57. *Works*, (151), 219, quoted by R. R. Palmer, *The Age of the Democratic Revolution* (Princeton, NJ: Princeton University Press, 1959), vol. 1, p. 223.

58. Quoted from a pamphlet published in 1774, in Becker, op. cit., p. 108.

59. See Ronald Hamowy, "Jefferson and the Scottish Enlightenment: A Critique of Garry Wills's *Inventing America: Jefferson's Declaration of Independence*," *William and Mary Quarterly*, 3rd ser., vol. 36, no. 4 (October 1979): pp. 503–23, and Harry V. Jaffa, *American Conservatism and the American Founding* (Durham, NC: Carolina Academic Press, 1984).

60. Jaffa, op. cit., pp. 104–5.

61. Pauline Maier, *American Scripture: Making the Declaration of Independence* (New York: Knopf, 1997), p. 87. For Locke's influence via Blackstone see H. N. Hirsch, *A Theory of Liberty: The Constitution and Minorities* (New York: Routledge, 1992), pp. 38–41.

62. Thomas Pangle, *The Spirit of Modern Republicanism: The Moral Vision of the American Founders and the Philosophy of Locke* (Chicago: University of Chicago Press, 1988), p. 276.

63. Robert K. Faulkner, *The Jurisprudence of John Marshall* (Princeton, NJ: Princeton University Press, 1968), pp. 16–19. The phrase comes from Marshall's opinion in the "Antelope" case (1825).

64. Stephen M. Dworetz, *The Unvarnished Doctrine: Locke, Liberalism, and the American Revolution* (Durham, NC: Duke University Press, 1990), p. 191.

65. Bailyn, op. cit., p. 27.

66. Letter to Samuel Kercheval (12 July 1816), Merrill D. Peterson, ed., *The Portable Thomas Jefferson* (New York: Viking, 1975), p. 555.

67. Alan Craig Houston, *Algernon Sidney and the Republican Heritage in England and America* (Princeton, NJ: Princeton University Press, 1991), p. 8.

68. In Venice only noble families listed in the "Golden Book" (of 1297) enjoyed the full rights of citizenship; somewhat more open, "the Florentine upper class was not in any formal sense a closed aristocracy . . . but a group of families, mostly with interests in long-distance trade and banking and who had come to consider the high offices of the state their natural birthright." Athanasios Moulakis, *Republican Realism in Renaissance Florence: Frances Guicciardini's "Discorso di Logrogno"* (Lanham, MD: Rowman & Littlefield, 1998), p. 90.

69. Isaac Kramnick, *Republicanism and Bourgeois Radicalism: Political Ideology in Late Eighteenth Century England and America* (Ithaca, NY: Cornell University Press, 1990), p. 13.

70. Hartz, op. cit., p. 61.

71. Wood, *Radicalism*, p. 369.

72. Ibid., p. ix.

73. Gordon S. Wood, review of Kramnick, *Republicanism and Bourgeois Radicalism*, *New Republic*, 11 February 1991, p. 33.

74. Hofstadter, *The American Political Tradition*, preface, p. xxxix.

75. Hartz, op. cit., p. 285.

76. See Bellah et al., op. cit.

77. See Gertrude Himmelfarb, *On Liberty and Liberalism: The Case of John Stuart Mill* (New York: Knopf, 1974), and William J. Bennett, *The De-Valuing of Our Culture: The Fight for Our Culture and Our Schools* (New York: Summit Books, 1992).

78. Cass R. Sunstein, *After the Rights Revolution: Reconceiving the Regulatory State* (Cambridge, MA: Harvard University Press, 1990), p. 12.

79. Hartz, op. cit., p. 12.

80. Herbert McCloskey and John Zaller, *The American Ethos: Public Attitudes toward Capitalism and Democracy* (Cambridge, MA: Harvard University Press, 1984), pp. 246–47.

81. Alan Wolfe, *One Nation, After All* (New York: Viking, 1998), especially pp. 319–21.

82. See inter alia the writings of Bruce Ackerman, Isaiah Berlin, Ronald Dworkin, William A. Galston, Stephen Holmes, Will Kymlicka, Charles Larmore, Harvey C. Mansfield Jr., Joseph Raz, Nancy L. Rosenblum, and Michael Sandel.

83. See John Rawls, *A Theory of Justice* (Cambridge, MA: Harvard University Press, 1971), and *Political Liberalism* (New York: Columbia University Press, 1993), and Robert Nozick, *Anarchy, State and Utopia* (New York: Basic Books, 1974).

84. Hobhouse anticipated Rawls's "difference principle" when he wrote that equality of opportunity implies that "whatever inequality of actual treatment, of income, rank, office, consideration, there be in a good social system, it would rest, not on the interest of the favoured individual as such, but on the common good. If the existence of millionaires on the one hand and of paupers on the other is just, it must be because such contrasts are the result of an economic system which upon the whole works out for the common good, the good of the pauper being included therein as well as the good of the millionaire; that is to say, that when we have well weighed the good and the evil of all parties concerned we can find no alternative open to us which could do better for the good of all." Hobhouse, op. cit., p. 70.

85. Rawls, *Political Liberalism*, p. 287.

86. For the contention that minority rights are implied by the constitutional guarantee of liberty, see Hirsch, op. cit.

87. Rogers N. Smith is right in contending that American civic development is not adequately understood as a dialectical encounter between liberalism and republicanism, and that "illiberal, undemocratic traditions" form part of the American tradition (*Civic Ideals*, p. 39), but wrong, I think, in supposing that because the American definition of citizenship has reflected illiberal, undemocratic "ascriptive doctrines" of racial, ethnic, and gender inequality, Hartz's thesis does not hold (ibid., p. 471). In arguing that American political thinking has been gripped by an "irrational" or mythic liberal consensus, Hartz hardly meant to suggest that this ideology was not contradicted, often flagrantly, by what he would have referred to as "social facts."

88. Harold J. Laski, *The Rise of European Liberalism* (London: Allen & Unwin, 1936).

89. C. B. Macpherson, *The Political Theory of Possessive Individualism: Hobbes to Locke* (Oxford: Oxford University Press, 1962).

90. "John Locke, the great enemy of all absolute and arbitrary power, was the last major philosopher to seek a justification for absolute and perpetual slavery." David Brion Davis, *The Problem of Slavery in the Age of Revolution, 1770–1823* (Ithaca, NY: Cornell University Press, 1975), p. 45.

91. Michael Lind, *The Next American Nation: The New Nationalism and the Fourth American Revolution* (New York: Free Press, 1995). See also the discussion of the United States as an example of civic or political nationalism in Sanford Lakoff, "Democracy," *Encyclopedia of Nationalism*, vol. 1 (San Diego: Academic Press, 2000), pp. 101–20.

92. Ralph Waldo Emerson famously saw "Reform" as "the party of hope" and "Conservatism" as "the party of memory." "The Conservative" (1841), *Essays and Lectures* (New York: Library of America, 1983), p. 173 (pp. 173–89). Some modern analysts stress differences of moral outlook. George Lakoff contends that liberal thinking is fixated on the metaphor of the "nurturant mother," conservative thinking on that of the "strict father." See his *Moral Politics: What Conservatives Know That Liberals Don't* (Chicago: University of Chicago Press, 1996). Harvey C. Mansfield Jr. suggests that liberals believe in moral choice whereas conservatives believe "that life is mainly a matter of consent, in which you must recognize your duties and live as duty requires." See his *America's Constitutional Soul* (Baltimore, MD: Johns Hopkins Press, 1978), pp. 128–34.

93. As has been shown to good effect by Diggins, op. cit., and by Steven M. Dworetz, op. cit., Dworetz, drawing on the work of John Dunn and Peter Hudson, argues effectively that Locke's political radicalism stems not from a fixation upon bourgeois property rights but from a "theistic philosophy" and that the loss of this foundation poses a problem for modern liberalism. An earlier example of how fruitful an examination of the links between religion and politics can be is Liston Pope's classic sociological study of the parallels between socioeconomic status and religious affiliation in a Southern town, *Millhands and Preachers: A Study of Gastonia* (New Haven, CT: Yale University Press, 1942).

94. "The main business of religions is to purify, control and restrain that excessive taste for well being which men acquire in times of equality." Tocqueville, op. cit., vol. 2, p. 448.

95. As is suggested by Will Herberg's remark: "By every realistic criterion, the American Way of Life is the operative faith of the American people." This faith, he contends, is a secularized version of Judeo-Christian religiosity: "It affirms the supreme value and dignity of the individual; it stresses incessant activity on his part, for he is never to rest but is always to be striving to 'get ahead'; it defines an ethic of self-reliance, merit, and character, and judges by achievement: 'deeds, not creeds' are what count." Herberg, "The Religion of Americans and American Religion," in *Religious Conflict in America*, ed. Earl Raab (Garden City, NY: Doubleday Anchor, 1964), pp. 104, 108.

96. Quoted by Lind, op. cit., p. 221.

# 4

---

# Conservatism

The term "conservative" first came into use early in the nineteenth century at around the same time as the word "liberal." Those who either adopted the designation or were so labeled were generally alarmed by the frenzy unleashed by the French Revolution and the broad challenge to the "Old Order" it posed. They were united not just by doctrine but by temperament and social standing: their champions had an almost visceral and usually self-interested attachment to the social order in which they enjoyed preeminence. They shared a profound distrust for those who wanted to destroy that order and reconstruct it on some abstract rational plan like the theory of the social contract or the physiocrats' economic laws of nature. They wanted to preserve traditional institutions, especially monarchy and aristocracy, but also the church, and were deeply skeptical of reforms that would have promoted a more egalitarian social order and popular government. The most unyielding also came to be called reactionaries, because they sought not just to conserve traditional institutions and customs but to reverse the radical social innovations, such as the abolition of monarchy and titles of nobility and their replacement by popularly elected parliaments, that challenged the very foundations of customary ways of life.

From the start, however, there was a subtle difference between those on the political right who hated "leveling" of any sort and others who were more conciliatory or pragmatic—who were prepared to accept efforts to expand access to the halls of political power, at least to the newly propertied middle class, so long as the changes were made incrementally and with regard to tradition and precedent, or what the Whig politician and writer Edmund Burke called "prescription." For much of the nineteenth century, conservatives and liberals were arrayed at opposite poles of the political world. As the century progressed, the liberal camp divided between those who adhered to the classical principles, especially the protection of property rights, and those who made common cause with socialists in recognizing the need to alleviate poverty and to improve the conditions of the new industrial working class. Conservatives, too, split between those who made common cause with ethnocentric nationalists and racists and those who moved toward an alliance with classical liberals against extremism on both the left and the right. In the twentieth century, conservatives in the first camp often supported fascism, even though it was hardly a movement spawned by aristocrats and monarchists, and conservatives in the other camp joined with classical liberals to form a hybrid "liberal conservatism."

## ORIGINAL CONSERVATISM

Originally, the contrast between conservatives and liberals was fundamental and broad. Whereas liberals were optimistic about the capacity for progress and perfectibility, conservatives were skeptical of such grandiose visions. They did not accept the view that the vices of mankind could be eliminated by improving social conditions or that human nature could be transformed by education and schemes like Robert Owen's for the elimination of poverty. The elements of conservatism had been around for a long time. They were the practices and rationalizations associated with the Middle Ages—the veneration of order, rigid status hierarchy, and the insistence on subservience and deference from the mostly peasant masses. As an English lord put it later, conservatism was inconspicuous in the Middle Ages not because there was little, but because there was little else. The first conservatives could readily be accused of wanting to maintain or return to the medieval way of life. Especially on the continent, they were often aristocrats and higher clergymen who had been victimized by forces unleashed in the French Revolution.

Thinkers later labeled conservative, like Edmund Burke, Joseph de Maistre, and Louis De Bonald, disagreed fundamentally with the liberal view of society. They did not think it was composed of discreet atomistic individuals living together by compact, either tacit or explicit, but rather that it was an organic entity, formed over long periods of time, and composed of groups, from the family to the village or township and finally to class. The "social contract," Burke declared memorably, "is a partnership in all science; a partnership in all art; a partnership in every virtue, and in all perfection . . . not only between those who are living, but between those who are living, those who are dead, and those who are to be born."[1] It prescribes duties as well as rights. It rests not only on reason and self-interest but even more on shared sentiments and attachments. Conservatives opposed the very idea of revolution, fearing the mass emotionalism that would be unleashed—the mob rule that would replace kings with demagogues. Unlike liberals, whose commitment to rationalism inclined them toward deism or secularism, conservatives were convinced not only that God exists but also that human life proceeds on a providential plan. If things are as they have been for a long time, they believed, the presumption must be that they are right, and that attempts to change them radically, to overthrow what is traditional, would bring nothing but the hardships of another expulsion from paradise. Government, they believed, should be left in the hands of those best fitted for it. It would be a terrible mistake to follow rabble-rousers relying on abstract theory rather than experience, in the hope that they could create a heaven on earth. The masses would inevitably be carried away just as the Jacobins were in France, by fantasies, fanaticism, ignorance, and a passion for revenge. Monarchy, they argued, provides stability, reverence for order, a stabilizing link to the past; overthrow kings and who would replace them? Some new Caesar who would make himself despot—a fear confirmed by the rise of Napoleon Bonaparte in the wake of the revolution in France. Fortunately, Burke remarked, in Britain these French delusions would meet rejection owing to national character:

> Thanks to our sullen resistance to innovation, thanks to the cold sluggishness of our national character, we still bear the stamp of our forefathers. We have not (as I conceive) lost the generosity of thinking of the fourteenth century, nor as yet have we subtilized ourselves into savages. We are not the converts of Rousseau; we are not the disciples of Voltaire; Helvetius has made no progress amongst us. Atheists are not our preachers; madmen are not our lawgivers. We know that we have made no discoveries, and we think that no discoveries are to be made, in morality; nor many in the great principles of government, nor in the ideas of liberty, which were understood long before we were born. . . . We fear God; we look up with awe to kings; with affection to parliaments; with duty to magistrates; with reverence to priests; and with respect to nobility.[2]

Burke and other conservatives were skeptical that even successful revolutions could produce lasting change. They were convinced that things would revert to what they had been previously because human nature would remain the same and efforts to degrade basic institutions like the family and the church would fail because, without them, society simply would become dysfunctional. Social subdivisions of all sorts had arisen for good reasons. Everyone, said Burke, marched in his own platoon.

"Prescription," not abstract human rights, is the basis of the social order: If a custom lasts, the presumption must be that it is worth preserving. Contrary to the philosophes, he thought prejudice a good thing and distrusted abstract reasoning. "The age of chivalry is gone," Burke said famously, "that of sophisters, oeconomists, and calculators has succeeded; and the glory of Europe is extinguished forever."[3] There should be gradual change, to be sure—"a state without the means of some change is without the means of its conservation"[4]—but change should proceed incrementally, not wholesale. For this reason, conservatives did not like the extension of the suffrage or the idea of educating the poor, because their minds would be filled with seditious ideas, and they would have at hand the means of achieving them. Democracy would threaten to reverse the old order in which the common people showed deference to their betters.

When they referred to the "lower orders," they included not only the poor and illiterate but also women, Jews, blacks, and even hairdressers and theater people. They were convinced that the seductive slogans of democracy like "one man one vote" were poisoning the minds of the lower orders, as Don Herzog has well shown. With Burke, they feared exactly what he feared: "the pernicious consequences of destroying all docility in the minds of those who are not fortified for finding their way in the labyrinths of political theory." Scholars whose pursuits were subsidized by aristocratic patrons were now turning against the hand that fed them. The result would only be that "[a]long with its natural protectors and guardians, learning will be cast into the mire, and trodden down under the hoofs of a swinish multitude."[5]

Burke was not the only prominent intellectual to embrace conservatism. The poet Coleridge said that political truth was too dangerous to put before "the multitude, who, ignorant and needy, must necessarily act from the impulse of inflamed Passions."[6] Dr. Samuel Johnson's *Dictionary* told middle-class townsmen that it is their duty "to lead back the people to their honest labor, to tell them, that submission is the duty of the ignorant, and content the virtue of the poor; that they have no skill in the art of government."[7] And in the House of Lords, Bishop Samuel Horsley observed that "he did not know what the mass of the people in any country had to do with the laws but to obey them."[8] As to Tom Paine's views, said another noble lord, they "were an attempt to persuade the Feet that, considering their importance and utility . . . it is a hardship and injustice for them to wade through the dirt and bear the weight of the whole body."[9] The Tory journal *John Bull* sounded the alarm: "We over-educate the poor and what do they say?—that they are superior to the drudgery of cotton-spinning or digging, or doing menial offices. . . . Who will sweep the chimneys and kill the pigs?"[10] Public opinion, said the poet Southey, was "the worst evil" threatening civilized society.[11]

The battleground on which the two sides clashed in domestic terms was formed by the opening up of education and the discussion of public affairs in such venues as the new circulating libraries, debating societies, workers' clubs, alehouses, coffeehouses, and newspapers. Already in 1821, newspapers had a circulation in London alone of 14 million, and 21 million in the entire country, which is really astonishing given the overall population. The enemies of democracy were desperately afraid of all this education and public information. Said Coleridge, "You begin with the attempt to popularize learning and philosophy, but you will end in the plebefication of knowledge."[12] And in the 1830s the battle erupted over the extension of the suffrage. The Reform Act of 1832 widened the suffrage even though it did not yet allow for universal manhood suffrage, let alone women's suffrage. The conservative strategy was to label the excluded as unfit and so warn off those who already had the vote from sharing it with these pariahs. They encouraged the opening of Sunday schools, which first came into being in the 1780s, with the aim of dispelling ignorance about what really mattered and to "bring men cheerfully to submit to their stations—to obey the laws of God and their country."[13] In effect they were agreeing with Marx that religion is the opiate of the masses, but unlike Marx they were prescribing more of it!

## INCIPIENT LIBERAL CONSERVATISM: TOCQUEVILLE AND BURKE

During much of the nineteenth century, liberalism and conservatism stood as polar opposites, bifurcating the political spectrum. In the middle and later decades, the growing appeal of socialism to the left and of authoritarian ideologies to the right caused both to fracture. In the late nineteenth and early twentieth centuries, many liberals moved leftward into the halfway house L. T. Hobhouse called "social liberalism," while many conservatives moved further to the right, embracing integral nationalism, imperialism, and fascism. More recently, disillusionment with socialism among liberals and with right-wing extremism among conservatives has led to a rapprochement. Center-right political parties blending elements of both traditions have attracted large followings everywhere in the West, and political theorizers like Raymond Aron, Michael Oakeshott, and the American neoconservatives have emerged as their intellectual counterparts. In important respects, the ground pattern of this convergence is prefigured in the thinking of Alexis de Tocqueville and Edmund Burke— both of whom also fit into neither category fully and were therefore looked upon as odd men out in their own times.

Although Tocqueville was not a political philosopher in the most restrictive sense of the term, John Stuart Mill remarked astutely that he had "changed the face of political philosophy."[14] Inasmuch as democracy had been considered an obsolete anomaly of earlier Western history (stored in the Attic?), Mill recognized that *Democracy in America* was a work of historic importance. But did the book reflect a point of view toward democracy? It had become popular in England, Mill thought, mainly "because luckily Sir R. Peel praised it, & made the Tories fancy it was a Tory book." "But I believe," he quickly added, "that they have found out their error." Mill preferred to think that Tocqueville's work transcended partisan controversy, marking the "beginning of a new era in the scientific study of politics."[15] Since then, other observers have given Tocqueville a philosophic face of his own, but their portraits vary. Some depict him as a dour conservative,[16] others as an upbeat if wary liberal,[17] while most describe him as a "liberal conservative"—an oxymoronic Janus frowning to one side and smiling to the other—or, as Roger Boesche puts it, a "strange liberal."[18]

The fact that Tocqueville should present such different faces to different observers is a tribute to his scrupulous empiricism, as well as to his breadth and equipoise. An observer first and foremost, he sought to understand history by unearthing evidence and recording the views of participants, not by imposing his own viewpoint. He was a practitioner of the Diltheyan ideal avant la lettre who could empathize with all perspectives while making his own quite clear. He also had a characteristically French fascination with irony and paradox. About some things he changed his mind over time or at least entertained differing hypotheses. But there is no warrant, in this instance or any other, for the deconstructionist dogma that since there are no self-explanatory texts, what an author believes is necessarily what any of his readers takes him to mean. To concede this in Tocqueville's case would be first of all to ignore his exceptional devotion to clarity of expression and his painstaking work habits.[19] He revised his writings with great care and did not publish anything until he was satisfied with it. More to the point, it would be to ignore the strong views he often expressed. No one with eyes not clouded by hermeneutic cataracts can read *Democracy in America* or *The Old Regime* and fail to recognize that Tocqueville, for all his doubts and equivocations, held strong opinions, especially about the implications of the transition to democracy. Although disagreement over textual interpretation in the study of political thought is not uncommon, it usually arises around those who changed their minds or who left writings of a patently divergent character. Tocqueville, by contrast, was single-minded in his preoccupations and point of view. Lukacs rightly remarks the "extraordinarily coherent and consistent nature of Tocqueville's philosophy."[20]

The problem is rather that Tocqueville does not fit neatly into the conventional categories. One alternative can be ruled out. No one claims to see in Tocqueville's brooding eyes the fiery glint of a socialist—unless too much is made of his critique of the brutalizing effects of industrialization[21] and his remark that no institution, including private property, is beyond alternation or abolition.[22] Tocqueville made clear repeatedly his fear that if democracy were to lead to socialism, the result would be a centralized despotism in which equality would become a euphemism for slavery. If he is not a socialist, is he then either a liberal or a conservative? Most readers of Tocqueville would probably agree with Drescher's description of him as "a liberal aristocratic landowner living in a post-revolutionary society"[23] or Saguiv Hadari's as "an aristocrat of conservative-liberal leanings,"[24] with their implication that he had a foot in both camps but was trying to influence the transition to democracy in the hope of protecting liberty.

Tocqueville himself deliberately contributed to the difficulty that later generations have had pinning a label on him when he asserted that he was not a partisan but an open-minded inquirer. "My critics insist on making me out to be a party-man," he wrote to his Tory friend and translator Henry Reeve, "but I am not that."[25] Some analysts agree with this self-portrait in seeing him as a political sociologist and psychologist in the tradition of Montesquieu and later, Saint-Simon, Comte, Durkheim, and Weber.[26] Political sociologist Tocqueville certainly was, but he was not "value neutral" in the sense that he avoided being judgmental or drew a sharp line between his scholarship and his politics. Nor was he "an ivory tower intellectual" indifferent to the conflicts embroiling his contemporaries. As an elected parliamentarian (and briefly foreign minister of the Second Republic), he acted on the reason he gave for investigating America: "I did not study America just to satisfy curiosity, however legitimate. I sought there lessons from which we might all profit."[27]

Although he was well aware of the complexity of making moral judgments in politics, he had one overriding concern. He had "only one opinion," he told Reeve, "an enthusiasm for liberty and for the dignity of the human race." In order to see how this moral principle took form in actual societies, however, it was important to recognize that all forms of government are "more or less perfect means of satisfying this holy and legitimate craving." Thanks to his own circumstances, he felt himself free of bias:

> When I entered life, aristocracy was dead and democracy yet unborn. My interest, therefore, could not lead me blindly to the one or the other. I lived in a country which for forty years had tried everything, and settled nothing. I was on my guard, therefore, against political illusions. Myself belonging to the ancient aristocracy of my country, I had no natural hatred or jealousy of the aristocracy, nor could I have had any natural affection for it, since that aristocracy had ceased to exist, and one can be strongly attached only to the

living. I was near enough to know it thoroughly, and far enough to judge it dispassionately. I may say as much for the democratic element. It had done me, as an individual, neither good nor harm. I had no personal motive, apart from my public conviction, to love or hate it. Balanced between the past and future, with no natural instinctive attraction towards either, I could without an effort look equally on either side of the question.[28]

## THE ORIGINS OF THE TERM

In retrospect, Tocqueville's struggle to come to grips with the rise of democracy mirrors the debate over this historic change of social context between conservatives and liberals in the nineteenth century. It is as though he were rehearsing in his own mind what they would play out on the stage of actual history. As is well appreciated,[29] the terms "conservative" and "liberal" were coined in the early decades of the century to take account of the polarization of opinion resulting from the French Revolution. *Le Conservateur* was the name of the journal started in 1818 by Tocqueville's uncle, Francois Rene de Chateaubriand, to champion the cause of monarchy and the church against partisans of the Revolution. The word "liberal" appeared fairly often in the journal as an epithet for supposed enemies of order and morality like Benjamin Constant, and to distinguish these enemies from the even more despised Jacobins. In England, "liberal" first became a common political label during the 1820s, inspired by the appearance of a Spanish political party, the *Liberales*. In France, the term "conservative" did not become the name of a political party. In England, it was used informally to designate those like the Duke of Wellington who sought to preserve the privileges of monarchy and aristocracy in opposition to the radicals who supported the Chartist movement and the extension of the suffrage. In the debate over the Reform Bill of 1830, the word "conservative" was attached to those in opposition, the word "radical" to those in favor, liberals being divided on the question. These categories were prime examples of what came to be called, after the coinage of Antoine Destutt de Tracy, "ideologies"—clusters of simplified ideas grounded in more elaborate political philosophies but designed to inspire political loyalties and to rationalize political action. Following Marx, Karl Mannheim invented the "sociology of knowledge" to describe the links between the new ideologies and the social classes. Liberalism, Mannheim noted, had two primary aspects: economic and political. In economics it meant "the release of the individual from all his bonds to either state or guild." Politically, it meant freedom "to do as he wishes and thinks fit," but particularly the possibility of exercising "the rights of man." Conservatism stood opposed to egalitarian leveling, republican government, and, especially in France, secularism and atheism.

It was espoused in the first instance by a "defensive alliance between the nobility, the monarchy, and the Church."[30] Although Mannheim oversimplified both ideologies, neglecting to note, for example, that liberalism originated in considerable part in efforts to achieve religious toleration while conservatism was inspired by the defense of religion—not just the church—against the Enlightenment, his class analysis served a useful purpose by identifying the primary groups to which the two doctrines appealed most at the outset.

Mannheim pointed out that there were significant national as well as ideological variations in the strands of conservatism. In Prussia, the major center of conservative thought in Germany, "the revolution precipitated a clash between the aspiration of the feudal forces and old estates, on the one side, and bureaucratic-absolutist rationalism on the other."[31] In his view, it transformed traditionalism into a deliberate opposition to everything stigmatized as "progressive": freedom of speech, looseness of manners, reliance on reason rather than faith, and more representative if not altogether republican government. English conservatives were certainly leery of bureaucratic absolutism and rationalism. But it would be more correct to say that at the outset their main concern was to refute the liberals' disparagement of monarchy and aristocracy—not representative government per se. English conservatives no less than English liberals accepted the important role for parliament established in the settlement of 1689—in their case more because they valued continuity than because they had confidence in popular self-government.[32] Wellington would hardly have repeated Charles I's observation on the scaffold that "a subject and sovereign are clean different things" or that the liberty of subjects "consists in having government, those laws by which their lives and goods may be most their own," but not in "having a share in the government."[33]

In France, conservatism was supportive of the old alliance of throne and altar against the forces undermining both unleashed by the French Revolution. Chateaubriand pledged that his journal would support "religion, the King, liberty, the Church, the [Restoration] Constitution, and respectable people (*honnêtes gens*)."[34] Those who sided with monarchy and aristocracy were thereafter called conservatives, and sometimes, especially by their enemies, reactionaries. At first in France they were usually known by the monarchical faction to which they belonged. (Thus supporters of the Bourbons' dynastic claims were called "legitimists.") In general, the "respectable people" who took this designation were bitter about the Revolution and were anxious to restore or preserve what the Revolution had set out to destroy. They insisted, however, that contrary to what their enemies claimed, they were not calling for a return to feudalism and the Inquisition, but rather for the ordered liberty that monarchy alone guaranteed. They opposed majoritarianism because it took no account of the moral and intellectual superiority of the titled and propertied.[35]

## TOCQUEVILLE AS A LIBERAL CONSERVATIVE

There were nevertheless some aristocrats disposed toward liberalism, Tocqueville among them, though his devotion was far from dogmatic. He drew on the work of one of the leading doctrinaires, Francois Guizot, in analyzing the events that precipitated the Revolution, and he was befriended by another, Pierre-Paul Royer-Collard. He became a close friend of English liberals like J. S. Mill and Senior. But those of his contemporaries considered liberals—the doctrinaires, the utilitarians, and the political economists—shared the belief that political and economic liberty could be grounded in abstract principles and that self-interest would lead to a more benevolent outcome than any paternalistic formula. Tocqueville, like Burke before him, was leery of abstract dogmas and of all else that smacked of *l'esprit de systeme*. He thought natural rights a doctrine of convenience used to justify revolution and property, and utilitarianism a modern version of Epicureanism, which he abhorred for its materialism far more than he did the doctrine of universal rights.

Unlike most liberals, Tocqueville came to his own belief in moral liberty from an acceptance of the Christian doctrine of freedom of the will.[36] In social terms, he thought that liberty had first arisen historically, not as liberals supposed in the revolt against feudalism, but paradoxically in the very bosom of feudalism, in the customary aristocratic "liberties" and fragmented authority of medieval corporatism. He acknowledged that the aristocratic ideal of liberty was less compelling than the democratic version, according to which every human being is endowed with the ability to govern himself "and possesses from birth the right to live independent from his fellow men, in all that concerns himself only, and to decide his destiny as he understands it."[37] But he saw democracies as more devoted to equality than to liberty, and he distrusted liberals who wanted governments to impose liberty through universal rules, as in the "legal despotism" of the physiocrats. He agreed with the economists in opposing poor laws, because they promote idleness and reward sloth, but he was also against such laws because they entailed state interference with civil society. At a time when liberals were beginning to want to use their newly won control over the state to protect property rights, Tocqueville urged that the state's power be limited in favor of local governments and voluntary association. He was as fervent a champion of the liberty of the individual and any middle-class liberal, but unlike them he wanted to preserve the bonds between the individual and the group so as to prevent both the expansion of state control and the tyranny of the majority. Well before pluralists like Leon Duguit and J. N. Figgis challenged both liberal individualism and the "omnicompetent state," Tocqueville championed decentralization and voluntary association.

Liberals were so intent strategically on destroying all remnants of feudalism that they regarded all "corporations" with suspicion, agreeing with Hobbes that they were "worms in the entrails of the body social" and naively supposing that society could be held together by no more than a hypothetical social contract among atomistic individuals. For their part, conservatives were too obsessed with restoring or maintaining monarchy to be as sensitive as Tocqueville was to the need to restrain and devolve political power.

Tocqueville was no radical either, in the sense in which that term was used in his lifetime, even though, in the 1830s, on a visit to England, he found himself drawn to radicals like George Grote and John Bowring who were promoting the extension of the suffrage. He agreed with the Chartists only because he thought it futile and even dangerous to social stability to deny the vote to those whom the rise of social democracy had in effect already morally enfranchised. But he could not share the radicals' enthusiasm for popular sovereignty. "My mind favors democratic institutions," he wrote in 1841, "but my heart is aristocratic: I despise and fear mobs. . . . I belong neither to the radical nor to the conservative party. Yet, after all, I incline rather to the second than to the first. For I differ with the conservatives rather in their means than in their ends, while I differ with the radicals both in their means and in their ends."[38] Tocqueville's conservative sympathies are hardly surprising in someone who by lineage and upbringing was the scion of noblemen, including a Norman ancestor who had fought at Hastings. In his nostalgia for the "old order," he might almost have been the model for Edward Arlington Robinson's "Miniver Cheevy." He thought the golden age of France had come during the second half of the seventeenth century, when wise men like Blaise Pascal wrote for themselves or solely for fame and addressed a small and highly cultivated public. He thought less well of the Enlightenment, with its utopian speculation and destructive criticism—and its effort to manipulate mass opinion.[39] Like the conservatives, Tocqueville believed strongly that social order required hierarchy and that only religious belief could provide the moral restraint that would prevent a descent into barbarism. His bond with them is evident in the doubts and fears he had about majoritarian democracy. Liberals like Benjamin Constant were generally more confident that an enlightened people could achieve autonomy in civil society with a stable representative government. Constant did not share Tocqueville's fear of the tyranny of the majority.[40]

But unlike most conservatives, Tocqueville thought it futile to try to resist the transition to democracy completely, and he had no illusions about the moral superiority of the aristocracy. He did not reject Chateaubriand's patronage and was certainly familiar with his writings. Before going to America, he read the romantic description of the landscape of the New World in Chateaubriand's novel *Atala*, and he may have been influenced by it in describing America as "the yet empty cradle of a great nation."[41] But he would not make common cause with the aristocrats, including his elder brother Hippolyte, who favored the return of the old regime. Although he thought monarchy best for France, he was no absolutist, and he refused to join his cousin Louis de Kergorlay and Kergorlay père in the failed legitimist coup aimed at restoring the Bourbon dynasty— something that may have cost him his welcome in the family household, though not the loyal friendship of "Loulou" himself, his lifelong friend. Although he held judicial appointments under two kings, swearing allegiances to both, he was no die-hard Bourbon loyalist like Kergorlay, who in 1819 denounced Constant in the pages of *Le Conservateur* for criticizing the ruling of the Chamber of Deputies barring the admission of regicides.[42] Tocqueville had the right, upon his father's death, to assume the title of count, but preferred not to use it. He married "beneath his class," to the chagrin of his friends, imitating the example of the English aristocracy which, as he remarked, differed from its continental counterparts in not behaving like a caste.[43] He did not contribute to Chateaubriand's journal, nor did he align himself with others who were labeled conservatives, such as de Maistre and de Bonald, who condemned the French Revolution as the work of Satan and pledged themselves to help extirpate all its works. Tocqueville differed from them in thinking that the old order had been swept away in part because of the failings and mistakes of the aristocracy and the Bourbon monarchy, especially Louis XIV, and in being prepared to work within the framework established by the Revolution for the sake of protecting its excesses. And if conservatism is defined broadly so as to include the "radical right" that developed in the late nineteenth and early twentieth centuries around the belief in racism, elitism, and integral nationalism as espoused by Maurice Barres, Charles Maurras, and the Action Française, then Tocqueville's sharp denunciation of the race theories of his protégé Arthur de Gobineau is an indication that he did not share this view either.

Tocqueville is therefore properly regarded as a hybrid "liberal conservative" who had mixed feelings about both democracy and aristocracy. He admired the ideal of inherited nobility because it represented a quest for honor and excellence, because its patronage of the arts allowed culture to flourish, and because at its best it was devoted to the ideal of service to others. But he was critical of the French aristocracy for selling titles of nobility and for allowing itself to be seduced by the pleasures of the court at Versailles to the neglect of its duty to superintend affairs in the provinces, and of the psychology of aristocracy for promoting a sense of haughty superiority and undignified inferiority, damaging to masters and servants alike. In these fundamental respects, he had leanings toward liberalism and conservatism but accepted neither completely. Just because he was born an aristocrat and was inculcated with Jansenist religious teachings, he may well have felt democracy to be a punishment by God visited upon the aristocracy for its sins—sins that he could expiate by his own good works aimed at preventing democracy from sliding into despotism.

## BURKE AND TOCQUEVILLE

Interestingly, much the same is true for Burke, whom Tocqueville resembles more closely than perhaps anyone else. Burke has been torn out of his historical context in order to be made the founder of an antiliberal conservatism, but neither of the two ideological labels fits him any better than they do Tocqueville. Despite generational and cultural differences, they resemble each other in striking and profound respects. Both prepared for careers in law but gained fame as men of letters. Both were absorbed by the study of history yet were active in contemporary politics. Both were traumatized, at a distance, by the French Revolution. Burke was scandalized by the unchivalrous execution of Marie Antoinette, the beautiful dauphiness he had once seen "glittering like the morning star."[44] Both Tocqueville's grandfather and his maternal great-grandfather, the lawyer Chrétien Guillaume de Malesherbes, were guillotined during the Terror—Malesherbes for defending the royal family before the revolutionary tribunal. Tocqueville's parents, who were also imprisoned but saved from execution by the timely fall of Robespierre, never recovered fully from their ordeal. Had Tocqueville been closer to these awful events, he might have denounced the Revolution and all its works as angrily as Burke had. Although Tocqueville was critical of Burke for failing to appreciate the sources and historical significance of the Revolution,[45] their analyses of its dangers were similar.[46] Tocqueville said that he wanted to honor Malesherbes by following his "double example" of defending the people before the king and the king before the people.[47] Like Tocqueville, Burke was no enemy to reform, as distinct from revolution—especially the Jacobin variety, which he thought gravely undermined liberty. "A state without the means of some change," he observed even in his polemic against the French Revolution, "is without the means of its conservation."[48] In 1790 he opposed the extension of the suffrage, lest it foment mob rule, but forty years later he might well have supported it as a measure whose time had come.[49] A Rockingham Whig, Burke was firmly attached to the principles of the settlement of 1689, as he made emphatically clear in his *Appeal from the New to the Old Whigs*. He came to be regarded as a conservative because, when he broke with Charles James Fox and other Whigs sympathetic to the French Revolution, he stressed the virtues of continuity over those of reform. Ironically, Burke's zeal for his principles "left this great exponent of the system of Party government isolated from both Whigs and Tories."[50] As in the case of Tocqueville, commentators on Burke tend to agree that he too straddles the ideological divide.[51]

On a number of specific issues, their views are quite close:

*For Colonial Liberty—and Colonialism.* To his contemporaries, Burke was known for his advocacy of the rights of colonials. His devotion to liberty led him to champion conciliation with the American colonies and religious liberties for Catholics in Ireland and to wage a relentless impeachment campaign against Warren Hastings, the governor general of India, for corruption and mistreatment of the native population. Tocqueville had a similar concern for the rights of French colonists in Algeria and Canada. But both also believed that colonialism was a legitimate enterprise that contributed to the strength of their respective nations. Burke wanted conciliation with the colonies so as to enable England to preserve her outposts in North America, and he did not favor independence for Ireland or India. Tocqueville accepted the right of Europeans to establish colonies in North America because he thought (erroneously) that the natives had not cultivated and therefore taken possession of the land. As Drescher observes, "Rejecting the principle of totally dependent individuals, Tocqueville and Beaumont embraced the principle of dependent peoples."[52]

*Against Equality But Not Necessarily for Aristocracy.* Both Tocqueville and Burke were leery of equality, but neither was an unqualified supporter of the traditional aristocracy of birth. Burke's fervent hostility to social and political equality arose in revulsion against the attack upon the nobility unleashed by the French Revolution. Burke insisted that society must have hierarchy, but he was no uncritical adulator of aristocracy:

> I am no friend to aristocracy, in the sense at least in which that word is usually understood. If it were not a bad habit to moot cases on the supposed ruin of the constitution, I should be free to declare, that if it must perish, I would rather by far see it resolved into any other form, than lost in that austere and insolent domination.[53]

Tocqueville sympathized with Americans like John Adams who believed in the need for a "natural aristocracy" of the propertied and educated, but doubted that democracy would tolerate any sort of aristocracy. Instead, he thought that the antisocial tendencies of democratic individualism could be countered by voluntary associations and political parties, which would serve as functional equivalents for aristocracy.[54] This preference for the play of factions and parties rather than for reliance on extraordinary statesmen also links him to Burke, who was among the first to appreciate the importance of political parties and partisanship for parliamentary government.[55]

*For Property But Not Dogmatic Laissez-Faire.* Burke believed in free trade, as C. B. Macpherson has shown, and the need for a docile working class. He thought "the love of lucre"—"this natural, this reasonable, this powerful, this prolific principle"[56]—though "sometimes carried to a ridiculous, sometimes to a vicious excess," the cause of prosperity.[57] To make accumulation possible, the common people "must be tractable and obedient" and government controlled by a "true natural aristocracy" reflecting the predominance of property, especially landed property.[58] Yet he condemned the age of "sophisters, oeconomists and calculators" as much as Tocqueville condemned "our economists"—the physiocrats—for helping to inspire the French Revolution. Tocqueville too thought that private property was an essential bulwark of freedom, but he thought that the writings of François Quesnay and Pierre-François Mercier de la Rivière revealed the true radicalism of the Revolution. Their targets were the institutions of the old order; their preferences were for those established by the Revolution. It had been a physiocrat who first denounced the existing division of France and called for its redivision into new provinces, before the map of France was redrawn forty years later by the Constituent Assembly. What Tocqueville especially disliked about the physiocrats was their opposition to any sort of diversity. They had no concern for contractual engagements or private rights but only for the public interest. And although they were amiable people and good administrators, they carried their views to fanatic lengths. They had a vast contempt for the past and no concern for political freedom. True, they were devoted to a system of laissez-faire in commerce and industry, but they were not in favor of political liberty. They were "thoroughly hostile to deliberative assemblies, to secondary organizations vested with local powers, and, generally speaking, to all those counterpoises which have been devised by free peoples at various stages of their history to curb the domination of a central authority." To Quesnay, "any system of opposing forces is highly objectionable." The only safeguard against bad government, they thought, is widespread education: "when a nation is fully educated, tyranny is ruled out." Tocqueville had no use for nostrums like natural law—the "vapourings of litterateurs." He much preferred solid institutional barriers to despotism. The physiocrats saw the old institutions, especially the *parlements*, as relics of the old order which stood in the way of reform. Like other advocates of "enlightened despotism," they wanted to enlist the royal power in the cause of reform. The state, they thought, should be all powerful. One of them remarked, "We must see to it that the state rightly understands its duty . . . and then give it a free hand." Tocqueville saw this very dogmatism as the basis of a new popular despotism:

> The form of tyranny sometimes described as "democratic despotism" (it would have been unthinkable in the Middle Ages) was championed by the Economists well before the Revolution. They were for abolishing all hierarchies, all class distinctions, all differences of rank, and the nation was to be composed of individuals almost exactly alike and unconditionally equal. In this undiscriminated mass man was to reside, theoretically, the sovereign power; yet it was to be carefully deprived of any means of controlling or even supervising the activities of its own government. For above it was a single authority, its mandatory, which was entitled to do anything and everything in its name without consulting it. This authority could not be controlled by public opinion since public opinion had no means of making itself heard; the State was a law unto itself and nothing short of a revolution could break its tyranny. De jure it was a subordinate agent; de facto, a master.[59]

It was no coincidence, Tocqueville thought, that Morelly's *Code de la Nature*, with its denunciation of private property, appeared in 1755, the year Quesnay founded his school, "so true is it that socialism and centralization thrive on the same soil."[60]

The fear of socialism and the need to rely on the holders of property to resist it led both Burke and Tocqueville to shy away from radical reforms that might have alleviated the plight of the poor.[61] Like modern liberal conservatives, they were so convinced that no amount of progress would altogether eliminate poverty and so paralyzed by fear that the working class would succumb to the siren calls of socialism that they prescribed nothing but private charity and imprisonment of the idle as a way of inculcating the work ethic.[62]

*Against Excessive Reliance on Rationalism.* Like Burke, who attacked the "literary cabal" whom he held responsible for the French Revolution,[63] Tocqueville distrusted uprisings led by men of letters, proceeding on the basis of abstract knowledge, rather than by practical politicians schooled in the hard realities of laws and institutions. There are few more Burkean passages outside the writings of Burke himself than Tocqueville's observations about the French Revolution being the work of *litterateurs*, with their spirit of abstraction and their penchant for radical experimentation:

> Our revolutionaries had the same fondness for broad generalizations, cut-and-dried legislative systems, and a pedantic symmetry; the same contempt for hard facts; the same taste for reshaping institutions on novel, ingenious, original lines; the same desire to reconstruct the constitution according to the rules of logic and a preconceived system instead of trying to rectify its

faulty parts. The result was nothing short of disastrous; for what is merit in the writer may well be a vice in the statesman and the very qualities which go to make great literature can lead to catastrophic revolutions.[64]

*In Favor of Religion as the Foundation of Social Order.* Burke and Tocqueville believed that religious belief was the necessary foundation of every good civil society. Classical liberals were often uncomfortable with religion. Some, like Locke and Jefferson, were deists; others like Paine could fairly be accused of atheism or a worship of reason. Burke was outspokenly in favor of religiosity, and was himself deeply religious. The English, Burke remarked, are so convinced of the need for religion that there is no "rust of superstition" that "ninety-nine in a hundred of the people of England would not prefer to impiety." Quoting Cicero's *De Legibus,* he described religion as "the basis of civil society, and the source of all good, and of all comfort."[65] He deplored the confiscation of church property in the French Revolution as an act of usurpation that set a precedent for the abolition of all prescriptive rights and betokened an anti-Christian fanaticism.[66] Tocqueville was very concerned about the danger of a loss of religious faith lurking in the materialist impulses of modern democracy. He thought that conventional religions were indispensable in giving people happiness in this life—whatever they might provide in an afterlife:

> When a people's religion is destroyed, doubt invades the highest faculties of the mind and half paralyzes all the rest. Each man gets into the way of having nothing but confused and changing notions about matters of greatest importance to himself and his fellows. Opinions are ill-defended or abandoned, and in despair of solving unaided the greatest problems of human destiny, men ignobly give up thinking about them. Such a state inevitably enervates the soul, and relaxing the springs of the will, prepares a people for bondage.

A concern for well-being was legitimate and necessary, but it could easily be carried to excess. He thought that the main business of religion should be to "purify, control, and restrain" the "excessive and exclusive" taste for well-being that equality brings. Catholicism was better than Protestantism for this purpose because it was more otherworldly, less concerned with rationalizing earthly vocations.[67] In his own faith, Tocqueville was troubled from the time he went through a spiritual crisis at the age of sixteen. André Jardin remarks that although Tocqueville was exposed in his youth to the religious classics and was devoted to his clerical mentor, he turned against the dogmatism of the church—to such an extent that he refused the importuning of his wife, a convert, to confess and receive communion on his deathbed.[68] But if he was a skeptic, he was also a deist and a Christian.[69]

*"A Salutary Bondage": Respect for Traditional Opinion.* Burke's readiness to defend prejudice against Enlightened skeptics is well known. He very deliberately threw back at the philosophes the very imprecation they hurled at defenders of the old order. Prejudices, he believed, embodied wisdom and served a useful purpose. In England, as opposed to revolutionary France, people still "bear the stamp of our forefathers," a stamp registered in "those inbred sentiments which are the faithful guardians, the active monitors of our duty. Even in "this enlightened age, I am bold enough to confess, that we are generally men of untaught feelings: that instead of casting away all our old prejudices, we cherish them to a very considerable degree, and, to take more shame to ourselves, we cherish them because they are prejudices; and the longer they have lasted, and the more generally they have prevailed, the more we cherish them."[70] Tocqueville put the same idea less polemically. He believed that there are many truths, of which everyday use is made, on which it is necessary to accept the common opinion based on what clever men have discovered, because it is impossible for any individual to gain enough information to decide for himself.[71] Even philosophers must do the same. To do so may be a form of bondage, but "it is a salutary bondage" because it allows the use of freedom, which would otherwise be paralyzed by indecision. Individuals may be independent, but they cannot expect to be completely so. "Somewhere and somehow authority is always bound to play a role in intellectual and moral life," he observed. "Men cannot do without dogmatic beliefs . . . it is desirable that they should have them."[72] In democratic times, he added, there is a general disposition to place intellectual authority in human sources, not to go beyond or outside humanity; to found new religions in such periods would invite ridicule.[73]

*The Need for Pluralism to Protect Liberty.* Burke detested the effort of the French revolutionaries to destroy all social distinctions and to rule out all social groupings except the presumably homogeneous body of citizens bound by the mysterious general will. He thought of society as an organic compound of families and estates—everyone marching in his own little platoon. Tocqueville was convinced that the prospects for liberty in any society rested above all with its pluralism. He believed that liberty had been protected by medieval corporatism until the rise of absolute monarchy instituted the centralization that made possible and was intensified by the Revolution. When Louis XIV drew all the strings of power to himself, replacing the nobility with his *intendants*, he effectively undermined the role of the French nobility and with it the justification of its privileges. The greatest danger in democracy, Tocqueville thought, was its natural tendency to make popular sovereignty a new form of absolutism. For just this reason, he was relieved to find that in America, federalism, voluntary association, widespread property ownership, and freedom of the press all promoted a devolution of power—indeed that in America power percolated up from the towns and villages rather than descending downward from the national capital. Tocqueville understood liberty not as the enjoyment of abstract natural rights but as a real condition that existed wherever there was no monopoly of authority. He paid practically no attention to the Bill of Rights in the American Constitution. For him, such paper guarantees were only valuable if implemented in institutions and sustained by mores. Like James Madison and latter-day political scientists, he thought that pluralism—the multiplicity of factions, the mutual checks on the power exercised by the various branches of government, and the federal division of authority between the central government and the states—was much the most reliable guarantee of American liberty.

*Fear of Mediocrity.* "Perhaps," Tocqueville remarked, "it was the will of God not to turn a few to excellence but to provide a mediocre well being among the mass of mankind."[74] He could not escape the fear that democracy would lead to cultural degradation because all taste would depend on the lowest common denominator. Mass society would lead to mass production and, in effect, mass culture. He thought the failure of the United States to produce a high aesthetic culture of its own was evidence that democracy simply would not maintain the taste for excellence and refinement introduced by aristocracy. He was afraid that this would apply to work in the "higher sciences" as well because in democratic times, people would be fixated on the superficial and the useful, to the neglect of the deeper forms of knowledge valued for its own sake.[75] Burke had the same fear that reliance on popular taste and judgment would lead to cultural as well as political degeneration: "Along with its natural protectors and guardians, learning will be cast into the mire, and trodden down under the hoofs of a swinish multitude."[76] Turning power over to "the sober incapacity of dull uninstructed men" could only bring results "both disgraceful and destructive." Without restraints, the people at large would no longer be content with habits of order, frugality, and industry. The more active of the lower orders would plunder the resources of government. It is then, "basking in the sunshine of unmerited fortune, that low, sordid, ungenerous and reptile souls swell with their hoarded poisons."[77] They have already erected statutes to their teacher, Rousseau, "the philosopher of vanity," who had hypocritically urged fatherly love and consigned his children to an orphanage—a "lover of his kind, but a hater of his kindred." Following his example, the leaders of the Revolution "infuse into their youth an unfashioned, indelicate, sour, gloomy, ferocious medley of pedantry and lewdness; of metaphysical speculations, blended with the coarsest sensuality."[78]

*Fearing the Tyranny of the Majority.* In the tumult unleashed by the French Revolution, Burke saw the specter of mob rule and in 1790 prophesied the rise of Napoleon—the commander of the army who would become "the master of your whole republic."[79] Tocqueville's "greatest complaint against democratic government" was "not its weakness, but its irresistible strength." A party suffering injustice cannot turn to public opinion, for it forms the majority. It cannot turn to the legislature because the legislature obeys the majority blindly. The police are "nothing but the majority under arms."[80] Burke shared the same fear. Even kings, he argued, cannot expect to rule without impediments to their power, because they need instruments; their power is therefore never complete, but the situation is different where the whole people exercises the sovereign power:

> Where popular authority is absolute and unrestrained, the people have an infinitely greater, because a far better founded, confidence in their own power. They are themselves in a great measure their own instruments. They are nearer to their objects. Besides, they are less responsible to one of the greatest controlling powers on earth, the sense of fame and estimation. The share of infamy that is likely to fall to the lot of each individual in public acts is small indeed: the operation of opinion being in the inverse ratio of the number of those who abuse power. Their own approbation of their own acts has to them the appearance of a public judgment in their favor. A perfect democracy is therefore the most shameless thing in the world. As it is the most shameless, it is also the most fearless.[81]

It is therefore wrong that subjects should be in a position to exact from their rulers "not an entire devotion to their interest, which is their right, but an abject submission to their occasional will."[82]

*History as the "Divine Tactic" or the Unspoken Will of God.* Finally, there is an affinity in their attitude toward history which puts both Burke and Tocqueville on the side of those liberals, like M. J. de Condorcet, who had come to believe that history was a process of progressive evolution. Tocqueville makes very clear at the outset of *Democracy in America* that he thinks of the tendency toward equality as the very expression of the will of God. Leo Strauss has shown that despite Burke's invocation of the principles of the "Glorious Revolution," he took a historicistic view of "natural right" in keeping with a movement of thought begun in the middle decades of the eighteenth century with Turgot's lectures on progress and culminating with Hegel's lectures on the philosophy of history and the materialist rendering of Marx. As Strauss puts it, Burke's "intransigent opposition to the French Revolution must not blind us to the fact that, in opposing the French Revolution, he has recourse to the same fundamental principle which is at the bottom of the revolutionary theorems and which is alien to all earlier thought."[83] For Strauss, Burke too is guilty of "secularization"—the "temporalization" of the spiritual.[84] In Burke this tendency leads to the acceptance of history as "the divine tactic," rather like Hegel's "cunning of reason"—an attitude of acceptance toward the march of history implying that to oppose the French Revolution would be to oppose the will of God. "They who persist in opposing this mighty current in human affairs," Strauss explains, "will not be resolute and firm, but perverse and obstinate." Ignoring Burke's protestations against the French Revolution and his later unwillingness to tolerate a "regicide peace" with revolutionary France, Strauss criticizes Burke for adopting a viewpoint that makes it wrong in principle to resist change:

> Burke comes close to suggesting that to oppose a thoroughly evil current in human affairs is perverse if that current is sufficiently powerful; he is oblivious of the nobility of last-ditch resistance. . . . It is only a short step from this thought of Burke to the supercession of the distinction between the progressive and the retrograde, or between what is and what is not in harmony with the historical process.

Strauss also observes that Burke's approach, with its emphasis on the peculiar excellence of the British constitution, is even more at variance with classical thinking than the ideology of the Revolution: "Political philosophy or political theory had been from its inception the quest for civil society as it ought to be. Burke's political theory is, or tends to become . . . an attempt to 'discover the latent wisdom which prevails' in the actual." Thus, transcendent standards can be dispensed with because the standard is inherent in the process, or immanent in history: "the actual and the present is the rational." "What could appear as a return to the primeval equation of the good with the ancestral is, in fact, a preparation for Hegel."[85] Had Strauss examined Tocqueville's attitude of acceptance toward democracy as the historical will of God, he might have made the same critique. Both Burke and Tocqueville are too ready to respect the verdict of history to satisfy a rigid conservative belief that fundamental principles must never be compromised to suit the exigencies of history.

## BURKE AND TOCQUEVILLE AS
## FORERUNNERS OF MODERN LIBERAL CONSERVATISM

Burke and Tocqueville wrote from different national and cultural traditions and with different temperaments and dispositions. Burke was English by citizenship, Protestant by confession (though often caricatured as a Jesuit[86]), and Irish by temperament. Burke did not scruple about using coarse anti-Semitic stereotypes; Tocqueville had great sympathy for all who suffered from prejudice and hatred. Burke's most "conservative" work, the *Reflections on the Revolution in France*, was written in the white heat of anger over what seemed to him a monstrous affront to order.

Tocqueville wrote during a later time, when the Revolution was a fait accompli, and in which it was possible to hope for a new synthesis of order and liberty—at least until 1848, when his thinking came to resemble Burke's in its despair and foreboding. Tocqueville's Catholicism gave him a Durkheimian preference for the Roman version of Christianity as a basis for social cohesion.

Despite these differences, they had in common an appreciation of the precious value of liberty; in that sense they certainly belong to the liberal tradition. As Tocqueville studied the history of France and was preoccupied by the transformation it was going through, so Burke studied English history and felt most comfortable when he could speak of English liberties in their own context. It may indeed be that this preference for the concrete over abstract political philosophy is itself a hallmark of conservatism, as Hearnshaw remarks,[87] but the larger significance of this affinity between Burke and Tocqueville is that it reveals a form of conservatism incorporating some but not all of the spirit of classical liberalism. Tocqueville and Burke were not full-fledged liberals, first of all because their belief in liberty was grounded neither in natural rights nor in economic liberalism. Burke's belief in liberty was based on the actual experience of English constitutional history, with its steady expansion of the privileges of the individual against arbitrary power. For Tocqueville, liberty was rooted in the belief in freedom of the will and was expressed politically in the absence of overweening central authority and the presence of what Montesquieu had called "intermediate powers." Both Tocqueville and Burke were also anchored in the conservative tradition. They accepted the historical/organic rather than the analytic/atomistic model of society, and with it the desirability of social hierarchy. Both favored monarchy and defended established religion. Their belief in property was less a result of an acceptance of laissez-faire economic thinking than an expression of the belief that widespread property ownership would check efforts to level all distinctions, which could only bring on despotism. Both feared that under popular sovereignty, ignorance would replace informed intelligence in the management of public affairs. Both deeply regretted the degradation of culture that they feared social equality would entail. Tocqueville in particular laid the groundwork for Tory democracy, with his confidence that an enlarged suffrage would bring conservative rural proprietors to the defense of order against revolution and against socialism.

In all these respects they resemble and prefigure right-of-center modern liberal conservatism, with its tough-minded approach to the use of power in international relations, its deep suspicion of big government and preference for devolution of authority to regional and local authorities, its disdain for utopian rationalism and the academic "new class," its crusades against moral license and welfare dependency, its efforts to form a coalition around "family values" with religious fundamentalists and "hard-hat" workers, and its pragmatic willingness to accept some social reforms, such as a minimal safety net, but not those that threaten conventional values or sap individual initiative. It should therefore not be altogether surprising that Margaret Thatcher, for example, a stalwart opponent of socialism and champion of political and economic liberty, should in modern times be labeled a conservative, even though her "conservatism" often seems to embody originally liberal principles of political and economic liberty. "I think of myself," Thatcher has said, "as a Liberal in the 19th century sense—like Gladstone." Samuel Beer suggests that Thatcher's stress on fiscal prudence and the free market removes the Tory element from traditional British conservatism, if Toryism is understood to mean paternalistic statism and an expectation of upper-class noblesse oblige and lower-class deference.[88] But it does not remove such other conservative characteristics as a lingering attachment to a colony like the Falklands or nationalistic opposition to integration with the rest of Europe. American neoconservatives have no Tory roots at all, but they too have much in common both with nineteenth-century liberals and conservatives. Like the liberals, they defend free-market capitalism and call for self-reliance rather than managerialism and welfare dependency. With nineteenth-century conservatives, however, they are leery of a liberty that they see as divorced from virtue and as too apt to cohabit with materialism and hedonism. Thus, Irving Kristol observes, in a reference to the antebellum Southern conservative George Fitzhugh, "if virtue is to regain her lost loveliness," a "combination of the reforming spirit with the conservative ideal seems to me what is most desperately wanted."[89]

This amalgam of liberalism and conservatism first found intellectual expression, in the aftermath of the Second World War, in the work of Aron and Oakeshott. Aron is often considered a latter-day Tocqueville,[90] as Oakeshott is often thought of as a "Burkean conservative," especially because of his objection to "rationalism in politics."[91] Burke and Tocqueville would have been in full agreement with their attacks on modern totalitarian collectivism in defense of liberal democracy. Aron, in an essay comparing Tocqueville and Marx, quotes the last lines of Tocqueville's preface to the *Old Régime* with approval:

> Even despots do not deny that freedom is an excellent thing; but they only want it for themselves, and they maintain that all other persons are completely unworthy of it. Thus, it is not on the opinion that they have of freedom that men differ, but on the degree of respect that they have for their fellows; and this is why one can say that the fondness that one shows for absolute government is exactly proportionate to the contempt one professes

for one's country. I hope that I may be permitted to wait a little longer before being converted to this feeling.[92]

Oakeshott observes, in an especially Tocquevillian passage:

> The opposition of collectivism to freedom appears first in the collectivist rejection of the whole motion of the diffusion of power and of a society organized by means of a multitude of genuinely voluntary associations. The cure proposed for monopoly is to create more numerous and more extensive monopolies and to control them by force. . . . Great power is required for the overall control of this organization—power sufficient not merely to break up a single over-mighty concentration of power when it makes its appearance, but to control continuously enormous concentrations of power which the collectivist has created. The government of a collectivist society can tolerate only a very limited opposition to its plans; indeed, that hard-won distinction, which is one of the elements of our liberty, between opposition and treason is rejected: what is not obedience is sabotage. Having discouraged all other means of social and industrial integration, a collectivist government must enforce its imposed order or allow the society to relapse into chaos.[93]

Liberals and conservatives split apart initially because liberals had greater confidence that the liberty unleashed by rationalism, religious toleration, the market economy, and representative government would produce a better society, while conservatives feared that these forces of change would imperil religion, social hierarchy, and order itself. But neither group favored dictatorship or collectivism. As fascism and Bolshevism created totalitarian systems abhorrent to both, the old division was replaced by a new alliance. Tocqueville and Burke, struggling to come to terms with an earlier social upheaval, were "liberal conservatives" ahead of their time.

## NOTES

1. Edmund Burke, *Reflections on the Revolution in France*, ed. L. G. Mitchell (New York: Oxford University Press, 1993), p. 96.
2. Ibid., p. 86.
3. Ibid., p. 76.
4. Ibid., p. 21.
5. Ibid., p. 79.
6. Don Herzog, *Poisoning the Minds of the Lower Orders* (Princeton, NJ: Princeton University Press, 1998), p. 177.
7. Ibid., p. 30.
8. Ibid., p. 32.
9. Ibid., p. 35.
10. Ibid., p. 93.

11. Ibid., p. 106.

12. Ibid., pp. 178–79.

13. Ibid., p. 78.

14. Alexis de Tocqueville, *Oeuvres, papiers et correspondance*, ed. J.-P. Mayer (Paris: Gallimard, 1945), vol. 6, *Correspondance anglaise*, p. 328.

15. "M. de Tocqueville on Democracy in America," in *The Philosophy of John Stuart Mill*, ed. M. Goldman (New York: Modern Library, 1961), p. 123.

16. See Bruce Frohnen, *Virtue and the Promise of Conservatism: The Legacy of Burke and Tocqueville* (Lawrence: University Press of Kansas, 1993).

17. See Judith N. Shklar, *After Utopia: The Decline of Political Faith* (Princeton, NJ: Princeton University Press, 1969), p. 226.

18. Roger Boesche, *The Strange Liberalism of Alexis de Tocqueville* (Ithaca, NY: Cornell University Press, 1987).

19. "No idea," Tocqueville told Beaumont, "should be shown in undress (*en deshabille*). To be received, it must be presented in as few words as is compatible with a perfect clarity." Conversation recorded 26 August 1860 by Nassau William Senior, *Oeuvres Complètes*, ed., D. W. and H. P. Kerr (Paris: Gallimard, 1991), p. 503. Out of respect for Tocqueville's fastidious work habits, his friend Beaumont thought that manuscripts Tocqueville left in draft form should not be published. Gustave de Beaumont, "Memoir," *Memoir, Letters, and Remains of Alexis de Tocqueville*, translated (Boston: Ticknor & Fields, 1862, reprinted University Microfilms International, 1983), vol. 1, pp. 81–82.

20. Alexis de Tocqueville, *"The European Revolution" and Correspondence with Gobineau*, ed. and trans. John Lukacs (Garden City, NY: Doubleday, 1959), introduction, p. 6.

21. Alexis de Tocqueville, *Democracy in America*, trans. G. Lawrence (Garden City, NY: Doubleday, 1969), vol. 2, p. 557.

22. Alexis de Tocqueville, *The Recollections of Alexis de Tocqueville*, trans. A de Mattos, ed. J.-P. Mayer (London: Harvill Press, 1948), p. 85.

23. Seymour Drescher, *Dilemmas of Democracy: Tocqueville and Modernization* (Pittsburgh: University of Pittsburgh Press, 1968), p. 92.

24. Saguiv A. Hadari, *Theory in Practice: Tocqueville's New Science of Politics* (Stanford, CA: Stanford University Press, 1989), p. 92.

25. Letter to Henry Reeve (22 March 1837) in *Memoir*, vol. 2, p. 39.

26. See the various references to Tocqueville as a political sociologist in the writings of Raymond Aron and also Jon Elster, *Political Psychology* (Cambridge: Cambridge University Press, 1993) and Hadari, op. cit.

27. *Democracy in America*, vol. 1, author's introduction, p. 18.

28. *Memoir*, vol. 2, pp. 39–40. Tocqueville's close collaborator, Gustave de Beaumont, faithfully endorsed Tocqueville's own view of himself. See *Memoir*, vol. 1, p. 42.

29. See Rudolf Vierhaus, "Conservatism," *Dictionary of the History of Ideas*, ed. Philip P. Wiener (New York: Scribner, 1974), vol. 1, pp. 477–85.

30. Karl Mannheim, *Conservatism: A Contribution to the Sociology of Knowledge*, ed. David Kettler, Volker Meja, and Nico Stehr (London: Routledge and Kegan Paul, 1986), p. 114.

31. Ibid., p. 112.

32. F. J. C. Hearnshaw suggests that conservatism embodies twelve "principles," none of which specifies or implies popular sovereignty: reverence for the past; the organic conception of society; communal unity; constitutional continuity; opposition to revolution; cautious or evolutionary reform; the religious basis of the state; the divine source of legitimate authority; the priority of duties to rights; the prime importance of character; loyalty; and common sense, realism, and practicality. F. J. C. Hearnshaw, *Conservatism in England* (New York: Howard Fertig, 1967), pp. 22–33.

33. Quoted in Antonia Fraser, *Cromwell: The Lord Protector* (New York: Knopf, 1973), p. 291.

34. *Le Conservateur* 1 (1818): p. xx.

35. Interestingly, the term "moral majority" first appeared in the pages of *Le Conservateur*, in an article denouncing merely "quantitative" voting and praising the Athenian class system and Roman group voting as a means of assuring the predominance of "moral majorities"—majorities that give "the enlightened and the propertied the predominance they deserve" (vol. 5 [1819]: p. 6). This usage resembles the Benedictine rule that the *sanior pars* (better part) should predominate. See Sanford Lakoff, *Democracy: History, Theory, Practice* (Boulder, CO: Westview Press, 1996), p. 92, and, for a more extensive treatment, Arthur P. Monahan, *Consent, Coercion, and Limit: The Medieval Origins of Parliamentary Democracy* (Kingston and Montreal: McGill-Queen's University Press, 1987), pp. 137–43.

36. André Jardin suggests that his view of freedom was "Pauline" but that his religious creed was closer to Unitarianism than to Catholicism. See Jardin, *Tocqueville: A Biography*, trans. L. K. Davis with R. Hemenway (New York: Farrar, Straus & Giroux, 1988), p. 385.

37. Quoted from "The Social and Political State of France before and after 1789," *London and Westminster Review* (1836) by Pierre Manent, *Tocqueville and the Nature of Democracy*, trans. John Waggoner (Lanham, MD: Rowman & Littlefield, 1996), p. 19.

38. Quoted in *The European Revolution*, op. cit., p. 20.

39. Conversation recorded by Nassau Senior, *Memoir*, pp. 114–70.

40. As Stephen Holmes points out, Constant thought that the real danger was posed by minorities who claimed to rule in the name of the majority. "The majority never oppresses," he asserted. "One confiscates its name, using against it the weapons it has furnished." Quoted in Holmes, *Benjamin Constant and the Making of Modern Liberalism* (New Haven, CT: Yale University Press, 1984), p. 25.

41. *Democracy in America*, vol. 1, p. 30.

42. *Le Conservateur* 4 (1819): pp. 32–34.

43. Conversation with Senior (25 October 1849), *Oeuvres Complète*, vol. 6, p. 257. *Le Conservateur* 4 (1819): pp. 32–34.

44. Burke, op. cit., p. 75.

45. While praising Burke's *Reflections* as "the work of a powerful mind" and describing his "insights into new institutions and their effects" as "masterful," Tocqueville faults him for failing to appreciate the novelty and universal significance of the revolution and that its "habits and ideas" were evident before in the weakness of the nobility, the vanities of the middle class, and the miseries of the lower class." *The European Revolution*, ed. Lukacs, pp. 163–64.

46. "The dependence of Tocquevillian analysis—in the measured language of scholarly objectivity and with no overriding suggestion of hostility—upon Burkean polemic has not been sufficiently appreciated." Robert Nisbet, "Sources of Conservatism," in *Edmund Burke: Appraisals and Applications*, ed. Daniel E. Ritchie (New Brunswick: Transaction Publishers, 1990), p. 279.

47. In a manuscript in the Tocqueville archive cited by Drescher, *Dilemmas of Democracy*, p. 103n.

48. Burke, op. cit., p. 21.

49. "We must all obey the great law of change," Burke wrote in 1792, in support of the enfranchisement of Irish Roman Catholics. "All we can do . . . is to provide that the change shall proceed by insensible degrees. . . . This gradual course . . . will prevent men, long under depression, from being intoxicated with a large draught of new power, which they always abuse with a licentious insolence. But wishing, as I do, the change to be gradual and cautious, I would, in my first steps, lean rather to the side of enlargement than restriction." From a letter to Sir Hercules Langrishe, quoted by Gerald Chapman, *Edmund Burke: The Practical Imagination* (Cambridge, MA: Harvard University Press, 1967), p. 168. And: "I reprobate no form of government merely upon abstract principles. There may be situations in which the purely democratic form will become necessary. There may be some (very few, and very particularly circumstanced) where it would be clearly desirable" (*Reflections*, ed. Mitchell, op. cit., p. 125).

50. Philip Magnus, *Edmund Burke* (London: John Murray, 1939), p. xi.

51. Conor Cruise O'Brien agrees with Philippe Raynaud that Burke can be said to be "at once liberal and counter-revolutionary" (O'Brien, *The Great Melody: A Thematic Biography and Commented Anthology of Edmund Burke* [London: Sinclair-Stevenson, 1992], p. 596), quoting Raynaud's preface to a French translation of the *Reflections*. Isaac Kramnick remarks: "Burke's conservatism . . . belongs to the liberal tradition, properly understood and translated to our time" (Isaac Kramnick, ed., *Edmund Burke* [Englewood Cliffs, NJ: Prentice Hall, 1974], p. 176). Chapman observes: "Burke means many things to many men. His prelacy in conservatism is commonly recognized; yet, as Harold Laski says, Burke also gives 'deep comfort to men of liberal temper.'" Chapman, op. cit., p. 1.

52. Drescher, op. cit., p. 194.

53. Quoted from *Thoughts on the Present Discontents* in Russell Kirk, *Edmund Burke: A Genius Reconsidered* (New Rochelle, NY: Arlington House, 1967), p. 87. Kirk also cites Burke's similar comments, eleven years later, in his speech on the bill for the repeal of the marriage act: "I am accused, I am told abroad, of being a man of aristocratic principles. If by aristocracy they mean the Peers, I have no vulgar admiration, nor any vulgar antipathy, towards them; I hold their order in cold and decent respect. I hold them to be of an absolute necessity in the constitution; but I think they are only good when kept within their proper bounds. . . . When, indeed, the smallest rights of the poorest people in the kingdom are in question, I would set my face against any act of pride and power countenanced by the highest that are in it; and if it should come to the last extremity, and to a contest of blood—God forbid! God forbid!—my part is taken; I would take my fate with the poor, and low, and feeble. But if these people came to turn their liberty into a cloak for maliciousness, and to seek a privilege of exemption, not from power, but from

the rules of morality and virtuous discipline, then I would join my hand to make them feel the force which a few, united in a good cause, have over a multitude of the profligate and ferocious" (pp. 87–88).

54. As Marvin Zetterbaum rightly observes, one of Tocqueville's most prominent themes is that the former place of aristocracy "may be filled in democratic times by voluntary associations, both social and political. These protect individuals against encroachment by the state (the modern analogue to the monarch), and provide that continuity in space and time thought to be an exclusive attribute of an aristocracy. It is essential to any society that these functions be served, but they need not be served by an aristocracy." Zetterbaum, *Tocqueville and the Problem of Democracy* (Stanford, CA: Stanford University Press, 1967), pp. 29–30.

55. See Harvey C. Mansfield Jr., *Statesmanship and Party Government: A Study of Burke and Bolingbroke* (Chicago: University of Chicago Press, 1965).

56. Quoted from Burke's *Third Letter on a Regicide Peace*, in C. B. Macpherson, *Burke* (Oxford: Oxford University Press, 1980), p. 54.

57. Quoted from Burke's *Third Letter on a Regicide Peace*, ibid.

58. Leo Strauss, *Natural Right and History* (Chicago: University of Chicago Press, 1952), p. 315.

59. Tocqueville, Alexis de, *The Old Regime and the French Revolution*, trans. S. Gilbert (Garden City, NY: Doubleday, 1955), pp. 158–62.

60. Ibid., p. 164.

61. Compare Drescher's discussion of Tocqueville's attitudes toward penal reform and the poor laws (in his *Dilemmas of Democracy*) with Macpherson's of Burke's similar views on the "relief of the able-bodied poor." C. B. Macpherson, *Burke* (Oxford: Oxford University Press), p. 55.

62. Burke objected that to grant the poor a right to obtain society's help would only create an idle and lazy class and reduce the incentive to work. See Macpherson, ibid., pp. 54–55. Similarly, in a memoir on pauperism, translated in Seymour Drescher, ed., *Tocqueville and Beaumont on Social Reform* (New York: Harper & Row, 1968), pp. 1–27, Tocqueville contended that in England public charity had only increased pauperism and that to grant a right to welfare would be to destroy initiative and perpetuate idleness.

63. Burke, op. cit., p. 11.

64. *The Old Régime*, p. 147.

65. Burke, op. cit., p. 90.

66. Ibid., pp. 122–23, 152–53.

67. *Democracy in America*, vol. 2, pp. 444–48. Manent examines Tocqueville's view of the importance of religion to democracy with exceptional sensitivity. "Religion," he points out, "occupies the strategic plane *par excellence* in the Tocquevillian doctrine. In it, he sees the practical possibility of securing access, in the framework of a democratic society, to an outside, to a thing *other* than democracy, to pure nature, but by naturally religious man, free from all convention, even the convention of equality" (Manent, op. cit., p. 106).

68. Jardin, op. cit., pp. 528–29.

69. Joshua Mitchell contends that Tocqueville's understanding of the "democratic soul" is informed by an "Augustinian conception of the self" oscillating between high and low, exalted and depraved. Mitchell, *The Fragility of Freedom:*

*Tocqueville on Religion, Democracy, and the American Future* (Chicago: University of Chicago Press, 1995). Peter Augustine Lawler sees the clue to Tocqueville's political views in his "Pascalian" understanding of the human condition. See Lawler, *The Restless Mind: Alexis de Tocqueville on the Origin and Perpetuation of Human Liberty* (Lanham, MD: Rowman & Littlefield, 1993). This too is an intriguing suggestion, especially inasmuch as Tocqueville admired Pascal's struggle to attain purity of belief: "When I see him, if one may put it so, tearing his soul free from the cares of this life, so as to stake the whole of it on this quest, and prematurely breaking the ties which bound him to the flesh, so that he died of old age before he was forty, I stand amazed, and understand that no ordinary cause was at work in such an extraordinary effort" (*Democracy in America*, vol. 2, p. 461).

70. Burke, op. cit., p. 87.

71. *Democracy in America*, vol. 2, p. 434.

72. Ibid., p. 442.

73. Ibid., p. 435.

74. *Oeuvres Complètes*, vol. 5, p. 425; quoted by J.-P. Mayer, *Alexis de Tocqueville: A Biographical Essay* (New York: Harper, 1960), p. 30.

75. *Democracy in America*, vol. 2, pp. 460–61.

76. Burke, op. cit., p. 79.

77. "Letter to a Member of the National Assembly, 1791," appendix to *Reflections*, pp. 258–59.

78. Ibid., pp. 273–74.

79. Ibid., p. 221.

80. *Democracy in America*, vol. 1, pp. 250–52.

81. Burke, op. cit., p. 93.

82. Ibid., p. 94.

83. Strauss, *Natural Right and History*, p. 316.

84. Strauss's argument resembles Eric Voegelin's critique of modern political theorizing as a variation on the Gnostic heresy. See Voegelin's *The New Science of Politics: An Introduction* (Chicago: University of Chicago Press, 1952).

85. Strauss, op. cit., p. 319.

86. Magnus, op. cit., p. 79.

87. Hearnshaw explains this reluctance to spell out principles as owing to the inherently defensive character of conservatism. Hearnshaw, op. cit., pp. 6–7.

88. Samuel Beer, "The Roots of New Labour: Liberalism Rediscovered," *Economist*, 7–13 February 1998, pp. 23–25.

89. Irving Kristol, *On the Democratic Idea in America* (New York: Harper & Row, 1972), p. 105.

90. "Aron saw in Tocqueville a truthful and forthright exemplar of thinking within and about and acting within modernity. . . . Aron's Tocquevillian voice stressed that what lay before today's citizen is neither a radiant future nor catastrophic doom, but an ever imperfect present characterized by antinomies and contradictions" (Daniel J. Mahoney, *The Liberal Political Science of Raymond Aron* [Lanham, MD: Rowman & Littlefield, 1992], p. 41).

91. See Frohnen, op. cit., pp. 153–54. Paul Franco objects to this conventional characterization on the ground that Oakeshott's notion of tradition arises out of a philosophical analysis and does not presuppose a belief in the "wisdom or

rationality of history." Franco, *The Political Philosophy of Michael Oakeshott* (New Haven, CT: Yale University Press, 1990), p. 7 and chap. 4. But while Franco is right about Oakeshott's resistance to historicism, his own analysis shows that Oakeshott resembles Burke and Tocqueville on other counts. Like Burke, Oakeshott strongly criticized reliance on any abstract doctrine of natural rights. Like Tocqueville, he condemned central planning as a threat to freedom and considered pluralism—"the absence of overwhelming concentrations of power"—to be "the most general condition of our freedom" (Michael Oakeshott, *Rationalism in Politics and Other Essays* [London: Methuen, 1962], p. 147).

92. Raymond Aron, *An Essay on Freedom*, trans. Helen Weaver (New York: World Publishing Company, 1970), p. 147.

93. Oakeshott, op. cit., p. 51.

# 5

───∞───

# Socialism

As a modern political movement, socialism arose in the early and middle decades of the nineteenth century. It attracted more and more adherents and gained political power in many countries until its appeal declined sharply late in the twentieth century. As an idea, however, it represents an old aspiration, evident much earlier in mythic, philosophic, and theological thought, and one that is likely to survive, though not as a warrant for radical revolution or a nationalized "command economy." In the simplest sense, socialism amounts to a belief that all producers ought to share equally in the fruits of combined labor. On a deeper level, socialism is more than an economic formula, and even more than a prescription for justice. It is an expression of faith in the capacity of the mass of mankind to overcome what is thought of as alienation or estrangement from its own essential nature, which socialists contend is far more creative, pacific, and altruistic than actual experience might indicate.

Until comparatively recently, this faith was usually circumscribed by an oppressive awareness of the constraints, both natural and artificial, preventing or distorting the expression of true humanity. Material scarcity and moral weakness were held to require and even to justify social systems in which inequality and hierarchy were assumed to be synonyms of order. All egalitarian alternatives were likely to be dismissed as impractical. Equality was thought of as a standard that may once have had bearing in the remote past, or that might apply in the distant future, but that could have no great relevance to present conditions, except as an invitation to chaos. Because it was treated as an impractical ideal, the idea of equality remained vague and undifferentiated, a catchall for panaceas of every description, and an easy target for skeptics.

Socialism was for a long time one facet of this relatively amorphous ideal, evident in romantic evocations of primitive innocence, in millenarian prophecies of future perfection, in the more radical theologies of the Protestant Reformation, in secular utopias, and in some of the social criticism of the French Enlightenment. In the nineteenth century these intimations were transformed into elaborate arguments for social change taking essentially two forms. One view held that cooperative communities are within the realm of possibility, provided they are constructed with careful attention to individual and social needs. The other, put forward by Karl Marx, conceived of socialism as a stage of historical development, destined to be achieved after a worldwide revolution by the working class against private property and those who benefit from it. In this view, the ideal community cannot be planned in advance and put into operation regardless of historical conditions; it must arise out of revolutionary activity and will be successful only when historically appropriate. This distinction between socialism as a theory of the planned community and socialism as the outcome of a historically determined revolution, starkly clear in the nineteenth century, was adumbrated even earlier but was not given much attention because of the tendency to think of socialism in all its forms as an impossible fantasy.

The first traces of socialism appear in the lament for a lost "Golden Age," a common theme in antiquity. Greek myths, recorded as early as the eighth century BC and derived from an even older oral tradition, recall an original state—the Age of Cronus—when all shared equally in the common lot, private property was unknown, and peace and harmony reigned undisturbed. These myths, as Lovejoy and Boas point out, describe either a "soft" or a "hard" primitivism: some depict a time of abundance and luxury in which human labor was unnecessary because the earth produced its bounty spontaneously; others depict a time of simple needs and satisfactions. Poetic renderings contrast the innocence of the original conditions with the degeneracy of actual society. The Golden Age, so the accepted interpretation ran, "was enjoyed by a different breed of mortals, in a different condition of the world and (in one version) under different gods, and no practical moral could therefore consistently be drawn from it for the guidance of the present race. It was by implication irrecoverable, at least by men's own efforts."[1]

The same melancholy reflection takes philosophic form in the Platonic dialogues. In the *Laws*, the "Athenian Stranger," who seems to express Plato's own view, pays tribute to the ancient ideal: "The first and highest form of the state [*polis*] and of the government and of the law is that in which there prevails most widely the ancient saying, that 'Friends have all things in common.'"² Although such perfection is beyond revival, he adds, no better system could be conceived. In the *Republic*, however, Socrates is represented as believing that even in an ideal society, communism could be a way of life only for a moral and intellectual elite. The superior philosophic capacity of the guardians or rulers would enable them to ignore the demands of appetite; their role would require that they be disinterested in all but the dispensing of justice. Otherwise, equality for unequals is criticized as a self-contradictory proposition that can only result in danger for society, as the chaotic experience of democracy proves all too well. In his *Politics*, Aristotle is skeptical of all proposals for communism, including the limited version advanced in Plato's *Republic*. Collective ownership flouts the most fundamental axioms of human nature; property held in common is likely to remain untended and uncultivated. Far better, in Aristotle's view, is the practice followed in Sparta, where goods were privately owned but made available by their owners for public use. The rightly ordered *polis* will apply the principle of distributive justice, or proportional equality. Absolute or numerical equality reflects only one of the claims that may legitimately be made by citizens—the claim that as members of society they deserve identical treatment. If equity and stability are to be served, however, other claims must also be recognized, such as those based upon superiority of intellect, contribution to the welfare of society, and birth or status.

The notion that differences in intellect justify social inequality was challenged by the Stoic school which arose in the third century BC in the waning years of the Greek *polis* and achieved considerable influence during the expansion of Rome. This influence was more ethical than political, however. Although the Stoics taught that the universality of reason rendered men equals by nature, they did not go on to argue that natural standards could be applied in conventional societies. Like the Cynics, they lamented the departure from the equality decreed by nature and criticized especially inhumane attitudes and practices, but they could see no way to return corrupt society to its natural innocence. The best that might be hoped for, according to such spokesmen for a mature Stoic view as Cicero and Seneca, was that less-fortunate classes, including slaves, would be treated charitably, in recognition of the essential unity of all mankind.

In Rome, the attitude shared by citizens and philosophers alike found expression in the festival of the Saturnalia. Once each year, the Age of Saturn (the Roman form of Cronus) was memorialized: slaves dined with masters and distinctions were temporarily forgotten. In at least one non-Roman version of this ceremony, the moral behind the festival is said to have been made explicit beyond any doubt: a criminal was elevated to the ruler's throne during the celebration and was executed as soon as it was over, as a warning to subject classes of what they might expect from attempts at revolution.

To these classes, Christian teachings may have seemed more radical than Stoicism, especially since the spiritual egalitarianism of the Gospels appeared to make the argument over degrees of rationality irrelevant. Of what consequence were differences of intellect if, in the eyes of God, every man had a soul and all souls were alike worthy? The "poor in spirit" (Luke 6:20, King James version) could well have read social significance into Saint Paul's announcement that with the advent of the Redeemer "there is no such thing as Jew and Greek, slave and freeman, male and female; for you are all one person in Christ Jesus" (Galatians 3:28).[3] According to Saint Luke, the apostles could be said to have practiced communism: "Not a man of them claimed any of his possessions as his own, but everything was held in common. . . . They had never a needy person among them, because all who had property in land or houses sold it, brought the proceeds of the sale, and laid the money at the feet of the apostles; it was then distributed to any who stood in need" (Acts 4:32–35).[4]

As the expectation of an imminent apocalypse receded, millenarian enthusiasm became an embarrassment and a threat to the order of society and the unity of the church. Authoritative interpreters of the Gospels insisted that they must not be read as a call to social revolution. An apostle had also declared that "the authorities are in God's service" (Romans 13:6).[5] Although God had intended men to live together as brothers in an earthly paradise, Saint Cyprian, Saint Zeno of Verona, and Saint Ambrose, the Bishop of Milan, all observed that human wickedness had frustrated this intention. Until the Parousia, or Second Coming of Christ, the Christian was obliged to endure worldly corruption with patience and obedience. The most influential of the church fathers, Saint Augustine, asserted in *The City of God* (AD 413) that the injustices of the earthly city were God's judgment upon human sinfulness. While the pious Christian lived "like a captive and a stranger"[6] in the unredeemed world, he was to cling to his faith but accept his station in life, whatever it might be.

The medieval canonists, who were the principal apologists for papal supremacy, added more positive justifications of inequality. Unity required subordination and discipline. Hierarchy in the church and society reflected the superiority of the soul to the body, as well as the order of the cosmos, the very architecture of God. Communism was appropriate only for those exceptional ascetic virtuosos in holy orders seeking to escape attachments to the flesh and the world. Movements outside the church, however, such as those of the Cathars, Waldenses, and Free Spirits, even though they aimed at a similar perfection, if not always through asceticism, were condemned as dangerous heresies.

Both the example and the teachings of monastic and sectarian movements nevertheless stood in pointed contrast to official dogma. As feudal society disintegrated under a complex network of strains, including princely ambition, conflicts over clerical appointments, splits within the church, the expansion of commerce, and the rise of independent cities, the hold of the orthodox view weakened and the appeal of alternatives rose. One distinctly unorthodox alternative was posed by a twelfth-century Calabrian monk, Joachim of Floris, who preached a historicized doctrine of the Trinity resembling that earlier condemned in Montanism. According to Joachim, the incarnation was to be understood as an evolutionary succession of three ages or dispensations: of the Father or law, of the Son or Gospel, and of the Holy Spirit. The process was to be completed between 1200 and 1260 under the aegis of a new order of monks that would direct the overthrow of the Antichrist. Through their triumph, the Holy Spirit would permeate all mankind, and servitude and obedience would be replaced by universal love. The Joachimite prophecy inspired a wing of the Franciscan order, the Franciscan Spirituals, to imagine themselves successors of the church appointed to lead Christendom toward the millennium.

Variations of the same prophecy assigned a messianic role to the Emperor Frederick II. Even after the death of Frederick, it was widely hoped that he would somehow reappear and usher in the last days by striking down the corrupt clergy. In the fourteenth and fifteenth centuries, peasant rebellions erupted in many parts of Europe in response to changing economic conditions as well as visionary preaching. Religious protests, such as those led by John Ball and John Wycliffe in England and by the Hussites and Taborites in Bohemia, weakened adherence to the church and eventually brought on the full-scale reformations of the sixteenth and seventeenth centuries. In the Protestant Reformation, the eschatological underground came to the surface in the general upheaval and made a noteworthy impact. Thomas Müntzer and Gerrard Winstanley, the leaders of two distinct movements on the "left wing of the Reformation,"[7] can fairly be regarded as among the most direct theoretical precursors of modern socialism.

Müntzer was a fiery zealot who broke with Martin Luther and raised a more radical and mystical standard than Luther and other moderate reformers were willing to accept. In 1525 he led an army of peasants in an abortive revolt that ended with his capture and execution. Although there is little in Müntzer's sermons and letters explicitly advocating communism, he was regarded by his contemporaries as a revolutionary in every respect—an "uproarious spirit" (*aufrührischen Geist*) in Luther's words. Müntzer earned this reputation by demanding total reform, temporal as well as ecclesiastical. Warmly acknowledging his debt to the "weighty testimony" of Joachim, Müntzer saw himself and his Allstedt

*Bund* performing the role the Franciscan Spirituals had earlier sought to assume. Unlike the monks, Müntzer saw no reason to refrain from violence against "godless" opponents. The "fifth monarchy" foretold by the prophet Daniel, he believed, could only follow the physical destruction of the first four, the last of which remained to be toppled.

Müntzer's "Revolutionary, or charismatic, Spiritualism"[8] rejected the view of more moderate reformers that the Bible and sacraments, but not a clerical hierarchy, should mediate between God and man. In order to become one with Christ (*Christformig*), he claimed, the believer had to experience an identification with God directly and without mediation. This theological radicalism enabled Müntzer to regard himself and his followers as "an élite of amoral supermen"[9] released from ordinary ethical injunctions in their role as a vanguard of the millennium. Sectarian quietism and withdrawal were also rejected in favor of the revolutionary activism of a mass movement. In contrast to Müntzer, the militant Anabaptists who took control of Münster and whose communism and polygamy seemed scandalous to all of Europe, were far more conventional in their views, since they continued to believe in the need to isolate themselves from worldly corruption in order to live a perfect life above the law.

Winstanley experienced a revelation in which he and his followers were instructed to seize certain lands and cultivate them in common so as to restore the "holy community," an ideal they shared with other Puritans. No one, he declared, ought to be "Lord or landlord over another, but whole mankind was made equall, and knit into one body by one spirit of love, which is Christ in you, the hope of glory."[10] The creation and redemption express a dialectic of separation and reunion: spirit and man are separate at first but in the end "man is drawne up into himselfe again, or new *Jerusalem* . . . comes down to Earth, to fetch Earth up to live in that life, that is a life above objects."[11] It is only a "strange conceit" to imagine a New Jerusalem "above the skies."[12] Winstanley and Müntzer share a mystical and socially activistic theological perspective. In Winstanley's case, this perspective issues in a pacifistic orientation toward labor in common; in Müntzer's, it serves to promote violent revolution. Had the left wing succeeded in impressing itself more fully upon the main carriers of reform, the distinction that was to arise in the nineteenth century between voluntaristic and revolutionary socialists might have been felt earlier. In fact, however, the impact of the left wing was ephemeral. The most significant social residue of the Reformation was the attitude Max Weber described as the "Protestant ethic," or the exhortation to economic individualism as proof of piety and predestination. Protestantism lent legitimacy to a limited egalitarianism by sanctioning economic competition and moral autonomy, but it offered no warrant for socialism, which continued to be regarded as "utopian."

The term "utopia" came into use after 1516, when Thomas More published his work of that name boldly denouncing the vicious effects of private property and commerce, especially as they were evident in the enclosure movement in England. The sheep, he wrote, had begun to devour men and to consume whole fields, houses, and cities; a true commonwealth, as distinct from those which go by the name but are merely conspiracies of rich men, would be possible only if property were held in common. More's hostility toward private property and his advocacy of communism joined a traditional Christian disapproval of worldly avarice and corruption with an attack upon contemporary economic inequities. Many later and more secular writers, including Francis Bacon and Thomas Campanella in the seventeenth century, followed More's example by inventing other utopias, both in order to give freer rein to the imagination and to publish more radical social criticism than might have been safe to broach in an essay or treatise. As a device and a literary genre, the utopia came to replace the prophecy of religious apocalypse as a vehicle for the expression of radically egalitarian sentiments.

The dominant tendency of social theorizing, in the period following the Reformation and culminating in the French Revolution, is more accurately reflected in the work of the natural rights/social contract school. These theorists secularized and transformed traditional natural law doctrines into justifications for limited government and civil liberty. In the process, the right of private property was established as one of the most fundamental of all natural rights. John Locke argued that while God had originally given the earth to men in common, He meant it for "the use of the Industrious and the Rational."[13] The right to appropriate was subject to the limits of the law of nature, but the introduction of money by tacit consent made evasion of these limits legitimate. The main objective of the social contract was therefore the protection of the right of property, broadly understood as life, liberty, and estate and more narrowly as material possessions. James Harrington argued in *Oceana* (1656) that agrarian republics could survive only if effective limits were put upon acquisition, especially of land, but neither Harrington nor any other English theorist of this century was in any sense an advocate of socialism.

The French physiocrats, who coined the term laissez-faire, agreed with Locke in regarding the right to private property as the foundation of law and economic progress. Otherwise, the leading writers of the French Enlightenment were rather less enthusiastic in their support for economic individualism. Generally, the attitude of the philosophes resembled that of the Stoics. Equality, Voltaire wrote, "is at once the most natural and at the same time the most chimerical of things." Although nature makes men equal, "on our miserable globe it is impossible for men living in society not to be divided into two classes, one the rich who command, the

other the poor who serve."[14] Similarly, although Rousseau issued a sting-
ing indictment of the evils of property, he did not propose that the right
of property be abolished. The most that could be hoped for, according to
Rousseau, Voltaire, Montesquieu, and Louis de Jaucourt in the *Encyclo-
pédie*, was that enlightened rulers would eliminate extreme inequalities
and alleviate the plight of the poor.

In the latter half of the eighteenth century, some theorists contended
that the natural condition of society must have been one of collective
rather than private ownership. Among them were Thomas Raynal, Jean
Meslier, Gabriel de Bonnot de Mably, Simon Linguet, and the all but
anonymous Morelly. But except for Morelly's *Code de la nature* (1755),
which advocated a return to communism, the others agreed with Mably
that although the communism of Sparta and the religious orders was
closer to nature than the modern worship of wealth and luxury, "where
property has once been established it is necessary to regard it as the foundation of order, peace, and public safety."[15]

The detached skepticism and critical resignation that characterized the
Enlightenment were swept aside by the enthusiasm for total renovation
accompanying the French Revolution. Even so, all but a handful of the
leading figures in the Revolution, including the Jacobins, were committed to the retention of private property. The demand for a more radical
reform emerged among a minority of disaffected revolutionaries. Their
major spokesman was François-Noël (Caius Gracchus) Babeuf, the leader
of a small "Conspiracy of the Equals" to which a larger number of Jacobins had attached themselves. Along with other conspirators, including
Sylvain Maréchal, the author of the provocative *Manifesto of the Equals*
(1796), Babeuf was arrested and tried for plotting to overthrow the Di-
rectory. In his defense, Babeuf insisted that he was acting in the service
of the Revolution, which would remain incomplete while there was still
inequality. Borrowing a distinction drawn by the moderate Girondin, the
Marquis de Condorcet, Babeuf argued that the Revolution had so far established only legal equality, but not "real" equality. Since even superior
intelligence and exertion do not "extend the capacity of the stomach," it
was "absurd and unjust" to distribute rewards on any basis other than
need.[16] The revolution of 1789 was therefore merely the forerunner of "another revolution, greater and even more solemn, which will be the last."[17]
It would be accomplished, however, not by legislative assemblies, but by
the broad masses of the people.

Although Babeuf's conspiracy was finally crushed, *babouvisme*, with
its emphasis on the revolutionary role of the working class, had a lingering influence on socialist theory. It was only after the Napoleonic Wars,
however, that modern socialism took definitive form. In the usage it
now has, the word "socialist" appeared in print for the first time in 1827

in the *Co-operative Magazine* published by the followers of the industrial reformer Robert Owen. In 1832, as *le Socialisme*, it made its debut across the Channel in *Le Globe*, the journal of a band of practical and visionary reformers inspired by the theories of Henri de Saint-Simon. In this germinal period, socialism had its greatest vogue in France, where the hold of more conventional ideas had been rudely shaken by waves of revolution. The aims and outcome of this series of upheavals were subjects of intense controversy, and socialism appeared to its adherents and even to some of its detractors as the logical fulfillment of the process of change that had begun in 1789. By about 1840, the term was commonly applied to a fairly wide array of doctrines, all sharing an intensely critical attitude toward existing social systems and a firm conviction that radical transformation was both possible and imperative.

Socialism probably seemed an apt name for this potpourri of dissenting views because in ways both critical and constructive, all these doctrines were focused on "social" rather than individual well-being. The "social question" was a subject of wide interest, but the prevailing view was that the wretched conditions endured by the poor were as inevitable as they were unfortunate. Those who challenged this complacency by subjecting social conditions to harsh criticism and by demanding that they be changed fundamentally were likely to be called socialists. All the doctrines, despite variations, stressed the need for greater collective responsibility and a "strengthening of 'socialising' influences," as Cole observed.[18] (The term "communism" was sometimes used as a synonym for socialism and sometimes to denote doctrines stressing the need for revolution and community of goods.)

The socialist view was advanced in direct opposition to the more widely accepted belief that the rights of the individual against society and the state were inviolable. The most popular writers on political economy in the first half of the nineteenth century generally claimed that since individual liberty was the source of all progress, its enhancement must be the paramount aim of public policy. To interfere with the freedom of exchange was to infringe upon the rights of man and to place dangerous obstacles in the way of industry and prosperity. Against this belief, the socialists argued that the legal protection of unlimited acquisition sanctioned the exploitation of wage laborers by the owners of capital. Any prosperity that resulted from industry could therefore benefit only the privileged few—the new aristocracy of wealth—at the expense of the many, who would remain at least as impoverished as ever.

On the most universal level—and perhaps the most fundamental—this objection to the gross inequalities flowing from the protection of private property expressed a profound and bitter moral indignation. Labor was said to have become a commodity, the laborer himself to have been robbed of his humanity and degraded into a brute instrument of production. "For the enormous majority," Karl Marx protested, the vaunted culture of European civilization amounted to no more than "a mere training to act as a machine."[19] Charles Fourier, in effect elaborating Rousseau's earlier indictment, drew up a meticulous catalogue of the vices due to selfish absorption with the accumulation of wealth. These vices included not only the misery of the poor but also the unhappiness and boredom of the rich. A phrase coined a generation earlier by the Girondin Jean-Pierre Brissot de Warville and popularized by Pierre-Joseph Proudhon summed up the socialist critique of conventional morality in an incendiary catechism: "What is property? It is theft."

The critics differed among themselves in the explanations offered of the sources of corruption and in proposals for reform. Some believed that moral regeneration could come only in new, planned communities. To Owen, the bedrock of social reconstruction was the principle that character is shaped by environment. Moral vices, he thought, could be reformed only by changing the conditions that produced them. Étienne Cabet imagined such a new community in his *Voyage in Icaria* (1840) in terms derived from earlier utopian speculation. Fourier sought to show that it was possible to diminish frustration and increase satisfaction without changing human nature, simply by establishing planned, but voluntary communities in which the diversity of human dispositions would be matched with the requirements of the division of labor. These ideas inspired the creation of model communities in Britain and America and generated great interest among social reformers in many countries.

Others who could see little or no hope in small-scale projects argued instead for grander efforts to reorganize society. The economist Jean-Charles Simonde de Sismondi pointed out, as early as 1819, that unless gains from increased productivity were more widely distributed, national economies would suffer not only from inequity but from periodic crises of overproduction. Saint-Simon declared that the enormous potentialities of the industrial system and of scientific research should be organized to serve the needs of society. The domination of society and government by aristocratic idlers (*les oisifs*) must be replaced by a combination of the producers (*les industriels*). Louis Blanc was convinced that the evils of the property system could be eradicated without revolution or expropriation if the state would extend public credit to "social workshops" (*ateliers*) in which artisans in the various branches of industry could form cooperative associations for production and distribution. By eliminating the need for private sources of capital, the state would make exploitation impossible. Proudhon, by vocation a tradesman, by temperament an anarchist, was suspicious of all central authority and all collectivist schemes. He preferred what he called "mutualism"—a series of decentralized exchanges in which producers would enter into contracts with each other to trade goods and services. The object would be to prevent exploitation but to retain the autonomy of the producers and avoid imposing an oppressive central authority in place of the market system.

Still others thought that changes of policy or institutions could be expected only after a change of heart. Constantin Pecqueur in France and Karl Grün, Moses Hess, and Wilhelm Weitling in Germany, believed that an ethical religion of humanity was needed either to fill the void left by the decline of Christian faith or to express common humanistic values to which all could subscribe, regardless of their attitude toward religion. The disciples of Saint-Simon, led by Barthélemy-Prosper Enfantin, Olinde Rodrigues, Saint-Armand Bazard, and Pierre Leroux, organized and directed a sect to propagate the master's call for a "New Christianity." The cult was outfitted with all the appropriate trappings, including clergy, ritual, and devotional services, and took as its cardinal dogma the "principle of association," the Saint-Simonian equivalent of Fourier's "law of attraction." It served the same purpose for the Saint-Simonians that Fourier's principle did for his followers, which was to provide a social and moral analogue of Newton's law of gravitation. Philippe Buchez and Proudhon, as well as Cabet—who preached a "true Christianity"—felt that Christianity itself, properly understood, was simply socialism by another, older name. In Britain, John M. F. Ludlow, with the help of Frederick D. Maurice and Charles Kingsley, both clergymen, founded a Christian Socialist movement.

None of these spokesmen for socialism had an impact comparable to that exerted by Karl Marx, whose writings became the touchstone of socialist thinking and action. Marx differed most strikingly from earlier socialists as well as from contemporaries in believing that socialism could not be established by an act of will, either through voluntary adoption or forced imposition, but would inevitably arise at an appropriate stage of history. He couched his views in a doctrine that was at once a philosophy of history, a science of society, and a handbook of revolution. As a thinker, his greatest talents were not so much those of an originator as of a trenchant critic, a skillful borrower, and a brilliant synthesizer. In the early stages of his thought, when he developed his philosophy of history, he was indebted most to Hegel. In the later period, he owed many of his sociological and economic ideas and more than a few of his revolutionary slogans to a host of other writers.

The influence of Hegelianism upon Marx is well recognized. It is not too much to say that all of Marx's work bears the impress of his early encounter with Hegel and the left Hegelians. What is less well appreciated is the degree to which the apocalyptic, quasi-religious character of Marxian socialism was shaped by Hegel's philosophical restatement of radical Christian theology. Hegel's first writings grew out of his study of theology at Tübingen. In them he struggled to come to terms with traditional Christianity and the new Kantian ethics. The resolution he came to is best expounded in his essay on "The Spirit of Christianity and Its Fate" (1799), where he offers an interpretation strikingly similar to the historical trinitarianism of Joachim. Kantian ethics is explained as a reversion to Judaism, or the religion of abstract law, a "juridical order" in which man is a dependent of a remote lawgiving deity. Christianity, as the incarnation of God in a single man, opens a second chapter in the unfolding of morality: Jesus, as "the beautiful soul," renounces property and all other ties to the juridical order and thereby transcends it. But Christianity, as a religion of faith in God rather than of universal participation in the divine, must be superseded by a final stage of development. In this age of fulfillment, contradictions of finite and infinite, subject and object, spirit and matter, are transcended by a total identification of the divine and the human.

These early speculations were the groundwork for *The Phenomenology of the Spirit* (1807), in which the whole of intellectual history is explained as the externalization, in the "phenomena" of human thought, of the mind of God. In two sections of the *Phenomenology*, Hegel hinted at the social implications of his philosophic history by describing self-consciousness in terms of the relations between lord and servant and by suggesting that the absolute freedom advocated in the Enlightenment generated, as its dialectical opposite, the reign of terror in the Revolution. In two other works, *The Philosophy of History* (1822) and *The Philosophy of Right* (1821), the externalization of the mind of God previously depicted in the development of theology and philosophy is described in terms of social history. Philosophically understood, history is the process in which the "Idea" expresses itself concretely and comprehensively through the medium of "world historical" nations and individuals. It assumes a final form in the constitutional state, which unites universal and particular will. The state was to be distinguished, however, from "civil society," in that the state expressed the union of public and private, while civil society was the sphere of the private alone.

Hegel's teachings had their most immediate result in the formation of two camps of disciples, the right and left Hegelians. While the right Hegelians saw in these teachings a powerful justification of existing institutions, the left Hegelians saw as Hegel's major achievement the undermining of traditional Christianity, in particular of its dualistic separation of God and man, spirit and matter. Bruno Bauer and Marx, who joined the group while a student, circulated what purported to be an attack on Hegel's atheism, intending to demonstrate Hegel's true views. David Friedrich Strauss argued in his *Life of Jesus* (1835) that the biblical account of Christ was not to be taken as literal fact but as a mythological reflection of an incomplete stage in human consciousness, as Hegel had suggested. Ludwig Feuerbach put the left Hegelian case more radically by contending that religion was simply a product of the mind of man. In *The Essence of Christianity* (1841), he described the idea of God as a projection of what was essential in human nature "purified, freed from the limits of the individual man, made objective."[20] The idea of heaven was simply the opposite of all that was disagreeable in actual existence: "The future life is nothing else than the present life freed from that which appears as a limitation or an evil."[21]

Marx broke with the Young Hegelians because he found their preoccupation with consciousness and the individual both narrow and reactionary. In *The Holy Family* (1845) and *The German Ideology* (1845–1846) he satirized "Saint Bruno" Bauer and "Saint Max" Stirner for continuing to think only in terms of ideal or spiritual freedom despite their rejection of traditional Christianity. Feuerbach had at least pointed in the right direction by making it clear that man was the source and not the product of consciousness, that "man makes religion; religion does not make man."[22] Feuerbach showed how Hegelianism must be transformed, or redirected: "The criticism of heaven is transformed into the criticism of earth, the *criticism of religion* into the *criticism of law*, and the *criticism of theology* into the *criticism of politics*."[23]

To make this transformation was to criticize the social conditions which Hegel and the Hegelians had, in Marx's view, only rationalized. Whereas Hegel had defined alienation as God's estrangement from Himself, Marx redefined it as the estrangement of man from his true or essential self and located the source of this estrangement in the relation of the laborer to the process of production. "The alienation of the worker in his product," Marx wrote in an early fragment, "means not only that his labor becomes an object, assumes an external existence, but that it exists independently, outside himself, and alien to him, and that it stands opposed to him as an autonomous power. The life that he has given to the object sets itself against him as an alien and hostile force."[24] Because he is compelled to work at the command of others and in occupations that exhaust and debase him, the laborer can scarcely scale the Promethean heights of creativity and self-determination that Marx saw as within his capacity. It followed that Hegel's attempt to distinguish between the state and civil society and to argue that universal and particular wills could be reconciled in the state while civil society was left inviolate was only an attempt to evade the inescapable logic of the dialectic. The political economy of civil society—precisely the subject Hegel had sought to exempt from philosophic scrutiny—must be studied critically and the contradiction between the general good and the particular interest of the propertied exposed for what it was.

Marx saw clearly where this criticism would lead. Moses Hess had no trouble persuading him of the ethical validity of communism. In 1842, Lorenz von Stein explained French socialism as an ideological outgrowth of the struggle for power within the "third estate" between the middle class and the proletariat. At stake, von Stein pointed out, was the control of the democratic system that had arisen out of the revolt against absolutism. Marx himself observed, in a commentary on Hegel, that because the proletariat was effectively excluded from civil society, it was the class with the most compelling interest in the overthrow of that society. He took as his personal objective the task of providing the proletariat not simply with an ideology but with a doctrine that would have the rigor and status of science. Only if it had such a doctrine, he believed, could the proletariat develop confidence in the success of revolution and an adequate resistance both to the seductions of bourgeois propaganda and the temptation to engage in premature revolts.

Consciousness, alone, however, would not assure the triumph of the proletariat or the achievement of socialism as a result of its triumph. Proletarian consciousness must be enhanced by revolutionary activity, or praxis. In such activity the proletariat would train itself to perform its historical role until eventually it would accomplish the real "negation of the negation." Alienated labor, itself a negation of human potentiality, would be negated by the proletarian revolution. In the fellowship of the revolutionary cause, the proletariat would experience the beginning of a return of its lost humanity. The establishment of communism would make possible "the return of man to himself as a *social*, i.e., really human being, a complete and conscious return which assimilates all the wealth of previous development."[25] Communism could not represent the final form of emancipation because it would still reflect a preoccupation, however negative, with production and possession. Genuine freedom or humanism, as Marx also described it, would become possible only when life activity was no longer constrained by the requirements of production or the limitations of material scarcity.

Marx came to a clear understanding of his own alternative to Hegelianism only gradually. At first he collaborated with the Young Hegelians in editing liberal political journals in Germany. In 1843, compelled to leave the country for his own safety, he went first to Paris, where he met Friedrich Engels, his lifelong collaborator and later his financial supporter, and profited from exposure to French socialist thinking. Expelled from France in 1845, he went to Brussels and from there to London, where after 1849 he made his permanent home. In 1847, at the request of the Communist League, which he and Engels were instrumental in forming, he outlined his views in the single most inflammatory document of nineteenth-century socialism, the *Manifesto of the Communist Party* (1848).

In the *Manifesto*, Marx summarized in bold and eloquent strokes the principal tenets of "scientific" socialism. The ponderous Hegelian and Germanic tone of the earlier writings is pushed into the background and replaced by a deceptively simple economic determinism. Material or economic conditions are said to be the main determinants of behavior and thought. Changes in economic conditions lead to changes in the relations among the producers, who invariably form antagonistic social classes. The ruling class's refusal to yield power compels its challengers to resort to violent revolution. Continuous change is inexorable because history is governed by laws of movement arising out of economic necessity. Under capitalist organization, the productive process reaches levels of size and integration at which capitalism itself, as a system of private ownership, becomes obsolete and a "fetter" upon further growth. Small-scale enterprise yields to large monopolies; society becomes increasingly divided into only two classes—the bourgeoisie, in whose hands all capital comes to be concentrated, and the proletariat, the wage earners who have only their labor power to sell. The contradictions between capitalism and the forces of production—the ensemble of technique and capacity—generate ever-deepening crises. The class consciousness of the proletariat is strengthened as workers are concentrated in large factories and as their conditions of life grow worse with every advance of capitalist production. Finally, under the leadership of the Communists, as the most advanced element of the proletariat, the working class must rise up in response to the ringing call with which the *Manifesto* closes: "The proletarians have nothing to lose but their chains. They have a world to win. Working men of all countries, unite!"[26]

In much of his later work, notably in *Capital* (1867), which remained incomplete at his death, Marx labored to explain in detail how capitalism had arisen and why it must fail, paradoxically—and dialectically—as a result of its very success. He drew upon the work of orthodox economists, including François Quesnay, Adam Smith, David Ricardo, and Jean-Baptiste Say, as well as such critics of capitalism as Sismondi and the British economists John Francis Bray, John Gray, Thomas Hodgskin, and William Thompson. The labor theory of value, which many other writers, from Aristotle to Locke and Smith, had also used in one form or another, became a cornerstone of Marxian theory.

Labor, according to Marx, was the sole source of value. Capital, however, did not represent an accumulation of individual labor. The "primary accumulation" of capital was a result of forceful usurpation. Although capital produced no value, to possess it in the form of means of production was to be able to draw profit from the labor of others. Profit represented the "surplus value" extracted from wage earners by capitalist exploiters, who paid the workers only enough to provide them with subsistence and appropriated for themselves that portion of the workers' product above what was required to maintain their subsistence. The wage rate was kept at this low level because the continuous introduction of machinery resulted in an "industrial reserve army" of the unemployed. In order to survive competition, however, each capitalist would be compelled to invest a part of his profits in machinery, or constant capital. Since machines could only repay their cost but could add no value independent of what was produced by labor, the increasing proportion of constant capital relative to variable capital, or wages, would inevitably lower the average rate of profit. Furthermore, as mechanization resulted in increased technological unemployment, the workers would be unable to purchase what was produced. The result would be crises of overproduction (or underconsumption), continually increasing in intensity, in which smaller capitalists would be wiped out and the proletariat would suffer "immiseration." Final disaster might be postponed by imperialistic investments in underdeveloped areas, where subsistence costs, and therefore wage rates, would still be low enough to provide a sufficient rate of profit. In time, nothing would avail: "The knell of capitalist private property sounds. The expropriators are expropriated."[27]

The suppression of the revolutions of 1848 and 1849 was a disappointment to Marx and Engels but not a disillusionment. Much of their prodigious intellectual energy in the years that followed was devoted to explaining the failure of these revolutions and to considering the tactics and strategy of insurrection. They generally believed that revolutionary acts would not succeed until the conditions were ripe and the class consciousness of the workers fully developed. They opposed sporadic and untimely acts of terrorism or coups d'état, such as had been organized by Auguste Blanqui in 1848. They conceded, however, that both tactics and strategy must be a function of national conditions. In England it was reasonable to work for the advance of socialism through parliamentary politics. In backward Russia, on the other hand, it might be possible to leap directly from agrarian populism to industrial socialism without waiting for the development of a mature capitalism.

Marx and Engels also participated in the formation of the International Working Men's Association in 1863, hoping to establish their doctrine as the theoretical basis of the socialist movement, and vied for control of the International with Ferdinand Lasalle, the German trade union leader, and Michael Bakunin, a Russian anarchist. Marx defended the revolt of the Paris Commune in 1871 in the name of the International, even though he thought it premature, and used the occasion to expound the need for a replacement of bourgeois parliamentarianism by a "dictatorship of the proletariat" to direct the transition to socialism. This argument, in particular, was to have great force with Lenin and other practical revolutionaries who declared themselves pupils of Marx and resorted to his works for guidance and vindication.

At Marx's death in 1883, socialism was still a marginal, heterogeneous, and highly fractious political movement. As a theoretical cause, it was firmly established throughout Europe and was beginning to win adherents elsewhere. The broad appeal of the doctrine was no doubt in part due to the restatement of traditional socialist objectives in modern terms, not only by Marx but also by Owen, Fourier, Saint-Simon, and Proudhon. These restatements were made possible and given special resonance by historical circumstances. Great advances in productivity due to increasing industrialization made it obvious that for the first time in history there was no need to accept material scarcity as an inevitable condition of social life. If scarcity was unnecessary, so were grinding poverty and long hours of labor for subsistence wages. For just this reason, the harsh conditions endured by factory workers, even though in some respects they may have been an improvement over rural poverty, were felt to be intolerable. Similarly, the democratic revolutions had challenged the traditional belief that inequality and hierarchy were also necessary, whether because they were divinely ordained or were essential to order. Socialism could be advocated as "the industrial doctrine," as Saint-Simon described his system, and as the ultimate form of democracy, the most perfectly egalitarian, the most truly libertarian.

If conservatives saw in the new creed only the ultimate form of mediocrity and mob rule and liberals only a revived and more bureaucratic state worship, the socialists could respond that the society of the future would resemble nothing in actual experience and therefore could not be judged by existing standards or by the failure of previous experiments. To votaries of science, socialism made a special appeal. Saint-Simon saw in "positive" science nothing less than the salvation of the modern world. Fourier compared his own discoveries in psychology with those of Copernicus, Linnaeus, Harvey, and Newton in the physical sciences. Marx was encouraged by the similarity between his view of history as a progressive outcome of dialectical conflict and the Darwinian hypothesis of biological evolution by natural selection. In an age when science was becoming an object of worship for the emancipated, socialism could claim to be the application of science to the problems of society, with its own theories of motion, its own laws of inevitability, its own calculus of motives, and its own explanations of deviations and anomalies.

To the young, to the workers, to the socially rejected of all ages, all classes, all countries, socialism was also the revolutionary doctrine par excellence, far more enticing than natural-rights liberalism which, despite efforts to extend its viability as a doctrine of social reform, was badly tarnished because of its association with such causes as laissez-faire, the inviolability of property rights, and the limitation of the suffrage to those meeting a property qualification. The internationalism of the doctrine appealed to some more than to others, but it was not impossible to be both an ardent nationalist and a socialist. The red banner borne by the socialists had first been raised in the French Revolution, and it continued to exert a powerful attraction on the romantic imagination, rekindling the age-old longing for primal innocence and paradise lost with a symbolism evoking images of fire and blood.

The revolutionary socialists were convinced, like the prophets of millenium before them, that the apocalyptic finale of history required a last cataclysmic conflict between the forces of light and darkness. But all socialists could believe that regardless of how it was to come about, the new society would make it possible for alienated man to recover his lost humanity. Neither the failure of premature and small-scale communitarian experiments nor initial departures from the ideal by revolutionary regimes are considered grounds for despair. "Socialist man," it is argued, can only be expected to make his appearance and keep himself from becoming corrupted when socialist institutions are firmly and widely established. Like earlier millenarians, modern socialists cling to the faith that once the soil is prepared, a genuine and lasting egalitarianism will become a practical possibility. Actual experience, like preredemptive history in religious doctrines, is thought of as a time of trial and testing when the work of preparation is to be accomplished.

In this faith lies the essence of the socialist idea. The forms of thought in which it has found expression, whether mythological, prophetic, utopian, or scientific, the disagreements over strategy between advocates of evolution and revolution, the policies that have in more recent times been taken to separate orthodoxy from heresy, such as nationalization and collectivization, are all adventitious to the idea itself. The most essential element of socialism—an element shared with democracy, liberalism, and other humanistic creeds—is the moral conviction that universal autonomy is the highest object of civilization. This conviction acquires a specifically socialist connotation when it is associated with the view that genuine autonomy depends upon an equal distribution of the proceeds of industry. The ultimate aim of socialism—and the standard by which systems claiming the name may properly be tested—is, in the words of Marx in the *Manifesto*, to create "an association, in which the free development of each is the condition for the free development of all."[28]

The blending of socialist and liberal conceptions produced movements for "social liberalism" or "welfare state liberalism" that have become the foundation of the political and social system in many countries, especially in Western Europe. At the same time, faith in socialism as a way of organizing the economy declined sharply because of the example of the failed

"command economy" of the Soviet Union and the failure of the nationalization of industry under social democratic governments.

The totalitarian character and ultimate collapse of the Soviet Union
dealt an especially heavy blow to the belief in socialism as an all-en-
compassing program for social reform. The Soviet failure amounts to an
indictment of socialism on multiple grounds, notably economics, politics,
and human psychology. Trotskyites blamed the repressions of the Bolshe-
vik Revolution on its supposed hijacking by Stalin, but the abuses started
with Lenin and have cropped up elsewhere in similar systems under
Mao Tse-Tung and Fidel Castro.

Experience has shown that Marx's economic theory, claiming that
capitalism would collapse of its own internal contradictions, is badly
flawed. Capitalism, or the regulated market economy, survived reces-
sions and depressions and has been credited with producing continued
economic growth. Plainly, what Marx identified as the "contradictions of
capitalism" did not necessarily have to lead to its destruction. He altogether failed to appreciate the strengths of the market economy and the
resilience of the capitalist system, especially as it was modified to allow
for government regulation, management via fiscal and monetary policy,
and guarantees of employment and welfare. Capitalism did go through
periodic crises, or what came to be called the business cycle, and later
economists, notably J. M. Keynes, made it clear that government intervention could soften the swings and prevent crises in which revolutions
might otherwise become likely. Other economists, notably Joseph A.
Schumpeter, showed that the greatest strength of capitalism was "creative destruction," the process whereby inefficient firms are replaced by
more efficient competitors and new and better processes and products
make older ones obsolete. Marx did not recognize that market incentives encourage entrepreneurs to develop new products and open new
markets, and that a market system offering risks and rewards is more efficient than a centralized command economy in sending price signals and
giving employers, managers, and workers incentives to become more
efficient. In addition, Marx paid too little attention to the serious weaknesses of socialism as an economic system, including the difficulty of
planning a complex economic system by substituting government plan-
ners for the millions of economic actors whose economic decisions and
transactions, registered in monetary terms, are more likely to enable a
balance of demand and supply. Government bureaucrats have tended to
protect government industries even when they have been inefficient, and
they have proven very vulnerable to political pressures not to close inefficient plants, raise commodity prices, or fire underperforming managers.
For such reasons, privatization has gained appeal even in partly social-
ized economies. Conditions were far worse in full command economies

like the Soviet Union, where apart from massive electrification projects, often using slave labor from the "gulag," the Soviet economy produced shoddy goods, poor harvests, and automobiles that nobody outside the country would buy.

Even so, Marx had one very good insight, which was that technology would increase productivity. Thomas Robert Malthus, in his famous *Essay on Population*, had forecast that rising population would outstrip available land for food, and mankind would suffer from famine, disease, and warfare as a result. Marx said this was a slander on the human race because Malthus did not realize that because of human ingenuity, advances in technology could increase the amount of food that could be grown on an acre of land—once the fetters of capitalism were removed. On this issue, he was right and well ahead of other political economists. But Marx thought that the owners of capital could not benefit from introducing new technology because new forms of production would take more and more of the surplus value they extracted from labor. Nor would the workers benefit because the employers would pay them only bare subsistence wages—as a result of the "iron law of wages." He failed to see that the introduction of labor-saving machinery would enormously increase the productivity of labor and thereby allow both profits and wages to rise and that the organization of workers into trade unions would compel employers to pay better wages and benefits.

Marx also proved naive in supposing that socialism would bring political equality and freedom. The Soviet, Chinese, and Cuban experience shows that an effort to achieve a complete socialist revolution inevitably creates a coercive, overbearing state. It undermines prospects for democracy by destroying civil society as a relatively independent sphere of social life and activity. When all wealth, all media, and all associations are controlled by the state, rule becomes authoritarian and at the extreme totalitarian because nothing can stand in the way of state power or protect the liberty of the individual from coercion by the state or public opinion. Violent revolutions put a premium on ruthlessness, which brings to the fore ruthless and often paranoid conspirators like Stalin. Once in power, Stalin purged rivals and potential enemies, instilling fear even in the ranks of the all-powerful Communist Party, and proceeded to remake society so as to eliminate all resistance, actual or potential. The Soviet effort to build communism resulted in the deliberate deaths, by execution or starvation, of between 15 and 20 million people. Maoism later had similar effects in China.

Ironically, the socialist state vaunted by Marx as a liberator became a police state in which the KGB set the model for the Gestapo, complete with concentration camps. In the Soviet Union, the socialist state also created a new class system, led there by the *"nomenklatura,"* an elite which gave itself special privileges. Ordinary people were expected to get by with what little the state allowed them. George Orwell's satire, *Animal Farm*, turned the state's egalitarian professions into the slogan "All animals are equal but some are more equal." Marx and his most determined followers (notably Lenin) were either naive or deceptive in supposing that once the state took over and established a "dictatorship of the proletariat," the elimination of classes would lead to the "withering away" of the state. Exactly the opposite actually happened. From the point of view of political theory, the biggest failure of socialism is in refusing to recognize that a state in total control of the means of production and managed by the one legitimate political party is bound to be oppressive. By disparaging liberalism as nothing more than a defense of property and democracy as its handmaiden, the socialists failed to recognize that liberals also defend other human rights, including freedom of opinion and the right to vote in free, competitive elections. Similarly they failed to appreciate that real democracy—not a sham "people's democracy"—would prevent the enormous abuse of power that socialism encouraged.

The failure of socialism on an involuntary, massive scale carries implications for social psychology missing in Marx's theorizing. While socialist ideology can inspire sacrifice in the cause of revolution and substitute symbolic rewards for material benefits, experience seems to show that most people will want the material benefits that only a competitive market economy brings and will not be willing to do their best with an Orwellian "Big Brother" monitoring their every move and thought. Economically, people seem to be most productive when they have some responsibility for their own success or failure. Politically, they will yearn for all the varieties of freedom—in expression, in belief, in ways of life—that are consistent with public order and that enrich life by allowing for toleration and diversity, not conformity. The ideal of socialism was designed to balance individualism, to check the impulse to selfishness, but when it put exclusive emphasis on the community, it went too far in the other direction. This is ironic and tragic because Marx believed that by overthrowing the unfairness and exploitation of capitalism, he was making freedom possible. Still, the ethical impulse underlying socialism retains its age-old appeal. Like other expressions of ethical humanism, it speaks to the oneness of mankind and the need for a sense of community to balance the individualism and indifference to the plight of the less fortunate that an exclusive focus on the liberty of individuals can engender.

## NOTES

1. A. O. Lovejoy and Franz Boas, *Primitivism and Related Ideas in Antiquity* (Baltimore, MD: Johns Hopkins Press, 1935), p. 16.

2. Plato, *Laws*, trans. B. Jowett (New York: Random House, 1937), vol. 2, p. 506.

3. *The New English Bible* (Oxford and Cambridge: Oxford University Press and Cambridge University Press, 1961), p. 323.

4. Ibid., p. 204.

5. Ibid., p. 274.

6. Augustine, *The City of God*, trans. Marcus Dods (New York: Modern Library, 1950), p. 696.

7. See Roland Bainton, *The Left Wing of the Reformation* (Chicago: University of Chicago Press, 1941).

8. George Huntston Williams, *The Radical Reformation* (Philadelphia: Westminster Press, 1957), p. 32.

9. Norman Cohn, *The Pursuit of the Millennium: Revolutionary Messianism in Medieval and Reformation Europe and Its Bearing on Modern Totalitarian Movements* (New York: Harper, 1961), pp. 149–68.

10. Gerrard Winstanley, *The Works of Gerrard Winstanley* (1648), ed. G. H. Sabine (Ithaca, NY: Cornell University Press, 1941), p. 323.

11. Ibid. (1650), p. 453.

12. Ibid. (1649), p. 226.

13. John Locke, *Two Treatises on Government* (1690), ed. P. Laslett (Cambridge: Cambridge University Press, 1964), *Second Treatise*, p. 309.

14. Voltaire, *Philosophical Dictionary* (1769), trans. P. Gay (New York: Basic Books, 1962), vol. 1, p. 245.

15. Grabriel Bonnot de Mably, *Oeuvres (Paris)*, vol. 9, p. 13.

16. V. Advielle, *Histoire de Gracchus Babeuf et du babouvisme* (Geneva: Slatkin, 1884), vol. 2, p. 38.

17. Ibid., vol. 1, p. 197.

18. G. D. H. Cole, *A History of Socialist Thought* (London: Macmillan, 1953), vol. 1, *Socialist Thought: The Forerunners, 1789–1850*, p. 4.

19. Karl Marx and Frederick Engels, *The Communist Manifesto* (1848), trans. S. Moore (London: Communist Party of Great Britain, 1948), pp. 146f.

20. Ludwig Feuerbach, *The Essence of Christianity*, trans. G. Eliot (New York: Harper, 1957), p. 14.

21. Ibid., p. 181.

22. Karl Marx, "Critique of Hegel's Philosophy of Right" (1844), trans. T. B. Bottomore, in *Marx's Early Writings* (New York: McGraw-Hill, 1964), p. 44.

23. Ibid.

24. Karl Marx, "Alienated Labor" (1844), Bottomore, op. cit., p. 122.

25. Karl Marx, "Private Property and Communism" (1844), Bottomore, op. cit., p. 155.

26. Marx and Engels, op. cit., p. 168.

27. Karl Marx, *Capital: A Critique of Political Economy*, trans. E. Paul and C. Paul (London, 1930), vol. 2, 7, chap. 24, p. 7.

28. Marx and Engels, op. cit., p. 153.

# 6

———— ❧ ————

# Nationalism

Nationalism is a doctrine invented in Europe at the beginning of the
nineteenth century. It pretends to supply a criterion for the determination of the unit of population proper to enjoy a government exclusively
its own, for the legitimate exercise of power in a state, and for the right
organization of a society of states. Briefly, the doctrine holds that humanity is naturally divided into nations, that such nations are known
by certain characteristics which can be ascertained, and that the only
legitimate type of government is national self-government. Not the least
triumph of this doctrine is that such propositions have become accepted
and are thought to be self-evident, that the very word nation has been
endowed by nationalists with a meaning and resonance which until the
end of the eighteenth century it was far from having.

—Elie Kedourie[1]

For all of its historical importance, "nationalism" is a term fraught with
ambiguity, mainly because it can suggest two very different though
related forms of association. Culturally, it expresses a shared sense of
identity, based on such ties as language or dialect, extended kinship or
ethnicity, and common traditions and folk legends. Politically, it refers
to a claim of sovereignty by a populace sharing historic attachments to
a particular territory. Combining both shadings, Anthony D. Smith offers a working definition of a "nation" as "a named human population
which shares myths and memories, a mass public culture, a designated
homeland, economic unity, and equal rights and duties for all members."[2]

Even when political and cultural nationalism are joined, however, as
in this definition, ambiguity recurs because the synthesis readily breaks

down into two very different forms—civic and ethnic—stressing the different elements of the term. Civic nationalism defines national identity by birth or naturalization, without regard to such differentia as ethnicity, religion, race, or language. Ethnic nationalism narrows the conditions of entitlement and challenges structures of state sovereignty that do not conform to its specifications, unless it can be accommodated by such political measures as autonomy, confederation, and multiculturalism. Both forms of nationalism may inspire chauvinism and expansionism, but ethnic nationalism is inherently expansionist or separatist when ethnicity does not coincide with territorial boundaries. The Nazi German dictator Adolf Hitler defined German nationality in ethnic terms (as *Grossdeutschland*) and set about expanding the boundaries of Germany to include those living in Austria, Sudeten Czechoslovakia, and Poland. Pan-Slavic and pan-Arab nationalists and a variety of irredentist movements have made similar claims. Separatist movements based on ethnicity remain active even in nation-states of long standing.

So long as nation-states remained under dynastic rule, nationalism was not an especially salient sentiment, since dynasts often ruled over different nationalities. The "nation" had previously been understood to mean a group of people belonging together by extended kinship, larger than a family but smaller than a clan or a people. Medieval universities often referred to groups of foreigners enrolled in them as various nations, and by extension the word was applied to groups of people sharing common characteristics, including, for political purposes, members of the nobility who could claim to represent or elect representatives for a particular territory. As popular forces began to play a larger role in affairs of state, nationalism became a subject of passionate concern. Flags and national anthems became precious symbols of belonging, and the most patriotic citizens believed that the highest calling was to sacrifice oneself on the altar of *la patrie*, the fatherland or motherland. Peoples subordinated in multinational units came to crave independence, and nation-states sought to expand their power by building empires, often rationalizing their ambitions by referring to the superiority of their national cultures. As a result, the middle decades of the nineteenth century came to be called "the springtime of nations," and the trend continued. By 1920, following the breakup of the Hapsburg and Ottoman empires, there were twenty-three nation-states in Europe; by 1994, there were fifty. The number has grown even larger as a result of the dissolution of Yugoslavia.

The emergence of the nation-state in Western Europe in the sixteenth and seventeenth centuries was a great turning point for the history of the continent and subsequently for the rest of the world. It became the foundation of modern international relations—sometimes referred to as the "Westphalian system" because the Peace of Westphalia in 1648 established the principle that territorial sovereignty was to be respected. Sovereignty was now defined as control, de jure or de facto, over a particular territory and all those who inhabited it. As a result, the nation-state became the recognized unit of political organization everywhere, and in time nationalism became its ideological expression. Paradoxically, the creation of regional systems like the European Union has made it more practical for "statelets" to secede without losing the security and economic benefits they enjoy from association with a larger country.

## CULTURAL AND POLITICAL NATIONALISM: ORIGINS AND DEVELOPMENT

Cultural nationhood has been identified as early as in the biblical account of the integration of the tribes of Israel, in the demarcation of Hellenes from "barbarians" in ancient Greece, and later in the separate identities of autonomous city-states in medieval and early modern times. In the modern history of Europe, cultural nationalism emerged before political nationalism, marked at first by the growing use of the vulgar tongues rather than Latin, the imperial language, and reinforced by the dissemination in the vernacular of national literatures and in Protestant countries by the translation and printing of the Bible.

Political nationalism emerged as a by-product of both cultural nationalism and the decentralization that ensued from the decline of the Roman Empire. In the sixteenth century, monarchs often asserted that they ruled by divine right over territories possessed by noblemen. They advanced a claim of "sovereignty," a concept developed by such influential political theorists as Jean Bodin, giving them complete and virtually unlimited territorial authority. Bodin defined sovereignty as supreme power over subjects, unrestrained by law. The sovereign was said to be the source of all law. The recognition of these claims began the process whereby statehood came to be associated with nationhood. The state, as the governing entity, came to be associated with the nation, as the entity to be governed.

At first, however, the aristocratic orders established by the new sovereign monarchs became the primary sponsors of the ideology of nationalism. As the custodians of the land, they saw themselves as bearers of nationality. The rise of commerce and mass discontent with feudalism led to revolts against both dynastic autocracy and aristocracy. As a result, the middle and lower classes came to see themselves, rather than kings and aristocrats, as the bearers of nationality. They often justified their rebellions by noting the foreign origins of their royal rulers, as in England, where the Puritan Revolutionaries compounded religious grievances with Saxon complaints against Norman "overseers," and in France, where the reigning queen, Marie Antoinette, was vilified as an "Autri-chien" (Austrian bitch) before being condemned to the guillotine.

## HERDER AND ROUSSEAU

Intellectuals rallied to the cause. In the eighteenth century, Gottfried Herder, a cosmopolitan and pacifistic intellectual, saw nationalism as a form of the expression of the particular genius of every distinctive people, and as a basis for harmony rather than antagonism. He blamed Roman expansionism for the evils that had befallen Europe. The answer to these evils, he thought, was to appreciate the reality of the *volk*—the national unit based on the common people. He emphasized the prepolitical, prerational foundations of nationhood—the mother tongue, ancient folk traditions, common descent, and what he thought of as the national spirit and sometimes the national genius. Herder put a great deal of emphasis on the differentiation embodied in myths, which he thought were necessarily national, because they expressed each peculiar people's spirit (*volksgeist*). Along with other Romantics, he celebrated an ethnolinguistic nationalism that especially suited Central and Eastern European societies where political differentiation along national lines was vaguer than it had become in Western Europe. Herder had great sympathy for underdog peoples like the Slavs and Latvians among whom he grew up and whose national aspirations had been suppressed by imperial rule. Each distinctive language, it was said by such theorists as Herder, Johann Gottlieb Fichte, and Friedrich Schleiermacher, is an expression of a particular way of life; to allow it to include foreign words is to contaminate and adulterate not only the language but also the national character it presumably reflects. Influenced by such thinking, nationalists in Germany, Italy, and the Balkans often rejected the ideals of liberal nationalism in favor of Romantic versions centered on the celebration of the "folk" and its special identity.

Like many other Europeans whose thinking was stimulated by Charles Darwin's discovery of the role of natural selection in evolution and Karl Marx's social analogue of history as progressive class struggle, they also came to believe that conflict among nations was inherent in social life, and that nature itself had ordained that only the strong would survive. Rather than adopt the liberal attitude of live and let live with respect to other nations, they were inclined to see international relations as a zero-sum game in which there could only be winners and losers. They called for protectionism in economics (preferring Friedrich List's mercantilist "national system" to the free market championed by Adam Smith and the physiocrats) and saw military strength and protection of the cultural patrimony as essential to national grandeur and survival.

Jean-Jacques Rousseau has been described as the father of modern political nationalism because he framed his social theory around the concept of "the general will" (*la volonté générale*). He did so in the hope of reviving the solidarity he revered in the classical polities. As a boy, he had dreamed of being a Spartan or Roman. He came to believe that if people could somehow strip themselves of all artificial accretions and consult their inmost natural or authentic selves, they would discover that they had exactly the same benevolent natural impulses or will as others and the same basic needs. A society whose law was founded on this "general will" would therefore be one that could command the fervent loyalty of all—one in which no one would be a subject and everyone would be a citizen. The spirit of such a society would resemble that of ancient Sparta, Israel, and the Roman republic. The modern social contract state envisioned by Rousseau was one in which all particular characteristics, including distinctions based on descent, property ownership, and religious confession, would be transcended by a common patriotic fervor, complete with a "civil religion"—the elements of which were to be determined by the civil sovereign, the people as a whole. While Rousseau warned that such a sense of community was possible only in small states like his native Geneva, whose small populations and geographical sizes allowed for self-government, he himself urged the Poles, at the time a nation of 11 million people dominated by several foreign powers, to prepare for their liberation by cultivating a distinctive national culture and establishing the republic in their hearts. He was so preoccupied with the Romantic dream of a patriotic community that he gave practically no thought to the potentially coercive character of the "general will" over nonconformists of various stripes.

Rousseau's thinking had a profound influence on the generation that rose in revolution in France in 1789. The first clear statement of the affinity between political nationalism and democracy appeared in the Declaration of the Rights of Man and the Citizen adopted by the revolutionary assembly, stating that "the principle of sovereignty resides essentially in the nation; no body of men, no individual, can exercise authority that does not expressly emanate from it." Because of this assertion of popular sovereignty, France came to be thought of as the paradigm of the modern nation and at the same time as the standard-bearer of the cause of liberty. The revolutionary anthem, the Marseillaise, aptly described by Simon Schama as a "great swelling anthem of patriotic communion,"[3] calls upon the *"enfants de la patrie"* to "irrigate the soil" with "the tainted blood of tyrants." Shock waves from the Revolution were felt by neighboring countries, and then throughout Europe, as the armies of Napoleon undermined the European status quo and extended the influence of French political ideas as far as Egypt. Discontented groups in many countries rallied to the vaguely related beliefs in national self-determination and popular, representative government associated with the French Revolution and its foundation in "the rights of man." The democratic revolutions of the late eighteenth and early nineteenth centuries dovetailed with the movements for national unification and the breakup of empires.

## THE EFFECTS OF THE FRENCH REVOLUTION

As the French declaration makes clear, political nationalism expresses the belief that all those who are citizens of some particular state ought to have the ultimate authority to declare its laws and choose its leaders. It may also express the wish for sovereignty among a people that aspires to political autonomy but does not yet possess territorial authority. The nineteenth-century Italians and Germans who campaigned for the unification of their respective provinces were the first to demand a political nationality they had not yet experienced. They were followed by Czechs, Slovaks, Ruthenians, and Hungarians in the Austro-Hungarian Empire; by the Greek and Armenian minorities in the Ottoman Empire; by the Baltic peoples and others on the periphery of the Czarist Russian Empire; and eventually by a host of anticolonial movements in Latin America, Asia, and Africa.

The link between the two concepts became strikingly explicit during the French and American revolutions, when the ideal of popular self-government was joined to the cause of national independence. Throughout the nineteenth century and well into the next, sentiments aroused in these revolutions, especially the French, inspired movements of national liberation in "sister republics" elsewhere. The seven Dutch provinces rebelled against the Prince of Orange and formed the United Netherlands. Belgians rose up against domination by the Austrian monarchy. Nationalist ferment agitated the Swiss cantons, producing a welter of short-lived minirepublics from which emerged a unified Helvetic Republic in 1798. City republics were established in Rome, Turin, and Naples, creating the groundswell from which issued the movement known as "Young Italy." Similar movements sprang up in many other regions, from the "Young Turks" to "Young India." The constitutions drafted for actual or would-be republics followed the model set by France. All incorporated declarations of rights, followed in some cases by a list of civic duties. All granted citizenship without regard to religion. All declared sovereignty to reside in "the citizenry as a whole"—though all restricted the right to vote to males, and some excluded servants and bankrupts.

The French Revolution had a decisive impact in replacing the dynastic conception of social order with one in which sovereignty was said to reside "essentially in the Nation." Now it came to mean any body of people associating together in order to create a common government. "What is a nation?" the Abbe Sieyes asked. His answer was, "A body of associates living under one common law and represented by the same legislature."[4] As Frenchmen began to experience a sense of national pride and power, France became known as *la grande nation*. Themselves newly emancipated, Frenchmen saw their armies as liberators of other peoples groaning under the yoke of kaisers, czars, and kings. But the early successes of the Napoleonic wars aroused fear of French domination in the nations invaded and inspired a nationalistic backlash. Although the army under Napoleon went forth in the name of the liberating slogan of the Revolution, "liberty, equality, fraternity," the message it sent to the rest of the world was that the French nation was bent on conquest and considered other nations inferior. The French Revolution, the nineteenth-century historian Lord Acton observed, spread nationalism "by its conquests, not its rise."[5]

The belief in political nationalism spread from Italy and France to Germany, which was still disunited. Fichte berated the German nobility, saying in effect that Germans were weak and vulnerable to Napoleon because they had not yet achieved unity but instead thought and acted as Prussians, Hessians, Saxons, and so forth, not as Germans. If they could overcome their parochialism, he declared, they, not the French, would be the masters of Europe. With similar sentiments, discontented groups in many countries rallied to the vaguely related beliefs in national self-determination and popular government associated with the French Revolution. In the nineteenth century, for the first time, chairs of national literature and history were established in European universities and doctoral dissertations were no longer written in Latin. The study of the ancient languages of Western civilization—Greek, Latin and Hebrew—ceased to form the core of the academic curriculum, replaced by a new appreciation of national epics and language.

From nationalism it was only a short step to rationales for imperialism. England, as the heart of an island state, first made itself into the United Kingdom, subjugating the Welsh, the Scots, and the Irish for a time, and then became the British Empire, over which, Britons could boast, the sun never sets, encompassing a vast expanse from North America to Malaya, India, Hong Kong, the Cape of Good Hope, and Australia and New Zealand. Even before the nineteenth century, European nations had turned voyages of exploration into missions of imperialism and colonialism, but in the nineteenth century, thanks to nationalism, it became much more than a form of adventure or casual economic enterprise, a search for gold or raw materials or fueling stations. It became a scramble for colonies as a means of enhancing national power and prestige vis-à-vis others—all rationalized as a sacred mission to bring Christianity and enlightenment to heathens and savages. The Spanish conquistadors set out to take possession of Latin America and thought they had both the right and the duty to bring Christianity to the pagan natives, even if that meant subjugating them and destroying their cultures. The French empire builders said they had a *mission civilisatrice*, a civilizing mission to spread French culture everywhere. The British writer Rudyard Kipling spoke of imperialism as "the white man's burden." Cecil Rhodes, the eponymous founder of the state that was called Rhodesia before it became Zimbabwe, said he would annex the stars if he could.

Everywhere in Europe, and then in the colonized areas, nationalism became a rallying cry among those who felt they were being denied greatness by being kept weak and divided. Italians and Germans campaigned for the unification of their respective provinces. They were followed by Czechs, Slovaks, Ruthenians, and Hungarians in the Austro-Hungarian Empire, by the Greek and Armenian minorities in the Ottoman Empire, and by the Baltic peoples and others on the periphery of the Russian Empire. The poet Byron went to Greece, where he died, it was said, for Greek liberty. Like a virus, nationalism spread widely, as far as the Russian Empire, where it took the form of the dream of pan-Slavic nationhood. Soon, much of the rest of the world caught the fever. When Napoleon landed in Egypt in 1798, he inspired nationalistic sentiments that took root in the Middle East and led to a backlash against both French and British colonialism in the name of Arab self-determination.

One by-product was the rise of political Zionism. On arriving near the Holy Land, Napoleon called upon Jews to reclaim their ancient homeland. At the time, European Jews were struggling to overcome the religious prejudice that kept them in ghettos. As nationalism rose all around them during the nineteenth century, they now found themselves doubly excluded, not just on religious grounds but because they were now doubly alien, doubly pariahs. Political Zionism emerged out of what had been a nostalgic memory of the Holy Land and a religious longing for a messianic return to it. Now that everyone else had a nationality, Zionist Jewish intellectuals argued that Jews would become a shadow people, unable to protect themselves or develop their own identity unless they too had a homeland. The Zionist movement even borrowed a Moldavian folk tune, based on an old Italian melody, and made it the Zionist anthem, *Hatikvah* (the hope). Jewish educators converted biblical Hebrew into a modern vernacular so that it could serve as a medium of national revival.

Even in America, where people took pride in having escaped the contentiousness of Europeans, nationalism expressed itself even before the Civil War in the movement called "Manifest Destiny." Thomas Jefferson had said that whereas Europe was a continent of war, America would be a nation of peace-loving yeomen farmers; but in the 1840s, as the tide of expansion reached the Pacific, American nationalists urged a "liberation"—that is, a conquest—of the remainder of North America. In 1845, when Congress approved the annexation of Texas, the leader of the American jingoists, John O'Sullivan, wrote, "Yes, more, more, more! . . . till our national destiny is fulfilled . . . and the whole boundless continent is ours!" The expansionists would not stop, as another of them put it, before we "embrace the whole hemisphere, from the icy wilderness of the North to the most prolific regions of the smiling and prolific south."[6] The press joined the jubilee. One New York newspaper editorial observed that "[t]he Mexican race is perfectly accustomed to being conquered, and the only new lesson we shall teach is that our victories will give liberty, safety, and prosperity to the vanquished. . . . Well may the Mexican nation, whose great masses have never yet tasted liberty, prattle over their lost phantom of nationality." Another, the *New York Herald*, went even further: if annexed to the United States, it claimed, Mexico would be "gorgeously happy." "Like the Sabine virgins, she will soon learn to love her ravisher." A Philadelphia newspaper proposed an elaborate plan for confederating Mexico with the United States, after a transitional occupation, concluding that General Winfield Scott "is the very fellow for the head of such a government. Our Yankee young fellows and the pretty senoritas will do the rest of the annexation, and Mexico will soon be Anglo-Saxonized, and prepared for the confederacy."[7]

## ETHNIC VERSUS CIVIC NATIONALISM

In this process of adoption, political nationalism acquired an ethnolinguistic cast, which could readily overshadow the more open civic definition. A "national" was now not just anyone who could claim citizenship but the embodiment of an organic and unique culture. When nationality was said to be a matter of belonging to some *volk*, nationalism became an exclusivist cause. In Nazi Germany, nationality meant to belong to the German *volk*, loosely linked to the "Aryan" or "Teutonic" race, perhaps the ultimate expression of this linkage.

This result was hardly what the early champions of civic nationalism anticipated and wanted. In the belief that liberation from all forms of dynastic and imperial oppression was progressive, liberals like John Stuart Mill and Giuseppe Mazzini supported nationalism as a worthy principle. "Where the sentiment of nationality exists in any force," Mill wrote, "there is a *prima facie* case for uniting all the members of the nationality under the same government, and a government to themselves apart. This is merely saying that the question of government ought to be decided by the governed."[8] "We shall be like the fingers of a hand," Mazzini proclaimed, "separate but cooperative." Free institutions, Mill asserted, "are next to impossible in a country made up of different nationalities."[9] He thought that "inferior and more backward" nationalities often benefited from ab- sorption by a dominant nationality, as in the case of a Breton and Basque in France, who gained the advantages of French citizenship and shared in "the dignity and prestige of French power," rather "than to sulk on his own rocks, the half-savage relic of past times, revolving in his own little mental orbit." The same was true, he added, for Welshmen and Scots.[10]

The historian Lord Acton took strong issue with Mill. He saw national- ism as one of several utopian delusions fostered by the French Revolu- tion. The Swiss had managed to separate political nationality from ethnic nationality, he noted, but in other cases nationalism would inevitably exalt one people over another. A state identified with and controlled by a particular people would be all too likely to tyrannize over other nation- alities contained in its boundaries. With chilling prescience he warned that in states dominated by ethnic nationalism, "inferior races" would be exterminated, or reduced to servitude, or outlawed, or put into a condition of dependence. Far better as a guarantor of liberty would be a state that combined different nationalities. The resulting diversity would help preserve liberty by creating a "firm barrier against the intrusion of government" beyond its basic sphere of authority. It would also dampen tendencies toward parochialism and self-centeredness:

> The co-existence of several nations under the same State is a test, as well as the best security of its freedom. It is also one of the chief instruments of ci- vilisation . . . and indicates a state of greater advancement than the national unity which is the ideal of modern liberalism.[11]

Acton's dissent from liberal orthodoxy did not deter more hopeful en- thusiasts for liberation in all its forms. Inspired by the dominant theme of nineteenth-century liberalism, which saw no conflict between political nationalism and democracy, President Woodrow Wilson made the "self-de- termination of nations" a key principle of American foreign policy when the United States entered World War I, a war that he also hoped would "make the world safe for democracy." To Wilson the two causes seemed inextrica- bly intertwined. No peace could last, he believed, unless it was founded on the principle of the self-determination of nations and guaranteed by a league of nations composed of democracies: "No autocratic government could be trusted to keep faith within it or observe its covenants. . . . Only free peoples can hold their purpose and their honor steady to a common end and prefer the interests of mankind to any narrow interest of their own."[12] In accor- dance with the announced war aims, the Ottoman and Austro-Hungarian empires were broken up by the Versailles Treaty and often-abortive efforts were made to establish new separate and democratic nation-states.

The principle was not immediately applied by the victorious powers after World War II, in large part because of the outbreak of the Cold War. The Soviet dictator Joseph Stalin insisted on controlling territories liberated by the Red Army, and the Western allies were anxious either to preserve their old colonies or to maintain friendly regimes in areas thought to be strategic barriers to the spread of communism. Throughout the colonized areas, however, nationalist movements arose to demand independence, often fueled by resentment that Westerners who claimed the right of independence and parliamentary democracy for themselves wanted to keep inhabitants of their overseas possessions in tutelary dependency. With only a few exceptions, notably India, success in achieving independence led to the installation of native autocracies. In the most recent period, the collapse of the Soviet Union and the end of its hegemony over the erstwhile countries of Eastern Europe again aroused the hope that independence would be accompanied by democracy—so far with mixed results.

## NATIONALISM AND DEMOCRACY

Many instances of nationalism have arisen out of efforts by a "people"— defined by territorial residence, ethnicity, or a sense of cultural affinity— to achieve collective autonomy. The demand for "home rule" served as the slogan of the struggle for Irish independence early in the twentieth century, as the desire to be *"maîtres chez nous"* continues to inspire separatist sentiment among Francophones in Quebec. The American Declaration of Independence began by noting that the time may come "when it becomes necessary for one people to dissolve the political bonds which have connected them with another." In such cases, even though the motives for asserting nationhood may include ethnic or cultural affinity, what is claimed is the right to *political independence*, not some other form of exclusivity. Neither Ireland nor presumably an independent Quebec, both predominantly Roman Catholic, would be considered democratic if they were to deny civic and political rights to Protestants. This distinction is important even when the nation's raison d'être is defined by ethnicity or religion, as in the case of modern Israel. Israel is a Jewish state in that it offers citizenship to all Jews and accords their religious customs special respect, and it is a democracy inasmuch as Arab, Druze, and other non-Jewish citizens enjoy the same political and civil rights.

Those forms of nationalism that exclude some inhabitants from full citizenship are another matter, whether they distinguish, as the nineteenth-century French statesman and historian François Guizot did, between *le pays légal* and *le pays réel* (the legal nation and the real nation) or deny equal legal status to those considered outsiders. If there is an established religion, tests of faith may bar some subjects from civic offices, rendering nonconformists second-class citizens, as most egregiously occurred in the seventeenth century, when Huguenots were driven from France and Puritans from Britain. Until 1865, the exclusion from eligibility for citizenship of Africans imported as slaves stood in blatant contrast to the democratic professions of American nationalism. The most notorious examples of such exclusivist nationalism were the fascist states that arose during the early middle decades of the twentieth century. Openly contemptuous of democracy, their leaders espoused chauvinistic, racist, and elitist ideologies that, in the extreme instance of Nazi Germany, led to an effort of genocide and a war of expansion aimed at expelling or enslaving supposedly inferior peoples. Ethnic nationalism has had similar consequences more recently in the breakup of Yugoslavia, leading to what has been euphemistically referred to as "ethnic cleansing." As the Yugoslav example suggests, this propensity is not specific to the racist version of fascism but is an inherent danger of all forms of ethnic nationalism. Political movements aiming to promote ethnic nationalism, such as those now active in France, Germany, and Russia, appeal to xenophobia in denouncing ethnic minorities and immigrants for destroying national homogeneity. In a similar vein, Muslim fundamentalists have openly declared that if they should gain power they would use the authority of the state to impose their religious laws upon nonbelievers (and quite possibly to ban political parties considered disrespectful of religious law, as in the Islamic Republic of Iran). Such movements take advantage of the opportunity that democracy offers to express even the most extreme points of view, but they are hardly themselves committed to the principles of democracy.

The political or civic form of nationalism is different and compatible with democracy because in principle (if not always fully in practice) it excludes no one who can claim the right of citizenship by birth or naturalization. On the contrary, it aims to unify all members of a particular society, regardless of their particular affinities, by emphasizing common loyalties, symbols, and institutions. Like democracy, political or civic nationalism entails a commitment to collective "self-determination" by the entire populace, without regard to ethnicity, race, religion, or any other cultural distinction, such as language or dialect. Both political nationalism and democracy are rooted in the assumption that those who either inhabit a particular territorial state or aspire to common statehood share a particular sense of *political* identity. Nationalism in this political or civic sense of the term is plainly consonant with democracy.

Similarly, democracy includes as one of its major premises the belief in popular sovereignty. The nationalist claim of self-determination and the democratic premise of popular sovereignty thus coincide—provided that self-determination is linked to universal and equal suffrage for all citizens. In the simplest example, a nation-state in which all citizens share equally in the making of basic laws, directly or through elected representatives, would exemplify both political nationalism and democracy. Conversely, a nation-state in which some or most inhabitants are excluded from full and equal citizenship could not be said to be either a specimen of political nationalism or of democracy—except possibly in an incipient sense.

This is, to be sure, an important exception because both political nationalism and democracy usually arise in a lengthy process of transition. Political nationalism has often had its beginnings in the assertion of nationhood by a social elite, or at least a militant faction, that challenges either dynastic or colonial rule in the name of the people. When constitutional authority passes from this elite to the populace as a whole, the transition to political nationalism may be said to be completed. Similarly, democracy has often arisen as a result of an overthrow of monarchy which leads in the short run to oligarchy and eventually, if the transition succeeds, to a more inclusive polity—or in Robert Dahl's terms, from a "closed" to an open, inclusive "polyarchy."[13]

In practice, the distinction between political and other forms of nationalism is sometimes fuzzy. Even in well-established democracies like the United Kingdom, France, the United States, and Germany, in which national identity is defined constitutionally by citizenship, whether acquired by birth or by naturalization, recent immigrants sometimes find that the performance of civic duties alone is not enough to assure them acceptance. Citizenship in the fullest sense is often associated with belonging to some dominant group or at least with the adoption of cultural norms imposed by a dominant group. Even when nationality is defined politically, the very fact that the word "nation" (and its analogues, "folk" or "people") is distinct from the word "state" hints at an important difference. Although, in ordinary usage, to be a citizen of a country is also to be a "national" of the country, there is at least an implicit difference. To be a national in the fullest sense of the term is to belong not just to the state (as in the German *staatsangehöriger*) but also to a social entity, usually one formed over a long time and distinct from the constitutional polity. Immigrants to the United States have often been torn between wanting to become "100 percent American" and maintaining their ties to the "old country." Those who came in great waves early in the twentieth century were often stigmatized as "hyphenated Americans," even after they became citizens. In more ethnically homogeneous societies, citizens who belong to religious or ethnic minorities may face even higher barriers to acceptance. In late nineteenth-century France, antidemocratic forces, led by the movement known as Action Française, arose after a military defeat at the hands of Prussia to exploit nationalist resentment at the loss of Alsace and Lorraine. Seeking someone to blame, they fastened on the small Jewish community of France, distinguishing between those who were presumably French in their heart and soul and those who could not truly be French by nationality, despite their citizenship. This campaign culminated in the bitterly divisive Dreyfus Affair, in which a Jewish army officer was accused on trumped-up charges of betraying military secrets to Germany. Even in modern France, which prides itself on the ethnic diversity of its sports teams, nationalist pressures sometimes require adherence to the cultural norms of the majority. A state law requires Muslim girls enrolled in public schools not to wear their traditional headdress. In Germany, the most intensely nationalistic movements display xenophobia, mixed with neo-Nazism, against immigrants and guest workers. These and other examples that could be cited indicate that even when nationalism is defined primarily in political terms, it may find other forms of expression hostile to democratic ideals.

Whereas nationalism could readily appear to satisfy the aspiration for liberation from foreign domination, it did not necessarily guarantee domestic democracy. Nationalism may even serve as a counterforce to democracy because it resembles democracy in its populist appeal but does not necessarily require respect for democratic norms; on the contrary, insistence on loyalty to the nation may override democratic concerns for freedom of speech and association, especially when national security is made a rationale for repression, and dissenters are stigmatized as "enemies of the people." Modern democracy rests on a distinction between the state (or public sector) and civil society (the private sector). This distinction is the single most definitive difference between ancient and modern democracy. A citizen of modern democracy has an equal share in the polity, expressed in the right to vote for representatives and to join with others in efforts to influence the outcome of elections. At the same time, each citizen also enjoys the right to be left alone in pursuing those activities that are thought to be "self-regarding," in John Stuart Mill's term, and the right to form associations. Where cleavages of culture, religion, race, and region are considered too intense to allow for unqualified majority rule, some democracies allow for power sharing and federal arrangements and are therefore considered instances of plural democracy in the fullest sense of the term.

Political nationalism coincides with democracy because citizens in a modern democracy experience a separate sense of identity and sphere of action as well as a common national identity. Despite this commonality, the two concepts are different and contain the possibility of antagonism. Nationalism locates the source of individual identity within a "people," which is seen as the bearer of sovereignty, the central object of loyalty, and the basis of collective solidarity. Modern democracy aims to empower all citizens equally, but unlike the ancient democracy of the Greek city-state, it allows citizens simultaneously to hold diverse forms of identity in a nonpublic space called civil society. A citizen is expected to take some of his identity from his nation, but he may also identify with his church, his region or locality, his family, with subcultural groups with which he may have an affinity, and with whatever quirks may be unique to his own personality. Modern democracy respects not only the principle of majority rule in matters of public policy but also the right of individuals and minorities to dissent and to act autonomously in the private sphere. Citizens of a modern democracy are protected in their right to take part in activities that are independent of the state and through which they may assert a sense of identity that is different from their political identity. Stable modern democracies allow for complex relationships that create cross-cutting cleavages and affinities, sometimes subnational, sometimes transnational. Subnational associations based on region, gender, lifestyle, ideology, or some other affinity may command a more passionate allegiance than the nation, even to the extent of promoting political apathy and withdrawal. Without in any way jeopardizing their political standing, religious believers may feel intense ties to coreligionists in other countries and accept the authority of an international church or foreign-headquartered clergy in matters of faith and morals. An employee may be loyal to a transnational corporation headquartered elsewhere. A scientist will feel ties to fellow members of a transnational, disciplinary "invisible college" and accept the norms of the cosmopolitan "republic of science." Environmentalists may be more concerned with the fate of "spaceship earth" than with some narrow national interest. As these instances suggest, modern democracy is a complex web of social organization and cross-cutting cleavages rather than a fixed hierarchical pyramid of social loyalties in which the nation is necessarily at the very top of the apex for everyone in every respect.

As a collective pursuit of self-determination, nationalism introduced an ambiguity into the understanding of natural rights. For nationalists, "national self-determination" became as legitimate a criterion of human rights as any right ascribed to individuals. This opened the door to the assertion of other "group rights" and to discriminatory treatment of citizens or residents not identified with the nation. The democratic commitment to personal and group freedom allows for a diversity of identities and associations, but all collectivistic ideologies, including nationalism, are potentially authoritarian—and the result is that there can be conflict between nationalism, even in its civic or political form, and modern democracy. Especially in times of social tension, patriotism is apt to promote xenophobia, which can be directed against inhabitants of foreign origin, as happened in the United States during World War I when Americans of German extraction became suspect as enemy aliens, and in World War

II when those of Japanese origin were removed from their homes and placed in relocation camps for fear they might be spies or saboteurs. Demands for conformity can also make dissent seem disloyal (in the case of the United States, "un-American") and subversive.

Thus, even though they share a common root in popular sovereignty, political nationalism and democracy may clash because democracy, in its generally accepted modern form, also includes guarantees of freedom of thought, expression, and association. For this reason, modern democracy is often referred to as liberal democracy, or sometimes as pluralist democracy. Democracy in this broader sense can be gravely undermined when political nationalism exalts group solidarity over individual liberty. If nationalist impulses give rise to demands for blind loyalty (on the principle of "my country right or wrong"), dissent may be stigmatized as unpatriotic and speech restricted. Despite the formal protections afforded by constitutional guarantees of individual rights, public pressure to conform can exert a chilling effect on freedom of speech and association.

In more extreme cases, when political nationalism exalts the fatherland as a sacred entity, loyalty to the nation becomes tantamount to a religious duty, and dissenters may be demonized as heretical and treasonous. Where nationalist fervor runs highest, individual and group liberty may be altogether extinguished. In the full-blown totalitarian state, only one political party—the party that presumably embodies the will of the people or folk—is allowed; all expressions of belief and all associations, from trade unions to professional groups, must be carefully monitored and integrated with the state. State security agencies hunt down and kill or imprison those considered actual or potential traitors. Inasmuch as it lacks a built-in concern for the rights of dissenters, political nationalism is open to this sort of manipulation. Just because it is exclusively devoted to the collective good, it is potentially at odds with the other characteristics of democratic thinking. By cloaking themselves in the mantle of political nationalism, demagogues and dictators can claim to be representing the popular will in denying democratic rights to their opponents. Among the people at large, a populist/patriotic version of democracy can reinforce this intolerance of dissent.

Many expressions of nationalism, moreover, are reactive in character—that is, based on hostility to other nations and rooted in an attempt to match and exceed their nationalism. The English sense of nationhood was forged and intensified in wars against France, Scotland, and Spain. German nationalism was a reaction against French nationalism, pan-Slavism and pan-Arabism were reactions against Western forms of nationalism, Zionism was in part a reaction against the exclusion of Jews from other expressions of nationality, and Palestinian nationalism was a reaction against the success of Zionism. The reactive character of these forms of nationalism does not necessarily make them hostile to democracy, but it may encourage feelings of chauvinism among some adherents that militate against the universalism of the democratic ideal. The nationalist movements of Central and Eastern Europe were often inspired by ethnic, religious, and cultural affinities. They emerged in areas where national political unity was weak and there was little experience with parliamentary democracy. They were therefore either indifferent to or hostile to democracy in practice and to its ideals of inclusiveness and equality, rejecting the individualism and rationalism of the Enlightenment for the view that individuals could only become full selves when absorbed into an organic, sometimes mythic conception of society as a unique entity.

Ethnic nationalism is often an invitation to secession and separatism. Old dynastic states like Austria-Hungary united groups of people who thought of themselves as belonging to different nations and who therefore chafed at being denied separate statehood. The same tensions have arisen in binational states like Canada and Belgium. Even in such settled nation-states as Spain and the United Kingdom, separatist sentiments have erupted in calls for dissolution, not just devolution or autonomy. Nationalism is, ironically, both a centrifugal and a centripetal force. If self-determination is to be granted to all those who constitute a distinct "people," the definition of exactly who constitutes a people is open to continual argument. Borders that seem settled and conventional can readily be challenged as accidental and improper. When nationalist sentiment first took hold in modern Europe, national identity was generally understood to be ascribed to all those who by virtue of language and culture could be said to belong to one or another separate community. At first, nationalists argued that subcommunities would benefit by setting aside local allegiances for the sake of the higher unity and thereby gaining greater security, prosperity, and pride. Giuseppe Garibaldi and Camillo Cavour were celebrated as Italian patriots because they struggled to unify the various elements of the country. As nationalism arose within the Russian, Austro-Hungarian, and Ottoman empires, however, those praised as patriots included not only integrationist pan-Slavists but also poets (like the Hungarian Sandor Petöfi) and local princes and politicians who championed parochial, breakaway forms of unity. Those who lived in mixed-ethnicity border communities like Alsace, Schleswig-Holstein, Danzig, and Trieste did not fit into any of the Procrustean beds, and these territories became flashpoints of conflict. Their existence was either ignored by nationalists as a marginal nuisance or was used to fan irredentism.

The net result of this nationalist agitation in Europe was "Balkanization," or the emergence of claims to nationhood on behalf of peoples integrated, often against their will, into states over which they had no significant control. The United States, formed originally as a union of former colonies composed of a largely homogenous and unilingual people, almost broke apart over the issue of slavery, only remaining "one nation, indivisible" thanks to the victory of the North in a fratricidal civil war. In Africa and Asia, as well as in the Middle East, the initial impact of nationalism was similarly toward integration rather than disaggregation, but there, too, countervailing tendencies may be setting in. The initial aim was to overcome tribalism by establishing nations, bound together wherever possible by common language and contiguous territory. But the divisions among the new nations were often arbitrary—lines drawn on a map by colonial powers dividing the spoils of war among themselves and to reward local satraps—and even when national boundaries were imposed by movements of national liberation, they sometimes overrode lingering sensitivities. Donald L. Horowitz has described Nigeria, Uganda, Benin, and the Indian Punjab as "coalitions of convenience" founded "to gain the requisite majority to form a government." Such coalitions, he adds, are easier to form than to sustain.[14] It remains to be seen whether the current divisions among many of the nation-states so established in developing areas will remain more or less constant or whether the example of the dissolution of the empires of Europe will be followed by the breakup of some of the larger nations of the other continents. The secessionist effort of the Ibos of Nigeria was beaten back, at great cost, and other tribal conflicts have led to horrendous slaughter elsewhere in Africa. The Afrikaners and Zulus of South Africa may or may not remain in South Africa. Such peoples as the Palestinians and the Kurds may succeed in achieving separate political status, as may many other outright or latent separatist movements in India, Indonesia, China (notably Tibet), and elsewhere.

The moral of this experience for the political theory of both democracy and nationalism is that the "self-determination of nations" is an uncertain formula. What constitutes a nation rests, rather like beauty, in the eye of the beholder. The formula can suit agglomerations of localities as well as splinter movements—Italians as well as Lombards; Spaniards as well as Basques; Britons as well as Scots and Welshmen; Yugoslavs as well as Serbs, Croatians, Bosnians, Slovenes, and Albanians; Russians as well as Chechnyans; and Canadians as well as Quebeckers, Cree, and Inuit. A seemingly well-established nation-state like the United Kingdom, which most observers would consider a single unified nation, can appear to some as an instance of "internal colonialism," needing not just devolution in the form of subnational parliaments but wholesale reconstruction into separate entities. The conflict in Northern Ireland has been so difficult to resolve peacefully and democratically because its people do not agree on which nation they belong to. The Supreme Court of Canada has held that although much of the Quebec population "certainly shares the characteristics of a people," the principle of federalism embodied in the Canadian constitution means that a decision to secede, even if adopted by a majority of the voting inhabitants of the province, could not legally take effect without the agreement of the other provinces. As to the claim that such a right could be claimed under international law, the court held that

> a right to secession only arises under the principle of self-determination of people . . . where "a people" is governed as part of a colonial empire; where "a people" is subject to alien subjugation, domination or exploitation; and possibly where "a people" is denied any meaningful exercise within the state of which it forms a part.[15]

It remains to be seen whether the court's interpretation will be respected in the event that a majority of Quebeckers vote for independence. They may well contend that the Canadian constitution was forced upon their forebears as a result of military defeat and is therefore nonbinding, and that their actual condition meets the standard of international law the court has invoked. In democratic theory, the question is inherently open and ambiguous.

In practice, however, there is at least one example, and it is a major one, of a country that has managed, albeit with difficulty—including civil war—to integrate different regions through federalism and to assimilate a population remarkably diverse in religion, ethnicity, and race. This is of course the United States of America, whose national slogan, *"e pluribus unum,"* embodies just this aspiration. Despite lingering difficulties, notably persisting racial tension, the United States has become the model of emulation for other nations seeking to enjoy both a sense of national unity and democracy. In its foreign policy, too, the United States has been, since the presidency of Woodrow Wilson, a leading champion of the belief in human rights and of "the self-determination of nations." Even though its domestic and foreign policies have not always reflected these values, it is a prime historical example of the confluence of democracy and nationalism.

But even in America, the ambiguity concerning the unit of nationhood led to a civil war, when slaveholding white southerners claimed the right to form their own confederacy. More recently, the separate ethnic and linguistic groups that lived together in Yugoslavia have become five separate nation-states. Should there be one Iraq or separate entities for Kurds, Shiites, and Sunnis? Nationalism provides no certain definition of the unit of nationhood. Everything depends on what the people concerned take to be the unit of population and whether they are willing to accept a multiregional, multiethnic, or multisectarian form of nationality or insist on a narrower one. Benedict Anderson has therefore emphasized that there is no such thing as an objective, "true" community, but all "communities larger than primordial villages of face-to-face contact (and perhaps even these) are imagined."[16] All stable nations are composed of people who come to think that they belong together; the others are inherently fractious combinations of people who suppose that they are distinct from each other and remain together in one state for reasons of convenience or by coercion.

## CIVIC VERSUS ETHNIC NATIONALISM

The difference between civic and ethnic nationalism sometimes shows up in immigration policy. Like the American Statue of Liberty, civic nationalism extends a welcome to immigrants, announcing in effect that anyone can belong to the nation who is born there or naturalized. Immigrants can become full-fledged citizens by embracing the national political values, respecting its symbols, and behaving loyally. Often, though not always, that means using the standard language. The United States, a nation of immigrants, is a prime example of this sort of nationalism—which, however, has been susceptible to the second, more malevolent form of nationalism.

Whatever the difficulty of achieving it, civic nationalism has a great deal to commend it. It evokes the kind of love of country people feel when they hear the national anthem, celebrate their attachment to their fatherland, or remember the fallen on days set aside for remembrance. American schoolchildren learn the frightening story by Edward Everett Hale about Philip Nolan, the man without a country, who was doomed to wander the world forever after he renounced his citizenship. The poem is a reminder that nationalism brings people together so that they feel a sense of community that transcends more parochial loyalties. The nation cherishes its traditions and inspires citizens to feel a sense of obligation toward each other. In the long history of civilization, which begins with families and tribes, fearful of each other, this sort of nationalism is a major advance. This is still poignantly clear in societies where tribalism and sectarianism prevent people from achieving the degree of cooperation and mutual respect they would feel if they thought of themselves as members of the nation rather than of some subnational unit.

But there is another face of nationalism—the one Dr. Johnson had in mind when he said that patriotism is the last refuge of a scoundrel. When the Nazis adopted the notion of *Grossdeutschland*, they called their regime the Third Reich and used nationalism as a rationale for racism and expansion, demanding *lebensraum* or living space, even if it belonged to other nations. Exclusionary nationalism turns others who live in the society into second-class citizens at best, or enemies and slaves at worst. In the most extreme cases, this sort of nationalism makes loyalty to the fatherland tantamount to a religious obligation. Dissenters are declared to be disloyal and even treasonous, and liberty may be crushed. Exclusivist national-ism can become chauvinistic and aggressive, as people are mobilized to engage in barbaric behavior that is euphemistically called "ethnic cleans-ing," to eradicate or expel those not considered members of the nation. And they can come to believe that it is their right and duty to subjugate other peoples by creating empires.

Has nationalism become an anachronism in a time when improved technologies of travel, communication, and warfare have shrunk the distances separating the continents and trade relations and transnational companies are more global than ever? The invention of supersonic air-craft and intercontinental ballistic missiles ended the era when the great moats of the Atlantic and Pacific allowed Americans to live in splendid isolation. Space exploration and warnings of rising ecological dangers due to human activity have aroused a new awareness that all human beings make up one species inhabiting "spaceship earth." Given these momentous changes, nationalism may well seem delusionary. For the time being, however, the end of nationalism is not in sight. So long as it is civic nationalism, it has virtues, as the political scientist Karl Deutsch pointed out:

> The nation-state . . . is still the chief political instrument for getting things done. The main basis of its power is, now more than ever, the consent of the governed, and this consent is easiest to obtain and to keep among popula-tions with the same language, culture, and traditions of nationality.[17]

## NOTES

1. Elie Kedourie, *Nationalism* (New York: Praeger, 1962), p. 9.

2. Anthony D. Smith, *Nations and Nationalism in a Global Era* (Cambridge: Polity Press, 1995), pp. 56–57.

3. Simon Schama, *Citizens: A Chronicle of the French Revolution* (New York: Knopf, 1989), p. 598.

4. Ibid., pp. 12–15.

5. J. E. E. Dalberg, Lord Acton, "Nationality" (1862), in *Essays in the Liberal Inter-pretation of History*, ed. William H. McNeill (Chicago: University of Chicago Press, 1967), p. 142. See Timothy Lang, "Lord Acton and 'the Insanity of Nationality,'" *Journal of the History of Ideas* 63, no. 1 (January 2002): pp. 129–49.

6. Quoted in Frederick Merk, *Manifest Destiny and Mission in American History* (New York: Vintage, 1966), p. 46.

7. Ibid., pp. 123–25.

8. J. S. Mill, *Considerations on Representative Government*, in *Utilitarianism, On Liberty and Considerations on Representative Government* (New York: J. M. Dent & Sons, 1972), pp. 360–61.

9. Mill, ibid., p. 361.

10. Ibid., pp. 363–64.

11. Acton, op. cit., pp. 149–50.

12. Quoted by Tony Smith, *America's Mission: The United States and the Worldwide Struggle for Democracy in the Twentieth Century* (Princeton, NJ: Princeton University Press, 1994), p. 94.

13. Robert A. Dahl, *Polyarchy: Participation and Opposition* (New Haven, CT: Yale University Press, 1971).

14. Donald L. Horowitz, *Ethnic Groups in Conflict* (Berkeley: University of California Press, 1985), pp. 369–78.

15. Supreme Court of Canada, Reference re Secession of Quebec, 20 August 1998, par. 154.

16. Benedict Anderson, *Imagined Communities: Reflections on the Origin and Spread of Nationalism* (London: Verso, 2006), p. 6.

17. Karl Deutsch, *Nationalism and Social Communication: An Inquiry into the Foundations of Nationality* (Cambridge, MA: MIT Press, 1966), p. 4.

# 7

## Fascism

The economic turmoil and social unrest that arose in much of Europe in the wake of World War I, coupled with widespread denigration of parliamentary democracy, produced a variety of movements attractive to ethnic nationalists, embittered war veterans, and others discontented by hardship and drawn to demagogic agitators promising relief and vengeance against their supposed oppressors. In a number of countries in Europe, these movements coalesced in fascism. Alongside them arose radical socialist movements that decried elected cabinets as "the executive committee of the ruling class," whose sole purpose was said to be to suppress the proletariat. Besieged between left and right, fledgling democracies succumbed in Italy, Germany, Spain, and Russia, and were assaulted elsewhere.

For all its uniqueness in generating efforts to construct totalitarian states and the tragic consequences it spawned, the ideology of fascism was not altogether unprecedented. The history of Western civilization is no unsullied record of freedom and self-determination contrasting neatly with "Oriental despotism." The same distrust of popular government that led to aristocratic reaction in ancient Athens and to the fall of the Roman republic reappeared in the nineteenth century. Again, popular assemblies were decried as faction-ridden "talking shops," and broadened suffrage was seen as an invitation to demagoguery and mob rule. As a doctrine and a movement, fascism exhibits elements of Greek tyranny, Spartan militarism, Caesarism, absolute monarchy, and imperialism. The very word is derived from a Roman symbol, the bound axe and rods of authority. Caesarism was echoed in the cult of the leader. Even the fascist salutations and salutes had classical origins: "Heil Hitler" is a version of "Hail Caesar," and both the Nazi and Italian extended-arm salutes were an imitation of the Roman version. A revived pagan religiosity led the Nazis to want to substitute Wotan for God and Hitler for the Christian savior.

Fascism is also to some extent another offshoot of the Renaissance, a bastard child perhaps, but still a descendant. While the rebirth of Western civilization recovered much of the classical legacy that was creative and humane, it also unearthed a toxic underside. The adulation of manliness and of fame and conquest inspired the blood-soaked career of the Borgias and enabled Machiavelli to describe princely conquests as an expression of a natural impulse of heroic men. The lust for gain unleashed by the revival of pagan *virtù* blinded Europeans of all classes to the iniquities of imperialism and led them to suppose that the slaughter, enslavement, and dispossession of native populations in the lands they explored and colonized was perfectly legitimate because it was their destiny to rule over inferiors.

Renaissance humanism produced a growing belief in universal human rights, manifest in such movements as liberalism, socialism, and democracy, but countermovements quickly emerged. Nineteenth-century critiques of egalitarianism were taken to an ultimate extreme in the twentieth century by the advocates of fascism, who spun fantasies of perfect social unity, unquestioning discipline, and obedience to the all-powerful state. The movement won adherents among conservatives who felt threatened by the growing strength of the political left and who supposed that fascism was a necessary blunt instrument for dealing with these threats. They deluded themselves into thinking it could serve their purpose or be turned to it. The major appeal of fascism, however, was to ordinary people who felt powerless and dispossessed in the turmoil that followed the First World War and who yearned for a return to the order and prosperity they identified with the authoritarian past. Conditioned by nationalism to blame their misfortunes on foreign enemies and internal minorities, and to suppose that they were uniquely endowed to rule over others, they were open to the inflammatory populist rhetoric of fascist demagogues. For just these reasons, neofascism remains a lurking threat whenever social breakdown—economic, cultural, or political—causes such anxiety as to undermine faith in democracy and revive suppressed yearnings for the imposition of order upon the strains and inefficiencies of liberty and pluralism.

## THE APPEAL OF FASCISM

The title of W. H. Auden's poem "The Age of Anxiety" captured the climate of opinion that nurtured the rise of fascism. Ideas and social conditions fit together in promoting its appeal. The charismatic spell of figures like Hitler and Mussolini was one factor that attracted people to it, inasmuch as hero worship was central to the mind-set. Those drawn to it wanted a leader they could follow blindly who seemed to embody their own determination and anger. Even while these leaders were still relatively unknown, fascism found a following in many countries. Mussolini's movement in the 1920s was the first to bear the name, but it was soon imitated in Spain, where Franco's rebellious Falangists aped the Italian and Nazi German example. Fascism also found true believers in Western and Central Europe—in movements like the Belgian Croix de Feu and Romanian Iron Guard—and an echo in the Peronist movement in Argentina. It had begun to have influence in the Middle East, among both Arabs and right-wing Zionists. Even in the United States, Charles Lindbergh, a national hero, admired the discipline the Nazis were imposing on Germany and was attracted by their notions of racial superiority and inferiority. The writer Lawrence Dennis wrote a tract for the times called *The Coming American Fascism*.[1] Louisiana's very popular governor, Huey Long, was assassinated by a doctor who feared he would become an American Hitler.

Fascism battened on perceptions of social distress. In 1919 and 1920, 160,000 officers in the Italian army were discharged in the midst of what was described as an economic earthquake. Unable to find work, they blamed the country's political establishment, and many joined the ranks of the Fascisti. In 1932, shortly before Hitler came to power, there were 6 million unemployed in Germany, and the country had been through a ruinous inflation, following the humiliation of defeat in World War I and the draconian terms imposed at Versailles. In both countries, cynicism and despair fused to create a receptive climate for movements clamoring for vengeance and a reassertion of national pride. Fascism emerged and gained strength in Germany because it seemed to empower the powerless, those inflamed by rage and resentment. *"Kleiner Mann, vass nun?"* (Little man, what now?), one early commentator asked. Another, Kurt Rauschnigg, called the Nazi takeover a "revolution of nihilism," a rejection of all the received pieties in favor of existential assertiveness. The same idea was expressed in positive terms by the film glorifying a party rally in Nuremberg entitled *Triumph of the Will*. Nazism began as a small movement, its hard core made up of discontented veterans and street toughs, and became a mass movement. The Nazis were not the only ones to call for a total overthrow of the existing system. Communists were also a strong force in Germany, and their battle with the Nazis for the streets proved impossible for the Weimar Republic to suppress.

In his history of the coming of the Third Reich, Richard J. Evans suggests that while elaborate theories expounded by fascist writers appealed mainly to the educated middle class, the mass of the following was electrified by more gut-level sentiments. Some recruits to the ranks of the SA, the Nazi mass movement, were drawn by anti-Semitic screeds, like a handbook on the Jewish question that reached its fortieth edition in 1933. The bulk of Hitler's core adherents were drawn to the movement by its ideology, which combined calls for racial purity with attacks on Weimar democracy, "Bolshevism," and cultural "degeneracy." Among ordinary party activists in the 1920s and early 1930s, however, "the most important part of Nazi ideology was its emphasis on social solidarity—the concept of the organic, racial community of all Germans—followed at some distance by extreme nationalism and the cult of Hitler."[2] Whatever brought particular individuals to embrace fascism, the ideas embodied in it made it seem like an answer to a sense of anger and despair that gripped a great many Germans. Indeed, the all but complete eclipse of fascism following the defeat of the Axis powers suggests that it was less a set of ideas than a fever or a nightmare that ended when Europeans who survived the war realized they had been in the grip of a delusion.

The delusion was a witches' brew of many elements. Chief among these was a backlash against liberalism, socialism, and democracy in favor of the sense of unity, solidarity, and purpose that dictatorship seemed to promise. Chauvinistic nationalism was another important common factor. A fascination with elite theory and elitism gave the cause intellectual ammunition, as did the popularity of new speculations about crowd psychology suggesting that the masses were easily led sheep. A romantic fixation on hero worship, perhaps sparked by the admiration of Napoleon Bonaparte, blended with the reaction against democracy and the supposed "revolt of the masses." A popularized version of social Darwinism made all life seem to be a struggle for survival and dominance. There was even a tinge of socialism. Mussolini came to fascism after having been a socialist, and the word "Nazi" was shorthand for "National Socialist." Mussolini was impressed by Georges Sorel's "myth of the general strike," which suggested that the masses could be mobilized by filling their minds with fantasies of political oppression. In the case of Nazism, the supposition that racial purity and national power were threatened by the integration of the Jews played a key role. Fascism was a blend of these elements, hardened by the adoption of military-style uniforms, marching, and other symbols of militancy.

Because they are such mélanges, the movements that went by the name fascism are not exactly alike. Italian fascism was racist mainly in the sense that race had come to be used loosely to mean peoples. The Italian fascists thought the Italian people, as descendants of the noble Romans, were destined to rule over inferior Africans and that the Mediterranean was *mare nostrum* (our sea). Otherwise the rest of the elements are quite visible in this first case: the disdain for democracy symbolized by the march on Rome, the shutting down of the parliament, and its replacement by an all-powerful dictatorship; chauvinistic nationalism playing upon the belief in restoring the grandeur or *grandezza* of the Roman Empire; elitism deriving from the work of Italian elite theorists, notably Gaetano Mosca and Vilfredo Pareto, and applied in the depiction of the black shirts of the Fascist Party as a new ruling class; and the belief in crowd psychology, exploited via marches, speeches from the balcony to adoring crowds below, using the new broadcasting medium of radio so that people far and wide could hear the bombast and the crowd worshipping the hero, shouting "Duce, Duce, Duce," accompanied by the grandiose gesture of the fascist salute. The propaganda in the schools and media inculcated the social Darwinist belief that life is a struggle in which the strong prevail and the weak perish. From socialism, fascists borrowed a call for social solidarity, except that fascism called for an end to class warfare and for crushing the forces of the left, presumably because they were really reactionary obstacles to the revolutionary transformation that fascism would bring. Whereas socialists promised that under communism the state would wither away, fascists saw it as the expression of the unity, strength, and wholeness they promised.

Racism was not a defining characteristic of all the variants. Spain's Falangists saw themselves as anticommunist, antirepublican, and devout Catholics, but they were not especially racist. Indeed many of the troops were from Spanish North Africa, the Moros or Moors, where the leader, called "El Caudillo," Generalissimo Francisco Franco, had been headquartered. By contrast, Nazi Germany's fascism was racist at the core, built on the idea that the Aryan race was superior to all others but was gravely threatened by the dark Semitic race. And the British, Dutch, Norwegian, French, Romanian, Croatian, and other fascist movements more or less hewed to the Nazi line.

What did they all have in common? As the case of Italian fascism shows, all of them drew upon an arsenal of diverse ideas that had been developed in reaction to liberal democracy and socialism. Members of the privileged classes, like Britain's Cliveden set before World War II, were apt to sympathize with fascism, and were led in a homegrown version in Britain by Oswald Mosley. But though they sympathized with fascists, they usually held themselves aloof from them, except for odd cases like one of the Mitford sisters or the Duke and Duchess of Windsor, because they had little in common with these mostly socially marginal rabble-rousers—the sort of riffraff Marx called the *lumpenproleteriat*. Conservatism was a frame of mind that appealed to people who valued privilege and refinement in taste and manners, whereas fascism came from the lower depths, from the impoverished haunts of hatred, brutality, and resentment. Some in the upper classes welcomed it because in an age when masses counted, thanks to the extension of the suffrage, fascism promised them the support of a mass movement. No longer did they have to fear that they were fighting a lost cause because liberals and socialists would ride to permanent power on the backs of popular majorities. Now they could suppose they had support from the very masses on whom their enemies were counting. In the end, they were disabused of the idea that they could control the monster they had helped to nurture.

It is tempting but too simple, however, to say that the conservative reaction of the nineteenth century mutated or morphed into fascism in the twentieth. Fascism was not some new version of the old conservatism of Burke and the continental aristocrats and clerics who formed the party of order, monarchy, and tradition. This new ultra-ultra-conservatism was radically reshaped by ideas that developed in the nineteenth century. It stood for a new order, not the old order, for dictatorship, not monarchy, for ethnic or racial purity, not religious piety. Fascism derived from and took to an extreme the conservative belief that hierarchy and discipline were essential for order and national greatness. At its core, fascism represented a rejection of the egalitarian ideals of both liberals and socialists, different as they were. All forms of democratization were condemned as agents of degeneration and mongrelization, not progress. Because of this resemblance, fascism was often welcomed by conservatives who thought it was a useful countermovement against what they saw as the dangers of a tyranny of the ignorant majority. Mussolini put the antidemocratic message of fascism starkly and clearly:

> Fascism attacks the whole complex of democratic ideologies and rejects them both in their theoretical premises and in their applications. . . . Fascism denies that the majority, through the mere fact of being a majority, can rule human societies; it denies that this majority can rule by means of a periodical consultation; it affirms the irremediable, fruitful and beneficent inequality of men, who cannot be leveled by such a mechanical and extrinsic fact as universal suffrage.[3]

Fascism was a compound of a number of key elements:

1. *Chauvinistic nationalism.* The chauvinistic form of nationalism, especially its ethnic variant, holds that the nation, not the individual, should be the central value and the focus of loyalty, and that it is quite wrong to make universal individual human rights a basis of citizenship or policy. A French conservative had said contemptuously that he knew Frenchmen, Italians, Britons, and Germans, but no universal men. From this rejection of universalism arose the chauvinistic conceit that nations are not only different but superior and inferior, and that the proof of superiority lay in outdoing others in acquiring colonies. This form of nationalism took shape in imperialism and the scramble for colonies and also in the

pan-movements, like pan-Slavism or pan-Germanism. Americans had a taste of it in the expansionist frenzy that led to the annexation of much of Mexico in the 1840s under the banner of Manifest Destiny. In Europe, it took on pandemic proportions, nowhere more than in Germany. In 1922, a chauvinistic German nationalist named Arthur Moeller van den Bruck wrote a book entitled *Das Dritte Reich* (The Third Reich), coining the term the Nazis were to seize upon as their vision of the future. In this work he praised inequality as the necessary basis of national greatness and railed against liberalism as the source of weakness. Germany's destiny, he said, was to become synonymous with Europe and to amalgamate kindred peoples into a grander and more powerful *Grossdeutschland* or integral Germany. In that form, nationalism became a bulwark of Nazi fascism, as in a similar way it reinforced Italian fascism. In the Nazi version, however, nationalism was fused with racism: Germany was seen as the spear point of the Aryan race.

2. *A popularized version of Social Darwinism.* In the middle of the nineteenth century, the biological discoveries of Charles Darwin and Alfred Russel Wallace revolutionized the understanding of nature in a way that was as unsettling as the Copernican revolution in cosmology or Newton's discovery of the laws of motion and optics. These earlier discoveries had altered the understanding of the physical universe and man's place in it. Darwin put life itself in a new light. He showed that all life forms, from the simplest to the most complex, developed through evolution and that the key to understanding evolution was the mechanism of natural selection. Nature produce variations; those best adapted to environmental change reproduced most successfully. The theory of evolution met resistance to this idea, especially because it suggested that human beings and apes were both mammals with a common ancestry. This seemed like a wild idea and one that somehow seemed insulting to human pride. And of course it flatly contradicted the account of creation in the Bible, a problem even today for evangelicals who want to see the schools give equal time to creationism or "intelligent design."

Darwinism also had the effect of greatly reinforcing the belief in progress that had emerged in the eighteenth century. Now progress could be understood as a result not just of the accumulation of knowledge but of the struggle to adapt displayed by all forms of life. It is easy to see why this idea should have appealed to Karl Marx. Having laid down that the history of all preceding society was the history of class struggle, Marx may well have thought he had discovered the social analogue to Darwinian natural selection. He even thought of dedicating *Das Kapital* to Darwin. But another nineteenth-century theorizer drew a very different moral from Darwin's theory—one that made him a hero to American tycoons. This was Herbert Spencer, who coined the phrase "the survival

of the fittest" and whose thinking came to be called "social Darwinism."
Through evolution, Spencer taught, a higher human species is evolving—
a species in which intelligence will be more widely diffused than in the
past and in which more and more individuals will be superior specimens,
capable of managing their own lives and making major contributions to
human welfare. To protect this progressive evolution, it was necessary
that the state not interfere with the competitive struggle. Spencer and his
champions—in America, notably William Graham Sumner—rested laissez-faire economics not on natural rights or utilitarian thinking, nor only
on the virtues of the market economy, but as a necessity for social evolution. The struggle might be hard on widows and orphans, or on small
"mom and pop" enterprises, they taught, but the state must not provide
welfare or curb big business lest it thwart the process of improvement.
Millionaires, decried as robber barons, were actually benefactors; thanks
to them and them alone, progress was being achieved. The right social
formula was therefore as little government as possible and no "handouts"
in the form of welfare for the poor and infirm.

But how did social Darwinism come to influence the rise of fascism?
Fascism was not laissez-faire economics given an up-to-date biological
underpinning. Social Darwinism became influential because the fascists
took the idea of the survival of the fittest from it and detached it from
the link to economic liberalism. They came to believe that as all life is
struggle, so the struggle for power is the very nature of international relations. Some nations survive; others perish or become enslaved. The very
title of Hitler's testament, *Mein Kampf* (My Struggle), is in keeping with
this idea. It is enough to read his speeches—better still to watch them
being delivered in his hypnotic fashion—to recognize a seething desire
to see Germans as a conquering people: "*Heute Deutschland, morgen die
welt*" (Today Germany, tomorrow the world). Social Darwinism also
helped inspired eugenics, the effort launched by Darwin's cousin Francis
Galton to improve the race by selective breeding and by eliminating the
unfit before they could reproduce. In the hands of the Nazis, that enterprise led to euthanasia of the mentally deficient, the SS breeding farms,
and the massacre of Jews and others deemed inferior. In a larger sense,
social Darwinism blended with other ideas emphasizing the struggle for
supremacy, like those of the sociologist Ludwig Gumplowicz, and the
geopolitical ideas of Karl Ernst Haushofer—one of whose pupils, Rudolf
Hess, became an admiring aide to Hitler. In this adapted, caricatured
form, social Darwinism reinforced the notion that Germany was threatened by the other imperial European powers and must either conquer or
be conquered.

3. *Racism.* Nationalism and the social Darwinist sense of struggle
shaded into racism. Race thinking had begun rather innocently in the

eighteenth century, inspired by the travel literature resulting from European exploration of other continents. On the basis of the reports of travelers and missionaries, some eighteenth-century theorists fashioned the myth of the noble savage—the idea that there was something noble, pure, and beautiful about the life of uncivilized or precivilized peoples before the corrupting effects of civilization set in. But most Enlightenment philosophers took a different view. They contended that civilization was vastly superior to the life of savages. As the belief in human rights took hold, however, pigmentation seemed accidental, and savages were seen as simply early human beings on the march of progress.

As scientists of all sorts began to make classifications, some set about trying to classify human groups. Thus entered the concept of race. The supposed differences among races raised questions about the assumption of Enlightenment thinkers like Locke and Claude Helvetius that all human beings are basically alike, that the differences among them are due to differences of nurture and environment, because the mind was simply a *tabula rasa*, a blank slate.

The writer who had the dubious distinction of popularizing the idea that different races had different characteristics was Arthur de Gobineau, a French aristocrat who wrote a four-volume work of pseudoscientific impressionistic anthropology called *The Inequality of the Human Races*. Gobineau argued that the white race was far superior to the black and yellow in intelligence and character, but that it was in danger of being engulfed and its blood adulterated by mixture with inferior dark races. Race mixing, he taught, was the path not to progress but to degeneration. According to Gobineau, the Aryans, who originated in India, were the best of the best, the cream of the white race. He made sure to add that his own group, the French nobility, was part of the Aryan subgroup and the bearer of civilization in France. When race mixing occurred, it was only natural that the mixed breeds that resulted from these unions would join with the lower races in championing the illusion of human equality. He saw America as a prime example of what would result from miscegenation. Nothing productive could result, he claimed, from the combinations of German, Irish, French, and Anglo-Saxon with Indians, Negroes, Spaniards, and Portuguese. "It is quite unimaginable that anything could result from such horrible confusion but an incoherent juxtaposition of the most decadent kinds of people."[4] It was precisely because Hitler held the same notion that he did not care whether the United States entered the war against him. What threat could such a mongrel people pose to the master race?

Gobineau's ideas were taken up by the composer Richard Wagner and German intellectuals who thought that the only thing wrong with Gobineau's thinking was that he was too pessimistic, too preoccupied with decline. It was not too late to arrest the pollution of the racial bloodstream, they contended, if a concerted effort were made to emphasize racial purity. Each national version of racism had its own particular notion of which people was superior, but they all agreed that one people living in Europe was a dangerous enemy because it could pollute the racial bloodstream. This of course was the Jews, the most obvious outsiders and traditional pariahs. Religious hostility to the Jews was long standing and universal throughout Christian Europe, instilled in the Gospels, church services, and passion plays, and it was compounded by the association of the Jews since medieval times with money lending. Forced to live apart in ghettos and forbidden from owning land or engaging in other professions, they were allowed to become moneylenders when this activity was forbidden to Christians. The immigration of Jews from Eastern Europe to Germany made all Jews, assimilated or not, perfect targets for German racism.

But although religious hostility to Jews and Judaism was long standing, "anti-Semitism" was new. Under the influence of the new interest in race and speculation about the link between race and language, the word was coined in Austria in the 1870s. The prominent historian Heinrich von Treitschke said famously, "The Jews are our misfortune." The midcentury literary critic Paul de Lagarde declared them to be a misfortune for all Europe, comparing them with vermin, for which the only remedy was extermination. In the 1890s, the Dreyfus case in France brought fury against the Jews to fever pitch, even in the country that was the home of human rights. In the Russian Empire, where the largest number of European Jews lived, confined to the western territories, they were subjected to regular restrictions and periodic pogroms. In 1905, the Okhrana, the czar's secret police, issued a forgery known as the *Protocols of the Elders of Zion*, which purported to reveal the conspiratorial plans of a cabal of Jewish rabbis plotting to destroy Christianity and take over the world by trickery. Parts of the document were plagiarized from a political satire written in the 1860s by a Francophone Swiss writer who imagined a dialogue between Machiavelli and Montesquieu in hell. The Okhrana simply put Machiavellian language in the mouths of these imagined rabbis. The *Protocols* have had a long and deadly life. In the 1920s, Henry Ford paid for their mass circulation in the United States; the king of Saudi Arabia handed a copy in English to Henry Kissinger the first time Kissinger paid a call on him as secretary of state; they continue to circulate in the Middle East.

Racism blended with anti-Semitism became a powerful organizing principle. Wagner's English-born son-in-law, Houston Stewart Chamberlain, wrote an influential book claiming that there were only two pure races in Europe, the Teutons and the Jews, whom he saw as alien infiltrators threatening the purity of the Teutonic race. A dense and lengthy excursion into European history, this two-tome work was reprinted twenty-four times and made a great impression on Hitler, who had acquired a hatred of Jews in Vienna, even though a sympathetic Jewish bookseller sought to encourage him by buying some of his amateurish drawings. The Nazis disseminated the *Protocols*; the propaganda minister Joseph Goebbels put the message out in films like *Jüd Süss*, and the party hack Julius Streicher did the same in the soft porn of the storm troopers' newspaper, *Der Sturmer*. Children's schoolbooks showed the same story with frightening illustrations in color of evil rapacious Jews.

Hitler planned to make the elite SS the agent of racial purification, and the "final solution" to the Jewish problem was designed to remove all possibility of contamination. The fate of Europe, Hitler said, would rest on the outcome of the struggle between the Aryan and the Semite. It would be a mistake to suppose that Hitler was merely using anti-Semitism to prop up his support among the German people. He was obsessed with the idea that he was leading a war against the supposedly all-powerful Jewish race, so much so that on September 3, 1939, when Britain honored its commitment to Poland and declared war against Germany, thus beginning World War II, Hitler explained the British decision to the German people as nothing more nor less than the result of a Jewish democratic plot. The Jewish democratic global enemy, he said, had succeeded in placing the English people in a state of war with Germany.

5. *Elitism*. Racism was reinforced by a doctrine that came to be called elitism. That, too, had started innocently. The very perceptive Italian political sociologist Gaetano Mosca wrote a book called (in English) *The Ruling Class*[5] in which he argued that all societies are governed by a political class. He was joined by Vilfredo Pareto, an economist and sociologist, who also wrote about "the circulation of elites," the process by which one succeeded another. Mosca deliberately advanced his thesis with the aim of refuting Marx's contention that it was possible to conceive of a future classless society. The implication was also that there could be no true democracy because there would always be a ruling class that would use one ideology or another—he called them "political formulas"—to justify its rule. Parliamentarism was simply an illusion because the ruling class used the system to manipulate the masses into supposing they were choosing their representatives. In reality, the representatives had themselves elected because they could easily control the electoral process.

Mosca lived to regret his early work and to appreciate the virtue of parliamentary government when Mussolini came to power and abolished it. But his and Pareto's ideas, and the notion of Roberto Michels that there was an "iron law of oligarchy"—in other words that democracy is an illusion because all organized social movements ended up with oligarchy— helped fuel the belief that fascism was a doctrine grounded in social and political science.

*6. Crowd Psychology.* Psychologists added fuel to the fire by describing the populace as essentially irrational and easily led by hypnotic leaders. They were sheep waiting to be led, ready victims of some new political religion promising them revenge against their enemies and heaven on earth. The masses crave a sense of power that they cannot experience for themselves, so they identify with some demagogue. Gustave Le Bon wrote, "As soon as a certain number of living beings are gathered together, whether they be animals or men, they place themselves instinctively under the authority of a chief."[6] Wilfred Trotter made a similar case in a book entitled *Instincts of the Herd in Peace and War.*[7] Despots would inevitably rise to power with their support, and once in power they would use the techniques of control made possible by science and crowd psychology to turn the masses into robots or army ants ready to do whatever the state told them to do.

*7. Hero Worship.* Writers like Thomas Carlyle and Friedrich Nietzsche celebrated not the common man but the uncommon man, Carlyle's hero or Nietzsche's overman (*übermensch*), sometimes translated as "superman." Both deplored the tendencies toward materialism and mediocrity they associated with the rise of the masses. Neither offered a political doctrine that could serve as an alternative to democracy but treated its apotheosis of the common man with contempt. Equality, Nietzsche's Zarathustra said, was the poison emitted by the liberal tarantula, the leveler of all greatness. Carlyle denounced liberalism and democracy for emphasizing rights rather than duties. He coined the term "dismal science" for economics because he said all it did was rationalize strivings for material gain rather than higher aspirations. Socialists applauded Carlyle's attack on what he called the cash nexus and his demand that the government take a paternalistic care of the working classes, but he was fixated on the role of heroes, not ordinary people. Nietzsche was a far subtler thinker, but he railed against the triumph of what he called slave morality, the beliefs of Judaism transmitted through Christianity, which undermined the old aristocratic ethos and produced a transvaluation of values. Although Nietzsche's overman was not a racist or a political demagogue but an ideal of aesthetic creativity, his attack on egalitarianism was warmly accepted by the Nazis and found echoes even in so astute a writer as H. L. Mencken, who said that democracy was like putting the inmates in charge of the insane asylum.[8]

*8. Pseudosocialism.* The fascists borrowed from socialism to emphasize the need to achieve social solidarity and to overcome or ignore class distinctions. The Nazis' *eintopf* meals—a one-pot dinner eaten in every neighborhood to emphasize shared sacrifice—harked back to the common tables of Spartan communism. Even Hitler's Volkswagen (literally "the people's car"), like vacations in the countryside for all in the Hitler

Youth, was designed to give the masses a sense of participation in the national enterprise, even as the Nazis singled out for membership in the SS those of the purest Aryan strain. The Nazis were able to appeal to industrialists by promising to use their companies to rebuild Germany, and they reassured them that unlike the communists they had no intention of nationalizing industry. At the same time, they could undercut the socialist and communist appeals to workers by promising full employment and an improved standard of living.

These currents in the realm of ideas served to reinforce skepticism about republican government and democratic values not only among the privileged but ironically also among the lower classes that were the greatest beneficiaries of egalitarianism. Peasant farmers began to resist the appeals of urban liberal and socialist parties and rallied instead to conservative parties, or to new fascist and populist movements. Some workers deserted the socialists for the fascists, and many in the middle classes found in fascism the promise of security and greatness they craved. All of these currents of nineteenth- and early twentieth-century ideas were absorbed by the fascist movements. Mussolini again was very explicit about what fascism would mean:

> The chief epithet of democracy is *all*, a word which has completely filled the nineteenth century. The time has come to say: the *few* and the *elite*. Democracy is on its last legs in every country in the world; in some of them as in Russia, it has been murdered, in others it is falling prey to increasingly obvious decadence. It may be that in the nineteenth century, capitalism needed democracy; today it has no such need. The War was revolutionary in the sense that it liquidated—in rivers of blood—the century of democracy, the century of majority, of numbers, of quantity.[9]

Only dictatorship, he believed, could enforce discipline, respond to the masses' craving for leadership and order, and provide a secular myth to encourage their sacrifice.

Hitler did not like the word "fascism." He preferred the traditional *Autorität*. But he would have agreed completely with Mussolini that

> the world seen through Fascism is not this material world which appears on its surface, in which man is an individual separated from all others and standing by himself, and in which he is governed by a natural law that makes him instinctively live a life of selfish and momentary pleasure. . . . The man of Fascism is an individual who is nation and fatherland, which is a moral law, binding together individuals and the generations into a tradition and a mission, suppressing the instinct for a life enclosed within the brief round of pleasure in order to restore within duty a higher life free from the limits of time and space: a life in which the individual, through the denial of himself, through the sacrifice of his own private interests, through

death itself, realizes that completely spiritual existence in which his value as a man lies.[10]

Fascism and other forms of totalitarianism encourage a belief in the necessity of violence. For Marxists, class struggle is the motor of history; conflict with capitalism is inevitable because the capitalists will not give up their privileges without a fight; the exploited must join together to battle the exploiters, the colonized the imperialists. For fascists, war is the health of the state. Filippo Marinetti, the artist who led the so-called futurist movement, was the most explicitly bloodthirsty:

> We want to glorify war—the only cure for the world—militarism, patriotism, the destructive gesture of the anarchists, the beautiful ideas which kill, and contempt for woman. . . . We want to demolish museums and libraries, fight morality, feminism, and all opportunist and utilitarian cowardice. . . . Standing on the world's summit we launch once again our insolent challenge to the stars.[11]

Taking up Marinetti's line, Mussolini openly challenged Christian pacifism and Immanuel Kant's hope for a world of eternal peace:

> Fascism believes neither in the possibility or the utility of perpetual peace. It repudiates the doctrine of Pacifism. . . . War alone brings up to their highest tension all human energies and puts the stamp of nobility upon the peoples who have the courage to meet it. . . . The Fascist looks on life as duty, ascent, conquest.[12]

Mussolini was hardly as effective at putting his boasts into action as his German partner. The Italian people proved less amenable than Germans to harsh discipline and calls for self-sacrifice in war, and Germany had more of the resources and will to conquest necessary for the mission set for it. Nazi Germany unleashed horrors upon the world and ultimately on the German people as well. In retrospect, it staggers the imagination to try to understand how such a pastiche of half-baked and misbegotten ideas came to be believed so passionately by so many people—in the country that gave so much to Western civilization, the country of humanitarians like Johann Wolfgang Goethe, Friedrich Schiller, and Ludwig von Beethoven and of gifted Jews like Heinrich Heine and the Mendelssohns. That the great mass of the German people could worship a madman and sacrifice their lives for a pathetic fantasy shows all too forcefully how intoxicating simplistic ideas can be when they are propounded by charismatic demagogues and disseminated with modern means of propaganda.

Even more disheartening was the attitude of so many German intellectuals. Despite the book burnings and the expulsion of non-Aryan teachers, the Nazi "new order" was welcomed by most of the faculty and students of the German universities, always excepting the heroic and honorable resistance of the small White Rose movement. The German philosopher who is now said by some to have been the foremost philosopher of the century was the existentialist Martin Heidegger, who joined the Nazi Party and paid his dues every year all the way into 1945. In May 1933, he became the rector of the University of Freiburg in a ceremony in which the anti-Semitic Nazi "Horst Wessel Song" was performed. Heidegger's inaugural address was couched in the metaphysical abstractions for which German thought is well known and which he raised to a new height of obscurity. But it is clear from the speech that he believed the university should be committed to Hitler's new order. He praises the elimination of academic freedom because it is merely "negative." The right course is to devote scientific studies to the nation by work service, military service, and spiritual service, by which he meant commitment to the national destiny as defined by the new National Socialist state. In November 1933, in time for a student celebration, he wrote an article for the student newspaper that was still more explicit:

> The National Socialist revolution rings in the total collapse of our German existence [Dasein]. . . . In you there must unceasingly develop the courage of your sacrifice for the salvation of the essence of our people within their state and for the elevation of its innermost force. Do not let principles and "ideas" be the rules of your existence. The Führer himself, and he alone, is the German reality of today, and of the future, and of its law.
>
> Heil Hitler, Rector Martin Heidegger[13]

After the war, the German refugee philosopher Herbert Marcuse wrote to him to ask how he could have supported Nazism. Heidegger answered evasively, saying that in 1933 he saw in Nazism "a spiritual renovation of all life," but in 1934 he thought differently and resigned his rectorship. Marcuse tried again, asking why he did not see what Nazism represented right away. "People in Germany were exposed to a total perversion of all concepts and feelings," Marcuse wrote,

> which so many among them readily accepted. It cannot be explained otherwise that you, who were able to understand Western philosophers like no one else, could see in Nazism "a spiritual rejuvenation of life in its totality." . . . This is not a political problem, but an intellectual one—I almost want to say a problem of knowledge, of truth. You, the philosopher, have you confused the liquidation of Western existence with its rejuvenation? Was this liquidation not already obvious in every word of the Fuhrer, in every gesture and act of the SA long before 1933?

Heidegger answered by equating the deportation and internment of Germans after the war at the hands of the allies with the Holocaust inflicted on the Jews. Marcuse expressed utter astonishment and castigated Heidegger for persisting in viewing Nazism as a form of spiritual renewal, even after he knew what it had done.[14]

> The failure of even highly intelligent Germans like Heidegger to appreciate the inhumane character of the Nazi version of fascism before it was too late is a cautionary reminder of the susceptibility to delusion that social breakdown can foster. It should have been obvious that the utopian promises of prosperity, unity, and national greatness offered by the Nazi movement (and others like it, including Peronism in Argentina[15]) would serve as excuses for the imposition of totalitarian statism and hate-filled aggressiveness. Nevertheless, millions of Germans rallied to its siren call.

Perhaps in the end it is better to see fascism less as a set of ideas than as what the Nazis called the triumph of the will—a will not to question, not to be skeptical, not to be rational, but to be possessed by a faith that is beyond reason. Fascism was the ultimate repudiation of that celebration of the dignity of man that emerged in the Renaissance. What is especially dismaying is that like an autoimmune disease, which uses the organism's very life-sustaining capacities against itself, fascism used the gifts of science and technology that humanism inspired to assault the human dignity that humanism exalted. The repudiation of individualism in favor of absorption into the state was designed to remake the social order so that it exhibited a pervasive sense of unity, reinforced by propaganda and secret police. The "new order" would be one in which all separateness would be regarded as inimical to the purposes of the society. All associations would be linked to the state and would serve the state in one form or another. Young boys were organized into the Hitler Youth, girls into the Bund Deutsches Mädchen. The Nazi Party became the only legitimate political party, and its function was to knit society and the state together. The SS was to be the elite core of the new society, and reproduction of the racially superior was made a state-supervised activity. The unfit were to be eliminated. The racially mixed were to be stigmatized as inferior. Culture was to be supervised so that art hostile to the ideals of the regime could be censored or eliminated. Italian fascism was hardly as thoroughgoing or ambitious, yet it was Mussolini who coined the term "totalitarian" and defined the goal of fascism as the total unification of the disparate elements of society.

It is some comfort that these regimes collapsed because in the end they could hardly deliver the fantasy they promised, and because they suffered from the effects of dictatorship. In the conduct of the war, they were not as creative, flexible, and productive as the democratic systems they sought to overthrow. There is some comfort, too, in knowing that when people follow a madman, they court their own doom. The Nazi regime, however, was at first very successful in achieving its aims. If there is a single lesson to be drawn from the phenomenon of fascism, it may be that those who value civilization must fight to preserve it by resisting, not appeasing, the enemies of its basic values. Fascism is the antithesis of democracy. In place of the ideal of universal autonomy it substitutes the ideal of submission, or immersion in the wholeness of the state and society. The leader, not the individual, is the master of personal and collective fate. Sacrifice for the nation is the highest duty, and individual fulfillment and diversity are considered anathema. Technology, industry, and art are to be bent to the service of the state. There can be no truly independent sector, whether that of the family, the church, the school, the profession, or industry. Insofar as these institutions are left unincorporated into the state, they are expected to be guided by state authority and bent to its purposes. The ideal of the society is supposed to be the success of the whole rather than the fulfillment of the individual or of subgroups. Fascists very deliberately rejected the individualism and pluralism of democracy in favor of social integration. They defined aesthetic creativity to mean propaganda for social integration and glorification. Censorship of the media of information was taken for granted and indeed was developed to a high art on the theory that, whether truthful or not, information should be disseminated for the purpose of promoting support for the state. Dissent was to be completely suppressed in the name of unity. In all these respects, fascism stood squarely against the traditional religious beliefs and the newer humanistic creeds that had come to define Western civilization.

Although the major fascist regimes of Germany and Italy did not last long enough to reveal their ultimate form, it is clear from what was attempted in their name and what was said in their justification that the aim was a radical transformation of ordinary ways of life in order to promote a disciplined, hierarchical, and totalitarian society in which the ruling elite would serve as controller and mentor, and all "anarchic" elements—free debate, collective bargaining, nonsecular religious ideals, and lifestyles that did not serve the goals of the society—would be eliminated. The adulation of a leader was hardly accidental. The leader was perceived as a kind of demigod whose unique intuitive grasp of the national destiny made him the embodiment of the populace and endowed him with godlike insight into what was needed. His orders were to be obeyed blindly, even when they contradicted the conventional wisdom of specialists like diplomats, industrialists, and generals. The Nazi fixation on Jews was not essential to fascism, but it did partake of the fascist perspective by denying that all people should enjoy the same universal human rights and by demonizing one group as an alien element whose influence would sap the national will and prevent it from realizing its destiny. Labor camps were created to sequester dangerous subversives and enemies and to remove social undesirables from the general population, but in the hands of the Nazis (and their Soviet imitators), they readily became extermination facilities. At bottom, then, fascism turned democracy upside down: it denied that all human beings were endowed with equal rights and proceeded from the assumption that the strong should dominate the weak and even eliminate elements that might somehow interfere with the aims of the state. Instead of empowering individuals, it aimed to use them as cannon fodder for the state, reducing the life of the individual to something of little value next to the survival and triumph of the state.

Nor is the bellicosity of fascist states an accident. However much Germans may have blamed the terms imposed at Versailles as unfair, their passion for the Nazis involved much more than simply a redress of grievance. There was a wish for revenge, to be sure, but also for conquest, on the assumption that the society was menaced by outside powers and ought to display its prowess by defeating and subjugating others. Conquest was at once a motivation and proof of the rightness of the ideology. It made the individual member of the society accepting of dictatorship and committed to the ideals of the state. Even as it inflicted hardships, these were borne as a necessary cost. Fascism encouraged the belief that other peoples were inferior and had to be conquered, either to be eliminated from the gene pool or to serve the ends of the master race.

## NOTES

1. Lawrence Dennis, *The Coming American Fascism* (New York: Harper, 1936).

2. Richard J. Evans, *The Coming of the Third Reich* (London: Penguin, 2003), p. 218.

3. Benito Mussolini (with Giovanni Gentile), "The Doctrine of Fascism" (1932), trans. Douglas Parmee, *Italian Fascisms from Pareto to Gentile*, ed. Adrian Lyttleton (New York: Harper & Row, 1975), p. 49.

4. Arthur de Gobineau, *Essai sur l'Inégalité des Races humaines* (Paris: Firmin-Didot, 1940), vol. 2, p. 536.

5. Gaetano Mosca, *The Ruling Class*, trans. Arthur Livingston (New York: McGraw-Hill, 1939).

6. Gustav Le Bon, *The Crowd: A Study of the Popular Mind* (London: T. Fisher Unwin, 1920), pp. 133–34.

7. Wilfred Trotter, *Instincts of the Herd in Peace and War* (London: Scientific Book Club, 1942).

8. H. L. Mencken, *Notes on Democracy* (London: Jonathan Cape, 1927), pp. 14–15.

9. Mussolini, "Which Way Is the World Going?" (1922), Lyttleton, op. cit., p. 66.

10. Mussolini, op. cit., pp. 37–38.

11. Filippo Tommaso Marinetti, "The Futurist Manifesto," Lyttleton, ed., op. cit., p. 212.

12. Mussolini, op. cit., p. 47.

13. Martin Heidegger, quoted in Richard Farias, *Heidegger and Nazism* (Philadelphia: Temple University Press, 1987), pp. 118–19.

14. Ibid., pp. 284–87.

15. Paul H. Lewis, "Was Peron a Fascist? An Inquiry into the Nature of Fascism," *Journal of Politics* 42, no. 1 (February 1980): p. 245.

# 8

—— ∞∞ ——

# Realism in Foreign Policy

"Let's face it: The emigration of Jews from the Soviet Union is not an objective of American foreign policy. And if they put Jews into gas chambers in the Soviet Union, it is not an American concern. It may be a humanitarian concern."

—Assistent to the President Henry Kissinger speaking privately to President Richard Nixon, March 31, 1973, as recorded on a White House tape recorder

"Realism" is the name given to the analysis of international relations that served as the matrix for the policy of containment adopted by the Western alliance during the Cold War and continues to influence thinking about foreign policy. Realists sharply criticize the tendency to rely on international law or to allow moral and humanitarian considerations to override concerns for the national interest. They start from the premise that the international system is an anarchic collection of sovereign states motivated by self-interest and the calculus of power, measured ultimately by the ability to prevail in war. They regard as naive "idealists" who hope that this anarchic system can be overcome by transferring the rule of law from domestic settings onto a global stage and erecting international systems of government. They point out that invoking moral standards ignores the reality of moral relativism and invests conflicts with self-righteous rationalizations that only make them harder to resolve. They distrust the expectation that transnational institutions such as the League of Nations and its successor, the United Nations, can become effective instruments for deterring aggression and punishing violations of international law and covenants protecting human rights. In their view, the best way to manage conflicts is by relying on traditional methods such as the balance of power.

Realism derives most immediately from Bismarckian *realpolitik*, the nineteenth-century attitude emphasizing the play of force. In essence, it is a venerable tough-minded understanding of the way the world works that can be traced back to Thucydides' *History of the Peloponnesian War*. In the famous dialogue of the Athenian ambassadors with the commissioners of the Spartan colonists on the island of Melos, the Athenians demanded that the Melians submit to their imperial power. When the Melians demurred, insisting on remaining neutral and independent, the Athenians replied that having saved all of Greece by defeating the Persians, they now expected acceptance of their leadership and control. The Melians objected that the demand was unjust since they had been neutral. At that point, the Athenian ambassadors are reported to have told them that "justice is what is decided when equal forces are opposed," but that otherwise the strong impose and the weak acquiesce.[1] In other words, as modern realists would say, national self-interest and calculations of relative power, not morality, dictate the options available to statesmen and the likely conduct of nation-states.

During the early period of the Cold War, this understanding was elaborated and expounded most influentially in the work of Hans J. Morgenthau, George F. Kennan,[2] and Reinhold Niebuhr.[3] They warned that if the leaders of two rival superpowers allowed themselves to be guided by considerations of moral superiority, the nuclear arms race might result in an apocalyptic conflict. The title of one of Niebuhr's books implied what the realists were thinking: *Moral Man and Immoral Society*. In other words, what holds for personal conduct, where moral considerations matter, cannot hold for statecraft. The world, Morgenthau contended, is an anarchic collection of sovereign states pursuing separate national interests and amassing whatever power they can in order to advance their objectives. To preserve peace it was essential for statesmen to recognize this reality and seek accommodations through alliances that would create a balance of power. Throughout history, the only sure basis for peace had been the balance of power. Wars resulted when the balance was allowed to break down.

In line with this way of thinking, Kennan wrote to his diplomatic colleague Charles E. Bohlen in 1945 that the United States should be prepared to make a "decent and definite compromise" with the Soviet Union, one that would "divide Europe frankly into spheres of influence . . . keep ourselves out of the Russian sphere and keep the Russians out of ours."[4] Instead of banking on some utopian dream of world government, they believed, it was far better to rely on the balance of power, which had worked in the past to keep the peace and could work again. Later "neorealists" adapted the theory to a world that was not totally anarchic but was stabilized by a bipolar system of alliances, in effect a new form of the balance of power. The realists also argued that containment would eventually lead to the reform of the Soviet system or its collapse. At the outset of the Cold War, they predicted—as it turned out, with great prescience—that if the West patiently pursued containment, the communist bloc would disintegrate from its own internal divisions, and the inefficiencies and inequities of Soviet communism would force fundamental reform.

## MORGENTHAU AS THE PRINCIPAL THEORIST

Morgenthau was the most theoretical and academically influential of the school. He came to America in the 1930s as a refugee from Nazi persecution. In his prime, he taught at the University of Chicago and wrote widely read books and articles. His gifts as a teacher, lecturer, and writer made him a person of great influence who challenged the conventional wisdom at a time when the United States was trying to come to grips with its new role in the world in the wake of the Second World War. On Morgenthau's death, Henry Kissinger wrote that "all of us teaching in this field had to start with the ground he had laid."[5]

Earlier theorists laid the foundations of realism. Both the identification of interest as the key motivation of social behavior and the general rejection of idealism in favor of realism had a pedigree. Already in the eighteenth century, David Hume had laid down the principle *"that it is only from the selfishness and confined generosity of man, along with the scanty provision that nature has made for his wants, that justice derives its origin."*[6] As Albert Hirschmann has shown,[7] the emphasis on interests as the founding category of behavior arose in early modern times out of uneasiness with the traditional view that destructive passions could be constrained by moral admonitions. Niccolò Machiavelli rejected the idealized picture of the Christian king in the "mirror of princes" writings and distinguished sharply between "the effectual truth of the matter rather than its imagined one," unlike those "who have imagined republics and principalities that have never been seen or known to exist in reality."[8] Machiavelli and many who followed in his footsteps, whether they acknowledged him or not, rejected the classical attempt to make the ideal either a model to be copied or a teleological essence immanent in reality. The stress on realism was reiterated by Spinoza when he attacked utopian philosophers who "conceive men not as they are but as they would like them to be."[9] This rejection of the link between ideal and real was also prefigured in the literature that arose in the Renaissance dealing with constitutional "reason of state"—the belief expressed by a host of political theorists following Machiavelli that in extreme circumstances, the moral law may need to be suspended in order to preserve the existence of the state, which is the sine qua non of any legal order.[10] Machiavelli said it is better for a prince to be feared than loved and that in matters of war and peace, "where there is no court of appeal, we must look at the final result . . . because the ordinary people are always taken in by the appearance or outcome of a thing; and in the world there is nothing but ordinary people."[11] Thomas Hobbes drew the logical conclusion that while it was possible for those in a state of nature to escape the terrors of civil war by accepting an all-powerful sovereign, international relations would remain in a state of nature, and therefore at risk of war, because no one sovereign would be capable of subordinating all the others.[12] Power, not justice, determined the order of the world when nations came into conflict, whatever theorists like Hugo Grotius might say about the bearing of the law of nations.

More proximately, Morgenthau's viewpoint is foreshadowed in the contrast drawn by Max Weber in his famous essay on "Politics as a Vocation" between the "ethic of ultimate ends"—the code of ethics that applies to personal conduct—and the "ethic of responsibility"—the pragmatic code that applies to political life. Weber's distinction goes some way toward a possible resolution of the paradox in Morgenthau's thinking. Like Weber, Morgenthau was not counseling amorality but rather recognition that peace is the necessary precondition of all morality and that to achieve peace it is necessary to accept inevitable differences in values and forge agreements based on shared interests. That recognition, rather than an insistence on following universal standards of good and evil, was for him, as it had been for Weber, the necessary condition of responsible statesmanship. The alternative was a quixotic posture that would inevitably lead to self-destruction.

In Morgenthau's case, this conception of politics probably attracted him in the first instance because of the vicissitudes of his upbringing and life experience. As a refugee, Morgenthau bore a double burden, the first of which was his Jewishness. Like other European Jews, whether religious or secularized, he was reared in a culture that revered the traditional prophetic insistence on the precepts of moral law but had come to look with skepticism on social ideologies that promised progress. The persistence of persecution despite the Enlightenment's call for toleration belied such promises. Already at the age of eighteen, in 1922, when he was asked by a teacher in his *gymnasium* to write about his aspirations, Morgenthau denounced as a "crying injustice and a dishonoring humiliation" the accusations directed against him solely on account of his Jewishness, accusations that were producing a "social ostracism destructive of the ties of love and friendship." "The pressure of anti-Semitism," he observed, "not only leads the mind astray, but it also shatters the foundations of morality. . . . When I see how little the enemy respects the law, how he declares me to be without the protection of the law, I easily might be persuaded that in dealing with such an enemy I could likewise dispense with justice and the law."[13]

This sting of exclusion may well have led Morgenthau to project his own experience onto a larger canvas by depicting the world as a place in which law and morality offered no protection to the weak and powerless. The same disillusionment with the promises of liberalism and Enlightenment led other German and Austrian Jews to clutch at a variety of alternatives. Freud's psychoanalysis allowed for the possibility of individual liberation from the tyranny of the instinctual, but not for social emancipation, because civilization rested on a renunciation of the instinctual that the "masses" were incapable of achieving; the best that could be hoped for would be that they would be ruled by superior men of reason.[14] Theodor Herzl embraced a liberal form of Zionism as the only answer to the persistence of anti-Semitism. Max Horkheimer, Theodor Adorno, Erich Fromm, and Herbert Marcuse became Marxists, convinced that socialism would resolve the economic inequities and moral alienation that bourgeois liberalism had produced. Hannah Arendt first adopted the existentialism of Karl Jaspers and Martin Heidegger before she developed her own idiosyncratic view of the human condition. Leo Strauss denounced not only liberalism, but the entire "modern project," with its absorption in hedonism, libertinism, nonteleological science, and survivalism, as a renunciation of the transcendental, teleological "natural right" foundation of Western civilization.[15]

The other burden Morgenthau brought with him to America was his German upbringing. This upbringing had imbued the younger Morgenthau with the teachings of Friedrich Nietzsche that life is an unending struggle for power and that belief in God was "dead,"[16] along with an acceptance of Bismarckian *realpolitik* inspired by political and intellectual developments in central Europe from the nineteenth century into the twentieth. Morgenthau was introduced to the study of international politics in two seminars taught by the historian Hermann Oncken, and he gradually became convinced by his historical research that the experience of the German states was in no way unusual, because all politics was a constant struggle for advantage, mitigated by the formation of alliances and stabilized by the balance of power.

When he was forced to leave Europe for America, Morgenthau set out to educate Americans out of what he thought was their seriously mistaken addiction to idealist illusions—one that was rooted in the country's beginnings. As historians have often noted, many early American settlers imagined themselves to be another chosen people, formed, like the biblical original, in an exodus from tyranny and determined to build a better world, even a New Jerusalem—"a city upon a hill"—in this Promised Land. This self-understanding brought with it a fervent moralism, a belief that there were standards of right and wrong and that governing authority was established by God to foster good and chastise evil.

In the early years of the republic, moreover, foreign policy was something Americans thought they could largely afford not to worry about. As president, George Washington famously advised his contemporaries to avoid foreign entanglements:

> The great rule of conduct for us, in regard to foreign nations is in extending our commercial relations to have with them as little political connection as possible. So far as we have already formed engagements let them be fulfilled, with perfect good faith. Here let us stop.
>
> Europe has a set of primary interests which to us have none, or a very remote relation. Hence she must be engaged in frequent controversies, the causes of which are essentially foreign to our concerns. Hence therefore it must be unwise in us to implicate ourselves by artificial ties, in the ordinary vicissitudes of her politics, or the ordinary combinations and collisions of her friendships, or enmities.
>
> Our detached and distant situation invites and enables us to pursue a different course. . . . Why forego the advantages of so peculiar a situation? Why quit our own to stand upon foreign ground? Why, by interweaving our destiny with that of any part of Europe, entangle our peace and prosperity in the toils of European ambition, rivalship, interest, humour, or caprice?[17]

Morgenthau contended, however, that the country had not been as isolationist or addicted to moralism as might be supposed. In 1793, the fledgling American republic was asked by revolutionary France to side with its Napoleonic regime against Britain and other monarchies, to repay the aid the French had given Americans in winning independence from their mother country. Washington declined and instead issued a neutrality proclamation. On his behalf, Alexander Hamilton explained that although the United States had an obligation to France, even a contract needs to be given a reasonable construction. Self-preservation is the first duty of a nation, he argued, and good faith does not require that a nation jeopardize its own existence, as the United States would if it were to enter this war on the side of France and by so doing risk going down to defeat with her. When the French helped us, he added, they were not being purely altruistic; they gave us support because they had an interest in seeing the British defeated.

The consequences of the action of a private person affect only himself, Hamilton went on—much as Morgenthau would have said—whereas the consequences of the action of a state affect all its citizens and may affect generations to come. An individual may decide to sacrifice himself by acting in a way that is not in his self-interest, but a state is not justified in doing the same, except only under dire conditions and with the narrowest constraints. We are told, Hamilton said, that the cause of France is the cause of liberty, and that if France falls, we will be next. We must ask two questions on this score: Is this so and if it is so, would the effects of our intervention be greater than evils that might flow from it? To both questions Hamilton answered that the national interest of the United States would be to remain neutral.

That was realism American style, and Morgenthau approved of it. American foreign policy began to go wrong when Jefferson injected moral considerations into the nation's strategic calculus and especially later on when President William McKinley claimed to have been inspired by the voice of God to annex the Philippines. Moralism reached its high point under Woodrow Wilson. Morgenthau's comments about Wilson inevitably carry over to several of his successors, notably Ronald Reagan and George W. Bush, but also to Franklin Roosevelt, Jimmy Carter, and Bill Clinton. Wilson, said Morgenthau,

> projects the national moral standards onto the international scene not only with the legitimate claim of reflecting the national interest, but with the politically and morally unfounded claim of providing moral standards for all mankind to conform to in concrete political action. Through the intermediary of the universal moral appeal, the national and the universal interest become one and the same thing. What is good for the crusading country is by definition good for all mankind, and if the rest of mankind refuses to accept such claims to universal recognition, it must be converted with fire and sword.[18]

Morgenthau thought that however admirable and successful American values had been in inspiring patriotic self-sacrifice, economic betterment, and continental expansion, these beliefs had given Americans a dangerously naive and potentially self-destructive view of their role in the world. For as they ventured outside their own hemisphere, from the turn of the twentieth century onward, they had failed to distinguish between domestic circumstances and the very different conditions that prevailed elsewhere and in relations among states. This was a Hobbesian, not a Lockean universe. Americans had come to confuse their national self-interest with the conviction that it was their calling—their quasi-religious mission—to lead a new crusade to remake the world in their image. Morgenthau thought this view a gross delusion. Wilson was wrong when he sought to destroy balance-of-power diplomacy and replace it by a scheme of world government. Franklin Delano Roosevelt followed in Wilson's footsteps when he agreed to the demand for "unconditional surrender" from the Axis powers, and when he imagined that the United Nations would be a form of world government that would make war obsolete and sweep away power politics and the balance of power, ignoring Churchill's misgivings. Roosevelt's secretary of state, Cordell Hull, said that with the founding of the United Nations, the age of power politics—with its balances of power, spheres of influence, and alliances, all aimed at national advantage and aggrandizement—would be replaced by an era of international collaboration. In fact, Morgenthau observed, the UN "did not put an end to power politics. . . . On the contrary it has become the forum where the nations of the world fight their battles for power neither with the weapons of war nor with those of traditional diplomacy, but through the legalistic manipulation of the procedures, especially those of voting, of international organization." By its structure and design, he added, the UN "is unable to make a substantial contribution to the peaceful settlement of conflicts among the great powers. On the contrary, its successful operation is predicated upon the absence of serious conflict among them."[19]

The great danger of the psychology induced by the Cold War, Morgenthau came to think, was that it was producing a new form of nationalism cloaked in universalistic moral disguise that could have catastrophic consequences. Inevitably, those who identified the national interest with some presumably universal mission, whether it was communism or the cause of "the free world," would delude themselves into thinking that their standard of what is right must be imposed on others. That impulse, if carried too far, would be resisted by the supposed beneficiaries, and the result would be war on an unprecedented scale:

> The morality of the particular group, far from limiting the struggle for power on the international scene, gives that struggle a ferociousness and intensity not known to other ages. For the claim to universality which inspires the moral code of one particular group is incompatible with the identical claim of another group; the world has room for only one and the other must be destroyed. Thus, carrying their idols before them, the nationalistic masses of our time meet in the same international arena, each group convinced that it executes the mandate of history, that it does for humanity what it seems to do for itself, and that it fulfills a sacred mission ordained by Providence, however defined. Little do they know that they meet under an empty sky from which the gods have departed.[20]

## THE PARADOX OF PERSONAL AND POLITICAL

To reflect on Morgenthau's character, his work, and his influence is to be struck anew by a long-recognized paradox at the heart of his beliefs and theorizing. Morgenthau believed as passionately as any religious believer or Kantian humanist that there is a universally valid moral code distinguishing right from wrong that must govern personal behavior. "I have time and again expressed my belief in an objective universal moral order," he wrote to a correspondent.[21] Walter Lippmann had good reason to tell him, "You are not the harsh realist you are painted but the most moral man I know."[22] But Morgenthau believed no less passionately that it was folly to suppose that this same universal moral code could apply to the conduct of states. "Justice among nations has no concrete universal meaning," he declared.[23] This distinction made him seem not only harsh but seemingly indifferent to questions of right and wrong in international relations. Morgenthau's realist theory, in other words, appears to have accepted the Hobbesian formula whereby, given the impossibility of supranational government,[24] international relations must remain in a state of nature, not subject to any moral law but rather in a condition of inherent insecurity in which the distribution of power, not justice or international law, determines the relations of states to each other.

In some respects, this apparent contradiction can be explained away, though not so fully as to allay all serious objections. On any careful examination,[25] it becomes clear that Morgenthau was not a Hobbesian *tout court*, content to leave international relations to the play of force, but rather an unsentimental analyst who contended, in the light of overwhelming evidence, that what holds for individual conduct, where codes of justice are enforceable, does not hold for the conduct of states, where such codes are unenforceable. Even while still a young scholar, Morgenthau concluded, against the views of most of his teachers, that international law could have little effect in the real world of statecraft because the force necessary to assure compliance was not the monopoly of a central government but dispersed among the states that were supposed to be held accountable. Its effectiveness "depends almost exclusively and most often very directly on the will of the individual nations and their representatives, in other words, on those who are at the same time the subjects of international law."[26]

But Morgenthau did not simply throw up his hands and accept the proverbial law of the jungle as the norm of interstate relations. He thought that a standard of morality for international relations could be identified, one that would arise from the primacy of self-interest in actual behavior, not from altruism or a sense of duty, and would be expressed in a willingness to achieve peace based on the accommodation of differing national interests. In other words, Morgenthau's conception of the national interest resembled Tocqueville's endorsement of "self-interest rightly understood." It was a false dichotomy, he maintained, to suppose that the choice in foreign policy is between political morality and political immorality. The real choice is between a set of moral principles divorced from political reality and another derived from that reality. "Self-preservation both for the individual and for societies is . . . not only a biological and psychological necessity but, in the absence of an overriding moral obligation, a moral duty as well. In the absence of an integrated international society, the attainment of a modicum of order and the realization of a minimum of moral values are predicated on the existence of national communities capable of preserving order and realizing moral values within the limits of their power."[27] The very character of the nation-state as the primary actor in world affairs, he thought, contains a latent injunction to moral behavior. Just as the sovereign state exists to prevent domestic anarchy, so the task of the statesman is to seek peace abroad in the interest of preserving the state from external dangers. The resort to war risks the state's very existence. Even if war results in victory, it is almost always costly in life and treasure and can inflict a sense of humiliation that may lead the defeated to nurse resentments and seek revenge. Negotiated settlements and the maintenance of a balance of power[28] are more likely to serve the interest of the state in self-preservation and the improvement of domestic prosperity. A policy of seeking and preserving peace is all the more important, he thought, now that the advent of total war and the looming threat of a nuclear doomsday have made the resort to force far more dangerous than ever. The moral path in international relations is therefore to strive for at least a modicum of civilized order and decency, and to try if at all possible to avoid the calamity that modern warfare would entail.

In developing this theory of international relations, Morgenthau began from the premise that the interpersonal is not the international. In the interpersonal realm, altruism will often be rewarded with respect, gratitude, and even love, but in international relations it can lead to quixotic crusades or invite disaster at the hands of those ready to take advantage of weakness. In relations with others we can usually assume that obligations will be reciprocal—if only because they are entered into in the context of a culture in which legal rights and duties are ultimately enforced by law and sanctions. By contrast, states operate in a setting in which, as the sophists liked to say, justice turns out to be what is in the interest of the stronger. An admirable adherence to moral principle in matters of individual conduct therefore becomes naive moralism in matters of foreign policy. The Melians insisted on appealing to the Athenians' sense of justice and paid the price for doing so. Realism amounted to restating a classical recognition of the moral implications of the critical difference between the personal and the political.

But this distinction was not as starkly amoral as it seemed because it did not leave international relations completely without a standard of right conduct. What Morgenthau objected to was the "utopian" or "perfectionist" view that insisted on applying only the highest standards of disinterested justice to the conduct of states. Such "idealists" were apt to suppose that human beings are basically well intentioned but sometimes misguided, and that they could be brought to a better standard of behavior by being reminded of what reason and morality dictate. Morgenthau sided with those who have a far more pessimistic attitude toward human nature. He thought that people were likely to be driven by considerations of self-interest and that states would always seek to aggrandize themselves at the expense of others. International relations were therefore inevitably governed by the pursuit of power. It was sheer self-delusion to suppose, as benighted idealists did, that "the era of power politics" could be brought to an end and that the balance of power could somehow be replaced as an instrument of stability by the adoption of universally binding rules and the creation of ostensibly supranational bodies that had no power of their own with which to constrain nation-states. The best that statesmanship could achieve would be a compromise peace based on the recognition of mutual interest. A foreign policy grounded in considerations of national interest was more likely to lead to a peaceful world of live-and-let-live than one directed by self-righteous moralism cloaking national interest in dogmatic ideology—and peace was after all something not only highly desirable from a moral point of view but the very sine qua non of civilized life. Indeed, Morgenthau added, states commonly recognize an obligation not to inflict death and suffering through mass killings in times of peace, even when such action can be thought to serve a "'higher purpose,' such as the national interest."[29]

Just as Machiavelli noted that armed prophets have succeeded and unarmed prophets have failed, Morgenthau noted that all successful statesmen had made the national interest the basis of their foreign policy, and all others, whether idealists like Wilson or power-mad dictators like Hitler, had invited disaster. Moralism all too readily disguises the sort of chauvinistic *Gott mit uns* fanaticism that sends innocent youth to war regardless of the consequences, whether out of nationalistic fervor, misguided idealism, or blind obedience to the classical maxim, *Fiat iustitia, pereat mundi* (Let justice be done even if the world perishes). The prudence required by realism would be guided by moral principles defined by consequences rather than good intentions. By conceiving of conflicts among nations as confrontations between good and evil and demanding total victory and unconditional surrender, the leaders of states risk far worse outcomes than might be achieved by accepting compromises that respect the basic interests of all parties. To allow a belief in the superiority of one's own way of life to override respect for the right of people elsewhere to follow a different way of life is to behave in an arrogant manner that is apt to be counterproductive and even self-destructive. This was, Morgenthau insisted, not a counsel of immorality or even of amorality but of prudence.

In 1959, Morgenthau became embroiled in a controversy that made perfectly clear his concern for personal morality. This was the result of a notorious scandal in that year over a television quiz show called

*Twenty-One* that paid out what was then a lot of money to contestants who answered twenty-one questions of increasing difficulty. The program proved to be very popular until a disgruntled former contestant caused a sensation by revealing that it was rigged: the producers were giving out the answers in advance to favored contestants. The main beneficiary of this covert coaching was Charles Van Doren, an instructor in English literature at Columbia University and the articulate and handsome son of the poet Mark Van Doren and nephew of the colonial historian Carl Van Doren. For weeks he had been a national celebrity who seemed to display a phenomenal range of knowledge coupled with a boyish anxiety that turned out to be an act. After being pressured to confess that he had been a party to a hoax, Columbia fired him and Morgenthau denounced him in the *New York Times Magazine* for betraying his calling as an intellectual and an academic. When many Columbia students sent in anonymous letters defending Van Doren and signed a petition calling for his reinstatement, Morgenthau laid into them in a memorable essay in the *New Republic* entitled "On the Sanctity of Moral Law." In it he made clear that Van Doren's behavior was a grave violation of the duty to be truthful that should guide everyone, especially intellectuals. It is a remarkable document that deserves to be quoted at some length not only because of what it says about Morgenthau's personal values but also because it exposes the essential difficulty of a thoroughgoing realism in foreign policy:

> You are sorry about losing an attractive teacher and you hate to see that teacher suffer; nothing else counts. But there is something else that counts and that is the sanctity of the moral law.
>
> All men—civilized and barbarian—in contrast to the animals, are born with a moral sense; that is to say, as man is by nature capable of making logical judgments, so is he capable by nature of making moral judgments. . . . Civilized man shares with the barbarian the faculty of making moral judgments, but excels him in that he is capable of making the right moral judgments, knowing why he makes them. He knows—as Socrates, the Greek tragedians . . . the Biblical prophets, and the great moralists and tragedians of all the ages know—what is meant by the sanctity of the moral law.
>
> The moral law is not made for the convenience of man, rather it is an indispensable precondition for his civilized existence. It is one of the great paradoxes of civilized existence that . . . it is not self-contained but requires for its fulfillment transcendent orientations. The moral law provides one of them. . . .
>
> . . . This connection between our civilized existence and the moral law explains the latter's sanctity. By tinkering with it, by sacrificing it for individual convenience, we are tinkering with ourselves as civilized beings, we are sacrificing our own civilized existence.[30]

These are clearly the words of a man for whom moral rectitude was no mere empty platitude, and of an intellectual who took his calling as a teacher as reverently as a monastic his vows. His eloquent rebuke brings to mind the verbal thunderbolts launched by the prophet Amos against those who were violating the Mosaic law. And a year later, in *The Purpose of American Politics*,[31] he made clear that he believed in the existence of a transcendental set of moral ideals not just as a matter of personal conviction but as standards for human conduct that do not arise from human nature but from reflection, and which alone imbue human existence and behavior with purpose.

In his lifetime and beyond it, Morgenthau's critique struck home. Not that the decision makers in Washington always followed Morgenthau's advice. Morgenthau supported Truman's decision to send American armed forces to protect South Korea from invasion by North Korea because it reflected a determination by the United States and its allies to maintain the balance of power in the Far East and regional stability in Asia. But when President Johnson decided to expand American support for the regime in South Vietnam, out of fear that its fall would jeopardize U.S. national interests in the region and damage the nation's credibility elsewhere, he strongly opposed that policy from the outset, contending that it reflected a gross exaggeration of the actual danger.

Given that precedent, he would probably have opposed President Clinton's decision to intervene forcibly in Bosnia and Kosovo in the 1990s to protect human rights because our national interest was not directly affected by whatever Serbs, Bosnians, Croatians, and Kosovars did to each other. He would surely have opposed the second Bush administration's decision to engage in a preventive war to topple Saddam Hussein merely on the supposition that he had weapons of mass destruction and might use them against us or our allies or pass them on to terrorists. And he would have condemned no less strongly the rationalization of this war as an effort to spread liberty and democracy in the Arab world. He taught that American foreign policy should not aim to export American-style democracy or protect the world from some other system. Its purpose should be the protection of national security, nothing more or less. To deviate from this policy would only invite enmity among those who would resent American interference in their own internal affairs. (Kissinger's private remark to Nixon, cited in the epigraph above, is in keeping with Morgenthau's view that national interest should not be confused with humanitarian considerations.)

Precisely the sense of national mission with respect to human rights or freedom and democracy that Morgenthau warned against reemerged as a motif of American foreign policy, especially in the administrations of Carter, Reagan, and George W. Bush. Morgenthau supported programs like the Marshall Plan and Point Four aid to developing countries because these were programs that would promote global stability and so serve the national interest. But he would surely have been critical of the renewed injection of morality into foreign policy in the name of advancing human rights and promoting democratization. He acknowledged that there was a deplorable lack of regard for human rights in many parts of the world, but he cautioned against framing foreign policy to allow for interventionism on this score. He denied that human rights are "of universal validity" or are as an "inalienable" as they are said to be in the U.S. Declaration of Independence:

> There exists of necessity a relativism in the relation between moral principles and foreign policy that one cannot overlook if one wants to do justice to the principles of morality in international relations. . . . Certain principles are obeyed by certain nations, by certain political civilizations, and are not obeyed by others.
>
> . . . Human rights are filtered through the intermediary of historic and social circumstances, which will lead to different results in different times and under different circumstances. . . .You have only to look at the complete lack of respect for human rights in many nations, or even most nations. . . .
>
> . . . We can tell the Soviet Union, and we should from time to time tell the Soviet Union, that its treatment of minorities is incompatible with our conception of human rights. But once we have said this we will find that there is very little more we can do to put this statement into practice. . . .
>
> . . . The United States is a great power with manifold interests throughout the world, of which human rights is only one and not the most important one, and the United States is incapable of consistently following the path of the defense of human rights without putting itself into a Quixotic position.[32]

In keeping with Morgenthau's teachings, realists believe that national security and the national interest require that force be used with the greatest possible restraint and only in self-defense, not preemptively or preventively. They argue that strong nations have no business imposing their values on other peoples, and that when they intervene unilaterally for whatever morally laudable motive, they risk making matters even worse. When it acts without restraint, the United States sets a bad example, weakening efforts to use diplomacy and build alliances, fomenting resentment, and creating divisions at home.

Realism can be a snare. A foreign policy based on narrow national self-interest can be ultimately self-defeating if it entails support for repressive regimes. When they are overthrown, as happened in Iran in 1979, popular backlash can turn against those countries that supported the regime or intervened on its behalf. In the absence of any standard of moral conduct in international relations, or any organizational mechanism for promoting collective security, it is hardly likely that the world will tend toward equilibrium based on a balance of forces as though it were a natural system guided by the laws of physics or biology.

Realism also raises serious questions about the character of the world community and the responsibility of those states with power to affect the course of civilization. Does not anarchy on any scale, whether in a neighborhood, a nation, or a world of nation-states, invite a lawless resort to violence that can embolden aggressors and make onlookers indifferent to the suffering of victims? Under modern conditions of "globalization," when there is so much interdependence, is there not a real and present danger that the use of force by even a distant regional actor can affect the vital interests of other states? Should there be no method and no agreed-upon principles for imposing common sanctions on regimes that are grossly oppressive to their own subjects? In other words, should respect for the sovereignty of the state preclude intervention to prevent "ethnic cleansing" or other campaigns of repression approaching genocidal proportions? Does not the threat posed by nonstate actors with potential access to weapons of mass destruction justify attacks against states that support and harbor them? Should the distinction between democratic and nondemocratic states be ignored as a moralistic diversion, or might it be true that democratic states are apt not to make war against each other whereas authoritarian regimes are likely to be more reckless?

If prudence is the standard of policy, it is not always clear that a policy of restraint is the best course, especially under conditions in which it is difficult if not impossible to foresee a looming threat in time to prepare for it. John Lewis Gaddis has argued that in the face of the threat from terrorism, prudence requires a preemptive strategy, though he admits that it entails a certain degree of arrogance:

> A nation that began with the belief that it could not be safe as long as pirates, marauders, and the agents of predatory empires remained active along its borders has now taken the position that it cannot be safe as long as terrorists and tyrants remain active anywhere in the world. That conclusion surely reflects prudence: where the nation's security is at stake, one can hardly be too careful.[33]

Realist theory may well be less relevant now than it was during the Cold War because the danger the world faces is posed not only by an unstable state system but also by the rise of shadowy nonstate actors who may attain access to destructive weapons formerly monopolized by states. These groups, moreover, are driven by an ideology that denies the very assumption on which the belief in self-interest rests, namely the view that all actors are driven by a concern for self-preservation. National self-interest is not for them a common coin for trade and bargaining. Realism enshrines a moral relativism that is useful as a counsel for peace but that can also blind people to gross injustice, including genocide, when they are not directly threatened, and provide an all too easy excuse for indifference to abuses. It seems to propose that those with the means to prevent injustice should simply turn aside from the systematic violation of human rights on the ground that peace among states is so overriding a moral concern that only violations of state sovereignty justify the use of sanctions. This very attitude paved the way for the Holocaust and for the slaughters of Cambodia and Rwanda. The reverse of this attitude helped bring about the end of apartheid in South Africa and of ethnic cleansing in Yugoslavia. Under modern circumstances of global shrinkage and interdependence, perhaps the only truly realistic policy is to recognize that national self-interest is bound up inextricably with the future of freedom and democracy in the world.

## NOTES

1. Thucydides, *The Peloponnesian War*, trans. Stephen Lattimore (Indianapolis: Hackett, 1998), p. 295.

2. See especially George F. Kennan, *American Diplomacy, 1900–1950* (Chicago: University of Chicago Press, 1984); *Around the Cragged Hill: A Personal and Political Philosophy* (New York: Norton, 1993); and George F. Kennan and John Lukacs, eds., *George F. Kennan and the Origins of Containment, 1944–1946* (Columbia: University of Missouri Press, 1997).

3. See Reinhold Niebuhr, *Moral Man and Immoral Society: A Study in Ethics and Politics* (New York: Scribner, 1932), and *Christianity and Power Politics* (Hamden, CT: Archon Books, 1969).

4. Charles E. Bohlen, *Witness to History* (New York: Norton, 1973), p. 175.

5. Henry A. Kissinger, "A Gentle Analyst of Power: Hans Morgenthau," *New Republic*, 2–9 August 1980, pp. 12–14.

6. David Hume, *A Treatise of Human Nature*, in Hume's *Moral and Political Philosophy*, bk. 3, ed. Henry D. Aiken (New York: Hafner, 1948), p. 64, italics in the original.

7. Albert O. Hirschman, *The Passions and the Interests: Political Arguments for Capitalism before Its Triumph* (Princeton, NJ: Princeton University Press, 1977).

8. Machiavelli, *The Prince*, trans. Mark Musa (New York: St. Martin's, 1964), p. 149.

9. Cited in Hirschman, op. cit., p. 13.

10. See Friedrich Meinecke, *Machiavellism: The Doctrine of Raison d'état and Its Place in Modern History*, trans. Douglas Scott (New Haven, CT: Yale University Press, 1957), and Carl J. Friedrich, *Constitutional Reason of State* (Providence, RI: Brown University Press, 1956). As Friedrich points out (p. 1), these theorists saw the protection of the state as "the essential prerequisite of virtue." Thus, *salus populi suprema lex est* was to be understood as an injunction allowing resort to extraordinary measures when necessary to preserve the fabric of civilization in which moral conduct is possible. When President Abraham Lincoln suspended

the right of habeas corpus to prosecute the war to preserve the union, he can be said to have been acting in accordance with this tradition.

11. Machiavelli, op. cit., p. 149.

12. Compare Morgenthau: "No society exists coextensive with the presumed range of a world state. . . . [T]he peoples of the world are not willing to accept world government, and their overriding loyalty to the nation erects an insurmountable obstacle to its achievement." Hans J. Morgenthau, *Politics among Nations: The Struggle for Power and Peace*, 3rd ed. (New York: Knopf, 1962), p. 511.

13. Hans J. Morgenthau, "Fragment of an Intellectual Autobiography: 1904–1932," in Thompson and Meyers, op. cit., p. 2.

14. See especially his letter to Albert Einstein entitled "Why War?" in Sigmund Freud, *Collected Papers*, ed. James Strachey (New York: Basic Books, 1960), vol. 5, pp. 273–87, and Philip Rieff, *Freud: The Mind of the Moralist* (New York: Viking, 1959), pp. 220–56.

15. See Leo Strauss, *Natural Right and History* (Chicago: University of Chicago Press, 1953).

16. This influence is stressed by Christopher Frei, *Hans J. Morgenthau: An Intellectual Biography* (Baton Rouge: Louisiana State University Press, 2001), pp. 99–113.

17. "Washington's Farewell Address," Richard D. Heffner, ed., *A Documentary History of the United States* (New York: New American Library, 1952), p. 63.

18. Morgenthau, *In Defense of the National Interest*, op. cit., p. 37.

19. Ibid., p. 100.

20. Morgenthau, *Politics among Nations*, 5th ed. (New York: Knopf, 1973), p. 256.

21. "Letter to Edward Dew, 22 August 1958," Morgenthau Papers; cited by Frei, op. cit., p. 213n. In the same letter he also wrote, "I affirm two basic moral values: the preservation of life and freedom in the sense of the Judaeo-Christian tradition and, more particularly, of Kantian philosophy." Cited ibid., p. 216.

22. According to Kenneth Thompson, "Philosophy and Politics: The Two Commitments of Hans J. Morgenthau," in *Truth and Tragedy: A Tribute to Hans J. Morgenthau*, ed. K. Thompson and R. Meyers (Washington, DC: New Republic Book Company, 1977), p. 26.

23. Hans J. Morgenthau, "The Primacy of National Interest," *American Scholar* 18 (Spring 1949), p. 211.

24. "No society exists coextensive with the presumed range of a world state. . . . [T]he peoples of the world are not willing to accept world government, and their overriding loyalty to the nation erects an insurmountable obstacle to its achievement." Hans J. Morgenthau, *Politics among Nations*, 3rd ed., p. 511.

25. See for example the account by Thomas Pangle and Peter Ahrensdorf, *Justice among Nations* (Lawrence: University of Kansas Press), pp. 218–38.

26. Hans J. Morgenthau, "La Realité des Normes, en particulier des Normes du Droit International" (Paris 1934), p. 242, cited and translated by Frei, op. cit., p. 139.

27. Hans J. Morgenthau, *In Defense of the National Interest: A Critical Examination of American Foreign Policy* (New York: Knopf, 1951), p. 38.

28. Some commentators contend that Morgenthau's approval of the balance-of-power diplomacy or "restrained power politics" that had kept the peace in the eighteenth and nineteenth centuries reveals him to be a "nostalgic idealist"

rather than a thoroughgoing realist. See Martin Griffiths, *Realism, Idealism and International Politics: A Reinterpretation* (London: Routledge, 1992), p. 35, for an elaboration of this description by Robert Berki. I would argue that he thought of the acceptance of the balance of power as a logical outgrowth of realism in international relations, much as Hobbes saw the natural law injunction to seek peace as a rational response to the anarchy of the state of nature.

29. *Politics among Nations*, 3rd ed., op. cit., p. 237.

30. Hans J. Morgenthau, "Epistle to the Columbians on the Meaning of Morality," in *The Decline of Democratic Politics* (Chicago: University of Chicago Press, 1962), pp. 372–74.

31. *The Purpose of American Politics* (New York: Knopf, 1962).

32. Morgenthau, "Human Rights and Foreign Policy," in *Moral Dimensions of American Foreign Policy*, ed. Kenneth Thompson (New Brunswick: Transaction Books, 1984), pp. 344–47.

33. John Lewis Gaddis, *Surprise, Security, and the American Experience* (Cambridge, MA: Harvard University Press, 2004), p. 110. Gaddis adds a note of warning: "But it reflects arrogance as well: there's more than a whiff of grandiosity about the insistence that one nation's security is coterminous with that of everyone else. What space is left for the American empire to expand into the next time there's a surprise attack? The self-servingness reflected in these reflections suggests the need for Americans themselves to reflect long, hard, and carefully—as [John Quincy] Adams would have wished them to—about where their empire of liberty is headed."

# 9

## Islamism

As I board the plane that takes me to Pakistan today, I carry with me a manuscript of a book. It is a treatise on the reconciliation of the values of Islam and the West and a prescription for a moderate, Modern Islam that marginalises extremists, returns the military from politics to their barracks, treats all citizens and especially women equally and selects its leaders by free and fair elections.

. . . The supporters of the Taleban and al-Qaeda have threatened my assassination. . . . I will not be intimidated. . . . Despite threats of death, I will not acquiesce to tyranny, but rather lead the fight against it.

—Benazir Bhutto[1]

The assassination of former Pakistani prime minister Benazir Bhutto shortly after she wrote these lines, by the very extremists she had set out to overcome, is one of many tragic signs of the incendiary passions that continue to be aroused by radical interpretations of the tenets of Islam. "Islamism" has been suggested as a catchall term for the highly politicized version of Islam that rejects looser renderings allowing for compromise with secular systems of law and government. Islamists demand a strict union of mosque and state via a restoration of the caliphate and application of Islamic holy law—the sharia—in personal as well as civic codes, in accordance with the precedent established by the founder of the faith, the prophet Muhammad. They "see in Islam as much a political ideology as a religion."[2] That ideology is a call to action to transform Muslim societies and regimes that are considered corrupt.[3] Islamism arose in the twentieth century as a reaction against both Western influences and indigenous efforts to modernize Islam and allow economic progress and secular nationalism to bring Islamic values into better harmony with beliefs in universal human rights, especially for women. It remains to be seen whether this reactionary movement will succeed in generating wider acceptance or whether its hostility to modernization in virtually all forms will provoke resistance that will weaken its appeal.

A further important distinction has been drawn between Islamism and "jihadism," the more extreme and violent doctrine embraced by the most zealous "radical Islamists."[4] The duty of jihad (literally "striving" or "struggle") may refer to the struggle of the believer to make himself a better Muslim, but traditionally it has been understood to require the defense of the faith against attack. The believer who engages in this struggle is called a *mujahid*. Hence the Afghan fighters against the Soviets were called "mujahideen." Bernard Lewis provides an authoritative explanation that makes clear why radical Islamists can claim that jihad is a basic obligation:

> According to Muslim teaching, *jihād* is one of the basic commandments of the faith, an obligation imposed on all Muslims by God, through revelation. In an offensive war, it is an obligation of the Muslim community as a whole (*fard kifāya*); in a defensive war, it becomes a personal obligation of every adult male Muslim (*fard 'ayn*). In such a situation, the Muslim ruler might issue a general call to arms (*nafir āmm*). The basis of the obligation of *jihād* is the universality of the Muslim revelations. God's word and God's message are for all mankind; it is the duty of those who have accepted them to strive (*jahada*) unceasingly to convert or at least to subjugate those who have not. This obligation is without limit of time or space. It must continue until the whole world has either accepted the Islamic faith or submitted to the power of the Islamic state.[5]

For moderate Islamists, jihad is a duty but not the defining commitment of their movements. Islamist political parties and movements, like the Justice and Development (AK) Party in Turkey and the Muslim Brotherhood in Egypt, hold that "Islam is the answer" to the challenges of secularism and the adoption of Western political ideologies and cultural notions that are considered dangers to faith. But they do not generally advocate a resort to violence in the absence of attack or suppression. They adhere to the views of Islamic scholars who have maintained that jihad must be declared by legitimate rulers and undertaken only as a last resort. Nor have scholars in the mainstream understood the obligation to jihad to include aggression against nonbelievers and "heretical" Muslims, or suicidal attacks against civilians. Terrorist assaults, such as those committed against the United States on September 11, 2001, are the work not of Islamists but of jihadists, though such attacks often arouse sympathy among Islamists and other Muslims, except when they target Muslims.

In practice, however, there are links between Islamism and jihadism. Islamist schools like the madrassas of Pakistan indoctrinate the young with beliefs that incline some of them to become jihadists. Islamist movements like Hamas in Gaza educate children to become militant defenders of the faith and to despise Jews as "apes and pigs." Leaders of the Islamic Republic of Iran not only use rhetoric similar to that of the jihadists but have also sponsored terrorism and offered rewards for assassinations of exiles and noncitizens (notably the novelist Salman Rushdie).

Modern Muslims are drawn to Islamism and its jihadist variant for reasons other than religious belief, including the failure of modernization in many Islamic-majority societies, resentment at past colonialism and repressive governments, and the persistence of tribalism and sectarianism, which cause *fitna* or civil strife. Inasmuch as Islam is the faith of over a fifth of the world's current population, the influence of both the Islamist and jihadist variants has been felt directly and indirectly both in the Muslim world and outside it. Both pose serious challenges to secular rulers and regimes in Muslim-majority countries; the jihadists, by engaging in acts of terror and threatening to acquire weapons of mass destruction, pose much the greater immediate danger to the non-Muslim world.

Conceivably, nonviolent Islamist movements will serve as an outlet for grievances and as an avenue toward reform that will facilitate modernization and gradually evolve into parties similar to those of Christian Democracy in Europe.[6] In one instance, however, that of Afghanistan, the triumph of an Islamist movement made it possible for jihadists to find a safe haven from which to orchestrate terrorist attacks. In another, that of Iran, the revolution that created an "Islamic republic" produced a militant and expansionist fusion of nationalism with religious fervor more than tinged with jihadist hostility toward those considered the enemies of Islam.

## ISLAM AS AN ABRAHAMIC FAITH

Islamism is not a necessary or inevitable outgrowth of Islam, but neither is it an artificial imposition. Islam is often described as an Abrahamic faith, one of the three monotheistic belief systems that claim ancestry from the original founding Chaldean patriarch.[7] It resembles the other two in serving as a comprehensive guide to a way of life as well as a set of theological principles. It also resembles them in having become fractious. Adherents of Judaism and Christianity are no less divided than Muslims in interpreting their sacred texts, in assigning authority over the faithful, and in working out the implications of holy writ for everyday life in modern times. Even though Orthodox, Conservative, Reform, and

Reconstructionist Jews accept monotheism and the moral injunctions of the Ten Commandments, for example, they differ over rites and liturgies and over such matters as conversion, marriage, dietary restrictions, observance of holy days, and even over who is a Jew. Christians have had to come to terms with schisms between the Western and Eastern churches and between Catholics and Protestants, and Protestants have produced a legion of denominations. Some professing Christians, like Copts, Quakers, Maronites, and Mormons, exist independently of the larger churches. Similarly, Muslims are divided into quite separate sects, notably the Sunni (about 84 percent) and Shiite (about 10 percent).[8]

The great majority of contemporary adherents of Islam have come to terms with the continued existence of non-Muslim peoples and societies, even as they may hope that eventually these people will see the light and embrace their faith. That tolerance does not go as far as allowing complete freedom of worship or conversion in countries under Muslim control, however. In some Muslim-majority states, non-Muslim prayer books and houses of worship are forbidden, and conversion from Islam is punishable by death. Most Muslims do not insist on the need to restore the caliphate, the institution that emerged after the death of the prophet Muhammad when he was succeeded by a caliph (or deputy) originally selected by the prophet's close followers. They have long grown accustomed to the split that developed in early Islamic history between secular dynasties and the bodies of learned religious scholars (the ulema). They do not interpret jihad to allow for the murder of innocents, and while they believe that women should be subordinate to men and must wear some form of head covering for the sake of modesty, most do not deny that women should have access to education and some opportunities to work outside the home. Indeed, defenders of Islam point out with pride that Islam represented a great step forward over earlier doctrines which made women virtually chattel.

The three religions differ in their prescribed attitudes toward the use of violence in defense of the faith. Interpreters of all three religions have sanctioned the use of violence to defend the religious community or to fulfill its commandments, but there is a striking textual difference on this score between the Christian Gospels and the Koran and its supplementary texts, the *ahadith* or sayings attributed to the prophet. The Gospel Sermon on the Mount is unambiguously pacifistic, whereas some passages in the Koran counsel tolerance while others exhort to intolerance. Believers are called upon to respect Jews and Christians—who are referred to as "people of the Book"—but not "polytheists." In the same holy scripture, however, God is reported to urge believers to "slay the idolaters wherever you find them" because "idolatry is more grievous than bloodshed" (2:191).[9] Muhammad's final words to his followers were, "I was ordered to fight all men until they say, 'There is no God but Allah.'"[10] Ibn Khaldun, the foremost Islamic philosopher of history, wrote in the fourteenth century that "in the Muslim community, the *jihad*"—meaning, in this context, righteous war—"is a religious duty because of the universalism of the Islamic mission and the obligation [to convert] everybody to Islam either by persuasion or by force." By contrast, "the other religions had no such universal mission and the holy war was [therefore] not a religious duty to them apart from self-defense."[11] In modern times, the Ayatollah Ruhollah Khomeini said of the Iranian revolution that "it is not exclusively that of Iran, because Islam does not belong to any particular people. . . . We will export our revolution throughout the world because it is an Islamic revolution. The struggle will continue until the calls 'there is no God but Allah' and 'Muhammad is his prophet' are echoed throughout the world."[12] As Mary Habeck has pointed out, the United States is the focus of attack by jihadists because they recognize it as the center of liberalism and democracy that "must be destroyed along with democracy itself."[13] A perpetrator of the 2000 bombing of a nightclub in Bali made clear that in the minds of the jihadists, the obligation to attack infidels of all sorts is central to their version of Islam:

> You who still have a shred of faith in your hearts, have you forgotten that to kill infidels and the enemies of Islam is a deed that has a reward above no other. . . . Aren't you aware that the model for us all, the Prophet Mohammed and the four rightful caliphs, undertook to murder infidels as one of their primary activities, and that the Prophet waged jihad operations 77 times in the first 120 years as head of the Muslim community in Medina?[14]

Otherwise there are important differences of experience and not just theological twists that distinguish Islam from the other Abrahamic faiths. The most significant of these is the merger of the political and the spiritual in Islam. In the case of the early Israelites, the priests are recorded in the Bible as having responded to the people's request by allowing them to have kings. Although the kings were adjured to follow the holy law, they had authority independent of the priesthood. Jesus said his kingdom was "not of this world" and adjured his followers to "render unto Caesar that which is Caesar's" because "the powers that be are ordained of God." Thus, in both cases, a separation of spiritual and temporal authority developed early. That separation persisted in medieval times for Christianity in accordance with the so-called "two-sword" theory allowing for the coexistence of sacred and temporal authority. By contrast, Muhammad was not only a spiritual leader or prophet but also a military commander, tax collector, judge, and political ruler.

Another important difference between Christianity and Islam appears in their very different attitudes toward secular authority. The followers of Jesus founded a religion that was persecuted; Jesus himself and many of the early adherents were martyred. Christianity begins with a sense that the secular power—the Roman Empire—is the enemy of the faith and of the community of the faithful. Saint Augustine warned Christians that they must choose between two loves—the love of God or the love of man—and therefore between loyalty to the city of God or to the city of man. The first city, he reminds his readers, was founded by the murderer Cain. God had brought Rome down to show the consequence of pride in the works of man and to bring the people of the empire to God through the church. Islam is very different in this respect. Its prophet and his followers did not see government as an enemy. On the contrary, they were at once religious leaders and political rulers. Muhammad founded a religion that was at the same time a polity, and a successful one at that. Again, Bernard Lewis puts this difference especially well:

> Moses was not permitted to enter the promised land, and died while his people went forward. Jesus was crucified, and Christianity remained a persecuted minority religion for centuries, until a Roman emperor, Constantine, embraced the faith and empowered those who upheld it. Muhammed conquered his promised land, and during his lifetime achieved victory and power in this world, exercising political as well as prophetic authority. As the Apostle of God, he brought and taught a religious revelation. But at the same time, as the head of the Muslim *Umma*, he promulgated laws, dispensed justice, collected taxes, conducted diplomacy, made war, and made peace. The *Umma*, which had begun as a community, had become a state. It would soon become an empire.[15]

As a result, from the beginning there was in Christianity a tension between church and state that was absent in early as well as later Islam. Early Christians were adjured to disdain the "earthly city." Their expectation was that the pagan state would soon pass away with the advent of the kingdom of God. When, after several centuries the secular realm did not disappear and Christianity became the religion of the empire, clashes erupted between pope and emperor, temporal and spiritual authorities, or *regnum* and *sacerdotium*. There was one *Respublica Christiana*, but two systems of authority. Christians were said to owe allegiance to the church in matters of faith and morals and to the state in other respects. The "investiture controversy" of the eleventh century arose over the question of whether the pope had the right to appoint the emperor or vice versa. As Christianity split into different versions, Eastern and Western, and then Roman Catholic and Reformed, many Christians felt all the more acutely the need to maintain a separation between church and state, lest their differences lead to civil and international wars, expulsions, and forced conversions. The American founders were especially anxious to avoid the outbreak of wars of religion such as had driven the Puritans from England and embroiled Protestants and Catholics in the Old World. Their answer was to erect what Jefferson called a "wall of separation" between church and state.

In classical Islam, there is no such wall of separation. In Medina, where Muhammad gathered his followers after his flight from Mecca, he was the head of the *umma*, or the community of adherents. He governed, dispensed justice, collected taxes, and made peace and war. Medina was a city-state and soon became the nucleus of an empire. Religious truth and political power were inextricably linked. Religion sanctified political power, and political power confirmed and gave effect to religion. Muhammad's early successors, the caliphs, were also at once religious and secular authorities. Even when dynastic regimes succeeded the rule of the caliphs, it came to be expected that the political ruler would enforce the sharia and respect the authority of the ulema. Most Muslim-majority states make religious law "the basis" of state law. (Turkey is a major exception. When Mustafa Kemal Ataturk established modern Turkey, he wanted it to be a secular state. Both the Ottoman sultanate and its religious counterpart, the caliphate, were dissolved.) A saying reported by a ninth-century Arab writer captures the unity of religion and society in a way bound to appeal to nomadic peoples:

> Islam, the government, and the people, are like the tent, the pole, the ropes, and the pegs. The tent is Islam, the pole is the government, the ropes and the pegs are the people. None will do without the others.[16]

## THE POLITICS OF RADICAL ISLAMISM

The demand that the state be based on Islamic law has important implications. It builds in a bias against legislatures that make law rather than simply interpret or apply the law given by God. Some Muslim authorities, like the Ayatollah Khomeini, have argued that for just this reason Islam and democracy are fundamentally incompatible. For most Muslims, there need be no irreconcilable conflict between religious law and authority and secular law and authority. Sunni and Shiite clerics alike are considered guides and teachers. Provided secular law does not contradict the tenets of Islam, it is thought to be a proper sphere of rule making. Shiite "Twelvers"—the great majority of Shiites—believe that the twelfth Imam went into hiding, remains invisible, and is to reappear, and therefore that no living person can claim both spiritual and political authority. They have therefore been politically quiescent. But that attitude changed for Iranian Shiites when Khomeini succeeded in leading the opposition to the shah in Iran and went on after the revolution to create an "Islamic Republic" under clerical control. Invoking the principle of *velayet-e faqih*, or rule of the jurisprudent, he laid down that until the return of the hidden Imam, the most religiously educated scholar should exercise overall social and political authority because otherwise God's law would not necessarily be rightly interpreted or enforced.

As Khomeini explained, government can be legitimate only when it accepts the rule of God. The rule of God means the implementation of the sharia. All laws contrary to it must be dropped because only the law of God will stay valid and immutable in the face of changing times. "Islam is a religio-political faith. . . . Its worship contains politics and its political affairs contain worship."[17] The form of government does not in itself matter so long as the law of Islam is enforced. If the government is a monarchy, the king should be appointed by the *mojtaheds*. They would choose a just monarch who does not violate God's laws. Government is expected to "follow religious rules and regulations and ban publications which are against the law and religion and hang those who write such nonsense in the presence of religious believers." The "mischief-makers who are corrupters of the earth should be uprooted so that others would avoid betraying religious sanctity. Western civilization and foreigners have in this respect "stolen the reason and intelligence from misguided Muslims."[18] Khomeini made clear that Islamic principles could not be reconciled with separate, secular forms of rule:

> The fundamental difference between Islamic government and constitutional monarchies and republics is this: whereas the representatives of the people or the monarch in such regimes engage in legislation, in Islam the legislative power and competence to establish laws belongs exclusively to God Almighty.[19]

As a result of Khomeini's revision of traditional Shiite teachings, Iran became a theocracy in which God's law empowers learned interpreters to become the ultimate guardians of the state. They exercise that power by vetting candidates for office and when necessary vetoing legislation that conflicts with Islamic precepts. The theocratic character of the state is limited insofar as the citizens are permitted the right to vote for political representatives, but the control of that process by the clerics makes it partially democratic in form but hardly so in substance. Over time, the paramilitary organization known as the Revolutionary Guard, nurtured by the clerical elite as an instrument of its control, has gained independent power, threatening to make Iran less a theocracy than a praetorian state with a theological veneer.

The ability of authoritarian rulers of various kinds to impose control is facilitated by the traditional Islamic teaching of respect for authority. Protestants could invent a right of resistance against any monarch who would deny them the right to worship God as they believed proper, because they could draw upon the traditional separation of church and state. Because there is no such recognized separation in Islam, a right of resistance is harder, though not impossible, to rationalize. Rulers are obliged to follow Islamic law, and religious authorities may counsel rejection of the edicts of secular rulers if they contradict religious laws, but generally speaking the Muslim attitude toward authority is one of acceptance. The Koran admonishes respect for authority in very clear terms: "Believers, obey God and obey the Apostle, and those in authority over you" (4:59). The oft-quoted maxim among Arabs is "Better sixty years of tyranny than one hour of anarchy."[20] Some authorities have gone so far as to contend that disobedience is not warranted even if the ruler is unjust. A saying attributed to the prophet held that the believer should obey his ruler, even if he sees anything in him he disapproves of, because when you meet God, if you say that you obeyed the caliph who was wrong, you will be absolved and he will be held responsible. But a Koranic injunction allows for resistance to rulers who do not follow Islamic law by declaring such rulers to be heretics: "Those who do not rule in accordance with God's law are unbelievers" (5:47). Just such authority has been claimed by modern jihadists as justification for the assassination of rulers they consider apostates or *kufr* (impure), a category which in Egypt has included presidents Gamal Abdel Nasser, Anwar Sadat, and Hosni Mubarak. The killers of Sadat regarded him as an apostate for "introducing a Western and therefore infidel system of law and adjudication, society and culture" and argued that "the penalty for apostasy is death."[21]

For similar doctrinal reasons, Muslims have often seen democracy as a system of government in conflict with the injunction to obey God's law. At first this distrust of popular government did not conflict with prevailing Western attitudes. When Islam was in its founding period, "democracy" was a very pejorative term everywhere. Many Muslim thinkers were well aware that Greek philosophers like Plato were critical of democracy, regarding it as a low and degraded regime in which the masses, governed by their appetites, replaced the rule of their betters and laid the foundations for tyranny. In the West, democracy became acceptable after many stages of transition away from authoritarian government. Over time, the idea that rulers rule by divine right and subjects must obey them as a matter of religious duty faded away or was repudiated. Instead the prevailing idea became the democratic idea that all people are born with equal rights, notably the right of self-government, and therefore that no political system is legitimate unless it rests on the consent of the governed, exercised by representatives chosen in free, fair, and frequent elections. Islam does not explicitly call for any of this. At most it calls for consultation, or *shura*, but the ruler is not obliged to respect the will of those he consults, any more than kings in the Western tradition were obliged to heed the advice of the knights and clergy they assembled in their courts.[22] It was only when these courts became parliaments, when their members were elected, when they used the power of the purse, when they forced kings to accept limitations on their power, that the institutional basis was laid for democracy.

While these developments were occurring in the West, especially during the nineteenth and twentieth centuries, they were not happening in the Muslim or Arab worlds, in part due to the fact that much of the territory was under the rule of foreign imperialists who hardly had any interest in encouraging self-government. Islam, however, posed a barrier to the adoption of democratic notions. Islam does not recognize the state as a specific territorial identity. The notion of the *umma* or community transcends territorial boundaries. *Dar al-Islam*, the abode of Islam, is anywhere Muslims exercise or have exercised dominion. Everywhere else is *dar al-Harb*—the abode of war. Islamic empires were more decentralized than the Roman version. What united the various Islamic-ruled territories was religious belief and practice. Although the secular dynasts who followed the caliphs lacked divine authority, the notion that they could be deposed in an election was beyond contemplation. On the contrary, it was a religious duty to obey the ruler because he maintained the religion, defended the territory in which it had been established, and enlarged its bounds. Rebellions by disgruntled or ambitious military leaders who sought to usurp existing authority would only bring turmoil and weaken the community in its struggles with outsiders. Religious leaders always condemned rebellion and praised obedience, no matter how the ruler came by his power or how he exercised it. As the esteemed scholar Ghazali put it in the twelfth century, "The tyranny of a sultan for a hundred years causes less damage than one year's tyranny exerted by the subjects against each other."[23]

The result was that a great gulf opened between rulers and ruled. The rulers did whatever was necessary to enhance their wealth and control, while the ruled sought to keep a low profile so as to enjoy the rulers' favor and not suffer their wrath. They did not try to set up representative bodies to engage in dialogue with the ruler, nor were they allowed to develop institutions of local self-government. It is sometimes said that the Ottoman Janissaries were a step toward democracy. These were Ottoman slave-soldiers who were originally the fiercest military supporters of the sultan. In the nineteenth century they became rebellious and unruly and sometimes deposed one sultan in favor of another. They were not acting on behalf of the populace, however, but only as a praetorian guard, much like more recent military juntas.

The biggest change in the Arab world due to Western influence in the nineteenth century was the recognition by rulers that they needed bureaucracies. The great example was Egypt under Mehmet Ali. He was an Ottoman officer sent to retake Egypt after the Napoleonic conquest. When he did so, he established himself as the ruler of the southern domains of the empire and hired European advisers to set up his government and his army. He took over all of Egyptian agriculture to support his ambitions and started a program of industrialization. He established a dynasty that survived until its overthrow in 1952 in a military coup, but his reforms did not succeed in laying strong foundations for constitutional monarchy and parliamentary government.

## ISLAMISM AND INTOLERANCE

The nineteenth-century colonization of the Middle East by Europeans produced a sharp backlash. Among the results was a politicized form of Islam that demanded unity to confront European, especially British, imperialism. Writers like Sayyid Jamal al-Din (1839–1897), Muhammed Abduh (1849–1905), and Rashid Rida (1865–1935) called upon Muslims to overthrow foreign domination and create Muslim political movements and parties. Some of these writers called for an Islamic Reformation, an effort to modernize the traditional religious doctrine so that it could take full advantage of modern science and industry so as to beat the West at its own game. Others reacted against imperialism by condemning Western influences and insisting on a return to the fundamental principles and practices of Islam. These became the sources of Islamism.

The turn toward Islamism also reflected a more radical intolerance. Although the Koran counsels tolerance toward other monotheistic faiths, hostility to Jews, along with wariness of Christians, is evident in the Koran and the *ahadith*. Muslims are warned not to befriend them: "O ye who believe! Take not the Jews and Christians for your friends and protectors." At first Muhammad tried to conciliate Jews in the hope of converting them, but he turned against them when the tribes he encountered in Arabia refused his message. He now said that God had transformed the Jews into pigs and monkeys. In one instance he approved the slaughter of six or seven hundred Jewish men, women, and children in one battle and ordered the killing of over ninety in another. A *hadith* often cited by jihadists reports the prophet as saying, "The Last Hour would not come until the Muslims fight against the Jews and the Muslims would kill them, and until the Jews would hide themselves behind a stone, or a tree would say 'Muslim or Servant of Allah[!], there is a Jew behind me; come and kill him.'"[24] Muslims often point out correctly that Jews found refuge from Christian persecution in Muslim countries, but Jews also encountered hatred and persecution in these countries as well. The yellow badge that

Jews were forced to wear by the Nazis was first introduced by a caliph in Baghdad in the ninth century, and it was from there that it spread to Europe in medieval times. The view promulgated by many imams is that Jews are a satanic force aiming to destroy Islam and rule the world. Israel is seen as the instrument of the West's attempt to subjugate Islam. Hence Muslims must fight the "Zionist-Crusader alliance." Just how bizarre thinking about Jews can get among radical Muslims can be seen in the charter of the Palestinian Hamas:

> The enemy [i.e., the Jews] has been planning for a long time . . . [and] has accumulated huge and influential material wealth. . . . With this money, it has taken control of the world's media. . . . With this money, it has ignited revolutions in various parts of the world. . . . It stood behind the French Revolution, the Communist revolution, and most of the revolutions we have heard about. . . . It is with this money that it has formed secret organizations throughout the world, in order to destroy societies and achieve the Zionists' interests. Such organizations are the [Free] Masons, Rotary Clubs, Lions Clubs, B'nai B'rith, and others. They are all destructive spying organizations. . . . [It] was [the trigger] behind the [outbreak of] World War I . . . and established the League of Nations in order to rule the world through that means. . . . No war broke out anywhere without its fingerprints on it.[25]

A similar intolerance has reinforced and sharpened Islam's subordination of women. The condition of women is especially deplorable in Muslim lands because of Koranic precedents. The Koran ordains that a husband can admonish a wife who is disobedient and that if she persists, he has the right to beat her: "Men have authority over women because God has made the one superior to the other. . . . Good women are obedient. . . . As for those from whom you fear disobedience, admonish them, forsake them in beds apart, and beat them" (4:34). Modern authorities caution that beatings should be administered so as not to inflict great injury, but this counsel is not easily enforced. Islam allows a man to take four wives at a time and to divorce any of them simply by saying "I divorce thee"—*talaq*. Osama bin Laden's father was a serial polygamist; before his death in a plane crash, he had no fewer than twenty-two wives who bore him fifty-four children.

In Egypt, female circumcision is widely practiced, although it is a pre-Islamic, African rather than Arab practice, unknown in other Muslim countries except Sudan and Somalia. Because Egyptian law is supposed to be based on Muslim law, the courts have had to apply that law. After a television program showed a ten-year-old girl being circumcised, the government banned the practice in public hospitals, but a coalition of Islamic authorities appealed to the courts, and the grand sheikh of Al Azhar, the leading Sunni school, issued a fatwa (religious ruling) calling on the government to execute anyone who opposed the practice. The sheikh explained that circumcision was as natural for women as shaving her armpit hair or clipping her fingernails. The court disagreed, saying it was not authorized by the Koran or the sharia, and the ruling was accepted without much protest because it was understood that the government was unlikely to enforce the ban. The practice continues, especially since the health ministries provided doctors with a convenient loophole by allowing circumcision in the case of medical necessity; virtually all Islamist doctors consider it necessary if the women are to remain healthy. The writer Geneive Abdo interviewed one of the doctors: "'Don't you think it is unjust to deprive women of having intense orgasms by clipping the clitoris?' I asked, shuffling in my seat after uttering words I knew were a bit extreme for his taste. 'No. This is why there is so much immorality in the West,' he replied in a matter of fact tone. 'At a young age, girls begin having sex. When they are older they tempt men because they can't control their desires.'"[26]

Both men and women who commit adultery can be subjected to very harsh penalties, including death by stoning, but it is hard to prove against a man because it requires four witnesses, whereas a woman who has a child out of wedlock carries the undeniable evidence of her crime. In northern Nigeria, a woman was sentenced to death for adultery under the harsh penalties of the sharia known as *huddud*, while the man she accused of being the father simply denied it and was not charged. As critics have pointed out, it is virtually impossible to prove rape under some interpretations of Islamic law. Unscrupulous men can commit rape with impunity as long as they deny the charge and there are no witnesses, because the victim's account is inadmissible. Even worse, if a woman accuses a man of rape, she may end up incriminating herself. If the required male witnesses cannot be found, the victim's charge of rape becomes an admission of unlawful intercourse. Many women imprisoned in Pakistan are committed for the "crime" of being a victim of rape.

Ayann Hirsi Ali, in her autobiographical book *Infidel*, explains that in her experience Islamic submission requires denial of the freedom and autonomy that are so central to Western values.

> Every Islamic value I had been taught instructed me to put myself last. Life on earth is a test, and if you manage to put yourself last in this life, you are serving Allah; your place will be first in the Hereafter. The more deeply you submit your will, the more virtuous that makes you.[27]

Islamism takes this essential belief in complete submission to the will of God as a rationale for total control of social life in order to make behavior conform to Islamic law, as initially understood, even if that requires intolerance toward other faiths and the rejection of secular science, literature, and education. Jihadists go further still by using this rationale as a justification for the use of violence against all those perceived as enemies of the faith, even to the extent of violating the traditional Islamic prohibition of suicide in committing acts of terrorism. Modern Muslims must now decide whether either of these paths will conduce to their own well-being and spirituality, but attempts to impose these ways of life on others are arousing stiff resistance and hostility to their faith, even when it is not understood to support Islamism or jihadism.

## NOTES

1. *London Times*, 18 October 2007, p. 17.

2. Olivier Roy, *The Failure of Political Islam*, trans. Carol Volk (Cambridge, MA: Harvard University Press, 1994), p. vii.

3. Ibid., p. 36.

4. See especially Mary Habeck, *Knowing the Enemy: Jihadist Ideology and the War on Terror* (New Haven, CT: Yale University Press, 2006).

5. Bernard Lewis, *The Political Language of Islam* (Chicago: University of Chicago Press, 1988), p. 73.

6. For the thesis that Islamists "may evolve into something akin to the 'Christian Democrats' in the West or the religious parties in Israel," see especially Saad Ibrahim, "Civil Society and the Prospects for Democratization in the Arab World" (1995), p. 263, and the other essays in Ibrahim, *Egypt, Islam, and Democracy: Critical Essays* (New York: American University in Cairo Press, 2002).

7. E. C. Peters, *The Children of Abraham: Judaism, Christianity, Islam* (Princeton, NJ: Princeton University Press, 2005).

8. These estimates are given by L. Carl Brown, *Religion and the State: The Muslim Approach to Politics* (New York: Columbia University Press, 2000).

9. All references to the Koran here are drawn from N. J. Dawood, trans., *The Koran* (London: Penguin Classics, 1956).

10. Quoted in Efraim Karsh, *Islamic Imperialism: A History* (New Haven, CT: Yale University Press), p. 63.

11. Quoted ibid.

12. Quoted ibid., p. 217.

13. Habeck, op. cit., p. 162.

14. Quoted in Robert Spencer, *The Truth about Muhammad* (Washington, DC: Regnery, 2006), p. 5.

15. Bernard Lewis, *The Middle East: A Brief History of the Last 2,000 Years* (New York: Scribner, 1995), p. 53.

16. Ibid., p. 156.

17. Quoted in Roger Moin, *Khomeini: Life of the Prophet* (New York: St. Martin's, 2000), p. 247.

18. Ibid., p. 63.

19. Quoted ibid., p. 155.

20. Cited by Brown, op. cit., p. 54.

21. Lewis, *The Political Language of Islam*, op. cit., p. 90.

22. See Sanford Lakoff, "The Reality of Muslim Exceptionalism," *Journal of Democracy* 15, no. 4 (October 2004), pp. 133–39.

23. Quoted in Ann K. Lambton, *State and Government in Medieval Islam: An Introduction to the Study* (New York: Routledge, 1981), p. 124.

24. Cited in the charter of Hamas, Saul Mishal and Avraham Sela, *The Palestinian Hamas: Vision, Violence, and Coexistence* (New York: Columbia University Press, 2000), app. 2, p. 180.

25. Ibid., pp. 189–90.

26. Geneive Abdo, *No God But God: Egypt and the Triumph of Islam* (New York: Oxford University Press, 2000), p. 178.

27. Aayan Hirsi Ali, *Infidel* (New York: Free Press, 2007), p. 219.

# 10

⎯⎯∞⎯⎯

# Democracy

"Democracy is not just about electoral ballots at the national level—it is about how you run your organization, how you run your small neighborhood, it is about having a say in every aspect of your life."

Ehab al-Kaharat, organizer of the
Egyptian Social Democratic Party[1]

Universal autonomy is the root idea of democracy. It has become the operative ideal of the most advanced societies of modern times and a widely held aspiration elsewhere. Since this ideal was first introduced in ancient Greece some 2,500 years ago, it has met with much criticism from philosophers and others hostile to its egalitarian premise and skeptical of its workability. For many centuries, the criticisms of its practicality appeared warranted. With the fall of Athenian democracy, the replacement of the Roman republic by an empire, and later the rise of feudalism and then the dynastic nation-state, popular government in the West came to seem anachronistic, except in the rudimentary form of tribal assemblies or small quasi-independent communities governed by councils of notables. Rule by local noblemen, a monarch, or an emperor appeared inevitable. In the late Middle Ages, however, several Italian city-states revived republicanism. Popular government on a larger scale was achieved in the union of Swiss cantons and later in the Dutch Republic. Finally, in the late eighteenth century, revolutions in America and France produced a representative form of democracy that became a model emulated since by the most stable and prosperous societies.

The revival again met resistance, and for a time the march of democracy was halted. To thwart its appeal, frustrated antagonists tried to empty the word of its real meaning and misuse it for antidemocratic ends. In response to the popular revolutions of the late eighteenth century, dispossessed aristocrats, clerics, and royalists claimed that democracy was somehow unnatural, even satanic, inasmuch as it denied the necessarily organic and divinely intended hierarchical structure of society. Some liberals feared that it would threaten the newly won right to hold private property and the political power that property made possible. Conservatives and liberals alike feared that a "revolt of the masses" could produce a "tyranny of the majority," leveling all distinctions and enforcing conformity, mediocrity, and materialism, with a despotic communism the likely outcome. Pluralists contended that democracy made a fetish of the "omnicompetent" state based on popular sovereignty, overriding the claims of group loyalty. Anarchists, whether individualistic or communitarian, opposed democracy because it, too, required a necessarily coercive state. In the twentieth century, fascists sharpened the attack by claiming that the fractious implications of democracy undermined national unity and discipline, denied the need for leadership and militancy, and substituted hedonistic individualism for willingness to sacrifice oneself in the cause of national greatness. Some socialists embraced democracy insofar as it opened the door to the expropriation of private property by an electoral majority, but radical socialists rejected representative government based on elections because it enabled capitalists to impose a "false consciousness" that would block proletarian solidarity and determination. They opted for a tightly disciplined movement that would seize power by revolution and create a presumably temporary "dictatorship of the proletariat." Apologists for the Soviet Union muddied the waters further by distinguishing between "bourgeois democracy" and "people's democracy"—a kind of virtual democracy in which a single party ruled by stigmatizing all opposition as counterrevolutionary and claiming to represent popular will without submitting to contested elections. Similarly, in developing societies, autocrats masked their dictatorships by referring to them as "guided democracies."

The defeat of fascism and the fall of communism helped clarify the meaning of democracy and underscore its appeals. Already in 1949, the newly created United Nations Social and Economic Council found that scholars throughout the world unanimously endorsed the concept, even though they thought it ambiguous. "There were no replies averse to democracy," the council reported. "Probably for the first time in history, 'democracy' is claimed as the proper ideal description of all systems of political and social organization advocated by influential proponents."[2]

A few years earlier, however, George Orwell stressed that because of its ambiguity, the term had become a cynical tool of propaganda:

> In the case of a word like *democracy*, not only is there no agreed definition, but the attempt to make one is resisted from all sides. It is almost universally felt that when we call a country democratic we are praising it: consequently the defenders of every kind of régime claim that it is a democracy, and fear that they might have to stop using the word if it were tied down to any one meaning. Words of this kind are often used in a consciously dishonest way.[3]

At the time, Orwell's complaint was still well justified, but the cloud of ambiguity has cleared considerably, thanks to the success of the model developed in Western Europe and North America and to the failure of authoritarian regimes that also claimed, for purposes of propaganda, the mantle of democracy. As a result, democracy is no longer an "essentially contested concept" in the sense that there is intractable disagreement over what the term means. Until relatively recently, the word was ambiguous enough to require qualifiers. Because democracy was thought to connote majority rule pure and simple, the qualifier "liberal" was often added to make clear that it meant majority rule limited by respect for individual rights. In Europe, the qualifier is apt to be "social," as in the case of the Social Democratic parties of Europe, where the aim is to suggest that majority rule is linked to concern for social welfare. In the days of Soviet, Chinese, and East German communism, the preferred term was "people's democracy" or "people's republic," Orwellian usages that actually connoted the absence of majority rule masquerading as popular self-government. In the third world, dictators used similarly propagandistic language in disguising autocracy as "guided democracy" or "African" or "Arab" democracy.

Much of the propagandistic usage has disappeared, and there is now widespread consensus that modern democracy means not only majority rule but also respect for human rights, including free speech; free, fair, and frequent elections; separation of church and state; civil control of the military; and the rule of law presided over by an independent judiciary. To a remarkable extent, it is now widely agreed that modern democracy aims to promote autonomy or self-government in constitutional regimes featuring representative governments chosen in elections that must be free, fair, and frequent.

There are differences between ancient and modern democracy even as there are parallels. Perhaps the most basic difference is that whereas ancient democracy and republicanism allowed for slavery, modern democracy is built on the assumption that all people should enjoy the same basic rights and therefore that suffrage must be universal. And there are others. An independent judiciary is considered essential to protect the rights of individuals against the state and to decide constitutional questions. Government is mainly representative, and voting in elections for representatives is a critical function of citizenship. Political parties are considered essential instruments for organizing electoral participation, and free media of communication are no less essential in providing the information that voters need and allowing for the expression of opinion and debates over policy. Federalism appeared early but in weak form and has been revived to allow for the distribution of power to local units. In modern democracy, civil society (everything that is considered private, including the family, business, professions, religious organizations, and civic associations) is held to be a sphere separate from that of the state or public sector, and the strength of civil society is thought to be essential to the preservation of democracy because it acts as a barrier against the encroachment of state authority. In modern democracies, religion and the state are kept separate; the separation need not be absolute, but it must be sufficient to allow for freedom of conscience and toleration and to remove religious affiliation as a barrier to office holding or the exercise of any civil rights. Civil control of the military is also considered essential to the preservation of democracy, lest military juntas be able to seize power and overthrow the constitutional order. Major continuities include a belief in the consent of the governed, expressed in discussion and debate and in voting, and adherence to the rule of law, making arbitrary decisions invalid.

In electoral terms, the main variants in modern democracy are majority/plurality and consensual.[4] In the former, two-party systems tend to predominate because the electoral system (single-member districts and "first past the post") discourages third parties. In the latter, proportional representation is generally the voting rule, encouraging a multiparty system. The adoption of either type is thought to reflect the character of the social system: majority systems tend to be more culturally homogenous, whereas those relying on proportional representation tend to have more permanent cleavages, such as ethnicity and language. Some democracies tend to be one-party dominant, though this is usually the case in the early stages of nationhood when one party is identified as the party of the revolution or the founding.

Structurally, the two main variants are presidential/congressional and cabinet/parliamentary. In both cases, demands for a strong executive have shifted power from the legislature to the president or prime minister (or in some cases a combination of both offices). In addition to the fact that presidents are elected directly whereas prime ministers are chosen by the party that wins a majority or plurality, the biggest difference remains that in a parliamentary system a cabinet that loses a vote of confidence can be dissolved, whereas in the presidential system the executive remains in office until the next prescribed election.

Some analysts contend that a distinction should be made between liberal and "illiberal" democracies.[5] An illiberal democracy is presumably one in which there is majority rule but no protection of minority or individual rights. To accept this distinction, however, it is necessary to posit a form of democracy in which political rights are denied. If so, however, how can the will of the majority be ascertained? If there is no protection of minority or individual rights—no free speech, no right to assemble or form political parties—elections cannot be free or fair. This conception of democracy therefore suffers from internal inconsistency. By modern standards, therefore, "illiberal democracy" is an oxymoron.

Otherwise, the controversies that now swirl around the idea of democracy mainly concern issues of implementation rather than meaning. There is great concern among political scientists, for example, with the question of how transitions to democracy are most likely to be achieved, especially in developing societies riven by tribalism and sectarianism. In the Muslim Middle East, democratization must overcome not only the ideological barrier posed by Islamic belief (see chapter 9), but also sectarian, ethnic, and regional cleavages. The same doubts apply to large and heterogeneous societies with a history of authoritarian government like Russia and China, where stability, order, and economic progress seem to require discipline and even repression. In China, an undemocratic regime maintains popular support because of fear that economic progress will be lost by another "cultural revolution," however different. Even with respect to stable democracies, there is disagreement over which electoral systems are fairest, are apt to encourage the widest and best-informed participation, and are most likely to provide stable government; whether societies with significant permanent cleavages (over language, ethnicity, or religion) are better served by power sharing or consensual democracy rather than by simple majoritarianism; how the public and its institutions—executive, legislative, and judicial—can judge among expert assessments in economic and scientific matters; over which voting method achieves the greatest fairness, allows for accountable government, and encourages participation; and over whether certain of the pathologies that democracy invites, like the corrupting role of large campaign contributions in elections, the manipulation of opinion by advertising, and the fixation on appearance and personality in a mass media culture, seriously undermine the ideal in practice.

## AUTONOMY AS THE KEY PRINCIPLE

These controversies need to be addressed for the sake of strengthening democracy in practice even if they cannot be fully resolved and are likely to be treated differently in accordance with varying cultural traditions, but they do not amount to a questioning of the ideal itself. The unifying impulse behind the belief in democracy is not just a yearning for equality of any and all sorts but for equal liberty or autonomy—a belief that has acquired wide acceptance as education and economic improvements have combined to encourage resistance to fatalism and subservience. In political terms, "autonomy" is a word with several dimensions. The word *autonomia* came into use with the very creation of an external conception of political order, an order, that is, in which individuals were expected to subordinate their personal concerns to some common standard. The term appears first in the middle of the fifth century BC when it was understood as the independence and self-determination of the community in its external and internal relations. Although sometimes used as a synonym for "freedom" (*eleutheria*), it had a different connotation. Freedom implied only the absence of external restraint, whereas autonomy implied the imposition of self-restraint, or more positively, the exercise of self-determination. The word acquired its democratic bearing when it came to identify the difference between Greeks as *autonomoi* and Asiatics as ruled by despots. Individual freedom came to be understood as a function of collective freedom in the formula appearing in Attic prose: "Because the demos rules, the city as a whole is free." In his funeral oration, Pericles recognizes that the neglect of duty by citizens is likely to be the ruin of the *polis*. The individual can be autonomous without being a good citizen, but the freedom of the city depends upon collective self-government. Autonomy, then, in the classical sense, refers especially to self-government by citizens but also to self-determination by individuals.

The opportunity for tensions between the two is well appreciated, as in Sophocles' *Antigone*, where Antigone is condemned by Creon and the chorus declares: "Power is not to be thwarted so. Your self-sufficiency (*autonomia*) has brought you down." The crucial protection against the dissolution of the *polis* is the adoption of basic laws that express the (collective) autonomy of the citizens and at the same time allow for individual autonomy in matters that do not affect the collectivity. In his justly celebrated funeral oration, Pericles sought to describe the balance:

> We have a form of government that does not emulate the practices of our neighbors, setting an example to some rather than imitating others. In name it is called a democracy on account of being administered in the interest not of the few but of the many, yet even though there are equal rights for all in private disputes in accordance with the laws, wherever each man has earned recognition, he is singled out for public service in accordance with the claims of distinction, not by rotation but by merit, nor when it comes to poverty, if a man has real ability to benefit the city, is he prevented by obscure renown. In public life we conduct ourselves with freedom and also, regarding that

suspicion of others because of their everyday habits, without getting angry at a neighbor if he does something so as to suit himself, and without wearing expressions of vexation, that inflict no punishment yet cause distress . . . we are especially law abiding . . . in our obedience both to anyone holding office and to the laws, above all those established to aid people who are wronged and those which, although unwritten, bring down acknowledged shame. We are free and tolerant in our private lives; but in public affairs we keep to the law. This is because it commands our deep respect.[6]

During the retrieval and reformulation of classical conceptions that began in the Renaissance and culminated during the eighteenth century, the renewed interest in freedom was not immediately recast in terms of autonomy. Even in the Italian republics, the preoccupation of thinkers like Guicciardini and Machiavelli was with the need for civic virtue to overcome or channel the passions and interests that ordinarily drive human conduct. It was only with the rise of social contract theory that the concept of liberty came to be clearly understood as the opportunity to engage in self-government through participation in the legislation and mutual acceptance of common legal norms. The main difference, in this respect at least, between the Lockean and Rousseauean formulations of the social contract is that for the former the contract involves acceptance of rights that are corollaries of a law of nature whereas for the latter the contract embodies a "general will" expressing the sentiment of compassion that all people naturally feel for each other in pronouncing the common law.

Better than anyone before him, Immanuel Kant provided critical reinforcement to social contract theory by making it unnecessary to rely on either natural law or moral sentiment. In effect, Kant argued that by reason alone it is obvious a priori that moral conduct must be defined as adherence to maxims capable of being practiced universally. Human beings are capable of autonomy because they are capable of reason, and they achieve autonomy when they follow the maxims reason dictates, that is, the categorical imperative, rather than the "heteronomous" influences of interest, desire, or external compulsion. Thus, while the freedom characteristic of the human mind makes it possible to will whatever human beings choose, that freedom only becomes autonomous when it is used to pursue the moral principles reason identifies. When the will is autonomous, as Ernst Cassirer explains, it

submits to no other rule than that which it has set up as a universal norm and proposed to itself. Wherever this form is achieved, wherever individual desire and wish know themselves to be participants in and subject to a law valid for all ethical subjects without exception, and where on the other hand they affirm that this law is their own, then and only then are we in the realm of ethical questions. . . . The concept of such a rational being, which must be regarded as legislating universally by all maxims of its will so as to judge itself and its actions from this perspective, leads directly to the correlative conception of a community of rational beings in a "realm of ends." If all rational beings stand under the law so that, in constituting their personhood, they are in relation with the moral individuality of others, and so that they demand the fundamental worth which they thus grant themselves from every other subject and acknowledge it in all other subjects, from this there springs a "systematic union of rational beings through common objective laws."[7]

Kant's formulation does not operate automatically. When Kantian actors enter into a social contract, they should legislate in accordance with the categorical imperative and experience an autonomy that is at once individual and collective. But what if they do not? Skeptics may well object that in practice self-interest would trump morality, but Kant's morality is in effect a recognition that basic law must protect everyone's basic self-interest. To guard against the need to rely too much on duty and altruism and against the danger of a misapplication of the Kantian standard by an autocratic ruler imposing the dictates of his own reason, a utilitarian conception of autonomy is a useful complement. Utilitarianism posits that all human beings wish for pleasure or happiness and that each is the best judge of what conduces either to pleasure or to pain. For those who reject the Kantian view and the theory of the social contract as well, utilitarianism is a plausible alternative, requiring that each individual "count for one and none for more than one" in the calculus of "the good of the greatest number." If the two formulations are brought together, the result is a strengthened concept of autonomy.

In effect, this is what John Rawls sought to do in developing his democratic theory of justice as fairness.[8] He combined Kantian and utilitarian approaches in imagining contractors ignorant of their self-interest (behind the famous "veil of ignorance") and guided solely by reason and self-interest—whatever it might be. In such a condition, he reasoned, they would seek to assure that all would enjoy not only equal liberty but also an equal share of "primary goods" (necessary to security and self-fulfillment) and a distribution of wealth that would satisfy the interest of the "least advantaged" while providing an incentive to the "most advantaged" to apply their talents to the common benefit. Whereas Locke would reward the diligent and industrious by allowing them to acquire property within the limits of natural law, and Kant would expect the categorical imperative to inspire people to use their talents to the fullest, Rawls, in the spirit of Bentham, prefers to provide material incentives tied to the general welfare. By appreciating the synthesis he attempted, it is also possible to understand why he sees the moral imperative decided upon by the contractors as hypothetical rather than categorical: it follows from their wish to protect their interests and to benefit from social cooperation, not from a priori reasoning alone.

## THREE TYPES OF AUTONOMY:
## COMMUNAL, PLURAL, AND INDIVIDUAL

Historically, the aspiration toward autonomy finds expression in three ideal-typical variations: communal, plural, and individual. Communal autonomy, the oldest form, emphasizes the self-determination of a cohesive political unit, such as a city-state or nation-state. It is evident in the exaltation of citizenship in Periclean Athens and in its modern echo, the call for a communitarian "civic republicanism." Plural autonomy emphasizes the need to accommodate and balance self-determining subgroups, often by formal power-sharing arrangements. In the "mixed constitution" of the Roman republic, two such groups, the patrician and plebeian "orders," shared authority and struggled for supremacy. In the early modern republics, a similar separation and tension existed between the wealthy and the poor. In present-day democracies, demands for plural autonomy arise on the basis of various cleavages: language, culture, religion, ethnicity, region, and shared interest. Individual autonomy, the most modern form, emphasizes personal self-determination, defined since the eighteenth century in terms of universal natural or human rights. Modern democracy compounds the three variations. Communal autonomy finds expression in patriotism, national self-determination, and the acceptance of the common good or public interest as an overriding standard. Plural autonomy takes form in the organization of subgroups based on affinities of identity, interest, and belief. Individual autonomy is manifest in the belief that citizens should be left alone to pursue ends of their own choosing and in their right to arrive at their own political judgments and to act upon them independently. Each form of autonomy has its strengths and weaknesses, from the point of view of social harmony, political stability, and the balance of liberty. All modern democracies express the compound, but in different measure, and there is likely to be disagreement as to the proper balance among the variants. The art of democratic politics consists to a considerable extent of constant efforts to mediate among the different autonomies.

## PLATO'S CRITIQUE AND THE DEMOCRATS' DEFENSE

Although there are significant differences between popular government in antiquity, both in Greece and Rome, and its modern manifestations, they share an essential belief in communal self-government. Democracy originally meant self-government by the mass of citizens (the *demos*), in contrast to monarchy and oligarchy. That is what it still means, with some important exceptions. Unlike ancient democracy, which allowed for slavery and excluded women and aliens from active citizenship, modern democracy limits majority rule through regard for individual rights and defines these rights to exclude discrimination by race, religion, ethnicity, or gender. Because of this emphasis on rights as checks on majority rule, it is therefore often described as "liberal democracy." There are other differences as well, arising from adaptations of democracy to societies larger than city-states, including especially three: the reliance on elected representation rather than direct participation, the use of federalism to allow for a combination of centrally and locally accountable government, and the protective role of an independent judiciary to assure conformity with the constitution and protect the rights of citizens.

As to the conditions that make democracy either possible or difficult to achieve and sustain, it is now generally agreed that a relatively high degree of prosperity, education, independence (such as is enjoyed by property-owning middle classes), and religious toleration, all allowing for the existence of a strong "civil society" (defined as every relationship outside the public sector), is essential, whereas poverty, ignorance, tribalism, and intense sectarianism make democracy hard to establish and maintain.

Beyond these social structural considerations, there is of course one more that is absolutely essential, and that is agreement on the norms of democracy. All political systems may be analyzed and compared along three dimensions: norms, institutions, and procedures. In the case of democracy, the essential norm is respect for moral autonomy—in the literal sense of giving law to oneself. Democratic political institutions, from courts to parliaments and government agencies, are designed to promote, respect, and facilitate the autonomy of citizens. Those outside the public sector, such as the family, the church, or the business corporation, are not required to conform to democratic norms and may exhibit more traditional, hierarchic patterns of government, but even they are bound to show the influence of democratic norms, in part because the democratic state protects the basic human rights of children and spouses and requires respect for civil laws that often restrict their ability to pursue undemocratic policies, such as racial discrimination. Procedurally, democracy stresses elections, encourages the formation of political parties, and allows for freedom of speech and debate—all in order to facilitate the realization of autonomy.

The autonomy that is the norm of modern democracy is a compound of three historical forms: communal, plural, and individual. Communal autonomy characterized the Athenian *polis*. Plural autonomy was the hallmark of the Roman republic, with its divisions between the two dominant "orders," patricians and plebeians. Individual autonomy arose with liberalism from the seventeenth century onward. This combination of different forms of autonomy breeds some confusion but also contributes to dynamic equilibrium. Democratic societies are apt to be preoccupied by conflicts over the rights of the individual, the power of groups, and the need for overriding loyalty to the common good. There is no escaping these tensions because they are implicit in the three forms of autonomy that characterize modern democracy.

The main strength of democracy, compared with all other forms of government, is that it provides an opportunity for citizens to choose representatives who will hold the reins of government for a time but cannot rule indefinitely or according to their own will. Even benevolent monarchy or enlightened despotism entrenches unaccountable rulers in power and makes it possible for their successors to be much less benevolent or enlightened. In democracies, moreover, those who lose an election can accept the outcome because they have had a chance to compete and know they will have it again and again. The main weakness of democracy is the obverse of its great strength: elections put a heavy burden on citizens, some of whom are apt to be poorly informed and poorly educated, to choose leaders who will be effective and not just emotionally appealing. As a result, many voters are subject to manipulation by artful campaign tactics and are susceptible to demagogic appeals (based on rhetoric, appearance, religious identity, etc.). The best remedy for these weaknesses is of course education, especially civic education, but the best form of political education is gained by experience in the process. Internships, service in campaign committees, membership in parties, participation in meetings with candidates, and the various forms of service on governmental boards (including parent-teacher associations and other civic organizations) give citizens a realistic view of the political process, which helps immunize them against slick campaign tactics.

Ironically, however, the leading philosopher produced by Athenian democracy has often been considered its arch critic. In the *Republic*, Plato denounced democracy as contrary to the ideal of justice, ostensibly because by giving the same share in authority to "equals and unequals alike," it violates the accepted view that justice means rendering to everyone his due. By empowering the uneducated *demos*, it invites demagogic leadership relying on rhetorical appeals to the ignorant rather than on reason. It can only lead to tyranny because the mass of the people, driven by hedonistic self-interest, would refuse to sacrifice for the common good or recognize what reason requires. As in other dialogues, such as the *Gorgias*, Plato takes issue with the sophist view that education should teach people how to function successfully in society as it is rather than how to discover the truth and remake their lives and society accordingly. Insofar as democracy makes uneducated opinion the basis of law, it cannot achieve true justice and must invite disorder.

In the same dialogue, however, Plato acknowledged the impracticality of the alternative he seemed to be proposing—the "ideal state" he conjured up, in which philosopher kings or guardians would rule, aided by a military caste. He admits that this elite would have a hard time winning the consent of the many to their rule. They might have to resort to propaganda, in particular the "noble" or "royal" lie—the "myth of the metals" whereby everyone would be said to be a fraternal creature of the same earth mother who simply admixed different metals ranging from gold to brass in each of them, giving them different levels of ability—to take the sting out of political inequality. Ordinary people, he recognized, might not accept this transparent falsehood. Besides, such a state would likely fail because the guardians would make mistakes in reproductive matching, as a result of which the caste system would lose its integrity.

It is open to question whether Plato intended this imagined state to be taken as a model or whether he designed it for an ulterior, instrumental purpose. At the midpoint of the dialogues, Socrates is reported to have proposed the construction of a state after he was unable to persuade his students that justice was something other than the interest of the stronger. His aim in constructing this imaginary state was to depict justice "writ large" in order to show by analogy how the elements of the soul—reason, spirit, and appetite—would be ordered in the just person. From this portrait, he proceeded to draw the conclusion. As the guardians, aided by the military, ruled the masses, so in the just individual, reason, aided by spirit, would govern appetite. The best evidence that this was his intention is the fact that, paradoxically, the supposedly "ideal state" depicted in the dialogue would not be composed of just individuals, with all three elements of the soul held in proper order, but rather of three castes—philosophers, soldiers, and commoners—each embodying one element to the exclusion of the others. The philosophers would be reared without personal property so as to be altogether detached from the temptations of appetite; the soldiers would be raised not to think for themselves or divert themselves in pleasure, but to be like Spartan soldiers, completely devoted to the arts of war; the ordinary people would be expected to concern themselves with producing and consuming, not with reflection or military service. In later dialogues, including the *Statesman* and the *Laws*, Plato offers more balanced and more practical portrayals of the social order, and in these (especially the *Laws*), democracy is looked on more sympathetically, as one element of the mixed constitution that he (and Aristotle after him) thought the best practical arrangement. It is also important to bear in mind that the democracy Plato was critical of relied on lot, or sortition, rotation in office, direct participation in the framing of laws, and a judicial process in which there were no judges or professional legal advocates—thus making his critique of democracy less relevant to its modern forms.

Other ancient philosophers, notably the sophist Protagoras, were apparently more sympathetic to democracy, although the evidence of his views is fragmentary. Protagoras accepted the order of the universe as it is rather than thinking of it as an imperfect copy of some transcendent ideal universe. In asserting that "man is the measure of all things," he apparently accepted human nature as it manifested itself and democracy as a process in which self-interested individuals accommodate their differences peacefully under law. The "good" or the "just" way of life that they thus achieve is not absolute but relative, a way of overcoming disagreements for the sake of living together. Participation in the *polis* turns individuals into citizens, who notice their neighbors and respect their needs and views. Unlike Plato, he and the other intellectuals and dramatists who favored democracy thought that ordinary people had the competence to make the necessary judgments and that open exchanges would assure good practical decisions. Socrates had often used the image of the flute player to point out that in a just society only those who could play well would be given flutes. The sophist answer was that if survival depended on playing the flute, the citizens who performed best would teach the others to play well enough.

Whether this speculation about Protagoras is historically accurate or not, it rests upon a compelling premise, which is that the rise of democracy must have inspired a democratic ethos, and that this ethos very likely rested on a belief that ordinary people are capable, thanks to their capacity to reason, of regulating their own lives, setting policies for society, and judging fairly in trials, together with other citizens. As Pericles observed, the most distinctive feature of Athenian democracy was that it made public affairs of even more concern to citizens than their private business. "We do not say that the man who takes no interest in politics is a man who minds his own business; we say that he has no business here at all."[9]

In rejecting democracy, Plato put himself in the awkward position of asserting that rational capacity, which all Greeks believed to be the defining characteristic of human beings compared to other animals, was so deficient in most people that they would be better off being ruled by philosophers like himself. The same equally awkward argument was used by ordinary Greek males to rationalize the exclusion of women from politics and the enslavement of "barbarians." The extraordinary achievements of Athenian civilization in its democratic period, both with respect to self-government and the encouragement of philosophic criticism and introspective drama, are themselves the best refutation of Plato's contention, for these achievements were hardly impositions of the few wise upon the many ignorant; they were made possible by the openness of democracy to criticism, dialogue, and creative expression.

As W. G. Forrest has observed, the greatest achievement of the Athenians was to have created,

> virtually *ab initio,* the idea of a state composed of citizens who by virtue of their citizenship alone had unquestionable rights and to do this without allowing either existing prejudices or existing institutions to interfere in any way with the exercise of those rights, without creating or permitting new prejudices and new institutions which might curb or distort their development. In a word, to invent the notion of an autonomous human being and to apply it rigorously throughout the society.

## DEMOCRACY IN HISTORY

How did the modern world become so enamored of democracy, and why is it now becoming ubiquitous? One major reason is disillusionment with alternatives, but the more fundamental answer can be found in the changes in social structure and expectations that have come with modernization. As the advance of commerce and technology has raised standards of living and public health and produced a greater sense of empowerment so that poverty and disease need not be accepted as altogether inevitable, masses of people have come to demand a voice in the decisions that affect their lives. The idea that most people should have to depend on the judgment or whims of a single individual or a privileged oligarchy has come to be rejected in modernizing societies where many people become quite capable of managing their own lives and are no longer willing to defer to their "betters." While there remain important instances in which democracy is looked upon as an invitation to disorder, and authoritarianism is preferred for the sake of economic growth and security, the belief that rulers should be held accountable and that people should be self-governing has become well nigh universal. Even authoritarian regimes are now expected to rule by law rather than caprice. As a result of these broad tendencies, in recent years a great many countries have moved toward adopting democracy. Some 121 countries are now considered electoral democracies.[10] It remains to be seen whether the authoritarian regimes of Russia, China, the Middle East, Africa, and Latin America will remain in a kind of twilight zone in which superficial bows toward democracy serve as a facade for continued dictatorship and oligarchy, or whether they are in transition.

The evidence of the past half century and more suggests that there is a pattern of evolution toward democracy—not that it necessarily takes hold easily. There have been waves and reverse waves, as Samuel Huntington has pointed out.[11] But the tendency toward democracy is a powerful force for reasons that become clearer in a long view of human social evolution. In very early times, humans lived in roving family bands, and then in tribes. The state first emerged when monarchs managed to rule over a collection of such tribes. In rare cases, notably in ancient Greece and Italy, monarchy was overthrown and replaced by oligarchy, tyranny, and democracy, or the mixed government the Romans called republicanism. These early experiments in popular government did not last because they were vulnerable to attack from within and from without and because monarchies were more effective in organizing and using military force to create empires. Monarchical absolutism eventually came under effective attack when the hold of feudal land tenure was broken and an urban middle class joined with landed gentry to compel a transfer of power. In recent times, popular revolts against authoritarian regimes have also produced transitions to democracy.

To take hold, democracy requires a number of conditions. Inasmuch as democracy requires active participation, if only at election time, citizens must be able to keep abreast of the news and come to informed judgments. Some degree of education is essential, as all advocates of democracy have recognized. In other forms of government, the opposite is the case: mass ignorance helps sustain dependence on authoritarian rulers, and fears and insecurities can be manipulated by clever politicians even though the interests of subjects are not being served. Prosperity is important to the achievement and maintenance of democracy for several reasons. People who are reasonably well off will not easily sell their votes. They will be independent enough not to have to follow the dictates of some landowner or factory owner. It has often been noted that democracies require a strong middle class, defined as people with enough income and property to come to independent judgments and to support causes they believe in. A high degree of inequality renders those at the top of the income pyramid far more influential in the political process than those with lower income, but this inequality can be offset to some extent by the sheer force of numbers, or by the role of organized labor unions and other pressure groups. A significant separation of church and state is essential because it assures that no citizen will be discriminated against because of adherence to a minority faith. Most modern societies tend to be multireligious or at least multisectarian, and these differences must be tolerated if the society is to live up to its ideals and not suffer from religious strains. The democratic state must not act as an arm of any religion, punishing heretics and apostates. It is now widely recognized that for democracies to flourish, not only is a separation between public and private necessary, but the institutions of the private sector—religious, economic, social, and cultural—must be strong enough to prevent dictation by government. The weakening of civil society weakens democracy by preparing conditions for the emergence of totalitarianism. The takeover of civil institutions by the Nazi and Soviet regimes made them increasingly totalitarian. The effort to create a transition, in Eastern Europe and Spain, involved the strengthening of the institutions of civil society. It is only when civil society is strong that individuals can form groupings to protect and advance their interests, that they can have assured access to means of communication, and so forth. In the transition to democracy, tribalism and sectarianism can be formidable obstacles. In Europe, these obstacles were overcome over many centuries by the creation of monarchical nation-states. Elsewhere, the effort to achieve the transition is often thwarted by the persistence of these primordial loyalties. The development of a national culture, including a single language, a national army or police, and an educational system following a single curriculum, may hasten the development of a national consciousness, but at the same time a respect for cultural differences may be necessary to overcome resistance. Elections have the distinct virtue of allowing factional conflict by peaceful means. Losers can accept defeat knowing they can hope for a better outcome before long. Victory in an election provides legitimacy, given the standards of democracy. It allows people to govern themselves even in very large societies. It makes officials accountable to the electorate and educates the voters concerning the issues.

Criticisms of modern democracy fall into several categories. Critics have often argued that it is too much to expect ordinary people, no matter how well informed they may be, or how capable they are of managing their own affairs, to decide complex matters involving scientific data (climate change, for example) or economic theory. Defenders of democracy answer that what the electorate can reasonably be expected to do is to tell politicians that the shoe is pinching and to decide who is best qualified to represent their will. Some have called this "democratic elitism," but it is implied by the design of the representative process. Although constituents choose candidates who are likely to reflect their concerns and values, they must delegate to them the authority to write laws based on expert testimony and advice and taking account of the interplay of concerns. As to intellectual capacity, many studies have shown that for reasons that are partly genetic and partly environmental, degrees of intelligence vary. Some critics of democracy have argued that this "bell curve" should be respected in the distribution of political authority. Even John Stuart Mill, who championed representative government, argued for giving graduates of Oxford and Cambridge doubly weighted votes. Some analysts, notably Gaetano Mosca and Vilfredo Pareto, have argued that in all societies power is apt to be concentrated in the hands of some particular category of people. Mosca called them the political or ruling class; Pareto referred to them as the social elite. Both argued that despite the forms of majority rule, power would devolve into the hands of those who best performed the functions the society valued most—whether priests or warriors in ear-lier times or businessmen in the modern era. Thomas Jefferson and John Adams both thought that republican societies would produce a "natural aristocracy" compatible with democracy because it would consist of those who could be trusted to exercise their best judgment on behalf of the elec-tors. Inasmuch as officeholders are held accountable by regular elections, this criticism is considerably weakened.

Democracy is often said to invite paralysis because of the difficulty of achieving consensus among self-interested individuals and interest groups. If everyone believes he has a right to his opinion, and all opinions count the same, there is bound to be difficulty achieving consensus on is-sues about which there is great contention. It is certainly true that gridlock is a frequent experience in legislatures and that vital, long-term issues tend to be given short shrift. In war conditions or in those tantamount to war, national security considerations can lead to the suspension of such democratic rights as freedom of speech and assembly and to the violation of the legal rights of individual citizens. There is no easy answer to this problem. People expect their governments to provide security above all else, and they are apt to tolerate deviations from democratic ideals when they are caught up in fear of some external or internal threat. In an analy-sis of Nazism, the psychologist Erich Fromm contended that dictatorship thrives on popular insecurity and the craving for leadership.[12] Whether this factor takes the extreme form it did then will depend on the extent to which conditions resemble those of the Weimar regime.

Winston Churchill said famously that democracy is the worst political system he knew—except for all the rest. Indeed, it is when we look at the alternatives to democracy that we see its virtues best. The trouble with reliance on dictatorship or monarchy, especially in democratic times, is that people are reduced to conspiring against it when they feel that their interests are not being served, and that the rulers are open to problems of succession, which are sometimes resolved by assassination. The diffi-culties of the Iranian effort to establish theocracy tempered by elections is another indication of the weakness of alternatives. When a regime aims to control the whole of society and to reshape it in accordance with some ideology, such as Nazism or communism, it becomes totalitarian, encompassing all activities of life, leaving nothing to the private sphere. In practice, no regime has yet succeeded in achieving full totalitarian control, but those of both Nazi Germany and the Soviet Union provided the template by outlawing any but the one state-approved political party, by gaining complete control of the media and using them to inculcate "the party line," and by using a highly intrusive secret police and punitive labor and death camps to intimidate, coerce, punish, and eliminate opponents.

But the pathologies of democracy are real and must be acknowledged. The need for vast amounts of campaign finance inevitably skews elections in favor of the interests of large contributors. Where judges are elected, their dependence on campaign contributions raises doubts about the fairness of the judicial process. Every organized interest group supports major lobbying programs designed to influence legislation, often to the detriment of the unorganized public. The lobbyists often include former elected and staff members of the legislature. They often manage to frame the way issues are debated, and sometimes they even draft the legislation that deals with their concerns. Even in systems where campaign spending is restricted and broadcast media are publicly owned and made available to parties and candidates free of charge, there are many other opportunities for interested groups and corporations to influence elected officials by campaign contributions, junkets, and the expectation of rewards after office via employment in the private sector.

Interest groups are an inevitable result of the democratic political process and the very existence of civil society. In the tenth *Federalist* paper, James Madison warned of the danger of factionalism, but acknowledged that factions were inevitable in a free society. "Liberty is to faction," he wrote, "what air is to fire, an aliment without which it instantly expires." By giving voice to concerns and providing information, interest groups play a constructive role in the democratic process, but they can also shape policy and legislation in accordance with narrow rather than broad public interests. In the United States, for example, the "gun lobby" is especially well organized and vocal, with the result that the U.S. has the loosest regulations of firearms of any modern democracy. Farm groups often succeed in gaining subsidies and tariffs against imports even though their behavior is adverse to the interest of the consumers who form a majority of the population.

Another problem affecting democracy is that even popular governments have a natural tendency to keep their procedures and policy findings secret, especially when power holders seek to avoid accountability and public debate. In the name of national security, governments may authorize intrusions into private lives that violate the civil liberties of citizens. At the same time, the idealization of individual liberty promotes suspicion of government and sometimes general antagonism, leading to tax revolts and a libertarianism that verges on anarchism.

Inevitably, too, in the modern world many decisions taken by governments require sophisticated analysis of data by natural and social scientists, as well as by a host of professional experts—doctors, lawyers, accountants, engineers, psychologists, and so forth. Ideally, democratic governments should encourage public discussion and debate so that representatives and the public can make informed decisions. In many cases, however, government agencies and legislative committees seek to predetermine the outcome by choosing experts with whose views they agree. Public interest groups in areas like environmental protection therefore play an important role in checking this tendency. But in areas of national security, much of the policy debate goes on behind a veil of secrecy and censorship, and decisions are adopted without much public discussion and debate. Even when there is adequate public airing, however, democracies run into the serious problem that most members of the public are not educated enough to follow the debate or interested enough to devote the time and effort needed for that purpose. The result is a tendency toward technocracy, modified by ill-informed resistance (as in the case of climate change, stem cell research, and the teaching of evolution).

## IN DEFENSE OF DEMOCRACY

It is not enough to defend democracy as the least bad form of government. Democracy's greatest appeal is that it reflects the acceptance of the belief in equal human rights—the basic rights of life, liberty, and economic well-being which are now all but universally recognized. No system of government that denies this charter of human freedom could possibly satisfy the aspirations of a reasonably well-educated human being. No one wants to be the slave of another. No one wants to be denied an opportunity to fulfill his or her natural talents, or to have a say in the decisions that affect his or her life and that of their families. Democracy can work well, however, only if the citizens it empowers gain enough understanding to fulfill their responsibilities, by voting, by running for office, by working in political parties and movements, by exercising their best judgment, and by remaining vigilant, lest governments trample on liberty or engage in behavior that endangers the society. The best argument for democracy is that it gives citizens no excuse for failed policies: they themselves must bear the responsibility for their own fate. It is a heavy responsibility, but it is a price worth paying for self-determination.

Plainly, for democracy to work, citizens must be informed about the conditions facing them and the options for dealing with them, as well as with the record of those who compete to be their leaders. This puts a considerable responsibility on the media of communication and also on the political parties and public interest groups. The media, parties, and public interest groups stand in a kind of middle ground between civil society and the public sector. They shape public opinion and articulate it; they create blocs and electoral groupings that vie for influence. When the media are controlled by the state, they may be inclined to peddle the official line and "manage the news." Journalists may also practice self-censorship to stay out of trouble. Independent media are much more likely to see themselves as public watchdogs or tribunes, ferreting out corruption and forcing officials to defend controversial policies. But privately owned media are liable to reflect the views of the wealthy interests who own them and the advertisers who support them. One solution is to create media that are publicly supported but independent of government control, like the BBC. But experience also suggests that reporting will be influenced by the predispositions of the reporter. There is no way of avoiding bias entirely. The best that can be hoped for is that enough competing voices will gain access and that a sense of public responsibility—buttressed by the threat of official sanction—will encourage media directors to give a fair hearing to all sides.

The problem is not simply the availability of information, but the interpretation put on the information. Democratic electorates need more and more sophisticated analysis of the ongoing flow of events, and analysis may not sell papers or attract viewers as well as the brute facts of violence or sensationalism. Democratic politics is bound to involve heated emotions, and so long as these do not boil over into hatred and violence, politics can be a kind of theatrical venue in which conflicts are played out in civil and even entertaining fashion. The trouble arises when the only news is what is considered entertaining. That tends to emphasize trivia at the expense of important concerns. Debate formats may satisfy the public's bloodlust at the same time as they are informative. Manipulative negative advertising is still another serious problem.

Although democracy has its own ethos, it does not serve as a complete philosophy of life. It is an enabler rather than a prescriptive dogma. A citizen of a democracy is free to devote himself to an infinite variety of ends, including his own self-expression and fulfillment, and if he wishes, whatever passion or religious or philosophical belief animates him. The only limitation is that what he does may not injure anyone else or interfere with their opportunities for self-expression. But democratic freedom does carry with it the obligation to respect and enhance democracy itself by fulfilling the duties of citizenship (such as voting, military, and other forms of public service) and being concerned with the public business. Democratic societies are complex and pluralistic. They present a kaleidoscope of group activities rather than a centrally orchestrated agenda. The very freedom that democracy entails promotes a competition for achievement in a host of areas. It may also promote self-indulgence and indifference to the commonweal, withdrawal into gated enclaves, or an emphasis on private satisfactions to the detriment of public amenities. To avoid these pathologies, democracies need to inculcate an appreciation of its many virtues and the risks attendant on allowing popular government to atrophy from neglect and apathy. Democracy requires patriotism but of a form that does not simply respect the symbols of unity but contributes actively to public debate and public service.

The debate between liberals and conservatives over the relative roles of government and the market hinge on considerations of efficiency and equity, but they do not put democracy itself in jeopardy because the debate presupposes that both regulation and independence from state control are critical for democracy. Democratic societies are bound to produce economic inequality, but democracy is undermined when inequality produces plutocracy and populist resentment. Similarly, illiteracy and lack of education are harmful because they produce an uninformed electorate too easily misled by demagogues and peddlers of panaceas.

Whether democracy will become the universal political norm remains uncertain. Poverty, illiteracy, and economic stagnation breed superstition, tribalism, and dictatorship. Democracy was successfully introduced in West Germany and Japan following World War II by external imposition, but the circumstances were extraordinary. Both societies had been devastated by war and were occupied by victorious powers in a position to reshape the society. The effort to install democracy in countries like Iraq and Afghanistan is a much more precarious undertaking. In such cases, tribalism and sectarianism are serious barriers that are hard to hurdle or remove. Eventually, their influence may be moderated as people come to see themselves as citizens of the nation with a strong sense of loyalty to it. In the near term, however, their subloyalties could well vitiate the force of democratization. Improvements in prosperity and education could counter these tendencies. It may be, however, that during the period of transition, the best that can be hoped for is a regime that will provide for stability and security, even if it is not democratic in the fullest sense or if it is nakedly authoritarian but at work in a society where ideas of democracy are percolating among the people. At the core of the appeal of democracy is the principle of self-government, for individuals and communities. As education and experience make it apparent that self-government enhances opportunities for the betterment of the human condition and the realization of liberty, the ideal of democracy is likely to attract more and more adherents.

## NOTES

1. *New York Times*, p. 1, April 8, 2011.

2. *Democracy in a World of Tensions* (Paris: UNESCO, 1951), app. 3, p. 527.

3. George Orwell, "Politics and the English Language," *A Collection of Essays* (Orlando, FL: Harcourt Brace Jovanovich, 1946), p. 162.

4. See especially Arend Lijphart, *Patterns of Democracy: Government Forms and Performances in Thirty-Six Countries* (New Haven, CT: Yale University Press, 1999).

5. See Fareed Zakaria, *The Failure of Freedom: Illiberal Democracy at Home and Abroad* (New York: Norton, 2003).

6. Thucydides, *The Peloponnesian War*, trans. Steven Lattimore (Indianapolis: Hackett, 1999), p. 92.

7. Ernst Cassirer, *Kant's Life and Thought*, trans. James Haden (New Haven, CT: Yale University Press, 1981), pp. 242–44. Quotation from Kant is in *Foundations for the Metaphysics of Morals*, first section.

8. John Rawls, *A Theory of Justice* (Cambridge, MA: Harvard University Press, 1971).

9. Thucydides, op. cit., p. 119.

10. See Arch Puddington, "The 2007 Freedom House Survey," *Journal of Democracy* 19, no. 2 (April 2008): p. 63.

11. Samuel P. Huntington, *The Third Wave: Democratization in the Late Twentieth Century* (Norman: Oklahoma University Press, 1991).

12. Erich Fromm, *Escape from Freedom* (New York: Holt, Rinehart & Winston, 1941).

# Epilogue

## Albion, Rome, and Athens: America as a State of Mind

During the visit of Queen Elizabeth II to the United States in 2007, the *New York Times* columnist David Brooks remarked that unlike Americans, Britons have a lively sense of history, partly because their monarchy is an ever-present reminder of their past. Americans, lacking a living link to their national pageant, are less attached to the nation's roots. When Americans say "That's history," they mean to dismiss whatever is "old hat," "horse and buggy," "yesterday's news," or, in the current teenage usage, no longer "cool." They may wax nostalgic about the country's pioneering origins, admire the practical wisdom of the founding fathers, and even reenact Civil War skirmishes, but as an art critic once observed, the tradition that is most venerated in American culture is the "tradition of the new." The dollar bill proudly proclaims the nation to be *novus ordo seclorum*, a "new order of the ages." Henry Ford, a prototypically irreverent specimen of can-do Yankee inventiveness, blithely declared that "history is bunk." Campaigning in 2008, both Barack Obama and Hillary Clinton, the leading Democratic candidates for the nomination, quoted Dr. Martin Luther King Jr. as saying that "we are guided by the fierce urging of now." Obama declared that "the choice in this election is not between regions or religions or genders. It's not about rich versus poor; young versus old; and it is not about black versus white. It's about the past versus the future." Not to be outdone, his Republican opponent Senator John McCain said, even as he sought to appeal to his party's presumably more nostalgic conservative base, "We're not a country that would rather go back than forward. We're the world's leader, and leaders don't pine for the past and dread the future. We make the future better than the past. We don't hide from history. We make history."

This tendency to cast history aside can be explained in various ways. America is a relatively young country and a nation composed mainly of immigrants, many of whom came to this "New World" anxious to shuck off the constraints of the Old. Relatively few Americans today can claim membership in the Daughters of the American Revolution, and only a diminishing fraction boast forebears who fought in the Civil War. The very novelty of the American experiment produced a buoyant sense of optimism that persists in the American character, despite the anxiety and foreboding evident in the country's culture from the writings of Herman Melville to William Faulkner and Arthur Miller and American film noir. Or the cause may be that America began as the world's first great democracy. "Democratic peoples," Tocqueville remarked in *Democracy in America*, "do not bother at all about the past, but they gladly start dreaming about the future, and in that direction their imagination knows no bounds, but spreads and grows beyond measure."[1] In *Democratic Vistas*, Walt Whitman observed that "for our New World I consider far less important what it has done, or what it is, than . . . results to come."[2] However it can best be explained, a restless refusal to be bound by the burdens of the past is a deep-set feature of the national character.

In some ways, this collective amnesia is psychologically healthy. "*Amerika, du hast es besser als unser Kontinent, der alte,*" Goethe remarked. America had it better than Europe, he thought, because its heart was not troubled by useless old remembrance and empty disputes. Even today, Europeans must struggle to keep memories of national animosities and stereotypical caricatures from spoiling their vision of a united, all but borderless continent. In the Middle East, where historical narratives are a fixation, ancient hatreds are nursed and serve as warrants for holy wars. Even though more than half a century has passed, many Japanese stubbornly refuse to admit that during World War II their army committed atrocities in China and forced captive women into prostitution. By contrast, Americans treat history like a palimpsest, overwriting everything— shrugging off the memory of the Malmedy massacre and the Bataan death march and now favoring German and Japanese cars and eating bratwurst and sushi without a twinge of remorse.

Americans readily acknowledge and apologize for such sins of the more distant past as Indian removal, slavery, xenophobic nativism, and patriarchalism, but they feel no need to pay reparations for the wrongs committed by previous generations. None of that happened on their watch! Instead, they focus on the need to "move on" by trying to realize ideals previously honored in the breach. The old Indian treaties, so often travestied, are reinterpreted to let tribes build gaming casinos in otherwise Puritanical precincts. People whose skin shade, ethnicity, or gender would once have all but disqualified them are regularly elected to high offices. Reared under the new politically correct dispensation calling for respect for diversity, the great majority of young Americans are, thankfully, free of prejudices that were once all too common.

But ignorance of the past is not necessarily bliss when it keeps a people from becoming aware of who they are and how and why they have come to hold the beliefs that shape their thinking. John Maynard Keynes famously remarked on the unconscious dependency on past ideas when he noted that "practical men who believe themselves to be quite exempt from any intellectual influences, are usually the slaves of some defunct economist."[3] In the same way, many Americans are probably unaware of the influence exerted on their ways of thinking by ideas and ideologies imprinted by the nation's political culture and the larger matrix of Western civilization.

Especially at the outset, American political thinking reflected a variety of influences, chief among them, as suggested in chapter 3, British natural rights/social contract theory. Two other influences were also strongly felt in the early period. One reflects a fixation on the experience of the Roman republic. The other, that of ancient Athenian democracy, came to be felt later, in the early and middle decades of the nineteenth century. At the risk of oversimplification, it can reasonably be said that the American political mind was framed as a synthesis of these three major historical influences. More specifically, it is a dynamic compound of British individualism, Roman pluralism, and Athenian communalism. Not that this synthesis is unique to America: every democracy exhibits these variations of autonomy in different combinations.

## BRITISH INDIVIDUALISM:
## RETHINKING TOCQUEVILLE'S ANALYSIS

British individualism is the most obvious and most determining influence. The United States, Tocqueville observed, was mainly the product of British settlement. The dominant force in its character would therefore be "Anglo-American."[4] The way of life of most early settlers, their nonconforming Protestantism, their taste for Georgian architecture, and their discomfort with arbitrary, unrepresentative authority, were all British in inspiration. In 1775, Edmund Burke gave his remarkable speech urging conciliation rather than confrontation with the colonies. Burke urged the British lawmakers to appreciate that the American demand for freedom was an inheritance from their mother country. "First, the people of the colonies," he said, "are descendants of Englishmen. England, Sir, is a nation which still, I hope, respects, and formerly adored, her freedom. . . . They are therefore not only devoted to liberty, but to liberty according to English ideas, and on English principles." "They augur misgovernment at a distance," he added in pungent prose, "and snuff the approach of tyranny in every tainted breeze."[5] Burke certainly understood the temper of the colonists. He saw that the belief in the liberty of the individual, first expressed by and for the benefit of barons in Magna Carta and finally flowering in the seventeenth century in the theory of natural rights and the social contract, was about to become the foundation of American liberal democracy.

Although many continental thinkers began the effort to revamp political theory to take account of this new direction, British political thinking came to predominate. It did so by rejecting the customary notion that the authority of monarchs was somehow ordained by God along with a social hierarchy in which the landed aristocracy and the clergy were the handmaidens of royalty. In this effort, the forerunner was Thomas Hobbes, but it was John Locke who had the greatest influence on American thinking. Like Hobbes, Locke imagined what conditions would be like in a "state of nature"—in order, as he said, to ascertain the true origins of civil government. In this state, life would be insecure, but since human beings are capable of reason, they would acknowledge the law of nature, a moral law that ordained principles of right conduct. The natural law implies as a corollary certain rights—including not only the right to be secure in one's life, but also the right to liberty and to property—the goods needed to sustain life that are drawn by labor from the bounty of nature. Life, liberty, and property were therefore rights of nature.

Still, the state of nature would have what Locke delicately referred to as "inconveniences." The lack of a common judge to settle disputes could turn it into a state of war. To remedy these inconveniences, reason would suggest the need for a social compact, in which individuals would create a civil government to protect their natural rights. To assure that this government would not become tyrannical, it would have to be one in which the compactors were equally represented, and the grant of authority would be revocable.

The Lockean formula was exactly what the American colonists needed to challenge royal authority. From Locke to Jefferson and Tom Paine went the message of natural rights and the social compact. The reason it appealed so strongly was the virtual absence of feudalism that Tocqueville noted. As Louis Hartz explained, as noted in chapter 3, Americans embraced "irrational Lockianism" not as one ideology competing with others, but as the rationale of the Revolution, so taken for granted that it was thought of as "Americanism," and competing ideologies were stigmatized as un-American.

That influence remains so enduring that it could well be considered defining. Every American leader, from Washington onward, has seen the

American mission to be the defense and propagation of the liberty of the individual. American political thought, lately expressed in the philosophical writings of social liberals like John Rawls and conservative liberals like Robert Nozick, has been similarly preoccupied with the primacy of liberty. Liberals or progressives (as they now sometimes style themselves) may differ from conservatives in their view of the role of the state in promoting liberty, but they disagree less about the end than about the means.

Tocqueville was among the first to appreciate the importance of the influence of British liberalism for America. He is especially remembered for making two remarkably prescient predictions. One was that the Anglo-Americans, who were the dominant element in the population, would spread across a swath of the continent almost as large as the whole of Europe, reaching a population of 150 million, all with the same civilization, language, religion, habits, and mores—this at a time when the population was just over 12 million. He did not anticipate the great diversity of religion and ethnicity that would come with immigration, but he was certainly right about the homogenizing effect of the country's dominant culture. The other was that because of the society's emphasis on individual liberty, America would come to hold the destiny of half the world in its hands while another rival nation, Russia, would command the other half. One, he added, would have freedom as its principal means of action, the other, servitude.

To describe American character, Tocqueville used a new word— "individualism"—coined in the 1830s to describe the new social order democracy was producing. As he explained, in the old order, everyone has his place and all are linked together by organic and hierarchical chains of identity. In democracy the chains are broken, and despite the persistence of families and communities, for the most part each individual lives by himself and for himself: "In ages of equality all men are independent of each other, isolated and weak."[6] Democracy makes up for this atomism by inducing people to recognize that they have common interests and concerns and need to cooperate. Voluntary associations become important, as does religion, which provides a much needed sense of community and moderates the preoccupation with the self and the absorption in material things.

Despite its cultural shortcomings, Tocqueville understood that America represented a turn of enormous importance in the history of civilization. He thought that this country was at the cutting edge of a great social transformation toward which all previous history had been leading. He called it "that irresistible revolution which has advanced for centuries in spite of every obstacle." It promoted what he called "a kind of religious awe." Although he confessed that he had fears as well as hopes for America, he thought this experiment in democracy would produce a different and better form of equality than the French Revolution had because Americans had been fortunate in having been "born equal" without having to endure a democratic revolution. In the absence of a feudal past, there was no need for a violent revolution to overthrow an old order; without feudalism, there would be no consciousness of class. All Americans, whether rich or poor, thought of themselves as members of one class, the middle class. Even now, in political campaigns, all candidates talk about relieving the problems of the "middle class," because few in America think of themselves as belonging either to the working class, the downtrodden proletariat, or the snobby upper class, whatever the objective reality may suggest.

The American Revolution was therefore mainly a rebellion for colonial liberation, not a social revolution. The struggle against the mother country had not entailed a civil war over class structure, nor had it left a residue of bitterness and division and disgruntled factions intent either on restoring some preexisting order or on carrying the revolution to a more radical conclusion. As a result, America would not be riven by class warfare. Primogeniture was outlawed, property was widely owned, and land was readily available, especially along the expanding western frontier. There would always be rich and poor, but in aristocracies, Tocqueville observed, servants are a class apart. In such societies there are families of masters as there are families of servants. Equality makes new men of them both and collapses the distance between them. It produces social mobility rather than fixity. Although this was more a statement of the American mythos than an accurate account of reality, it very much reflected a popular mind-set that determined behavior and expectations.

Tocqueville recorded deep misgivings over the problems posed by America's racial diversity, but he was less prophetic about the future in this respect than in others. He wrote with great sympathy of the terrible plight inflicted by European settlement on both American Indians and on the Africans who had been brought here as slaves. He thought that the enslavement of the Africans was a terrible evil and would have to end, but he feared that emancipation would lead to a racial civil war unless the Africans were repatriated. Like Jefferson, he could not imagine that whites and blacks could ever live together on an equal footing in America.[7]

Although Tocqueville's perspective needs to be broadened to include other influences, he was profoundly right about American individualism, and right, too, in thinking that it had a lot to do with a British heritage. And it is probably true that individualism remains, more than any other belief, at the center of American values. Americans disagree about the extent to which individualism should be constrained, both with respect to moral behavior and to economic incentives and rewards, but they agree on the principle. Despite sharp differences of interpretation between liberals and conservatives, they share a consensus on the underlying value of the equal liberty of all individuals.

## ROMAN PLURALISM

Another influence on the framers was the experience of the Roman republic. From the neoclassical architecture of the federal style to the architecture of the country's mixed constitution, with authority divided between a senate and a popular assembly, the American nation came to birth with the example of the Roman republic very much in mind. Hamilton, Jay, and Madison signed their contributions to the *Federalist Papers* with the name Publius, after Publius Valerius, one of the founders of the Roman republic. As Bernard Bailyn observed, the cavalcade of Roman history was a fixation among the rebellious colonials:

> They found their ideal selves, and to some extent their voices, in Brutus, in Cassius, and in Cicero, whose Catilinarian orations the enraptured John Adams, aged 23, declaimed aloud, alone at night in his room. They were simple, stoical Catos, desperate, self-sacrificing Brutuses, silver-tongued Ciceros, and terse, sardonic Tacituses eulogizing Teutonic freedom and denouncing the decadence of Rome. England, the young John Dickinson wrote from London in 1754, is like Sallust's Rome: "Easy to be bought, if there was but a purchaser." Britain, it would soon become clear, was to America "what Caesar was to Rome."[8]

To appreciate the initial fixation on Rome, no more is necessary than to look around the nation's capital. Congress meets on Capitol Hill, with its Capitol building and rotunda. The neoclassical architectural style of our public buildings here and in the state capitals, complete with marble and columns, is deliberate and unmistakable, even though sometimes incongruously an Indian sentry is posted atop the capitol building, as if still on the lookout for pale-faced invaders, and tobacco leaves are chiseled into the marble facings. (Interestingly, the first portraits of Indians showed them to be not just noble savages but noble Romans, complete with togas, on the naive assumption that as primitive peoples they were at the stage Europeans had been at during the time of Rome.)

American political language is shot through with Latinisms. Even though our word for politics is from the Greek, most of our political terminology is either Anglo-Saxon or Latin in derivation: "liberty," from *libertas*, "equality" from *aequalitas*, "president," "president pro tem," "referendum," "senator," "candidate," "nominee," "federalism," "municipality," "justice," "jurisprudence," "consul," "veto," "magistrate," "patronage," "legislature," "legislative sessions sine die," and innumerable legal provisions like habeas corpus and the writ of mandamus used in *Marbury v. Madison*. Our veterans are called "legionnaires." Our national slogan is *"e pluribus unum,"* and we sometimes indulge in other Latin tags like *"Salus populi suprema lex est."* We speak of the "commonwealth" of Virginia, Pennsylvania, and Massachusetts, a translation of the Roman "republic." In the frieze atop Langdell Hall at the Harvard Law School, the inscription reads *"Non sub homines, sed sub deo et leges."* *"Nolo mi tangere"* is the motto of our oldest infantry regiment. The founders, when they took pseudonyms for self-protection, signed themselves Cato, Cicero, Brutus, and Agricola, never Cleisthenes or Pericles.

The reasons Rome was so much on the minds of the founding generation are well appreciated. As numerous historians have shown, the founders looked to Rome and the revival of republicanism in the Italian city-states, as restated by the Whig "Commonwealthmen" of England (among them Milton and Harrington), because they were afraid that their bold experiment in popular government might fail, just as the ancient republic had failed, and for the same reasons: first, because the civic virtue that republics required could succumb to corruption and factionalism, and second because the republican form had proven impossible to maintain under the expansion it ironically made possible. Montesquieu had emphasized the importance of virtue to a republic (as honor was the principle of aristocracy and fear of monarchy), and he had also attributed the decline of the Roman republic to imperial expansion, which required a monarchy. The framers of the Constitution were therefore preoccupied with the need to build formal institutions that would create a mixed government—one that would protect against corruption by dividing power, creating several branches of government to check each other. They followed the English example in creating representative institutions to allow for the size of the country and to prevent overweening central government.

It is certainly not the case that well-educated early Americans were ignorant of the heritage of ancient Greece. John Adams and Thomas Jefferson read all the classical authors, Greek as well as Roman, though Adams sheepishly admitted that he had taken Plato for a friend of popular government until he had actually read *The Republic*.[9] But for their political bearings they looked to Rome, for reasons that are easy to discern. Rome had done more than experiment with popular government. It had achieved it and maintained it for a long time. That experience was transmitted through the Roman Empire, even though the institutions that survived from republican times were only a shell of what they had been. Indeed, what Montesquieu saw as the degradation of the Roman republic into the empire, what Machiavelli had also lamented, became the schoolbook of the framers. How to avoid factions? Make sure there are enough of them to check each other. How to avoid dictatorship? Hamstring the executive. How to avoid the struggle of the orders? Institutionalize it by creating a bicameral legislature so there would be no need for plebeians to fight for a *Lex Hortensis* and all the rest. How to avoid a proletariat? Create a nation of farmers. How to avoid slave revolts? Here of course the framers hesitated to draw the lesson they knew from Rome because they needed to preserve the unity of the colonies, and the result was that they sowed the harvest of a civil war.

The Roman republican model the Americans sought to emulate thus puts a premium not only on civic virtue but also on civil pluralism. It is based on the assumption that individual citizens become effective in influencing affairs of state only as they organize into groups. In Rome, there were two major such groups, or as they were known, "orders," the patricians and the plebeians. To later observers, beginning with Polybius, the "struggle of the orders" and the mixed constitution it produced was the guarantor and matrix of Roman republicanism and the foundation of the Roman idea of liberty—the idea that tyranny or despotism was best prevented by power sharing among the major groups in society. "The government of Rome was admirable," observed Montesquieu, the most revered writer on law and politics of the eighteenth century. "From its birth, abuses of power could always be corrected by its constitution, whether by means of the spirit of the people, the strength of the Senate, or the authority of certain magistrates."[10] Liberty, according to Montesquieu, required divided government: "To prevent the abuse of power, 'tis necessary that by the very disposition of things power should be a check to power."[11]

The Roman republic collapsed not just because a new order, the proletariat—a Latin derivation of a term that literally means those who own nothing but their offspring—had been left out of the social bargain. The republic was also weakened because it expanded so far and wide that the power of the Caesars, founded on the loyalty of the enlarged Roman legions, became too great a force to be contained. The republican form of government, based on the direct participation of citizens, proved unable to control the empire it created. Unlike the Greeks, who restricted citizenship to natives, the Romans made citizenship available to those among their captives they thought deserving, which is to say, who were willing and able to serve in its legions. This policy helped the republic expand its boundaries, but it also contributed to its fall and replacement by the empire of the Caesars. The subsequent fall of the empire could conceivably have been avoided had the Romans transformed it into a commonwealth, extrapolating their domestic pluralism to create a federation of republics.

The American founding fathers sought to learn from the Roman experience. They counted on the patriotic fervor forged in the battles of Bunker Hill and Concord and Lexington and in the campfires of Valley Forge to foster the spirit of civic virtue that had animated the Roman republic. The first constitution, the Articles of Confederation, created a federal system that was initially a league of independent states, though they soon realized that the Congress would be hamstrung unless the states ceded some of their authority to it. Because they recognized that it was physically impossible for an enlarged republic to rely on direct participation, they modified Roman republicanism to allow for representation. To protect against Caesarism, they made sure to subordinate the military to the civil authority, making the president the commander in chief of the armed forces. Finally, they made a virtue out of a Roman vice, arguing that the best safeguard against the corrosive effects of the factionalism that had weakened the Roman republic was the multiplicity of interest groups to be found in so large and diverse a society as this one. In *Federalist* 10, James Madison argued that factions—groups of citizens, whether a minority or a majority, activated by interests adverse to those of others—are both natural and potentially beneficial. "Liberty is to faction," he wrote, "what air is to fire—an aliment without which it instantly expires."[12]

The best remedy for the evils of factionalism was therefore not to try to outlaw interested groups but to have so many that they would check each other—or, as John Kenneth Galbraith would later put it, exercise mutually "countervailing power." Indeed, Arthur F. Bentley, an early twentieth-century political scientist who founded the study of interest groups, observed famously, "When the groups are stated, all is stated. And I mean all."[13] However much he may have exaggerated, there can be no doubt that interest groups continue to exert considerable influence—at times to an overbearing and corrupting degree—on policy outcomes both domestic and foreign. In our checks and balances and our interest group pluralism, we remain very much under the influence of the Roman model.

## ATHENIAN COMMUNALISM

A third influence, less well appreciated, is Athenian. This influence emphasizes loyalty to the community in preference to individualism and pluralism, and it was this identification with the society rather than with individualism or pluralism that came to the fore as Americans embraced a spirit of nationalism, especially in the aftermath of the Civil War. The historical importance of the Greek *polis* in providing a basis for democratic community, not only in America but wherever democracy is adopted, is of paramount importance. The *polis* arose as an advance over tribalism, a way for people of varying kinship affiliations to live together peacefully. It represented, as one classical scholar noted, the triumph of social justice over private vengeance. "The mature polis becomes the means," wrote Humphrey Kitto, "by which the Law is satisfied without producing chaos, since public justice supersedes private vengeance; and the claims of authority are reconciled with the instincts of humanity."[14] The reforms of Cleisthenes, who created the democratic constitution of Athens, were designed to stabilize this transition by promoting loyalty to the community over loyalty to the family and the larger kinship unit, the tribe. One way he did this was to create ten artificial tribes, mingling citizens from different families, in order to provide a counterweight to their kinship affiliations. It is hard to exaggerate the historical significance of this transition and its continued bearing. As we have lately been compelled to appreciate, a major reason democracy has proven so hard to achieve in the Middle East and Africa is the tenacity of tribalism.

Greek influence on American thinking came into play later than British and Roman influence, as the country underwent democratization and especially as a sense of national unity welled up in the wake of the Civil War. The modern Greek struggle for independence struck a chord among early Americans, as the theft of the Elgin marbles—however it justified Byron's outrage—rekindled interest in Greek art and artifacts. At first, the Greek influence on America was mainly architectural: the discovery of the monuments of antiquity in the early nineteenth century made the Greek Revival all the rage. But as the franchise was broadened and political power shifted to populist leaders like Andrew Jackson, the Athenian example came to be viewed more favorably than it had been by the founding federalists, who were leery of popular government.

The founders might have taken the Athenian model more seriously if Aristotle's constitution of Athens, only discovered in the beginning of the twentieth century, had been known to them, but even then it would probably not have been as influential as the histories of Rome. The Greek democracies, after all, were small city-states, considered unstable, whereas the Roman republic had expanded, though it too was only a cautionary model, like the Italian city-states. This attitude was in keeping with what the founding generation learned from Plato, whose *Republic* and *Laws* denounced democracy as a way station en route to tyranny. By giving equality to equals and unequals alike, by making even art a function of a "theatrocracy," and by giving rein to opinion rather than knowledge, democracy undermined the rule of the wise and led to the rule of greed. Follow that example, the founders thought, and the result would be a tyranny of the majority. The framers did not accept Plato's remedies, rule by philosopher kings or guardians or a nocturnal council, complete with noble lies or the "myth of the metals." Without realizing it, they strove for Aristotle's idea of the polity, or mixed constitution, the golden mean between extremes that would prevent revolution by giving all social classes a stake in the system.

Even when democracy began to emerge, as the suffrage was extended and the Jacksonians took office, there were few explicit references to Greek models, but there was a sense that the spoils system was somehow a return to rotation in office, in the sense that now everyone was considered eligible for patronage. This was of course consistent with the pejorative connotation attached to the Athenian experience, thanks to the survival of ancient texts by philosophers critical of the very democracy that had nurtured them! And so was the more explicit reference to Athenian civilization on the part of slaveholders. They tried numerous rationales to defend the South's "peculiar institution." One of them was that the Bible had sanctioned slavery. Another was that Africans were not only different but inferior, and were destined to be slaves. Another was that slavery was a harmonious, organic relationship, as contrasted to the dog-eat-dog style of capitalism. And they tried one other rationale, which was that Athens had achieved a great culture because slavery allowed for the leisure that enabled a creative class of citizens to flourish. Leisure, as was later said, was the basis of culture; the very word meant contemplation. The slave, as Aristotle had declared, was merely an animate tool, destined for this role by nature and not just by the conventions of conquest.

The first sign of a very different interest in Athenian democracy occurred during the period in the early decades of the nineteenth century that has been called America's Greek Revival. Archeology had rekindled interest in Greece just as modern Greece began its struggle for independence from the Ottoman Turks. This was the period celebrated by Byron who died fighting for Greek liberty, by Keats in his "Ode on a Grecian Urn," and by Shelley in *Hellas*: "We are all Greeks—our laws, our literature, our religion, our arts have their roots in Greece. But for Greece, Rome . . . would have spread no illumination with its arms, and we might still have been savages." In Germany the romantics, led by Hölderlin, also celebrated the glory that was Greece and lamented its fall. The Elgin marbles had been plundered, removed from their place on the Parthenon, to the British Museum in 1806, where they helped stimulate a new appreciation for all things Greek. American architecture shifted from Roman to Hellenic models. From about 1820 to 1850, the Greek Revival became America's first national style of architecture, in homes as well as public buildings. Thomas Strickland's Second Bank of the United States in Philadelphia is an adaptation of the style of the Parthenon, with north and south Doric porticoes. Lyceums were created in American cities where workingmen and others could hear speakers discussing current events. The Young Men's Lyceum at Springfield, Illinois, where Lincoln made a major address calling for a respect for law rather than mob rule, was designed to provide a place where young men could hone their skills as orators.

The Athenian influence came to a head in the Gettysburg addresses of Lincoln and Everett—the former magnificent, the latter only grandiloquent—with their parallels to Pericles' funeral oration. Lincoln's exquisitely crafted speech, though at first little noted, became a critical event in American history because it gave meaning to the Civil War, reaffirming and restating the essential national goals and rationalizing the struggle against secession and the inequality of slavery. Until then, the United States was confused about its identity, still very much a nation of separate states, regionally divided with only a fragile sense of national unity, the division exacerbated by the increasingly sharp disagreement over the morality of slavery.

Gettysburg was the battle that had saved the union as Marathon had saved Greece. As Garry Wills has skillfully shown, both Lincoln's address, and the much longer but unremembered address by Edward Everett, were modeled on Pericles' famous funeral oration of almost 2,400 years earlier. But this revival of the ancient tradition was much more than a mere imitation in style; it amounted to a recognition that the Athenian model was now as important as the Roman model had been previously. As Wills puts it, the conception of "America as a second Athens was an idea whose moment had come in the nineteenth century."[15] The constitution was a doctrine reflecting the Roman acceptance of class inequality, but the Gettysburg address returned to the egalitarian promise of the Declaration of Independence, now explicitly extended beyond the white race. In a very real sense, the end of the Civil War, followed by the adoption of the Thirteenth, Fourteenth, and Fifteenth amendments, restored the spirit of the Declaration to the center of the American political ideal, whereas the Constitution had made it peripheral to the need to create a federal union, even at the price of allowing slavery. Lincoln was keenly aware that he was appealing to the Declaration against the compromises embodied in the Constitution, in effect rewriting the Constitution to make it not only the shield of union but of a nation dedicated to universal emancipation. Wills is certainly right in concluding that Lincoln and not just the war itself brought forth a new nation out of the blood and turmoil of the Civil War, and that he did so by reaffirming and enlarging the promise of equality in the Declaration. It is that promise of equality which, despite the existence of slavery in both societies, comes closest to the Athenian ideal.

After the Civil War and what Lincoln called America's "new birth of freedom," communalism reappeared in several forms. It was evident in calls for urban socialism, based on the religion of solidarity manifested in nationalism, rural populism, and the movement that Theodore Roosevelt called "the New Nationalism"—at once expansionist abroad and calling for vigorous government at home. This was followed by two movements for collective uplift, Progressivism and the New Deal, and lately by otherwise quite different calls for communitarianism and national unity against the threat of terrorism. Throughout, the spirit of Athenian democracy has animated the political process, allowing for dialogue and adaptation. The classicist Josiah Ober has described this spirit well, in a way that bears not only on Athenian experience but on that of modern democracy as well:

> Athens was a democracy, not just because the ordinary citizen had a vote, but because he was a participant in maintaining a political culture and a value system that constituted him a free agent and the political equal of his elite neighbor. Through publicly performed speech acts, democratic institutions were implicated in an ongoing process of defining and redefining the contingent truths used in political decision-making and of assimilating local knowledges into an overarching democratic knowledge.[16]

## THE AMERICAN SYNTHESIS

The net result is that American political thinking came to embody the three basic forms of democratic autonomy: individual, plural, and communal. By the standards of individual autonomy, society exists to promote the liberty of the individual, not to subordinate that liberty to the good of the whole or a potentially tyrannical majority—even a presumably moral majority. Pluralists contend that a free society is inevitably a strong civil society in which people will band together in groups, based on economic interest, ideology, or cultural, religious, and ethnic affinity, and that government should be structured so as to promote voluntary cooperation or give and take among these groups rather than to require their suppression or subordination to the will of some omnicompetent state. They therefore often prefer consensual, federal systems of government to unitary, majoritarian forms, consider proportional representation the fairest and most appropriate form of election for democracy, and sometimes prefer that group rights be acknowledged alongside the rights of individuals. Those who believe in communal autonomy, whether they are communitarians or strong nationalists, contend that democratic governments should aim to be guided by the common good, even if this means restricting individual liberty and the play of interest groups. In varying ways, they believe that the state should not be simply a night watchman, but an enabler and a reflection of common purpose. They do not think that the ends of democracy are properly satisfied when individuals are allowed to fend for themselves, to experience what Isaiah Berlin called negative freedom or "freedom from," or when organized interest groups are allowed to twist public policy to their own advantage.

The interplay among proponents of these three forms of autonomy shapes the democratic dialogue and finds expression in public policy. When they are artfully blended, the policies tend to be most successful; when one predominates to the detriment of the others, the policy outcome tends to arouse resentment and dissatisfaction at home and—in the case of extreme nationalism—the kind of hostility abroad that the Athenians found when they treated the other members of the Delian League as imperial satrapies rather than sister democracies.

In the twentieth century, democracy had formidable enemies who could cite the critiques of democracy by elite theorists, racists, and radicals, all of whom argued that democracy was inefficient as well as wrongheaded. H. L. Mencken, the acerbic "sage of Baltimore," said that democracy meant putting the inmates in charge of the asylum. Today, democracy still has enemies, notably militant Islamists, but these are much less formidable intellectually because the critique they offer is embedded in an abhorrent theology celebrating terrorism as martyrdom, and the alternative social order they propose is so retrograde and stultifying that it can appeal only to those who have not experienced the opportunities for fulfillment that freedom offers.

The larger problem facing democracies stems, oddly enough, from tensions produced when the ideals that are its very strengths come into conflict rather than coexist. Excessive individualism risks weakening social cohesion, but too much social control, even in the name of assuring welfare, stifles initiative and discourages responsibility. It is well to remember that Athenian communalism coexisted for a time with the practice of ostracism. There was no respect for the rights of the individual that would preclude the punishment of exile. During the era of McCarthyism, Americans made a fetish of loyalty to the community, stigmatizing all dissent as disloyalty or un-American and overriding the concern for individual liberty, oddly enough in the name of supporting the free world against a totalitarian enemy. Taken to an extreme, pluralism promotes multiculturalism, weakening the ties that bind all Americans to a common identity and loyalty. It produces a crazy quilt of varying state laws that penalize sexual conduct in one place but not another and ethnic enclaves that seek to prevent assimilation and demand that schools inculcate multicultural diversity rather than a sense of national unity. A balance blending the liberty of the individual with respect for the interests of groups and concern for the common good produces a tempered vitality.

Finally, one other factor that shapes America as a state of mind is a capacity for adaptation, the capacity that Darwin saw as the basis of species' perpetuation in nature. The economist Joseph Schumpeter said that the secret to the strength of capitalism is "creative destruction." Thanks to the spirit of entrepreneurs, old industries are made obsolete and new ones take their place. Max Lerner expressed confidence that we would not go through a decline like the Roman Empire because of our capacity for "extended genesis," or, in other words, for remaking ourselves as conditions change.[17] Walter Russell Meade contends that both Britons and Americans have shown more adaptability than others because they have resisted rigid government, rigid economic systems, and rigid religions.[18] Even Edmund Burke, the founding father of conservatism, said that a government without the means of change is without the means of its own preservation. The greatest danger now facing Americans is less the threat of any outside power so much as the danger of becoming too inflexible, too deadlocked by ideological polarization, so as to lose that capacity for adaptation. If the synthesis of benign Western values that shaped the country's mind remains resilient, whichever way the electorate tilts, to one side or the other of the American consensus, the country will remain an example to be emulated.

## NOTES

1. Alexis de Tocqueville, *Democracy in America*, trans. George L. Lawrence (Garden City, NY: Doubleday, 1966), vol. 2, p. 485.

2. Walt Whitman, *The Complete Prose Works of Walt Whitman* (New York: Putnam, 1902), vol. 2, p. 50.

3. J. M. Keynes, *The General Theory of Employment, Interest, and Money* (London: Macmillan, 1936), p. 383.

4. Tocqueville, op. cit, conclusion, pp. 408–11.

5. Edmund Burke, *Speech on Conciliation with America*, ed. D. Thompson (New York: Henry Holt, 1911), pp. 19–25.

6. Tocqueville, op. cit., vol. 2, p. 439.

7. Ibid., vol. 1, p. 336.

8. Bernard Bailyn, *The Ideological Origins of the American Revolution* (Cambridge, MA: Harvard University Press, 1967), p. 26.

9. Ibid., pp. 24–25.

10. Charles Secondat Baron de Montesquieu, *Considerations on the Greatness of the Romans and Their Decline* (New York: Free Press, 1965).

11. Charles Secondat Baron de Montesquieu, *The Spirit of Laws*, ed. D. W. Carruthers (Berkeley: University of California Press, 1977), vol. 6, p. 200.

12. Alexander Hamilton, John Jay, and James Madison, *The Federalist Papers*, ed. Clinton Rossiter (New York: Penguin, 1961), no. 10, p. 78.

13. Arthur F. Bentley, *The Process of Government: A Study of Social Pressures* (Chicago: University of Chicago Press, 1908), p. 208.

14. H. D. F. Kitto, *The Greeks* (Harmondsworth: Penguin, 1951), p. 77.

15. Garry Wills, *Lincoln at Gettysburg: The Words That Remade America* (New York: Simon & Schuster, 1992), p. 44.

16. Josiah Ober, *Political Dissent in Democratic Athens* (Princeton, NJ: Princeton University Press, 1998), p. 40.

17. Max Lerner, *America as a Civilization: Life and Thought in the United States Today* (New York: Simon & Schuster, 1957), p. 39. See also Sanford Lakoff, *Max Lerner: Pilgrim in the Promised Land* (Chicago: University of Chicago Press, 1998), pp. 153–86.

18. Walter Russell Meade, *God and Gold: Britain, America, and the Making of the Modern World* (New York: Knopf, 2007).

# Bibliography

Abdo, Geneive. *No God But God: Egypt and the Triumph of Islam*. New York: Oxford University Press, 2000.

Ackerman, Bruce. *Social Justice in the Liberal State*. New Haven, CT: Yale University Press, 1980.

Advielle, V. *Histoire de Gracchus Babeuf et du babouvisme*. Geneva: Slatkin, 1884.

Ali, Aayan Hirsi. *Infidel*. New York: Free Press, 2007.

Amiel, Barbara. *Locke and America*. Oxford: Oxford University Press, 1996.

Anderson, Benedict. *Imagined Communities: Reflections on the Origin and Spread of Nationalism*. London: Verso, 2006.

Appleby, Joyce O. *Liberalism and Republicanism in the Historical Imagination*. Cambridge, MA: Harvard University Press, 1992.

Arendt, Hannah. *The Human Condition: A Study of the Central Dilemmas Facing Modern Man*. Garden City, NY: Doubleday Anchor, 1959.

Aron, Raymond. *An Essay on Freedom*. Trans. Helen Weaver. New York: World Publishing, 1970.

Augustine. *The City of God*. Trans. Marcus Dods. New York: Modern Library, 1950.

Bailyn, Bernard. *The Ideological Origins of the American Revolution*. Cambridge, MA: Harvard University Press, 1967.

Bainton, Roland. *The Left Wing of the Reformation*. Chicago: University of Chicago Press, 1941.

Baron, Hans. *The Crisis of the Early Italian Renaissance: Civic Humanism and Republican Liberty in an Age of Classicism and Tyranny*. Rev. ed. 2 vols. Princeton, NJ: Princeton University Press.

Bartlett, Irving H. *The American Mind in the Mid-Nineteenth Century*. New York: Thomas Y. Crowell, 1967.

Beaumont, Gustave de. *Memoir, Letters, and Remains of Alexis de Tocqueville*. Boston: Ticknor & Fields, 1862. Reprinted University Microfilms, 1983.

Becker, Carl L. *The Declaration of Independence: A Study in the History of Political Ideas*. New York: Knopf, 1942.

Beer, Samuel H. "Liberalism and the National Idea." In *Left, Right and Center: Essays on Liberalism and Conservatism in the United States*, ed. Robert A. Goldwin. Chicago: Rand McNally, 1965.

———. "The Roots of New Labour: Liberalism Rediscovered." *Economist*, 7–13 February 1998, pp. 23–25.

Bellah, Robert, Richard Madsen, William M. Sullivan, Ann Swidler, and Steven M. Tipton. *Habits of the Heart*. Berkeley: University of California Press, 1985.

Bennett, William J. *The De-Valuing of Our Culture: The Fight for Our Culture and Our Schools*. New York: Summit, 1992.

Bentham, Jeremy. *Rights, Representation, and Reform: Nonsense upon Stilts and Other Writings on the French Revolution; The Collected Works of Jeremy Bentham*. Ed. Philip Schofield, Catherine Pease, and Cyprian Blamires. Oxford: Oxford University Press, 2002.

Bentley, Arthur F. *The Process of Government: A Study of Social Pressures*. Chicago: University of Chicago Press, 1908.

Berlin, Isaiah. *Liberty: Incorporating Four Essays on Liberty*. Ed. Henry Hardy with an essay on Berlin and his critics. Oxford: Oxford University Press, 2002.

Boesche, Roger. *The Strange Liberalism of Alexis de Tocqueville*. Ithaca, NY: Cornell University Press, 1987.

Bohlen, Charles E. *Witness to History*. New York: Norton, 1973.

Bouwsma, William J. *Venice and the Defense of Republican Liberty*. Berkeley: University of California Press, 1968.

Brown, L. Carl. *Religion and the State: The Muslim Approach to Politics*. New York: Columbia University Press, 2000.

Bultmann, Rudolf K. *The Theology of the New Testament*. Trans. K. Grobel. New York: Scribner, 1951.

Burckhardt, Jacob. *The Civilization of the Renaissance in Italy* (1860). Trans. S. G. C. Middlemore. London: Phaidon, 1951.

Burke, Edmund. *Reflections on the Revolution in France*. Ed. L. G. Mitchell. New York: Oxford University Press, 1993.

———. *Speech on Conciliation with America*. Ed. D. Thompson. New York: Henry Holt, 1911.

Carlyle, A. J., and R. W. Carlyle. *A History of Mediaeval Political Theory in the West*. New York: Barnes & Noble, 1953.

Cassirer, Ernst. *Kant's Life and Thought*. Trans. James Haden. New Haven, CT: Yale University Press, 1981.

Chapman, Gerald. *Edmund Burke: The Practical Imagination*. Cambridge, MA: Harvard University Press, 1967.

Cohn, Norman. *The Pursuit of the Millennium: Revolutionary Messianism in Medieval and Reformation Europe and Its Bearing on Modern Totalitarian Movements*. New York: Harper, 1961.

Cole, G. D. H. *A History of Socialist Thought*. London: Macmillan, 1953.

Croly, Herbert. *Progressive Democracy*. New York: Macmillan, 1914.

Dahl, Robert A. *Polyarchy: Participation and Opposition*. New Haven, CT: Yale University Press, 1971.

Dalberg, J. E. E., Lord Acton. "Nationality" (1862). In *Essays in the Liberal Interpretation of History*, ed. William H. McNeill. Chicago: University of Chicago Press, 1967.

Davis, David Brion. *The Problem of Slavery in the Age of Revolution, 1770–1823.* Ithaca, NY: Cornell University Press, 1975.

Dennis, Lawrence. *The Coming American Fascism*. New York: Harper, 1936.

Deutsch, Karl. *Nationalism and Social Communication: An Inquiry into the Foundations of Nationality.* Cambridge, MA: MIT Press, 1966.

Diggins, John. "Knowledge and Sorrow: Louis Hartz's Quarrel with American History." *Political Theory* 16, no. 3 (1988): pp. 335–76.

———. *The Lost Soul of American Politics: Virtue, Self-Interest, and the Foundations of Liberalism.* New York: Basic Books, 1988.

Drescher, Seymour, ed. *Dilemmas of Democracy: Tocqueville and Modernization.* Pittsburgh: University of Pittsburgh Press, 1968.

———. *Tocqueville and Beaumont on Social Reform.* New York: Harper & Row, 1968.

Dudden, C. Homes. *The Life and Times of St. Ambrose.* Oxford: Oxford University Press, 1935.

Dworetz, Stephen M. *The Unvarnished Doctrine: Locke, Liberalism, and the American Revolution.* Durham, NC: Duke University Press, 1990.

Dworkin, Ronald. *Taking Rights Seriously.* Cambridge, MA: Harvard University Press, 1977.

Elster, John. *Political Psychology.* Cambridge: Cambridge University Press, 1993.

Emerson, Ralph Waldo. *Essays and Lectures.* New York: Library of America, 1983.

Engels, Frederick. "On the History of Early Christianity" (1894–1895). In Karl Marx and Friedrich Engels, *Basic Writings on Politics and Philosophy*, ed. L. Feuer. New York: Doubleday, 1959.

Evans, Richard J. *The Coming of the Third Reich.* London: Penguin, 2003.

Farias, Richard. *Heidegger and Nazism.* Philadelphia: Temple University Press, 1987.

Faulkner, Robert K. *The Jurisprudence of John Marshall.* Princeton, NJ: Princeton University Press, 1968.

Feuerbach, Ludwig. *The Essence of Christianity.* Trans. G. Eliot. New York: Harper, 1957.

Franco, Paul. *The Political Philosophy of Michael Oakeshott.* New Haven, CT: Yale University Press, 1990.

Fraser, Antonia. *Cromwell: The Lord Protector.* New York: Knopf, 1973.

Frei, Christopher. *Hans J. Morgenthau: An Intellectual Biography.* Baton Rouge: Louisiana State University Press, 2001.

Freud, Sigmund. *Collected Papers.* Ed. James Strachey. New York: Basic Books, 1960.

———. *Group Psychology and the Analysis of the Ego.* Trans. J. Strachey. New York: Norton, 1949.

Friedrich, Carl J. *Constitutional Reason of State.* Providence, RI: Brown University Press, 1956.

Frohnen, Bruce. *Virtue and the Promise of Conservatism: The Legacy of Burke and Tocqueville.* Lawrence: University Press of Kansas, 1993.

Fromm, Erich. *Escape from Freedom.* New York: Holt, Rinehart & Winston, 1941.

Gaddis, John Lewis. *Surprise, Security, and the American Experience*. Cambridge, MA: Harvard University Press, 2004.

Gallie, W. B. "Essentially Contested Concepts." *Proceedings of the Aristotelian Society* 56 (1956): pp. 167–98.

Galston, William A. *Liberal Purposes*. Cambridge: Cambridge University Press, 1991.

Gobineau, Arthur de. *Essai sur l'inégalité des races humaines*. Paris: Firmin-Didot, 1940.

Green, T. H. *Lectures on Political Obligation*. London: Longmans, 1941.

Griffiths, Martin. *Realism, Idealism and International Politics: A Reinterpretation*. London: Routledge, 1992.

Habeck, Mary. *Knowing the Enemy: Jihadist Ideology and the War on Terror*. New Haven, CT: Yale University Press, 2006.

Hadari, Saguiv A. *Theory in Practice: Tocqueville's New Science of Politics*. Stanford, CA: Stanford University Press, 1989.

Hamilton, Alexander, John Jay, and James Madison, *The Federalist Papers*. Ed. Clinton Rossiter. New York: Penguin, 1961.

Hamilton, Edith. *The Echo of Greece*. New York: Norton, 1957.

Hamowy, Ronald. "Jefferson and the Scottish Enlightenment: A Critique of Garry Wills's *Inventing America: Jefferson's Declaration of Independence*." *The William and Mary Quarterly*, 3rd ser., vol. 36, no. 4 (October 1979): pp. 503–23.

Hartz, Louis. *The Liberal Tradition in America: An Interpretation of American Political Thought since the Revolution*. New York: Harcourt Brace, 1955; reissued, Harcourt Brace Jovanovich, 1980.

Hearnshaw, F. J. C. *Conservatism in England*. New York: Howard Fertig, 1967.

Herberg, Will. "The Religion of Americans and American Religion." In *Religious Conflict in America*, ed. Earl Raab. Garden City, NY: Doubleday Anchor, 1964, pp. 101–25.

Herzog, Don. *Poisoning the Minds of the Lower Orders*. Princeton, NJ: Princeton University Press, 1998.

Higgonet, Patrice, *Sister Republics: The Origins of French and American Republicanism*. Cambridge, MA: Harvard University Press, 1988.

Himmelfarb, Gertrude. *On Liberty and Liberalism: The Case of John Stuart Mill*. New York: Knopf, 1974.

Hirsch, H. N. *A Theory of Liberty: The Constitution and Minorities*. New York: Routledge, 1992.

Hirschman, Albert O. *The Passions and the Interests: Political Arguments for Capitalism before Its Triumph*. Princeton, NJ: Princeton University Press, 1977.

Hitchens, Christopher. *God Is Not Great: How Religion Poisons Everything*. New York: Hachette, 2007.

Hobhouse, Leonard. *Liberalism*. New York: Oxford University Press, 1964.

Hofstadter, Richard. *The American Political Tradition and the Men Who Made It*. New York: Vintage, 1989.

———. *The Progressive Historians: Turner, Beard, and Parrington*. New York: Knopf, 1968.

Holmes, Stephen. *Benjamin Constant and the Making of Modern Liberalism*. New Haven, CT: Yale University Press, 1984.

Horowitz, Donald L. *Ethnic Groups in Conflict*. Berkeley: University of California Press, 1985.

Houston, Alan Craig. *Algernon Sidney and the Republican Heritage in England and America*. Princeton, NJ: Princeton University Press, 1991.

Hume, David. *Hume's Moral and Political Philosophy*. Ed. Henry D. Aiken. New York: Hafner, 1948.

Huntington, Samuel P. *American Politics: The Promise of Disharmony*. Cambridge, MA: Harvard University Press, 1981.

———. *The Third Wave: Democratization in the Late Twentieth Century*. Norman: Oklahoma University Press, 1991.

Ibrahim, Saad. *Egypt, Islam, and Democracy: Critical Essays*. New York: American University in Cairo Press, 2002.

Jaeger, Werner. "The Greek Ideas of Immortality." *Harvard Theological Review* 52, no. 3 (July 1959): pp. 135–48.

Jaffa, Harry V. *American Conservatism and the American Founding*. Durham, NC: Carolina Academic Press, 1984.

Jardin, André. *Tocqueville: A Biography*. Trans. L. K. Davis with R. Hemenway. New York: Farrar, Strauss & Giroux, 1988.

Jefferson, Thomas. *The Portable Jefferson*. Ed. Merrill Peterson. New York: Viking, 1975.

Karsh, Efraim. *Islamic Imperialism: A History*. New Haven, CT: Yale University Press, 2006.

Kedourie, Elie. *Nationalism*. New York: Praeger, 1962.

Kennan, George F. *American Diplomacy, 1900–1950*. Chicago: University of Chicago Press, 1984.

———. *Around the Cragged Hill: A Personal and Political Philosophy*. New York: Norton, 1993.

Kennan, George F., and John Lukacs, eds. *George F. Kennan and the Origins of Containment, 1944–1946*. Columbia: University of Missouri Press, 1997.

Keynes, J. M. *The General Theory of Employment, Interest, and Money*. London: Macmillan, 1936.

Kierkegaard, Søren. "On Authority and Revelation." In *The Book on Adler, or a Cycle of Ethico-Religious Essays* (1848), trans. W. Lowrie. Princeton, NJ: Princeton University Press, 1955.

Kirk, Russell. *Edmund Burke: A Genius Reconsidered*. New Rochelle, NY: Arlington House, 1967.

Kissinger, Henry A. "A Gentle Analyst of Power: Hans Morgenthau." *New Republic*, 2–9 August 1980, pp. 12–14.

Kitto, H. D. F. *The Greeks*. Harmondsworth: Penguin, 1951.

Kohn, Hans. *The Idea of Nationalism*. New York: Macmillan, 1944.

The Koran. Trans. N. J. Dawood. London: Penguin Classics, 1956.

Kramnick, Isaac, ed. *Edmund Burke*. Englewood Cliffs, NJ: Prentice Hall, 1974.

———. *Republicanism and Bourgeois Radicalism: Political Ideology in Late Eighteenth Century England and America*. Ithaca, NY: Cornell University Press, 1990.

Kristol, Irving. *On the Democratic Idea in America*. New York: Harper & Row, 1972.

Kymlicka, Will. *Liberalism, Community, and Culture*. Oxford: Clarendon Press, 1989.

Lakoff, George. *Moral Politics: What Conservatives Know That Liberals Don't*. Chicago: University of Chicago Press, 1996.

Lakoff, Sanford A. "Democracy." *Encyclopedia of Nationalism*, vol. 1. San Diego: Academic Press, 2000, pp. 101–20.

———. *Democracy: History, Theory, Practice*. Boulder, CO: Westview Press, 1996.

———. *Equality in Political Philosophy*. Cambridge, MA: Harvard University Press, 1964.

———. *Max Lerner: Pilgrim in the Promised Land*. Chicago: University of Chicago Press, 1998.

———. "The Reality of Muslim Exceptionalism." *Journal of Democracy* 15, no. 4 (October 2004): pp. 133–39.

Lambton, Ann K. *State and Government in Medieval Islam: An Introduction to the Study*. New York: Routledge, 1981.

Lang, Timothy, "Lord Acton and 'the Insanity of Nationality.'" *Journal of the History of Ideas* 63, no. 1 (January 2002): pp. 129–49.

Larmore, Charles. *The Morals of Modernity: An Introduction to Contemporary Philosophy*. New York: Oxford University Press, 2002.

Laski, Harold J. *The Rise of European Liberalism: An Essay in Interpretation*. London: Allen & Unwin, 1936.

Lawler, Peter Augustine. *The Restless Mind: Alexis de Tocqueville on the Origin and Perpetuation of Human Liberty*. Lanham, MD: Rowman & Littlefield, 1993.

Le Bon, Gustav. *The Crowd: A Study of the Popular Mind*. London: T. Fisher Unwin, 1920.

Lerner, Max. *America as a Civilization: Life and Thought in America Today*. New York: Simon & Schuster, 1957.

Levy, David W. *Herbert Croly of the New Republic*. Princeton, NJ: Princeton University Press, 1985.

Lewis, Bernard. *The Middle East: A Brief History of the Last 2,000 Years*. New York: Scribner, 1995.

———. *The Political Language of Islam*. Chicago: University of Chicago Press, 1988.

Lewis, Paul H. "Was Perón a Fascist? An Inquiry into the Nature of Fascism." *Journal of Politics* 42, no. 1 (February 1980): pp. 242–56.

Lijphart, Arend. *Patterns of Democracy: Government Forms and Performances in Thirty-Six Countries*. New Haven, CT: Yale University Press, 1999.

Lind, Michael. *The Next American Nation: The New Nationalism and the Fourth American Revolution*. New York: Free Press, 1995.

Lipset, Seymour M. *The First New Nation*. Garden City, NY: Doubleday, 1963.

Locke, John. *Two Treatises on Government* (1690). Ed. P. Laslett. Cambridge: Cambridge University Press, 1964.

Lovejoy, A. O. *Essays in the History of Ideas*. Baltimore, MD: Johns Hopkins University Press, 1948.

Lovejoy, A. O., and Franz Boas. *Primitivism and Related Ideas in Antiquity*. Baltimore, MD: Johns Hopkins Press, 1935.

Luther, Martin. *A Commentary on St. Paul's Epistle to the Galatians* (1535). Ed. P. S. Watson (London: James Clarke, 1953).

———. *Three Treatises*. Philadelphia: Fortress Press, 1943.

———. *Works of Martin Luther*. Philadelphia: A. J. Holman, 1930.

Lyttleton, Adrian, ed. *Italian Fascisms from Pareto to Gentile.* New York: Harper & Row, 1975.

Mably, Gabriel Bonnot de. *Oeuvres.* Paris, 1796.

Macedo, Stephen. *Liberal Virtues: Citizenship, Virtue, and Community in Liberal Constitutionalism.* Oxford: Clarendon Press, 1986.

Machiavelli, Niccolò. *The Prince.* Trans. Mark Musa. New York: St. Martin's, 1964.

Macpherson, C. B. *Burke.* Oxford: Oxford University Press, 1980.

———. *The Political Theory of Possessive Individualism: Hobbes to Locke.* Oxford: Oxford University Press, 1962.

Magnus, Philip. *Edmund Burke.* London: John Murray, 1939.

Mahoney, Daniel J. *The Liberal Political Science of Raymond Aron.* Lanham, MD: Rowman & Littlefield, 1992.

Maier, Pauline. *American Scripture: Making the Declaration of Independence.* New York: Knopf, 1997.

Manent, Pierre. *Tocqueville and the Nature of Democracy.* Trans. John Waggoner. Lanham, MD: Rowman & Littlefield, 1996.

Mannheim, Karl. *Conservatism: A Contribution to the Sociology of Knowledge.* Ed. David Kettler, Volker Meja, and Nico Stehr. London: Routledge and Kegan Paul, 1986.

———. "Conservative Thought." *Essays on Sociology and Social Psychology,* ed. Paul Kecskemeti. New York: Oxford University Press, 1953.

Mansfield, Harvey C., Jr. *America's Constitutional Soul.* Baltimore, MD: Johns Hopkins Press, 1978.

———. *The Spirit of Liberalism.* Cambridge, MA: Harvard University Press, 1978.

———. *Statesmanship and Party Government: A Study of Burke and Bolingbroke.* Chicago: University of Chicago Press, 1980.

Marx, Karl. *Capital: A Critique of Political Economy.* Trans. E. Paul and C. Paul. London, 1930.

———. *Marx's Early Writings.* Trans. T. B. Bottomore. New York: McGraw-Hill, 1964.

Marx, Karl, and Frederick Engels. *The Communist Manifesto* (1848). Trans. S. Moore. London: Communist Party of Great Britain, 1948.

Mayer, J.-P. *Alexis de Tocqueville: A Biographical Essay.* New York: Harper, 1960.

McCloskey, Herbert, and John Zaller, *The American Ethos: Public Attitudes toward Capitalism and Democracy.* Cambridge, MA: Harvard University Press, 1984.

McKitrick, Eric L., ed. *Slavery Defended: The Views of the Old South.* Englewood Cliffs, NJ: Prentice Hall, 1963.

Meade, Walter Russell. *God and Gold: Britain, America, and the Making of the Modern World.* New York: Knopf, 2007.

Meinecke, Friedrich. *Machiavellism: The Doctrine of Raison d'état and Its Place in Modern History.* Trans. Douglas Scott. New Haven, CT: Yale University Press, 1957.

Mencken, H. L. *Notes on Democracy.* London: Jonathan Cape, 1927.

Merk, Frederick. *Manifest Destiny and Mission in American History.* New York: Knopf, 1963.

Mill, John Stuart. "M. de Tocqueville on Democracy in America." In *The Philosophy of John Stuart Mill,* ed. M. Goldman. New York: Modern Library, 1961.

———. *Utilitarianism, On Liberty and Considerations on Representative Government.* New York: J. M. Dent & Sons, 1972.

Mishal, Saul, and Avraham Sela. *The Palestinian Hamas: Vision, Violence, and Coexistence.* New York: Columbia University Press, 2000.

Mitchell, Joshua Mitchell. *The Fragility of Freedom: Tocqueville on Religion, Democracy, and the American Future.* Chicago: University of Chicago Press, 1995.

Moin, Roger. *Khomeini: Life of the Prophet.* New York: St. Martin's, 2000.

Monahan, Arthur P. *Consent, Coercion, and Limit: The Medieval Origins of Parliamentary Democracy.* Kingston and Montreal: McGill-Queens University Press, 1987.

Montesquieu, Charles Secondat Baron de. *Considerations on the Greatness of the Romans and Their Decline.* New York: Free Press, 1965.

———. *The Spirit of the Laws.* Trans. Anne M. Cohler, Basia Carolyn Miller, and Harold Samuel Stone. Cambridge: Cambridge University Press, 1989.

Moore, George Foot. *Judaism in the First Centuries of the Christian Era, the Age of the Tannaim.* Cambridge, MA: Harvard University Press, 1962.

Morgenthau, Hans J. *The Decline of Democratic Politics.* Chicago: University of Chicago Press, 1962.

———. *In Defense of the National Interest: A Critical Examination of American Foreign Policy.* New York: Knopf, 1951.

———. *Politics among Nations: The Struggle for Power and Peace.* 3rd ed. New York: Knopf, 1962. 5th ed., 1973.

———. "The Primacy of National Interest." *American Scholar* 18 (Spring 1949): pp. 207–12.

———. *The Purpose of American Politics.* New York: Knopf, 1964.

Morison, Samuel Eliot. *The Oxford History of the American People.* New York: Oxford University Press, 1965.

Morone, James A. *The Democratic Wish.* New York: Basic Books, 1998.

Mosca, Gaetano. *The Ruling Class.* Trans. Arthur Livingston. New York: McGraw-Hill, 1939.

Moulakis, Athanasios. "Civic Humanism." *Stanford Encyclopedia of Philosophy,* ed. N. Zelta. Fall 2008 edition.

———. *Republican Realism in Renaissance Florence: Frances Guicciardini's "Discorso di Logrogno."* Lanham, MD: Rowman & Littlefield, 1998.

*The New English Bible.* Oxford and Cambridge: Oxford University Press and Cambridge University Press, 1961.

Niebuhr, Reinhold. *Christianity and Power Politics.* Hamden, CT: Archon Books, 1969.

———. *Moral Man and Immoral Society: A Study in Ethics and Politics.* New York: Scribner, 1932.

Nietzsche, Friedrich. *The Philosophy of Nietzsche.* Trans. H. B. Samuel. New York: Modern Library, 1927.

Nisbet, Robert. "Sources of Conservatism." In *Edmund Burke: Appraisals and Applications,* ed. Daniel E. Ritchie. New Brunswick: Transaction Publishers, 1998.

Nozick, Robert. *Anarchy, State and Utopia.* New York: Basic Books, 1974.

Oakeshott, Michael. *Rationalism in Politics and Other Essays.* London: Methuen, 1962.

Ober, Josiah. *Political Dissent in Democratic Athens.* Princeton, NJ: Princeton University Press, 1998.

O'Brien, Conor Cruise. *The Great Melody: A Thematic Biography and Commented Anthology of Edmund Burke*. London: Sinclair-Stevenson, 1992.

Orwell, George. *A Collection of Essays*. Orlando, FL: Harcourt Brace Jovanovich, 1946.

Paine, Thomas. *Collected Writings*. New York: Library of America, 1995.

Palmer, R. R. *The Age of the Democratic Revolution*. 2 vols. Princeton, NJ: Princeton University Press, 1959.

Pangle, Thomas. *The Spirit of Modern Republicanism: The Moral Vision of the American Founders and the Philosophy of Locke*. Chicago: University of Chicago Press, 1988.

Pangle, Thomas, and Peter J. Ahrendorf. *Justice among Nations*. Lawrence: University of Kansas Press, 1999.

Patterson, Orlando. "The Liberal Millennium." *New Republic*, 8 November 1999, pp. 54–63.

Peters, E. C. *The Children of Abraham: Judaism, Christianity, Islam*. Princeton, NJ: Princeton University Press, 2005.

Pico della Mirandola, Gian Francesco, "Oration on the Dignity of Man." In *The Renaissance Philosophy of Man*, ed. Ernest Cassirer, Paul Oscar Kristeller, John Herman Randall, et al. Chicago: University of Chicago Press, 1948.

Plamenatz, John. "Equality of Opportunity." In *Aspects of Human Equality, Fifteenth Symposium of the Conference on Science and Religion*, ed. Lyman Bryson et al. New York: Harper, 1957.

Plato. *Laws*. Trans. B. Jowett. New York: Random House, 1937.

Pocock, J. G. A. *The Machiavellian Moment: Florentine Political Thought and the Atlantic Republican Tradition*. Princeton, NJ: Princeton University Press, 1975.

———. "Virtue and Commerce in the Eighteenth Century." *Journal of Interdisciplinary History* 3, no. 1 (1972): pp. 119–34.

Pope, Liston. *Millhands and Preachers: A Study of Gastonia*. New Haven, CT: Yale University Press, 1942.

Puddington, Arch. "The 2007 Freedom House Survey." *Journal of Democracy* 19, no. 2 (April 2008): pp. 61–73.

Rawls, John. *Political Liberalism*. New York: Columbia University Press, 1993.

———. *A Theory of Justice*. Cambridge, MA: Harvard University Press, 1971.

Raz, Joseph. *The Morality of Freedom*. Oxford: Clarendon Press, 1986.

Reich, Charles. *The Greening of America: How the Youth Revolution Is Trying to Make America Livable*. New York: Random House, 1970.

Rieff, Philip. *Freud: The Mind of the Moralist*. New York: Viking, 1959.

Roazen, Paul. "Louis Hartz's Teaching." *Virginia Quarterly Review* 64, no. 1 (Winter 1988): pp. 108–25.

Robb, David M., and J. J. Garrison. *Art in the Western World*. New York: Harper & Brothers, 1942.

Robbins, Caroline. *The Eighteenth-Century Commonwealth-Man*. Cambridge, MA: Harvard University Press, 1959.

Rodgers, R. *Contested Truths: Keywords in American Politics since Independence*. New York: Basic Books, 1987.

Rosenblum, Nancy L. *Another Liberalism: Romanticism and the Reconstruction of Liberal Thought*. Cambridge, MA: Harvard University Press, 1987.

Ross, Dorothy. "The Liberal Tradition Revisited and the Republican Tradition Addressed." In *New Directions in American Intellectual History*, ed. John Higham and Paul K. Conkin. Baltimore, MD: Johns Hopkins University Press, 1979.

Roy, Olivier. *The Failure of Political Islam*. Trans. Carol Volk. Cambridge, MA: Harvard University Press, 1994.

Sabine, George H., and Stanley B. Smith. Introduction to Marcus Tullius Cicero, *On the Commonwealth*, trans. Sabine and Smith. Columbus: Ohio State University Press, 1929.

Sandel, Michael J., ed. *Democracy's Dilemma: America in Search of a Public Philosophy*. Cambridge, MA: Belknap, 1996.

———. *Liberalism and Its Critics*. New York: New York University Press, 1984.

Schama, Simon. *Citizens: A Chronicle of the French Revolution*. New York: Knopf, 1989.

Senior, Nassau William. *Oeuvres complètes*. Ed. D. W. and H. P. Kerr. Paris: Gallimard, 1991.

Shklar, Judith N. *After Utopia: The Decline of Political Faith*. Princeton, NJ: Princeton University Press, 1969.

———. *American Citizenship*. Cambridge, MA: Harvard University Press, 1991.

Skinner, Quentin. *The Foundations of Modern Thought*. 2 vols. Cambridge: Cambridge University Press, 1978.

Smith, Anthony D. *Nations and Nationalism in a Global Era*. Cambridge: Polity Press, 1995.

Smith, Rogers N. *Civic Ideals*, New Haven, CT: Yale University Press, 1997.

Smith, Tony. *America's Mission: The United States and the Worldwide Struggle for Democracy in the Twentieth Century*. Princeton, NJ: Princeton University Press, 1994.

Spencer, Robert. *The Truth about Muhammad*. Washington, DC: Regnery, 2006.

Strauss, Leo. *Natural Right and History*. Chicago: University of Chicago Press, 1953.

Sullivan, William. *Reconstructing Public Philosophy*. Berkeley: University of California Press, 1986.

Sunstein, Cass R. *After the Rights Revolution: Reconceiving the Regulatory State*. Cambridge, MA: Harvard University Press, 1990.

Thompson, Kenneth, and R. Meyers, eds. *Moral Dimensions of American Foreign Policy*. New Brunswick: Transaction Books, 1984.

———. *Truth and Tragedy: A Tribute to Hans J. Morgenthau*. Washington, DC: New Republic Book Company, 1977.

Thucydides. *The Peloponnesian War*. Trans. Stephen Lattimore. Indianapolis: Hackett, 1998.

Tocqueville, Alexis de. *Democracy in America*. Trans. George L. Lawrence. Garden City, NY: Doubleday, 1966.

———. *"The European Revolution" and Correspondence with Gobineau*. Trans. John Lukacs. Garden City, NY: Doubleday, 1959.

———. *Oeuvres, papieres et correspondance*. 6 vols. Ed. J.-P. Mayer. Paris: Gallimard, 1945–1952.

———. *The Old Regime and the French Revolution*. Trans. S. Gilbert. Garden City, NY: Doubleday, 1955.

———. *The Recollections of Alexis de Tocqueville*. Trans. A de Mattos. Ed. J.-P. Mayer. London: Harvill Press, 1948.

Troeltsch, Ernst. *The Social Teaching of the Christian Churches*. Trans. O. Wynn. New York: Harper, 1960.

Trotter, Wilfred. *Instincts of the Herd in Peace and War*. London: Scientific Book Club, 1942.

Tuchman, Barbara. *The March of Folly: From Troy to Vietnam*. New York: Ballantine, 1984.

Vierhaus, Rudolf. "Conservatism." *Dictionary of the History of Ideas*, 5 vols., ed. Philip P. Wiener. New York: Scribner, 1974.

Voegelin, Eric. *The New Science of Politics: An Introduction*. Chicago: University of Chicago Press, 1952.

Voltaire. *Philosophical Dictionary* (1769). Trans. P. Gay. New York: Basic Books, 1962.

Washington, George. "Washington's Farewell Address." In *A Documentary History of the United States*, ed. Richard D. Heffner. New York: New American Library, 1952.

Weber, Max. *The Protestant Ethic and the "Spirit" of Capitalism, and Other Writings*. Trans. Peter Baehr and Gordon C. Wells. New York: Penguin, 2002.

West, Thomas G. "The Classical Spirit of the Founding." In *The American Founding: Essays on the Formation of the Constitution*, ed. L. Jackson Barlow, Leonard W. Levy, and Ken Masugi. New York: Greenwood Press, 1988.

Whitman, Walt. *The Complete Prose Works of Walt Whitman*. New York: Putnam, 1902.

Williams, G. H. *The Radical Reformation*. Philadelphia: Westminster Press, 1964.

Williams, G. H., and A. Mergal, eds. *Spiritual and Anabaptist Writers*. Louisville, KY: Westminster John Knox Press, 2006.

Wills, Garry. *Head and Heart: American Christianities*. New York: Penguin, 2007.

———. *Inventing America: Jefferson's Declaration of Independence*. New York: Vintage, 1979.

———. *Lincoln at Gettysburg: The Words That Remade America*. New York: Simon & Schuster, 1992.

Winstanley, Gerrard. *The Works of Gerrard Winstanley*. Ed. G. H. Sabine. Ithaca, NY: Cornell University Press, 1941.

Wolfe, Alan. *One Nation, After All*. New York: Viking, 1998.

Wood, Gordon S. *The Creation of the American Republic*. New York: Norton, 1972.

———. *The Radicalism of the American Revolution*. New York: Vintage, 1993.

———. Review of I. Kramnick, *Republicanism and Bourgeois Radicalism*. *New Republic*, 11 February 1991, pp. 32–36.

Zakaria, Fareed. *The Failure of Freedom: Illiberal Democracy at Home and Abroad*. New York: Norton, 2003.

Zetterbaum, Marvin. *Tocqueville and the Problem of Democracy*. Stanford, CA: Stanford University Press, 1967.

Zinn, Howard. *A People's History of the United States*. New York: Harper, 1967.

# Index

# About the Author

**Sanford Lakoff** is Edward A. Dickson Professor Emeritus of political science at the University of California, San Diego, where he served as founding chair of his department. He has received accolades for teaching and the Chancellor's Associates Award for promoting discussion of public affairs. He taught previously at Harvard, Stony Brook, and the University of Toronto, and has been a visiting lecturer at the University of Rochester, MIT, and the European University Institute in Florence, Italy. Lakoff is the author of numerous book and scholarly articles on the history of political thought and relations of science and government, including *Equality in Political Philosophy, Democracy: History, Theory, Practice; Max Lerner: Pilgrim in the Promised Land*; and *A Glossary of Political Ideas* (edited, with Maurice Cranston).